*Third Edition*

# FUNDAMENTALS OF
# OPERATIONS MANAGEMENT

**MARK M. DAVIS**
*Bentley College*

**NICHOLAS J. AQUILANO**
*The University of Arizona*

**RICHARD B. CHASE**
*University of Southern California*

**Irwin**
**McGraw-Hill**

Boston   Burr Ridge, IL   Dubuque, IA   Madison, WI   New York   San Francisco   St. Louis
Bangkok   Bogotá   Caracas   Lisbon   London   Madrid
Mexico City   Milan   New Delhi   Seoul   Singapore   Sydney   Taipei   Toronto

# *Irwin/McGraw-Hill*

*A Division of The* **McGraw·Hill** *Companies*

FUNDAMENTALS OF OPERATIONS MANAGEMENT

Domestic:      4 5 6 7 8 9 0 VNH/VNH 9 3 2 1 0
International:  1 2 3 4 5 6 7 8 9 0 VNH/VNH 9 3 2 1 0 9 8

ISBN 0-256-22557-5

Vice president/Editorial director:   *Michael W. Junior*
Publisher: *Jeffrey J. Shelstad*
Senior sponsoring editor:   *Scott Isenberg*
Senior developmental editor:   *Gail Korosa*
Senior marketing manager:   *Colleen J. Suljic*
Senior project manager:   *Susan Trentacosti*
Senior production supervisor:   *Heather D. Burbridge*
Freelance design coordinator:   *Laurie J. Entringer*
Cover illustrator: *Andy Davis*
Senior photo research coordinator:   *Keri Johnson*
Photo research:   *Connie Gardner*
Supplement coordinator:   *Becky Szura*
Compositor:   *Interactive Composition Corporation*
Typeface: *10/12 Times Roman*
Printer:   *Von Hoffmann Press, Inc.*

**Library of Congress Cataloging-in-Publication Data**

Davis, Mark M. (date)
    Fundamentals of operations management / Mark M. Davis, Nicholas J.
Aquilano, Richard B. Chase. -- 3rd ed.
        p.   cm. -- (Irwin/McGraw-Hill series in operations and
decision sciences)
    Includes index.
    ISBN 0-256-22557-5
    1. Production management.   I. Aquilano, Nicholas J.   II. Chase
Richard B.   III. Title.   IV. Series.
TS155.D248   1999
    658.5--dc21                                                    98-40391

# Contents

## Chapter 3

### PROCESSES IN MANUFACTURING AND SERVICES  42

## Supplement 3

### FINANCIAL ANALYSIS IN OPERATIONS MANAGEMENT  76

## Chapter 4

## PROCESS MEASUREMENT AND ANALYSIS 104

## Chapter 5

## QUALITY MANAGEMENT 132

"We Are
Ladies and
Gentlemen
Serving
Ladies and
Gentlemen"

THE RITZ-CARLTON

CREDO

The Ritz-Carlton Hotel is a
place where the genuine care
and comfort of our guests is ou
highest mission.
We pledge to provide the fines
personal service and facilities fo
our guests who will always enjo
a warm, relaxed yet refined
ambience.
The Ritz-Carlton experience
enlivens the senses, instills wel
being, and fulfills even the
unexpressed wishes and
needs of our guests.

## Chapter 10

# PROJECT MANAGEMENT   348

## Chapter 11

# SUPPLY CHAIN MANAGEMENT   380

## Chapter 12

# JUST-IN-TIME SYSTEMS   396

## Chapter 13

## AGGREGATE PLANNING   430

## Chapter 14

## INVENTORY SYSTEMS FOR INDEPENDENT DEMAND   460

"Something's got to go, Fenton. You, me or this inventory—and it's not going to be me."

## Chapter 15

## INVENTORY SYSTEMS FOR DEPENDENT DEMAND   494

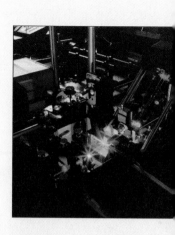

## Chapter 16

## SCHEDULING   532

## APPENDIXES   561

## PHOTO CREDITS   581

## NAME INDEX   583

## SUBJECT INDEX   589

# FUNDAMENTALS OF
# OPERATIONS MANAGEMENT

# Chapter

# 1

# INTRODUCTION

## Chapter Objectives

- Demonstrate that operations management addresses issues in both manufacturing and service organizations, and that manufacturing and services are becoming integrated within an organization rather than being treated as two separate and distinct entities.

- Introduce the application of OM tools to other functional areas within an organization such as marketing and human resources.

- Present an overview of the book.

- Show the impact of a changing and increasingly complex environment on business decision making and on the operations management function and the organization.

- Demonstrate that the operations management function takes a broader global perspective as a company increases its international activities.

- Define the operations management (OM) function and understand how it adds value to the goods and services provided by an organization.

- Present an historical perspective of operations management and how it has evolved to its current role in an organization.

"**D**irect marketing? You want me to manage a direct marketing operation?" Mark Longa, the operations manager at Bose Corporation's stereo speaker manufacturing facility in Westboro, Massachusetts (shown here talking to a worker on an assembly line), stared in disbelief at the telephone, trying to comprehend why this conversation was even taking place. "But I've spent my entire career in manufacturing and have absolutely no experience in direct marketing," Mark continued. "We know that," said the voice at the other end of the line, "but we've finally recognized that the key to our success depends on our ability to develop a smooth running operation that can be responsive to the needs of our customers, and you were recommended as just the person to accomplish this for us." ■

Source: Special thanks to Mark Longa, Bose Corp., Westboro, Massachusetts.

## INTRODUCTION

MARKETING    While Mark Longa didn't take the job as operations manager for the direct marketing firm, the fact that he was asked is important. Ten years ago, it would never have occurred to a direct marketing firm's top management that they might need an operations manager on its senior management team. Today, however, there is growing recognition that the various elements that typically comprise the operations management function aren't limited solely to the production line, but have applications in the other functional areas within an organization.

Mark Longa's experience isn't an isolated incident; similar conversations with operations managers are becoming very common. Senior managers in manufacturing and services, in for-profit organizations, and not-for-profit organizations and in both the public and private sectors are now recognizing the important contribution of operations management. This renaissance in operations management has created a growing need for highly skilled operations managers like Mark Longa.

## SPECIFIC OBJECTIVES OF THIS BOOK

Most students do not major in operations management. In fact, many schools and colleges do not even offer a major in operations management. Nevertheless, it is important for you to understand how the operations management function contributes to the overall success of an organization. The reasons are twofold. First, understanding how the different elements within the OM function fit into the overall organizational structure will provide you with a broader perspective which, in turn, will allow you to do your own job better. In addition, as we stated above, the concepts developed initially within the OM function have application in all of the other functional areas within an organization. Understanding and applying these tools and concepts can improve your ability to be both effective and efficient in the way you do your work.

Many students don't appreciate the importance of operations management until after they graduate and begin work (see the OM in Practice box: Excerpts from Two Letters from Former Students). For example, consider the "hot" employment area of information technology (IT). Specialists in IT should really have a working knowledge of the best practices in process management, forecasting, quality control, and project planning to correctly apply many of the software tools that they will encounter on the job.

For these reasons, the specific objectives of this book are to:

1. Introduce the various elements that comprise the field of operations management, and some of the new and evolving concepts within OM.
2. Identify some of the OM tools and concepts that can be applied to a wide variety of situations, including non-OM related areas.

   3. Develop an appreciation of the need for interaction between operations management and the other management functions within an organization.
4. Explain the role of technology in operations management and its impact on the different OM elements.

   5. Describe the growing trend toward globalization among firms and how it affects operations management.

   6. Demonstrate that manufacturing and services are becoming more integrated within companies.
7. Provide an integrated framework for understanding the field of OM as a whole and its role in an organization.

# Operations Management in Practice

## EXCERPTS FROM TWO LETTERS FROM FORMER STUDENTS

". . . part of an audit for a CPA firm includes learning about the systems of a client. A by-product of the audit is a management letter which suggests how the client might improve their systems. By systems I am referring to the accounting information systems, the inventory control systems, as well as the production process.

In evaluating these systems, one must first understand the generalities underlying all systems. OM explains these generalities as they apply to production processes. The better one understands how processes work, the easier it is to apply this understanding to different systems and provide your client with good suggestions for improving the efficiency of their operations . . .

The course you teach in Operations Management is invaluable, and any student of accounting would be a fool to blow it off and try to just get by without learning anything. . . ."

**Gary S. Fortier**
B.S.B.A., C.P.A.
Atlanta, GA

". . . if I were to call you on the phone and tell you what I do for work, I think I would hear some of the following from you:
  'I told you so.'
  'You should have paid more attention the second time you took the course.'
  'Maybe if you even went to class . . .'

Well, I have been busy working for the Gillette Company as a production analyst. Basically, it's OM all over again, making sure that the production is running smoothly and keeping management pleased. It's unreal how much of your class takes place in my everyday work.

Scrap rates, net average hours of production, efficiency, sample sizes, shifts, the number of hours a machine can run with a certain product. I tell you I'd take your course a third time if I could squeeze it into my schedule. Putting in 60–70 hours a week and learning OM all over again just kills me, because if I had given some effort in your class, . . . who knows?

I am sure that you are giggling to yourself and saying ha ha, that ought to teach him not to have missed any of my classes. I thought that maybe some of your students that are like me could benefit from this e-mail. . . ."

**Erik Geagan**
B.S.B.A.
Boston, MA

With respect to the last objective, our goal is to demonstrate that operations management is not just a loosely knit aggregation of tools but rather a *synthesis* of concepts and techniques that relate directly to operating systems and enhance their management. This point is important because OM is frequently confused with operations research (OR), management science (MS), and industrial engineering (IE). The critical difference between OM and these fields is this: OM is a field of management, whereas OR and MS are branches of applied mathematics and IE is an engineering discipline. Thus, while operations managers use the tools of OR and MS in decision making, and are concerned with many of the same issues as IE, OM has a distinct business management role that differentiates it from OR, MS, and IE.

## WHAT IS OPERATIONS MANAGEMENT?

### A Corporate Perspective

**operations management**
Management of the conversion process which transforms inputs such as raw material and labor into outputs in the form of finished goods and services.

MARKETING

FINANCE

From a corporate perspective, **operations management** may be defined as the management of the direct resources that are required to provide an organization's goods and services.

The marketplace—the firm's customers for its goods and services—shapes the corporate strategy of the firm. This strategy is based on the corporate mission, and in essence reflects how the firm plans to use all of its resources and functions (marketing, finance, and operations) to gain a competitive advantage. The operations strategy specifies how the firm will employ its production capabilities to support its corporate strategy. (Similarly, the marketing strategy addresses how the firm will sell and distribute its goods and services,

**EXHIBIT 1.1**

Role of OM within an
Organization

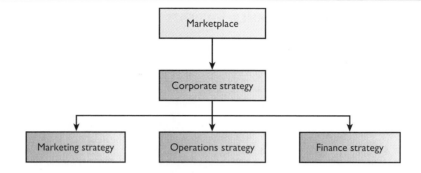

and the finance strategy identifies how best to utilize the financial resources of the firm, as shown in Exhibit 1.1.)

Within the operations function, management decisions can be divided into three broad areas:

- Strategic (long-range) decisions.
- Tactical (medium-range) decisions.
- Operational planning and control (short-range) decisions.

**EXHIBIT 1.2**

Hierarchy of
Operations Planning

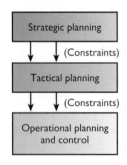

The hierarchical relationship between these three planning functions is shown in Exhibit 1.2.

The strategic issues are usually very broad in nature, addressing such questions as:

- How will we make the product?
- Where do we locate the facility or facilities?
- How much capacity do we need?
- When should we add more capacity?

Consequently, by necessity, the time frame for strategic decisions is typically very long, usually several years or more, depending on the specific industry.

Operations management decisions at the strategic level impact the long-range effectiveness of the company in terms of how well it can address the needs of its customers. Thus, for the firm to succeed, these decisions must be aligned with the corporate strategy. Decisions made at the strategic level then define the fixed conditions or constraints under which the firm must operate in both the intermediate and short term.

At the next level in the decision-making process, tactical planning primarily addresses the issue of how to efficiently schedule material and labor within the constraints of the strategic decisions that were previously made. Thus, some of the issues on which OM concentrates at this level are:

- How many workers do we need?
- When do we need them?
- Should we work overtime or put on a second shift?
- When should we have material delivered?
- Should we have a finished goods inventory?

These tactical decisions, in turn, define the operating constraints under which the operational planning and control decisions are made.

The management decisions with respect to operational planning and control are very narrow and short term, by comparison. For example, issues at this level include:

At Ford Motor Company's Valencia, Spain, plant more than 20 suppliers are located in an adjacent industrial park that feed parts, like these bumpers, directly to the assembly line as needed.

be extremely valuable in solving technical problems during production. As shown in the OM in Practice box, Foxboro Company's Customer Friend Program provides a good example of how manufacturing is now directly interacting with customers.

More and more firms are recognizing the competitive advantage achieved when the transformation process is not isolated, as when customers are invited to view their operating facilities firsthand. For example, Green Giant believes that the tours of their production facilities that they provided to Japanese distributors was a major factor in their ability to penetrate that market with their Green Giant food products.[5] Similarly, National $R_x$ Services, which offers a mail-order prescription service, encourages insurance companies and HMOs to visit their facilities to assure themselves of the high quality of its prescription-filling process.

In a like manner, companies are working more closely with suppliers. Firms like Toyota, for example, have suppliers deliver product directly to the factory floor, eliminating any need for a stockroom. General Scanning of Watertown, Massachusetts, encourages its vendors to automatically replenish items on the factory floor without purchase orders or incoming reports.

**value chain**
Steps an organization requires to produce a good or a service regardless of where they are performed.

This trend toward having the transformation process work more closely with both suppliers and customers alike is often referred to as a product's **value chain.** We can define a value chain as consisting of all those steps that actually add value to the product without distinguishing where they are added. This concept attempts to eliminate all nonvalue-added steps (such as inspections and inventory), and consequently results in a higher degree of dependence among the value-added functions that are linked in the chain. The relationship between the transformation process, its support functions, and the other value-added functions is shown in Exhibit 1.8.

[5]J. Ammeson, "When in Rome," *Northwest Airlines World Traveler,* March 1993.

**EXHIBIT 1.8**

The Value Chain and Its
Support Functions

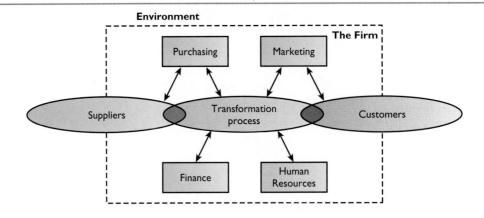

**EXHIBIT 1.9**

Line and Staff Jobs in
Operations Management

| Organizational Level | Manufacturing Industries | Service Industries |
|---|---|---|
| Upper | Vice president of manufacturing | Vice president of operations (airline) |
| | Regional manager of manufacturing | Chief administrator (hospital) |
| Middle | Plant manager | Store manager (department store) |
| | Program manager | Facilities manager (wholesale distributor) |
| Lower | Department supervisor | Branch manager (bank) |
| | Foreman | Department supervisor (insurance company) |
| | Crew chief | Assistant manager (hotel) |
| Staff | Production controller | Systems and procedures analyst |
| | Materials manager | Purchasing agent |
| | Quality manager | Inspector |
| | Purchasing agent | Dietician (hospital) |
| | Work methods analyst | Customer service manager |
| | Process engineer | |

This integration of both suppliers and customers into the transformation process begins to blur the boundaries between what were previously totally independent organizations. What appears to be emerging now is a concept known as the **virtual enterprise,** which is a full integrated and interlocked network in *inter*dependent organizations. With this new approach, it is often difficult to determine where one organization leaves off and the next one begins. As one example, FedEx has several employees who work full time at the L.L. Bean Mail Order Distribution Center in Freeport, Maine.

**virtual enterprise**
Company whose boundaries are not clearly defined due to the integration of customers and suppliers.

## Job Opportunities in Operations Management: Relating OM to Other Business Functions

Exhibit 1.9 lists some of the line and staff jobs that are frequently viewed as relating to the operations function. There are more staff specializations in manufacturing than in services because of the focus on materials management and control.

Operations Management is a required course in many business schools, not only because it deals with the basic question of how goods and services are created, but also because many of the concepts developed in OM have applications in every other functional area within an organization. As seen in Exhibit 1.10, processes exist within every function.

I n 1995, 70 percent of product sales at Hewlett-Packard (HP) were from new products that were less than two years old. The operations strategy in the Medical Products Group (MPG) has focused on developing manufacturing processes that are both fast and flexible: fast, in terms of time-to-market in new product development and in delivery time after receipt of customer orders; flexible, in terms of quickly introducing new products into production while at the same time accommodating a wide variety of product types and configurations.

The average time-to-market for developing new products has been significantly reduced over the years. This reduction can be attributed to the use of defined product generation processes, product platforms (standardized building blocks), and product evolution strategies. Because manufacturing is an integrated part of the new product development process, MPG can quickly introduce new products into production.

Moreover, production processes have been designed to minimize final assembly and test time. The final assembly and test for a typical patient monitoring system (which has an average list price of $20,000) is 30 minutes. Thus products are built to order because the process is sufficiently flexible to accommodate different product configurations.

The rapid build times of products and subassemblies eliminates the need to keep track of work-in-process (WIP) inventories at every stage in the manufacturing process. Instead, using bar code technology, all of the components and raw material that go into completed components and end products are "backflushed" from inventory, much in the same way that all of the ingredients in a Whopper at Burger King are subtracted from inventory when that item is rung up on the cash register. This alignment between business and manufacturing strategies has been a key ingredient in the success of the Medical Products Group. Sales and profit margins have continued to increase in recent years in a market that is considered to be highly competitive. ■

Source: Special thanks to Rick La Fratta and Steve Smyth, Hewlett-Packard Medical Products Group, Andover, Massachusetts.

# BEING COMPETITIVE IS ALL ABOUT WINNING

Competition in most industries has intensified significantly in recent years, especially among international firms, and this trend is expected to continue. This increase in competition is largely because the world is quickly becoming a global village.

This movement towards a single world economy has occurred for several reasons, including: (a) continued advances in information technology which facilitate the rapid transfer of data across vast distances, (b) the growing trend to lower trade barriers as evidenced by NAFTA and the formation of the European Union, (c) the lowering of transportation costs, and (d) the emergence of high-growth markets with associated high-profit margins, in **newly industrialized countries (NIC).**[1] These new markets can be compared to the saturated markets and shrinking profit margins that are being experienced in the more highly developed countries. For example, McDonald's growth in the United States between 1984 and 1994 was 6.4 percent annually while its international sales grew 19.0 percent annually during this same time period.[2]

As a consequence, in order to not only survive but also prosper in such a fiercely competitive marketplace, a company needs to differentiate itself from its competition. In such an environment, customers will buy solely on the basis of price, thereby driving prices down and shrinking profit margins. In this highly competitive situation, only the low cost producer in an industry can be successful and Michael Porter, a professor at the Harvard Business School and perhaps today's leading authority on competitive strategy, has suggested that even this isn't guaranteed.[3]

He recommends, therefore, that beyond a **low cost strategy**, there are two other business strategies that a firm can adopt: **market segmentation** and **product differentiation**. Companies that are considered to have world-class operations have been able to develop an operations strategy that is properly aligned with corporate strategy which, in turn, is compatible with the overall goals and mission of the firm.

## Definitions

There often develops within an industry or company a unique set of terms that are familiar only to those associated with that industry or company. This is also true for the functional areas within an organization. Since operations strategy is a relatively new and evolving concept, several of the terms more commonly used are defined here.

Today, many corporations, especially the larger conglomerates, consist of several stand-alone businesses which are often referred to as **strategic business units** or **SBUs**. Within this context, **corporate strategy** pertains to the overall *financial strategy* that has been adopted by the umbrella organization, in terms of how capital is generated (that is, debt versus equity), which SBUs receive infusions of investment, and which are treated as cash generators or "cash cows."

**Business strategy** refers to the individual strategy adopted by each SBU, in terms of how it addresses the specific markets that it serves and the products that it provides.

---

**newly industrialized countries (NIC)**
Emerging countries that compete in global markets with their goods and have populations with a high standard of living.

**types of business strategies:**
**low cost**
Producing the lowest cost products.
**market segmentation**
Satisfying the needs of a particular market niche.
**product differentiation**
Offering products that differ significantly from the competition.

**strategic business unit (SBU)**
Stand-alone business within a conglomerate which operates like an independent company.

**corporate strategy**
Overall financial strategy adopted by the parent corporation.

**business strategy**
How a strategic business unit (SBU) addresses the specific markets it serves and products it provides.

---

[1] J. Naisbitt and P. Aburdene, *Megatrends 2000* (New York: William Morrow and Co., 1990).

[2] G. Loveman, "The Globalization of Services: Four Strategies That Drive Growth across Borders," *Proceedings of the 4th International Research Seminar in Service Management,* Agelonde-LaLonde les Maures, France, June 4–7, 1996.

[3] M. Porter, *Competitive Strategy: Techniques for Analyzing Industries and Competitors* (New York: The Free Press, 1980).

**functional strategy**
Strategy developed by a function within an organization to support the business strategy.

**competitiveness**
Company's position in the marketplace relative to its competition.

**operations strategy**
How the operations function contributes to competitive advantage.

**competitive priorities**
How the operations function provides a firm with a competitive advantage.

**Functional strategies** (for example, operations, marketing, human resources) are developed to support or align with the established business strategy.

A company or SBU's **competitiveness** refers to its relative position in the marketplace in terms of how it competes with the other firms in its industry. **Operations strategy** refers to how the operations management function contributes to a firm's ability to achieve its competitive advantage in that marketplace.

Operations strategy can be divided into two major categories: *structural elements* consisting of facility location, capacity, vertical integration, and choice of process (all of which are considered to be long term or "strategic" in nature) and *infrastructural elements* consisting of the workforce (in terms of size and skills), quality issues, planning and control, and organizational structure (all of which are often viewed as "tactical" because they can be changed in a relatively short time).

Operations strategies are developed from the **competitive priorities** of an organization which include (a) **low cost,** (b) **high quality,** (c) **fast delivery**, (d) **flexibility,** and (e) **service.**

Core capabilities are the means by which competitive priorities are achieved. Consequently, core capabilities must align directly with competitive priorities.

## OPERATIONS STRATEGY—AN OVERVIEW

MARKETING
FINANCE

In the period following World War II, corporate strategy in the United States was usually developed by the marketing and finance functions within a company. With the high demand for consumer products that had built up during the war years, U.S. companies could sell virtually everything they made at comparatively high prices. In addition, there was very little international competition. The main industrial competitors of the United States today, Germany and Japan, lay in ruins from massive bombings. They could not even satisfy their own markets, let alone export globally.

Within the business environment that existed at that time, the manufacturing or operations function was assigned the responsibility to produce large quantities of standard products at minimum costs, regardless of the overall goals of the firm. To accomplish this, the operations function focused on obtaining low-cost, unskilled labor and installing highly automated assembly line type facilities.

### The Emergence of Operations Strategy

With no global competition and continued high demand, the role of operations management (that is, to minimize costs) remained virtually unchanged throughout the 1950s and early 1960s. By the late 1960s, however, Wickham Skinner of the Harvard Business School, who is often referred to as the grandfather of operations strategy, recognized this weakness among U.S. manufacturers. He suggested that companies develop an operations strategy that would complement the existing marketing and finance strategies. In one of his early articles on the subject, Skinner referred to manufacturing as the missing link in corporate strategy.[4]

---

[4]C. W. Skinner, "Manufacturing—The Missing Link in Corporate Strategy," *Harvard Business Review* 47, no. 3 (May–June 1969), pp. 136–45.

Subsequent work in this area by researchers at the Harvard Business School, including Abernathy, Clark, Hayes, and Wheelwright, continued to emphasize the importance of using the strengths of a firm's manufacturing facilities and people as a competitive weapon in the marketplace, and also take a longer-term view of how to deploy them.

## What Is Operations Strategy?

Operations strategy is thus concerned with the development of a long-term plan for determining how to best utilize the major resources of the firm so that there is a high degree of compatibility between these resources and the firm's long-term corporate strategy. Operations strategy addresses very broad questions about how these major resources should be configured in order to achieve the desired corporate objectives. Some of the major long-term issues addressed in operations strategy include:

How big do we make the facilities?

Where do we locate them?

When do we build them?

What type of process(es) do we install to make the products?

Each of these issues is addressed in greater detail in subsequent chapters. In this chapter we want to take a more macroscopic perspective to better understand how these issues are interrelated.

In developing an operations strategy, management needs to take many factors into consideration. These include: (a) the level of technology that is or will be available, (b) the required skill levels of the workers, and (c) the degree of vertical integration, in terms of the extent to which outside suppliers are used.

As shown in Exhibit 2.1, operations strategy supports the long-range strategy developed at the SBU level. One might say that decisions at the SBU level focus on being effective, that is, "on doing the right things." These decisions are sometimes referred to as **strategic planning.** Strategic decisions impact intermediate-range decisions, often referred to as **tactical planning,** which focus on being efficient, that is, "doing things right." Here the emphasis is on when material should be delivered, when products should be made to best meet demand, and what size the workforce should be. Finally, we have **operational planning and control** which deals with the day-to-day procedures for doing work, including scheduling, inventory management, and process management.

**strategic planning**
Long range planning such as plant size, location, and type of process to be used.

**tactical planning**
Focuses on producing goods and services as efficiently as possible within the strategic plan.

**operational planning and control**
Scheduling of daily tasks to determine which operator is assigned to work on which job and machine.

**EXHIBIT 2.1**
Hierarchy of Operational Planning

| Type of Planning | Time Frame | Typical Issues |
|---|---|---|
| Strategic | Long range | Plant size, location, type of process |
| Tactical | Intermediate range | Workforce size, material requirements |
| Operational planning and control (OPC) | Short range | Daily scheduling of workers, jobs, and equipment; process management; inventory management |

# COMPETITIVE PRIORITIES

competitive priorities
**cost**
Providing low cost products.
**quality**
Providing high quality products.
**delivery**
Providing products quickly.
**flexibility**
Providing a wide variety of products.
**service**
How products are delivered and supported.

The key to developing an effective operations strategy lies in understanding how to create or add value for customers. Specifically, value is added through the competitive priority or priorities that are selected to support a given strategy.

Skinner and others initially identified *four basic competitive priorities*. These were **cost, quality, delivery,** and **flexibility.** These four priorities translate directly into characteristics that are used to describe various processes by which a company can add value to the products it provides. There now exists a fifth competitive priority—**service**, and it currently is the primary way in which companies are differentiating themselves in the 1990s.

## Cost

Within every industry, there is usually a segment of the market that buys strictly on the basis of low cost. To successfully compete in this niche, a firm must necessarily, therefore, be the low-cost producer. But, as noted earlier, even doing this doesn't always guarantee profitability and success.

Products sold strictly on the basis of cost are typically commodity-like. (Examples of commodities include flour, petroleum, and sugar.) In other words, customers cannot distinguish the products made by one firm from those of another. As a result, customers use cost as the primary determinant in making a purchase.

However, this segment of the market is frequently very large and many companies are lured by the potential for significant profits, which are associated with large unit volumes of product. As a consequence, the competition in this segment is exceedingly fierce—and so is the failure rate. After all, there can only be one low-cost producer, and that firm usually establishes the selling price in the market.

## Quality

Quality can be divided into two categories: product quality and process quality. The level of quality in a product's design will vary as to the particular market that it is aimed to serve. Obviously, a child's first two-wheel bicycle is of significantly different quality than the bicycle of a world-class cyclist. The use of thicker sheetmetal and the application of extra coats of paint are some of the product quality characteristics that differentiate a Mercedes-Benz from a Hyundai. One advantage of offering higher-quality products is that they command higher prices in the marketplace.

The goal in establishing the "proper level" of product quality is to focus on the requirements of the customer. Overdesigned products with too much quality will be viewed as being prohibitively expensive. Underdesigned products, on the other hand, will lose customers to products that cost a little more but are perceived by the customers as offering much greater benefits.

Process quality is critical in every market segment. Regardless of whether the product is a child's first two-wheeler or a bicycle for an international cyclist, or whether it is a Mercedes-Benz or a Hyundai, customers want products without defects. Thus, the goal of process quality is to produce error-free products.

## Delivery

Another market niche considers speed of delivery to be an important determinant in its purchasing decision. Here, the ability of a firm to provide consistent and fast delivery allows

The flexibility of the manufacturing process at John Deere's Harvester Works in Moline, Illinois, allows the firm to respond to the unpredictability of the agricultural industry's equipment needs. By manufacturing such small volume products as seed planters in "modules" or factories within a factory, Deere can offer farmers a choice of 84 different planter models with such a wide variety of options that farmers, with a choice of 1.6 million different types of planters, can have planters virtually customized to meet their individual needs. Its manufacturing process thus allows Deere to compete on both speed and flexibility.

it to charge a premium price for its products. George Stalk, Jr., of the Boston Consulting Group, has demonstrated that both profits and market share are directly linked to the speed with which a company can deliver its products relative to its competition.[5] In addition to fast delivery, the reliability of the delivery is also important. In other words, products should be delivered to customers with minimum variance in delivery times.

## Flexibility

Flexibility, from a strategic perspective, refers to the ability of a company to offer a wide variety of products to its customers. Flexibility is also a measure of how fast a company can convert its process(es) from making an old line of products to producing a new product line. Product variety is often perceived by the customer to be a dimension of quality.

 ## Service

With product life cycles becoming shorter and shorter, the actual products themselves tend to quickly resemble those of other companies. As a consequence, these products are often viewed as commodities in which price is the primary determinant in deciding which one to buy. A good example of this is the personal computer (PC) industry. Today, the differences in the products offered among the different PC manufacturers are relatively insignificant, so price is the prime selection criterion.

---

[5]George Stalk, Jr., "Time—The Next Source of Competitive Advantage," *Harvard Business Review* 66, no. 4 (July–August 1988), pp. 41–51.

To obtain an advantage in such a competitive environment, firms are now providing "value-added" service. This is true for firms that provide goods and services. The reason is simple. As Sandra Vandermerwe puts it, "The market power is in the services, because the value is in the results." For example, Hendrix Veeders, a Dutch producer of livestock feed for pig farmers, now provides a range of value-added services for these farmers, including consulting on pig breeding, nutrition management, delivery of pigs to the slaughter house, and distribution of pork products to retail outlets. Another example is SKF, a Swedish manufacturer of ball bearings that advises its customers on spare parts management, training and installation, and good preventive maintenance practices to extend the life of ball bearings.[6]

Within the service sector Putnam Investments in Boston offers a wide range of mutual funds through independent brokers. To obtain a competitive advantage over other mutual fund companies, Putnam now provides brochures and prospectuses of their mutual funds to brokers within 24 hours of request.

### The Next Competitive Advantage?

Companies are always looking toward the future to find the next competitive advantage that will distinguish their products in the marketplace. Currently, there appears to be a trend toward offering environmentally friendly products that are made through environmentally friendly processes. As consumers become more aware of the fragility of the environment, they are increasingly turning towards products that are safe for the environment. Ford now advertises an environmentally friendly automobile. The Body Shop, an international retail chain headquartered in England, sells various cosmetics and skin lotions that are made without harming the environment. Veryfine Products of Westford, Massachusetts, which produces a line of fruit drinks, promotes its concern for the environment by noting that it uses a very high percentage of recycled products in its containers and packaging.

## BUILDING AN OPERATIONS STRATEGY FROM COMPETITIVE PRIORITIES

### Factory Focus and Trade-Offs

The notion of factory focus and trade-offs was central to the concept of operations strategy during the late 1960s and early 1970s. The underlying logic was that a factory could not excel simultaneously on all four competitive priorities. Consequently, management had to decide which priorities were critical to the firm's success, and then concentrate or focus the resources of the firm on those particular characteristics. For firms with very large manufacturing facilities, Skinner suggested the creation of a Plant-within-a-Plant (PWP) concept, in which different locations within the facility would be allocated to different product lines, each with their own competitive priority. Even the workers, under the PWP concept, would be separated in order to minimize the confusion associated with shifting from one type of priority to another.[7]

For example, if a company wanted to focus on speed of delivery, then it could not be very flexible in terms of its ability to offer a wide range of products. As an example,

---

[6]S. Vandermerwe, *From Tin Soldiers to Russian Dolls: Creating Added Value through Services* (Oxford, England: Butterworth-Heinemann, 1993).

[7]C. W. Skinner, "The Focused Factory," *Harvard Business Review* 52, no. 3 (May–June 1974), pp. 113–22.

McDonald's provides very fast service but offers a very limited menu of highly standard-ized products; in contrast, Wendy's makes your request to order but takes longer to deliver. Similarly, a low-cost priority was not seen to be compatible with either speed of delivery or flexibility. High quality was also viewed as a trade-off to low cost.

The need for focus has been recognized in other service operations as well. Hotel chains like Marriott and Holiday Inn have segmented the hotel industry and now offer a variety of products, each focused on a different market segment. For example, within the Marriott group there is Fairfield Inns for economy-minded customers; Marriott Hotels and Resorts for conferences and for customers wanting full-service hotels; Residence Inns for customers wanting more than just a hotel room; and Marriott Courtyards for those wanting certain hotel conveniences like meals, but who are still concerned about price. Skinner's PWP concept is now also being applied to the healthcare industry where "hospitals-within-hospitals" allow specialized firms to focus only on specific ailments. For example, Inten-siva accepts only long-term acute patients and operates independently within the facilities of St. Francis Hospital in Beech Grove, Indiana. Because it specializes in only one area (intensive care), Intensiva's operating costs are 50 percent lower than those of a typical intensive care ward.[8]

Other examples of focused operations in the service sector include BankBoston's Private Bank Division, which focuses on providing a full line of banking services to wealthy customers ("A bank within a bank," which is again not unlike Skinner's Plant-within-a-Plant concept) and Shouldice Hospital in Toronto, Canada, which performs only one type of hernia operation. The benefits of a focused operation can be readily demonstrated at Shouldice Hospital, whose very unusual product is a "hernia vacation." Patients are admit-ted to a mansionlike hospital in a beautiful setting outside Toronto. Every detail of the hos-pital's operations is focused on providing high-quality hernia care and a congenial, restful atmosphere. Patients mingle, mix, and generally relax, enjoying the experience so much that the annual reunion dinner is oversubscribed. This highly focused care permits Shouldice to keep operating costs low while maintaining high quality, both in terms of med-ical care and customer service. However, by becoming a specialist facility, Shouldice does not have the capabilities to perform other types of medical treatments.

## Questioning the Trade-Offs

With the world becoming a single global village, there has emerged a group of companies that have adopted an international perspective toward both manufacturing and marketing. Within this global arena, competition is significantly more intense, due to both the greater number of "players" and the tremendous profit opportunities that exist.

Those companies that have excelled on this global level have often been referred to as *world-class operations*. Events in the world marketplace during the 1970s and 1980s, in terms of the growing intensity in competition, forced these companies to reexamine the concept of operations strategy, especially in terms of the so-called "necessary" trade-offs. Managers began to realize that they didn't have to make trade-offs to the same extent that they had previously thought. What emerged instead was a realization of the need to establish a hierarchy among the different priorities, as dictated by the marketplace. Exhibit 2.2 presents the sequence or priorities in which these priorities were introduced over time.

[8]Keith Hammonds and Nicole Harris, "Medical Lessons from the Big Mac," *Business Week,* February 10, 1997, pp. 94–98.

**EXHIBIT 2.2**

Time Line for Operations Strategies

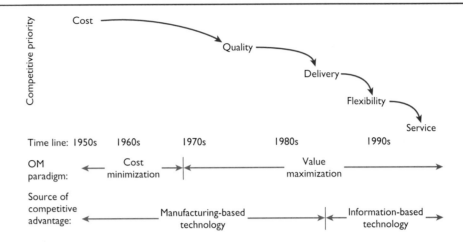

Specifically, in the late 1960s and early 1970s, cost was the primary concern, a holdover from the philosophy of the 1950s that manufacturing's only objective was to minimize production costs. However, as more and more companies began to produce low-cost products, the need became apparent to develop other ways to differentiate themselves from their competitors. The priority thus shifted to quality. Companies at this time obtained a competitive advantage by producing high-quality products, which allowed them to charge more—although price still was a factor in the consumer's buying decision. However, competition again soon caught up, and everyone was offering high-quality products that were reasonably priced.

Companies, in looking to obtain another competitive advantage in the marketplace, turned to speed and reliability of delivery as a means of differentiating themselves from the rest of the pack. Now the ante into the "game" was high-quality products that were reasonably priced and which could be delivered quickly and reliably to the customer.

In the 1980s, George Stalk, Jr., a leading management "guru," as previously noted, identified speed of delivery as a major factor in determining the success of a company.[9] Companies therefore concentrated their resources on reducing product lead times with very dramatic results. Products that once took weeks or months to deliver were now being shipped within hours or days of the receipt of an order.

Eventually, the competition again caught up and the more aggressive firms looked for still another means to obtain a competitive advantage. This time flexibility was selected, as manifested by the ability of the firm to produce customized products. Now the marketplace dictated that for firms to be successful, they had to produce reasonably priced, customized products of high quality that could be quickly delivered to the customer.

 A good example of a firm that has accomplished this is the National Bicycle Company in Japan.[10] (See the OM in Practice box on Japan's Personalized Bike Production.) An example of a retail operation that competes on more than one dimension is Custom Foot of Westport, Connecticut, that offers custom-fitted shoes on a mass-market basis (see the OM in Practice box).

---

[9]George Stalk, Jr., "Time—The Next Source of Competitive Advantage," *Harvard Business Review,* July–August 1988, pp. 41–51.

[10]Susan Moffat, "Japan's New Personalized Production," *Fortune*, October 22, 1990, pp. 132–35.

# Operations Management in Practice

## JAPAN'S PERSONALIZED BIKE PRODUCTION

Does your bike fit you to a "t"? Would you like one that does? If you are willing to pay 20 to 30 percent more than you would pay for a mass-produced bike, you can get a Panasonic bike manufactured to exactly match your size, weight, and color preference. You can even get your bike within three weeks of your order (only two weeks if you visit Japan). This is accomplished via a process called the Panasonic Individual Customer System (PICS), which skillfully employs computers, robots, and a small factory workforce to make one-of-a-kind models at the National Bicycle Industrial Company factory in Kokubu, Japan.

The National Bicycle Industrial Company (NBIC), a subsidiary of electronics giant Matsushita, began making the bikes under the Panasonic brand in 1987. With the introduction of its personalized order system (POS) for the Japanese market (PICS was developed for overseas sales), the firm gained international attention as a classic example of mass customization—producing products to order in lot sizes of one.

The factory itself has 21 employees and a computer-aided design (CAD) system, and is capable of producing any of 8 million variations on 18 models of racing, road, and mountain bikes in 199 color patterns for virtually any size person.

The PIC system works in the following way. A customer visits a local Panasonic bicycle store and is measured on a special frame. The storeowner then faxes the specifications to the master control room at the factory. There an operator punches the specs into a minicomputer, which automatically creates a unique blueprint and produces a bar code. (The CAD blueprint takes about three minutes as opposed to three hours required by company draftspeople prior to computerization.) The bar code is then attached to metal tubes and gears that ultimately become the customer's personal bike. At various stages in the process, line workers access the customer's requirement using the bar code label and a scanner. This information, displayed on a CRT terminal at each station, is fed directly to the computer-controlled machines that are part of a local area computer network. At each step of production, a computer reading the code knows that each part belongs to a specific bike, and tells a robot where to weld or tells a painter which pattern to follow.

Despite the use of computers and robots, the process is not highly automated. Gears are hand-wired, assembly is manual, and the customer's name is silk-screened by hand with the touch of an artisan. The entire manufacturing and assembly time required to complete a single bike is 150 minutes, and

---

As the "rules" for operations strategy shifted from that of primarily reducing costs to that of including quality, speed of delivery, flexibility and service, the strategy for the operations management function has also shifted. The strategy of minimizing production costs has been replaced with that of maximizing the value added.

This emphasis on being competitive on more than one dimension might lead to the conclusion that there are no longer any trade-offs. This is not the case. As Wickham Skinner said at a breakfast meeting of the Boston P/OM Pancake Society in April 1995, "There will always be trade-offs." Today, however, those trade-offs occur on what can be described as a higher performance curve, as shown in Exhibit 2.3. A firm can either improve delivery at the same cost ($A_1$ to $B_1$) or reduce cost while maintaining the same speed of delivery ($A_2$ to $B_2$) or any combination of the two ($A_3$ to $B_3$).

### Order Qualifiers and Order Winners

**order-qualifiers**
Minimum characteristics of a firm or its products to be considered as a source of purchase.

**order-winners**
Characteristics of a firm that distinguish it from its competition so that it is selected as the source of purchase.

Terry Hill of the London Business School has developed the strategic concept of **order-qualifiers** and **order-winners**.[11] Order qualifiers can be defined as the minimum elements or characteristics that a firm or its products must have in order to even be considered as a potential supplier or source. In Europe, for example, the vast majority of companies today require that their vendors be ISO-9000 certified. (This certification ensures that a firm has documented all of its processes.) Thus, ISO-9000 certification is an order-qualifier in

---

[11]T. Hill, *Manufacturing Strategy: Text and Cases*, 2nd ed. (Burr Ridge, IL: Irwin, 1994).

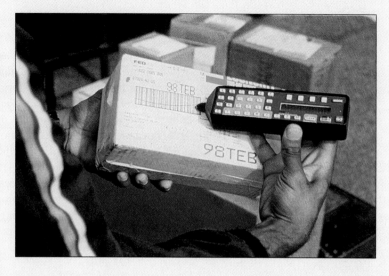

**P**rocess management at FedEx is viewed as a systematic examination of how the actual work of operating a business gets done. This approach, which cuts across divisional, functional, and departmental lines, entails collaborative investigation, analysis, and then refinement of the basic processes, activities, and tasks by which a business operates.

The five core business processes defined at FedEx are: (*a*) providing direction, (*b*) acquiring and retaining customers, (*c*) servicing customers, (*d*) moving, tracking, and delivering the product, and (*e*) invoicing and collecting payment. Process management at FedEx is customer-driven. It focuses first on customer requirements to assure that the process is designed to meet the expectations of the customer. It utilizes analytical techniques to identify high-leverage opportunities for standardizing work processes, as well as for creating opportunities for continuous improvement.

Measurement is also important at FedEx. The old business maxim, "You cannot manage what you cannot measure," has been an inspiration for measuring both customer satisfaction and service quality. Measurement is accomplished through the use of process quality indicators (PQIs), which measure the outputs of processes, as well as other process indicators, which measure such factors as the quality of the process results, the cycle time of each operation within a process, and the cost of the process. An example of a PQI within the moving, tracking, and delivering the product core process is "the total number of conveyances (trucks and aircraft) arriving late at Hubs, destination ramps, and destination stations, which is measured on a daily basis at the corporate level."

FedEx recognizes that its future success depends on many factors, including its ability to improve its business processes. It believes that only if it can adopt and fully utilize analytical business tools, such as process management, to improve operations will it be able to compete against other companies in the marketplace. However, the full utilization of the techniques of process management depends on the motivation and competencies of its front-line management. Its managers must have analytical, communication, and decision-making skills, and that the training is available to ensure that these managers obtain these required skills. ∎

Source: Adapted from a letter from Fred Smith, CEO, FedEx, to FedEx management, October 7, 1996.

As confirmed by Fred Smith at FedEx, managers today recognize that processes exist everywhere within their organizations. We define a *process* as any step or series of steps that are involved in the conversion or transformation of inputs into outputs. We use the terms *process, conversion process,* and *transformation process* interchangeably throughout this text. Exhibit 3.1 presents some examples of the various types of processes that can exist within an organization. Within the operations function, some processes focus on the development of new products; some focus on the day-to-day production of existing products; still others focus on customer service.

This chapter provides a framework for addressing some of the basic issues that are associated with the design and on-going production of goods and services. We also identify the factors that need to be considered in selecting the proper processes for producing these products. We include here a discussion of the product/process relationship and how technology can impact these processes.

# THE ORIGINS OF NEW PRODUCTS

Davis and Tumolo have identified five different types of new products that are a function of the process by which they are developed. These include: (*a*) revolutionary products, (*b*) evolutionary products, (*c*) product extensions, (*d*) core research products, and (*e*) partnership products. How a firm decides to develop new products can have a significant impact on resources (such as plant and equipment), cash flow, and scheduling.[1]

## Revolutionary Products

Revolutionary products are the result of major breakthroughs in science and technology, in terms of new product materials and/or new processes by which the product is made. Ford's Model T car, nylon fabric, the Polaroid camera, Xerox copiers, and compact disks (CDs) provide good examples of revolutionary products.

Typically, a firm with a revolutionary product has a tremendous advantage in the marketplace over its competition. Such new products are often protected by patents, which prevent competition from producing identical or similar products for a significant amount of time. Consequently, these companies often enjoy a captive audience for the first few years

---

**EXHIBIT 3.1**

Examples of Processes within an Organization

Inputs → | Transformation process | → Outputs

| Process Description | Inputs | Outputs |
|---|---|---|
| Market research | Surveys, interviews, focus groups | Customer preferences, suggestions |
| Payroll | Time sheets, time cards | Paychecks |
| Customer service | Complaints, inquiries | Resolution of issues |
| Hiring new employees | Advertisements, interviews, tests | New employees |

---

[1]Mark M. Davis and Paul L. Tumolo, *Operations Management in Manufacturing* (Watertown, MA: American Management Association, 1994), pp. 29–31.

**EXHIBIT 3.4**

Design Change to Reduce the Number of Parts in a Bracket

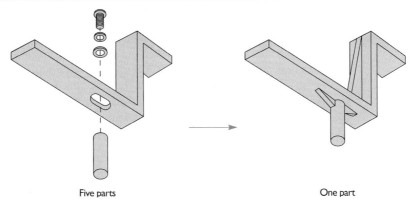

Five parts                                    One part

Source: Bart Huthwaite. "Managing at the Starting Line: How to Design Competitive Products," Workshop at the University of Southern California–Los Angeles, January 14, 1991, p. 7.

## Customer Support Services

MARKETING

More and more firms are looking to service as a means for obtaining a competitive advantage in the marketplace. This includes customer support services after the purchase has been made. It is important that these services properly focus on the needs of the customer and do so in a customer-friendly manner that will continue to foster customer loyalty. Properly designed customer support services understand how a customer uses a product. This information can be obtained through focus groups, and more recently, with "storytelling." With storytelling, market researchers seek out real-life anecdotes that reflect how customers behave and what they actually feel. These stories provide some newfound insights into what customers really want in a product. Using this approach, Kimberly-Clark developed a new $500 million diaper market and Intuit similarly was able to develop software that totally changed the way in which people conduct their financial transactions.[3] Information gathered through these various approaches reduces the need for customer support services by anticipating customer issues before they occur. In addition, when these support services are requested, the firm can respond quickly and properly to satisfy the customer.

## Frequency of Design Changes

Should products be changed every year, twice a year, every two years? How often a firm changes designs depends, in large part, on its marketing strategy. An example of very frequent design changes is Sony Corporation's Walkman cassette player. Sony introduced its Walkman to the market in 1979. It was an immediate success. Two years later, Sony brought out a new model to keep ahead of its competitors. Since 1979, the rate of new Walkman products introduced by Sony has accelerated; Sony has brought out more than 160 models of the Walkman.

Sony has relied on "design-based incrementalism." That is, product families are upgraded and enhanced throughout their life cycles. Such changes are small, frequent, and both technological and topological. *Technological innovation* is introducing new technology that enhances the function, adds higher quality, and/or lowers production costs (e.g., developing a new motor). *Topological design* is the rearrangement or remanufacture of well-understood components (e.g., making smaller parts, a more compact unit, easier functioning,

---

[3]Ronald B. Lieber, "Storytelling: A New Way to Get Close to Your Customer," *Fortune,* February 3, 1997, pp. 102–10.

a more appealing product, or creating product distinction, etc.). Due to its policy of incrementalization, Sony could bring out its "My First Sony" line for children in less than one year because it was built on existing products.

One of the main reasons for the success of Japanese companies is their ability to quickly introduce new products to the market. Their speed of introduction is also compatible with their philosophy of "Ready, Fire, Aim." In the same time that a typical U.S. company takes to conduct extensive and time-consuming market analyses, their Japanese counterparts will launch several new products, letting the market itself determine which ones are good and which ones are not. The key in successfully implementing this strategy is the flexibility of the manufacturing function to easily convert existing production capacity from one product to another.

**Opportunity for Product Design Change**   In the overall development of a new product, the concept and design phases typically commit about 70 percent of the product's manufacturing costs while expending only about 5 percent of the total costs. (Committed costs are defined here as the production costs directly resulting from the design, including materials, labor, processes and so forth.[4]) Often, manufacturers spend far too little time and resources in identifying all the flaws during the design stage of a new product. Therefore, a more prudent approach might suggest expending a bit more to ensure a good, reliable user-friendly design and expecting to profit through reduced committed cost.

**Concurrent Engineering**   A major trend in manufacturing companies is early and continuing involvement with new products by production, materials planning, and engineering support groups and even vendors to ensure that the products are effectively managed throughout their life cycles. At Hewlett-Packard, this responsibility is seen as carrying through product development, transition to manufacturing, volume production, and obsolescence.

**concurrent engineering**
Integration of functional areas in an organization which results in faster design and development of new products.

MARKETING
PURCHASING

**Concurrent engineering** can be used interchangeably with the terms *simultaneous engineering* or *concurrent design*. Obviously, as these terms imply, continual interaction and parallel actions are necessary throughout that entire process from initial product design through production. Other areas such as marketing and purchasing need to be involved and interact with the different phases of design and development. Their input is critical concerning production planning, productive capacity, and the availability of parts and materials. The sequence from product design to delivery to the marketplace is not a series of consecutive steps. Continual interaction throughout the process ensures that a well-designed product is released to the market at a good price and on time.

## New Product Design and Development Processes in Services

Services differ from manufacturing operations in many respects. In services, customers typically interact directly with the service delivery process, and production and consumption take place simultaneously. Services are considered to be intangible, and they cannot be stored. An empty seat on an airline or a vacant hotel room cannot be saved for a busy period when all of the available seats or rooms are being used.

Because of these differences, specifically the direct interaction of the customer with the process, the analysis of service systems must be broader in approach and also include the marketing and human resource management functions within an organization.

[4]Bart Huthwaite, "Managing at the Starting Line: How to Design Competitive Products," Presented at a Workshop at the University of Southern California, Los Angeles, CA, January 14, 1991.

Karl Albrecht and Ron Zemke's *Service America!* gets to the heart of the issue of managing service operations in stating: "Every time a customer comes into contact with any aspect of the company it is a 'moment of truth,' and it can create either a positive or a negative impression about the company."[5] How well these moments of truth are managed depends on a carefully designed service delivery system.

In order to better understand the various processes with respect to services, we begin by presenting several approaches to classifying services. Next, we introduce different service strategies and how to design a service delivery system that is compatible with a specific strategy. Finally, we present three different approaches to designing service delivery systems.

## A Framework for Designing Service Processes

Service systems are generally classified along industry lines (financial services, health services, transportation services, and so on). These groupings, though useful in presenting aggregate economic data, are not particularly appropriate for OM purposes because they tell us little about the process. In manufacturing, by contrast, there are fairly well-defined terms for classifying production activities that transcend industry lines (such as *intermittent* and *continuous production*); when applied to a manufacturing setting, they readily convey the essence of the process. While it is possible to describe services in these same terms, we need another item of information to reflect the level of customer involvement in the process. That item, which we believe operationally distinguishes one service system from another in its production function, is the extent of customer contact in the creation of service.

*Customer contact* refers to the presence of the customer in the system, and *creation of the service* refers to the work process that is involved in providing the service itself. *Extent of contact* here may be roughly defined as the percentage of time the customer must be involved in the system relative to the total time it takes to perform the customer service. Generally speaking, the greater the percentage of contact time between the service system and the customer, the greater the degree of interaction between the two during the production process.

From this concept of customer contact, it follows that service systems with a **high degree of customer contact** are usually more difficult to manage and consequently harder to justify than those with a **low degree of customer contact.** In high-contact systems, the customer can affect the time of demand, the exact nature of the service, and the quality of service since the customer is involved in the process.

Exhibit 3.5 illustrates the difference between high- and low-contact service systems in a bank. Here we see that each design decision is impacted by whether or not the customer is present during the service delivery. We also see that when work is done behind the scenes (in this case a bank's processing center), it is performed on substitutes for the customer, that is, customer reports, databases, and invoices. We can, therefore, design these behind-the-scenes operations according to the same principles we would use in designing a factory. That is, to maximize the amount of items processed during the production day.

Obviously, there can be tremendous diversity of customer influence and hence system variability within high-contact service systems. For example, a bank branch offers both simple services such as cash withdrawals that take just a minute or so, as well as complicated services such as loan application preparation that can take in excess of an hour. Moreover, these activities may range from being self-service through an ATM, to coproduction

**high degree of customer contact** Service operations which require a high percentage of customer contact time.

**low degree of customer contact** Service operations which require a low percentage of customer contact time.

---

[5]Jan Carlson, president, Scandinavian Airlines System, quoted in Karl Albrecht and Ron Zemke, *Service America! Doing Business in the New Economy* (Homewood, IL: Dow Jones-Irwin, 1985), p. 19.

| Design Decision | High-Contact System (a branch office) | Low-Contact System (a check processing center) |
|---|---|---|
| Facility location | Operations must be near the customer. | Operations may be placed near supply, transport, or labor. |
| Facility layout | Facility should accommodate the customer's physical and psychological needs and expectations. | Facility should focus on production efficiency. |
| Product design | Environment as well as the physical product define the nature of the service. | Customer is not in the service environment so the product can be defined by fewer attributes. |
| Process design | Stages of production process have a direct, immediate effect on the customer. | Customer is not involved in majority of processing steps. |
| Scheduling | Customer is in the production schedule and must be accommodated. | Customer is concerned mainly with completion dates. |
| Production planning | Orders cannot be stored, so smoothing production flow will result in loss of business. | Both backlogging and production smoothing are possible. |
| Worker skills | Direct workforce constitutes a major part of the service product and so must be able to interact well with the public. | Direct workforce need only have technical skills. |
| Quality control | Quality standards are often in the eye of the beholder and hence variable. | Quality standards are generally measurable and hence fixed. |
| Time standards | Service time depends on customer needs, and therefore time standards are inherently loose. | Work is performed on customer surrogates (e,g., forms), thus time standards can be tight. |
| Wage payment | Variable output requires time-based wage systems. | "Fixable" output permits output-based wage systems. |
| Capacity planning | To avoid lost sales, capacity must be set to match peak demand. | Storable output permits capacity at some average demand level. |

where bank personnel and the customer work together as a team to develop the loan application.

In another attempt to better understand services in general, Roger Schmenner proposes a method for classifying services along two dimensions.[6] The first dimension, degree of customer interaction and customization, closely parallels the degree of customer contact we discuss above. In addition, Schmenner also includes the degree of labor intensity required to deliver the service. From these two factors he develops a service process matrix, as shown in Exhibit 3.6.

Within this matrix, Schmenner defines four broad categories of services:

1. *Service factory* is characterized by a low degree of labor intensity and a low degree of customer interaction and customization.

2. *Service shop* has the same low degree of labor intensity, but has a higher degree of customer interaction and customization.

---

[6]Roger W. Schmenner, "How Can Service Businesses Survive and Prosper?" *Sloan Management Review* 27, no. 3 (Spring 1986).

**EXHIBIT 3.6**

The Service Process Matrix

| | | Degree of Interaction and Customization | |
|---|---|---|---|
| | | Low | High |
| Degree of Labor Intensity | Low | Service factory:<br>Airlines<br>Trucking<br>Hotels<br>Resorts and recreation | Service shop:<br>Hospitals<br>Auto repair<br>Other repair services |
| | High | Mass service:<br>Retailing<br>Wholesaling<br>Schools<br>Retail aspects of<br>commercial banking | Professional service:<br>Doctors<br>Lawyers<br>Accountants<br>Architects |

Source: Roger W. Schmenner, "How Can Service Businesses Survive and Prosper?", *Sloan Management Review* 27, no. 3 (Spring 1986), pp. 21–32, by permission of publisher. Copyright 1986 by Sloan Management Review Association. All rights reserved.

3. *Mass service* is defined by a high degree of labor intensity, but has a relatively low degree of customer interaction.

4. *Professional service* requires both a high degree of labor intensity as well as a high degree of customer interaction and customization.

This type of classification scheme provides service managers with some insights in developing strategies for their respective organizations. For example, those services that exhibit a low degree of labor intensity are usually capital intense with high fixed costs. These firms cannot easily adjust capacity to meet changes in demand and must, therefore, attempt to smooth out the demand during peak periods by shifting it to off-peak times.

The issues confronting service managers with high labor intensity operations require a different focus. Here, workforce management is paramount, with emphasis being placed on hiring, training, and scheduling.

More important, this approach to classifying services cuts across industry lines, providing service managers with a better understanding of the strengths and weaknesses within their own operations. Through this perspective, managers can look to similar operations in other service industries to seek ways for improving their respective operations.

## Designing a New Service Organization

Designing a service organization entails the execution of four elements of what James Heskett refers to as the "Service Vision."[7] The first element is identification of the target market (Who is our customer?); the second is the service concept (How do we differentiate our service in the market?); the third is the service strategy (What is our service package and the operating focus of our service?); and the fourth is the service delivery system (What are the actual processes, staff requirements, and facilities by which the service is created?).

Choosing a target market and developing the service package are top management decisions setting the stage for the direct operating decisions of service strategy and delivery system design.

Several major factors distinguish service design and development from typical manufactured product development. First, the process and the product must be developed simultaneously; indeed, in services the process is the product. (We make this statement with the

[7]James L. Heskett, "Lessons from the Service Sector," *Harvard Business Review,* March–April 1987, pp.118–26.

general recognition that many manufacturers are using such concepts as concurrent engineering and DFM [design for manufacture] as approaches to more closely link product design and process design.)

Second, although equipment and software that support a service can be protected by patents and copyrights, a service operation itself lacks the legal protection commonly available to goods production. Third, the service package, rather than a definable good, constitutes the major output of the development process. Fourth, many parts of the service package are often defined by the training individuals receive before they become part of the service organization. In particular, in professional service organizations (PSOs) such as law firms and hospitals, prior certification is necessary for hiring. Fifth, many service organizations can change their service offerings virtually overnight. Routine service organizations (RSOs) such as barbershops, retail stores, and restaurants have this flexibility.

### Designing the Customer Service Encounter

**service-system design matrix**
Framework for relating sales opportunities with ways a service can interact with a customer.

Service encounters can be structured in a number of different ways. The **service-system design matrix** in Exhibit 3.7 identifies six common alternatives.

The top of the matrix shows the degree of customer/server contact: the *buffered core,* which is physically separated from the customer; the *permeable system,* which the customer can penetrate via phone or face-to-face contact; and the *reactive system,* which is both penetrable and reactive to the customer's requirements. The left side of the matrix shows what we believe to be a logical marketing proposition, namely, that the greater the amount of contact, the greater the opportunity to generate additional sales; the right side shows the impact on production efficiency as the customer exerts more influence on the operation.

**EXHIBIT 3.7**

Service-System Design Matrix

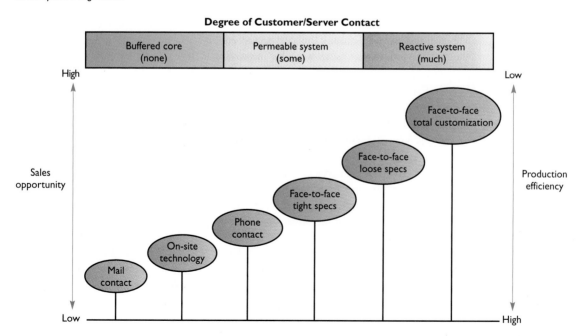

As one would anticipate, production efficiency decreases as the customer contact time increases, thereby giving the customer more influence on the system. To offset this, however, the face-to-face contact provides greater opportunity to sell additional products. Conversely, low contact, such as mail, allows the system to work more efficiently because the customer is unable to significantly affect (or disrupt) the system. However, there is relatively little, if any, sales opportunity for additional product sales at this end of the spectrum.

There can be some shifting in the positioning of each entry. Consider the "face-to-face tight specs" entry in Exhibit 3.7. This refers to those situations where there is little variation in the service process—neither customer nor server has much discretion in creating the service. Fast-food restaurants and Disneyland come to mind. "Face-to-face loose specs" refers to situations where the service process is generally understood, but there are options in the way it will be performed or the physical goods that are a part of it. A full-service restaurant or a car sales agency are examples. "Face-to-face total customization" refers to service encounters whose specifications must be developed through some interaction between the customer and server. Legal and medical services are of this type, and the degree to which the resources of the system are mustered for the service determines whether the system is reactive or merely permeable. Examples would be the mobilization of an advertising firm's resources in preparation for an office visit by a major client, or an operating team scrambling to prepare for emergency surgery.

**Strategic Uses of the Matrix**    The service-system design matrix has both operational and strategic uses. Its operational uses are reflected in its identification of worker requirements, focus of operations, and innovations previously discussed. Some of its strategic uses are

1. *Enabling systematic integration of operations and marketing strategy.* Trade-offs become more clear-cut, and, more important, at least some of the major design variables are crystalized for analysis purposes. For example, the matrix indicates that it would make little sense relative to sales for a service firm to invest in high-skilled workers if it plans to operate using tight specs.
2. *Clarifying exactly which combination of service delivery the firm is actually providing.* As the company incorporates the delivery options listed on the diagonal, it is becoming diversified in its production process.
3. *Permitting comparison with other firms in the way specific services are delivered.* This helps to pinpoint a firm's competitive advantage.
4. *Indicating evolutionary or life cycle changes that might be in order as the firm grows.* Unlike the product-process matrix for manufacturing, where natural growth moves in one direction (from intermittent to line-flow as a volume increases), the evolution of service delivery can move in either direction along the diagonal as a function of the trade-off between efficiency and the potential to generate additional sales.
5. *Providing flexibility.* The user of the matrix can go into depth, placing particular service products of a small firm or individual department on it, or cover a large service organization at a more aggregated level.

# PROCESS SELECTION IN MANUFACTURING

## Types of Processes

Manufacturing operations, as shown in Exhibit 3.8, are categorized into three broad types of process structures, each category depending to a large extent on the volume of item(s) to be produced. These three categories are often referred to as **project processes, intermittent**

**EXHIBIT 3.8**

Types of Processes

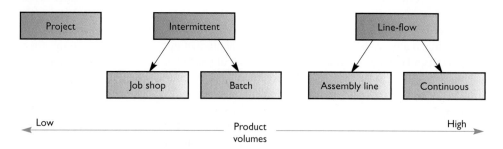

processes, and **line-flow processes.** While we identify three discrete categories, we should emphasize that the different types of manufacturing processes that exist should be viewed as a continuum, and that any one company may incorporate a combination of these processes in the manufacture of its products.

**project process**
Process that focuses on making one-of-a-kind products.

**Project Process**    A project-oriented process usually involves the manufacture of a single, one-of-a-kind product. Examples here include the production of a movie and the erection of a skyscraper. Building a customized car to compete in the Indianapolis 500 race is another good example. The major strength of a project-type process is that it is totally flexible to meet the individual needs of the customer. Projects are usually analyzed using network-solving techniques like those presented in Chapter 10.

Variable costs in this category are comparatively very high. On the other hand, fixed costs are negligible or even nonexistent. (In the extreme case, when there is truly only one product to build, all costs are expensed and consequently there are no fixed costs.)

Highly skilled personnel are usually required for this type of process, as they must often work independently, with minimal guidance and supervision. In addition, workers here need to be well trained in a variety of tasks.

**intermittent process**
Process that produces products in small lot sizes.

**Intermittent Process**    As shown in Exhibit 3.8, intermittent type processes can be further subdivided into job shop and batch processes. We define a *job shop* as a process where a specific quantity of a product is produced only once. Numbered prints from a painting, programs for concerts, and T-shirts commemorating specific events are good examples of products made in a job shop process.

A batch process produces the same item again and again, usually in specified lot sizes. McDonald's is a good example of a batch process where hamburgers are cooked throughout the day in lot sizes of 12. The manufacture of shoes provides another example of a batch process. Here a batch consists of one size and style of shoe.

Variable costs are still relatively high with intermittent processes, although they are usually lower than those of a project-type process. However, higher fixed costs are incurred with these processes. Similarly, worker skills remain high, though somewhat less than those required for projects.

**line-flow process**
Continuous process that produces high volume, highly standardized products.

**Line-Flow Process**    As with intermittent processes, line-flow processes are also frequently subdivided into two processes: assembly line and continuous. Assembly-line processes manufacture individual, discrete products. Examples here include electronic products such as VCRs and CD players, as well as automobiles and kitchen appliances. Continuous processes are exactly what their name implies—continuous, producing products that are not discrete. Petroleum refineries and chemical plants provide good examples of continuous processes.

Line-flow processes can produce a wide variety of products ranging from filling and capping of bottled beer in a continuous flow process at the Miller Brewing Company to motorcycles that are made on an assembly line at Kawasaki Motors Manufacturing Company.

Line-flows are characterized by high fixed costs and low variable costs, and are often viewed as the most efficient of the three types of processes. Labor skill, especially in assembly-line operations, is typically very low, as workers are required to learn only a very few simple operations. Line-flows are used for only the highest volumes of products, are very focused, and consequently are the most inflexible of the three processes.

## The Product-Process Matrix

The relationship between the different types of processes and their respective volume requirements is often depicted on a product-process matrix, shown in Exhibit 3.9, which is adapted from the widely cited Hayes and Wheelwright product-process matrix. In this matrix, as volume increases and the product line narrows (the horizontal dimension), specialized equipment and standardized material flows (the vertical dimension) become economically feasible. This evolution in process structure is frequently related to the different stages of a product's life cycle (introduction, growth, and maturity).

The industries listed within the matrix are presented as ideal types that have found their process niche. It certainly is possible for an industry member to choose another position on the matrix, however. For example, Volvo makes cars on movable pallets rather than on an assembly line. Thus, on the matrix it would be at the intersection of process stage II and product stage III. Volvo's production rate is lower than its competitors because it is giving up the speed and efficiency of the line. On the other hand, the Volvo system has more flexibility and better quality control than the classic automobile production line. Similar kinds of analysis can be carried out for other types of process-product options through the matrix.

In looking at Exhibit 3.9, it is interesting to note that companies that try to operate in either of the corners opposite the diagonal are doomed to failure. Companies in the upper right-hand corner reflect those firms that are too slow to react to changes in the marketplace. As a result, they try to compete in a market that requires high volume, low-cost products with a project-type process that not only has very high variable costs, but also has very limited capacity. As a consequence, these firms incur very high opportunity costs from lost sales because high prices encourage customers to take their business elsewhere.

---

## EXHIBIT 3.9

Matching Major Stages of Product and Process Life Cycles

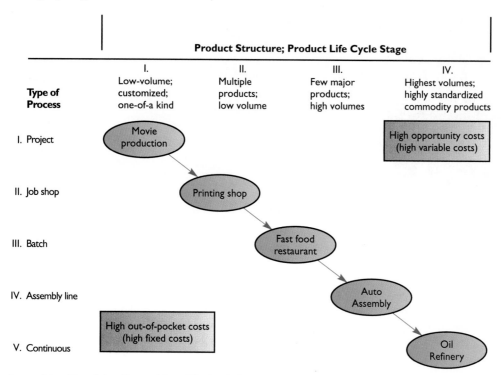

Source: Adapted from Robert Hayes and Steven Wheelwright, *Restoring Competitive Edge: Competing through Manufacturing* (New York: John Wiley & Sons, 1984).

In the lower left-hand corner are companies that anticipated selling greater volumes of product than actually materialized. As a result, these firms have incurred very high out-of-pocket costs in the form of very high fixed costs, which are associated with the capital intensive processes that were installed.

It may be a little easier to understand the logic of a product-process matrix if we divide it into its component parts. Part A of Exhibit 3.10 shows a traditional product life cycle from product conception through product termination. Part B relates the frequency of changes made in the product design to the stages of the product life cycle. Logically, most of the product changes occur during the initial stages of the life cycle, before major production starts. This suggests that a project-type process is appropriate for this stage. The product then tends to go through many changes—simplification, adding features, newer materials, and so forth. The motivation here is for more performance and perhaps greater appeal to a broader market. The flexibility of an intermittent-type process allows for these changes. During the maturity stage of the product very few additional changes are made and the focus is on low costs, which can be provided by a line-flow process.

Changes in the production process, as shown in Part C of Exhibit 3.10, occur most rapidly during the early stages of production design and startup. This is where choices are made in the production layout, equipment, tooling, and so on. The goal here is to reduce production costs. Also, both product and process engineers work together to reduce costs and increase product performance. When full production occurs, few additional changes

**EXHIBIT 3.10**

Product and Process Life Cycles

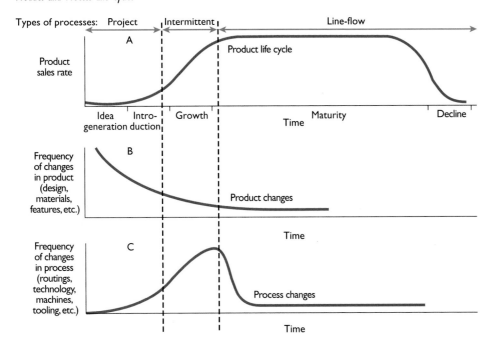

are made. During the decline phase of the product, however, some additional process changes occur; these are due in part to switching the smaller production volumes to different equipment and facilities.

During the early stages in a product's life cycle when production quantities are small (certainly during the product research and development stages), manufacturing likely takes place in a functional type layout, which we usually call a *process-oriented layout.* Here, all similar machines and processes are grouped together in one location and are used for many different products. As production volumes increase, machines and processes may be grouped to simplify the product's flow through the factory. This ultimately results in assembly lines, which are considered to be *product-oriented layouts.*

## Choosing among Alternative Processes

**break-even analysis**
Determination of product volume where the costs associated with two alternative processes are the same.

A standard approach for deciding which among several alternatives is best suited for a particular business is to use **break-even analysis.** (The specific steps involved in conducting a break-even analysis are presented in Chapter 3S which follows this chapter.)

The results of such an analysis can be presented in graph form, as shown in Exhibit 3.11. The horizontal axis represents the volume of product to be produced, while the vertical axis represents the total costs. As discussed previously, projects have little or no fixed costs but very high variable costs. On the other hand, line-flow processes have very high fixed costs but very low variable costs. Intermittent processes fall in between. Using a lowest cost criterion, the choice of which process to adopt is therefore dependent on the volume to be produced. For example, if the anticipated volume is less than $V_1$, then the project process should be selected; if the volume is expected to be between $V_1$ and $V_2$, then the intermittent process is the proper choice; and if the volume will be greater than $V_2$, then the line-flow

**EXHIBIT 3.11**

Determining the Least Cost Process as a Function of Volume

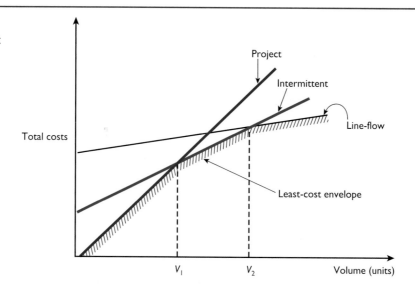

**least-cost envelope**
Lowest total costs to produce various volumes of a product.

process gives us the lowest total cost and unit cost. The lowest cost line for each type of process is often referred to as the **least-cost envelope,** as noted by the shaded area on the graph.

# PROCESS SELECTION IN SERVICES

 ## Types of Service Organizations

Service management issues exist in three broad organizational contexts:

**1.** *Service businesses* are organizations whose primary business requires interaction with the customer to produce the service. Familiar examples of service businesses include banks, airlines, hospitals, law firms, retail stores, restaurants, and so on. Within this category, we can make a further major distinction: **facilities-based services,** where the customer must go to the service facility, and **field-based services,** where production and consumption of the service take place in the customer's environment (e.g., cleaning and home repair services).

**facilities-based services**
Services which require the customer to go to the service facility.

**field-based services**
Services which can be performed at the customer's location.

Technology has allowed for the transfer of many facility-based services to field-based services. Dental vans bring the dentist to your home. Some auto repair services have repairmobiles. Telemarketing brings the shopping center to your TV screen.

**2.** *Customer support services* provide support to external customers who have already purchased the goods and/or services of the company. Included here are 800-numbers for registering complaints and obtaining additional information on the firm's products. Product maintenance and repair services also fall into this category.

**3.** *Internal services* are the services required to support the activities of the larger organization. These services include such functions as data processing, accounting, engineering, and maintenance. Their customers are the various departments within the organization that require such services. (It is not uncommon for an internal service to start marketing its services outside the parent organization and become a service business itself.)

MIS
ACCOUNTING
ENGINEERING
MARKETING

The three general approaches to delivering on-site services are the production line approach made famous by McDonald's Corporation, the customer involvement approach made famous by ATMs and gas stations, and the personal attention approach made famous by Nordstrom department stores.

## The Production Line Approach

The production line approach pioneered by McDonald's refers to more than just the steps required to assemble a Big Mac. Rather, as Theodore Levitt notes, it is treating the delivery of fast food as a manufacturing process rather than a service process.[8] The value of this philosophy is that it overcomes many of the problems inherent in the concept of service itself. That is, service implies subordination or subjugation of the server to the served; manufacturing, on the other hand, avoids this connotation because it focuses on things rather than people. Thus, in manufacturing and at McDonald's, "the orientation is toward the efficient production of results not on the attendance on others." Levitt notes that besides McDonald's marketing and financial skills, the company carefully controls "the execution of each outlet's central function—the rapid delivery of a consistently uniform, high-quality mix of prepared foods in an environment of obvious cleanliness, order, and cheerful courtesy. The systematic substitution of equipment for people, combined with the carefully planned use and positioning of technology, enables McDonald's to attract and hold patronage in proportions no predecessor or imitator has managed to duplicate."

Levitt cites several aspects of McDonald's operations to illustrate the concepts:

- The McDonald's french fryer allows cooking of the optimum number of french fries at one time.
- A wide-mouthed scoop is used to pick up the precise amount of french fries for each order size. (The employee never touches the product.)
- Storage space is expressly designed for a predetermined mix of prepackaged and premeasured products.
- Cleanliness is pursued by providing ample trash cans in and outside each facility (and the larger outlets have motorized sweepers for the parking area).
- Hamburgers are wrapped in color-coded paper.
- Through painstaking attention to total design and facilities planning, everything is built integrally into the (McDonald's) machine itself—into the technology of the system. The only choice available to the attendant is to operate it exactly as the designers intended.

## The Customer Involvement Approach

In contrast to the production line approach, C. H. Lovelock and R. F. Young propose that the service process can be enhanced by having the customer take a greater participatory role in the production of the service.[9] Automatic teller machines (ATMs), self-service gas stations, salad bars, and in-room coffee-making equipment in motels are good examples of where the burden of providing service is shifted to the consumer. Obviously, this philosophy requires some selling on the part of the service organization to convince customers that this is beneficial to them. To this end, Lovelock and Young propose a number of steps, including developing customer trust, promoting the benefits of cost, speed, and convenience, and following up to make sure that the procedures are being effectively used. In essence, this turns customers into "partial employees" who must be trained in what to do and be compensated primarily through low prices charged for the service.

---

[8]Theodore Levitt, "Production-Line Approach to Service," *Harvard Business Review* 50, no. 5 (September–October 1972), pp. 41–52.

[9]C. H. Lovelock and R. F. Young, "Look to Customers to Increase Productivity," *Harvard Business Review* 57, no. 2, (May–June 1979), pp. 168–78.

## The Personal Attention Approach

 The following example by Tom Peters describes how Nordstrom department store operationalizes its personal attention philosophy.[10]

> After several visits to a store's men's clothing department, a customer's suit still did not fit. He wrote the company president, who sent a tailor to the customer's office with a new suit for fitting. When the alterations were completed, the suit was delivered to the customer—free of charge.
>
> This incident involved the $1.3 billion, Seattle-based Nordstrom, a specialty clothing retailer. Its sales per square foot are about five times that of a typical department store. Who received the customer's letter and urged the extreme (by others' standards) response? Co-chairman John Nordstrom.
>
> The frontline providers of this good service are well paid. Nordstrom's salespersons earn a couple of bucks an hour more than competitors, plus a 6.75 percent commission. Its top salesperson moves over $1 million a year in merchandise. Nordstrom lives for its customers and salespeople. Its only official organization chart puts the customer at the top, followed by sales and sales support people. Next come department managers, then store managers, and the board of directors at the very bottom.
>
> Salespersons religiously carry a "personal book," where they record voluminous information about each of their customers; senior, successful salespeople often have three or four bulging books, which they carry everywhere, according to Betsy Sanders, the vice president who orchestrated the firm's wildly successful penetration of the tough southern California market. "My objective is to get one new personal customer a day," says a budding Nordstrom star. The system helps him do just that. He has a virtually unlimited budget to send cards, flowers, and thank-you notes to customers. He also is encouraged to shepherd his customer to any department in the store to assist in a successful shopping trip.
>
> He also is abetted by what may be the most liberal returns policy in this or any other business: Return *anything,* no questions asked. Sanders says that "trusting customers," or "our bosses" as she repeatedly calls them, is vital to the Nordstrom philosophy. President Jim Nordstrom told the *Los Angeles Times,* "I don't care if they roll a Goodyear tire into the store. If they say they paid $200, give them $200 (in cash) for it." Sanders acknowledges that a few customers rip the store off—"rent hose from us," to use a common insider's line. But this is more than offset by goodwill from the 99 percent-plus who benefit from the "No Problem at Nordstrom" logo that the company lives up to with unmatched zeal.
>
> No bureaucracy gets in the way of serving the customer. Policy? Sanders explains to a dumbfounded group of Silicon Valley executives, "I know this drives the lawyers nuts, but our whole 'policy manual' is just one sentence, 'Use your own best judgment at all times.'" One store manager offers a translation, "Don't chew gum. Don't steal from us."

No matter what approach is taken, seven common characteristics of well-designed service systems have been identified:

1. *Each element of the service system is consistent with the operating focus of the firm.* For example, when the focus is on speed of delivery, each step in the process should help to foster speed.

2. *It is user-friendly.* This means that the customer can interact with it easily—that is, it has good signage, understandable forms, logical steps in the process, courteous service workers that are available to answer questions, and is easily accessible.

3. *It is robust.* That is, it can cope effectively with variations in demand and resource availability. For example, if the computer goes down, effective backup systems are in place to permit service to continue.

4. *It is structured so that consistent performance by its people and systems is easily maintained.* This means that the tasks required of the workers can be performed

---

[10]Tom Peters, *Quality!* Palo Alto, CA: TPG Communications, 1986, pp. 10–12.

repeatedly with a high level of consistency, and the supporting technologies are truly supportive and reliable.

5. *It provides effective links between the back office and the front office so that nothing falls between the cracks.* In other words, the barriers between the different functional areas are reduced or eliminated.

6. *It manages the evidence of service quality in such a way that customers see the value of the service provided.* Many services do a great job behind the scenes but fail to make this visible to the customer. This is particularly true where a service improvement is made. Unless customers are made aware of the improvement through explicit communication about it, the improved performance is unlikely to gain maximum impact.

7. *It is cost-effective.* There is minimum waste of time and resources in delivering the service.

# THE ROLE OF TECHNOLOGY

## Technology in Manufacturing

The term *automation* is familiar to all, but a commonly agreed upon definition still eludes us. Some authorities view automation as a totally new set of concepts that relate to the automatic operation of a production process; others view it simply as an evolutionary development in technology in which machinery performs some or all of the process-control function. Automation is a set of concepts, but it is also evolutionary in the sense that it is a logical and predictable step in the development of equipment and processes.

Some major developments in manufacturing automation include machining centers, numerically controlled machines, industrial robots, computer-aided design and manufacturing systems, flexible manufacturing systems, computer-integrated manufacturing, and islands of automation.

**machining centers**
Operations where machine tools are changed automatically as part of the process.

**Machining centers** not only provide automatic control of a machine but carry out automatic tooling changes as well. For example, a single machine may be equipped with a shuttle system of two worktables that can be rolled into and out of the machine. While work is being done at one table, the next part is mounted on the second table. When machining on the first table is complete, it is moved out of the way and the second part is moved into position.

**numerically controlled (NC) machines**
Manufacturing equipment that is directly controlled by a computer.

**Numerically controlled (NC) machines** are under the control of a digital computer. Feedback control loops determine the position of the machine tooling during the work, constantly compare the actual location with the programmed location, and correct as needed. This eliminates time lost during setups, and applies to both high-volume, standardized types of products as well as low-volume, customized products.

**industrial robots**
Programmable machines that can perform multiple functions.

**Industrial robots** are substitutes for human manipulation and other highly repetitive functions. A robot is a reprogrammable machine with multiple functions that can move devices through specialized motions to perform any number of tasks. It is essentially a mechanized arm that can be fitted with a variety of handlike fingers or grippers, vacuum cups, or a tool such as a wrench. Robots are capable of performing many factory operations ranging from machining processes to simple assembly.

One of the major contemporary approaches to the product design process is **computer-aided (or -assisted) design (CAD).** *CAD* may be defined as carrying out all structural or mechanical design processes of a product or component at a specially equipped computer terminal. Engineers design through a combination of console controls and a light pen that draws on the computer screen or electronic pad. Different perspectives of the product can be visualized by rotating the product on the screen, and individual components can be enlarged to examine particular characteristics. Depending on the sophistication in software, on-screen testing may replace the early phases of prototype testing and modification.

CAD has been used to design everything from computer chips to potato chips. Frito-Lay, for example, used CAD to design its O'Grady's double-density, ruffled potato chip. CAD is also now being used to custom design swimsuits. Measurements of the wearer are fed into the CAD program, along with the style of suit desired. Working with the customer, the designer modifies the suit design as it appears on a humanform drawing on the computer screen. Once the design is decided upon, the computer prints out a pattern, and the suit is cut and sewn on the spot.

**Computer-aided design and manufacturing (CAD/CAM)** uses a computer to integrate component design and processing instructions. In current CAD/CAM systems, when the design is finalized, the link to CAM is made by producing the manufacturing instructions. Because of the efficiency of CAD/CAM systems, design and manufacture of small lots can be both fast and low in cost.

Even though CAD/CAM systems are usually limited to larger companies because of the high initial cost, they do increase productivity and quality dramatically. More alternative designs can be produced, and the specifications can be more exact. Updates can be more readily made, and cost estimates more easily drawn. In addition, computer-aided process planning (CAPP) can shorten and, in some cases, even eliminate traditional process planning.

A **flexible manufacturing system (FMS)** actually refers to a number of systems that differ in the degree of mechanization, automated transfer, and computer control and are sufficiently flexible to produce a wide variety of products.

A flexible manufacturing module is a numerically controlled (NC) machine supported with a parts inventory, a tool changer, and a pallet changer. A flexible manufacturing cell consists of several flexible manufacturing modules organized according to the particular product's requirements. A flexible manufacturing group is a combination of flexible manufacturing modules and cells located in the same manufacturing area and joined by a material handling system, such as an automated guided vehicle (AGV).

A flexible production system consists of flexible manufacturing groups that connect different manufacturing areas, such as fabrication, machining, and assembly. A flexible manufacturing line is a series of dedicated machines connected by automated guided vehicles (AGVs), robots, conveyors, or some other type of automated transfer devices.

**Computer-integrated manufacturing (CIM)** integrates all aspects of production into one automated system. Design, testing, fabrication, assembly, inspection, and materials handling may all have automated functions within the area. However, in most companies, communication between departments still flows by means of paperwork. In CIM, these islands of automation are integrated, thus eliminating the need for the paperwork. A computer links all sectors together, resulting in more efficiency, less paperwork, and less personnel expense.

---

**computer-aided (or -assisted) design (CAD)**
Designing a product using a specially equipped computer.

**computer-aided design and manufacturing system (CAD/CAM)**
Integration of design and production of a product through use of a computer.

**flexible manufacturing system (FMS)**
Manufacturing facility that is automated to some extent and produces a wide variety of products.

**computer-integrated manufacturing (CIM)**
Integration of all aspects of manufacturing through computers.

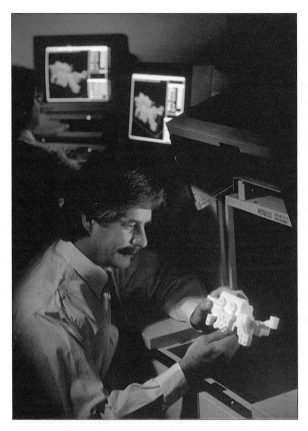

The speed with which a company can design and develop new products is a critical element in its ability to quickly introduce new products into the marketplace. Rapid prototyping machines are a new generation of CAD equipment that can quickly produce three dimensional prototypes early in the product design cycle. These rough draft models of new designs result in higher quality products and lower development costs.

This flexible manufacturing system from Cincinnati Milacron automates the machining of structural aerospace components at Boeing's plant in Auburn, Washington. The demand for this technology is driven by industry's need to shorten lead times and improve flexibility.

**islands of automation**
Automated factories or portions which include NC equipment, automated storage/ retrieval systems, robots and machining centers.

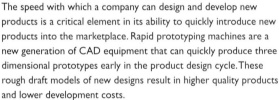

MIS

**Islands of automation** refers to the transition from conventional manufacturing to the automated factory. Typical islands of automation include numerically controlled machine tools, robots, automated storage/retrieval systems, and machining centers.

## Technology in Services

The advances in technology, especially information technology, have had a significant impact on how services are provided. Technology, in one form or another, has penetrated almost every type of service. In-room check-out at hotels, automatic teller machines (ATMs) at banks, airline reservation systems, and the emergence of the Internet provide good examples of how technology affects the delivery of services. As an illustration, using e-mail to provide technical support instead of a telephone allows a company to "inventory" demand, and thus level out the workload over a 24-hour period. In addition, by making documents available at a Web site, the cost and time to obtain these documents are placed on the customer. At the same time, these documents are always available when the customer wants them.

However, management must clearly understand how the technology is to be used and then define its role in the overall organization to avoid many of the pitfalls that have been previously experienced. For example, many service firms have looked to technology to increase worker productivity and ultimately to increase profits. However, as Roach has pointed out, the large investments in technology that these service companies have made have not yielded the expected increases in productivity.[11] In order to better understand the various ways in which technology can contribute to services, Quinn and Bailey have identified the following reasons, other than increasing productivity, that a company would want to invest in technology:

- Maintaining market share.
- Avoiding catastrophic losses.
- Creating greater flexibility and adaptability.
- Improving responsiveness for new products.
- Improving service quality.
- Enhancing quality of life.
- Increasing predictability of operations.[12]

When investing in technology, service managers must therefore realize that technology investments may not result in increased productivity. In fact, managers must realize that such investments are often required just to maintain the status quo (and the lack of such investments would have resulted in significant decreases in sales and associated profits) with respect to competition. Managers must also realize that some of the benefits of technology investments are difficult to measure and quantify in dollars, such as improved worker morale and shortened customer service times, both of which may be of considerable importance to the organization. As an example, Norwalk Furniture Corporation of Norwalk, Ohio, uses technology to simplify a customer's furniture selection process. (See OM in Practice box.)

Technology can significantly alter the way in which a company does business. Adopting the proper strategy and associated technology can result in substantial increases in market share and profits. Failure to do so can result in customers defecting to competitors. We suggest there are four major strategies that service firms can adopt in terms of why they should invest in technology. These are: (*a*) strengthen customer relations, (*b*) provide rapid and controlled growth, (*c*) improve performance, and (*d*) increase efficiency.

**Strengthen Customer Relationships**   One reason why services are adopting new technologies is to strengthen their relationships with their customers. For example, during the 1950s, Holiday Inn was probably one of the first companies to recognize the importance of information technology as a way in which it could achieve a competitive advantage. With its *Holidex* reservation system network, customers were able to make reservations at any Holiday Inn in the country from any other Holiday Inn with only a single, toll-free telephone call. Similarly, American Airlines SABRE system has linked that airline's reservation systems directly to travel agents, thereby giving them online, real-time capability to provide information to customers. Instead of dealing with a reservation agent, which can be time consuming and inefficient, the travel agent, with the SABRE system, can quickly explore all of the flight and pricing options for a customer.

---

[11]S. S. Roach, "Services Under Seige—The Restructuring Imperative," *Harvard Business Review,* September–October 1991, pp. 82–91.

[12]J. B. Quinn and M. N. Bailey, "Information Technology: Increasing Productivity in Services," *Academy of Management Executive* 8, no. 3, 1994, pp. 28–51.

# Operations Management in Practice

## COMPUTERS ASSIST CUSTOMERS IN CHOOSING FABRICS AT NORWALK— THE FURNITURE IDEA STORES

When customers visit a retail outlet of Norwalk Furniture, they can actually see what a chair or sofa will look like with different types of fabrics. To simplify the customer selection process, Norwalk has installed in each of its retail locations a computer with a software package that will allow customers to view a particular style of sofa or chair with a variety of fabric designs. The computer and software are part of a larger overall process that Norwalk has recently developed which allows it to deliver customized furniture to its customers in about five weeks—half the normal delivery time in the furniture industry.

Even though it is the leader in the industry, in terms of fast delivery, Norwalk isn't resting on its laurels. Instead, Norwalk is continuously looking at new ways and processes which will allow them to deliver furniture even faster than they currently do.

Source: Special thanks to Barb Myers at Norwalk Furniture.

---

**Provide Rapid and Controlled Growth**   A second reason that service companies are investing in new technologies is to achieve rapid and controlled growth. Services that interact directly with their customers must be located where these customers are. Examples include retail operations, restaurants, hotels and car rental agencies. For example, one of the key factors to the sustained and managed growth of Mrs. Fields' Cookies was the management information system that was custom designed and installed for its operations. As a result, the headquarters for Mrs. Fields' Cookies, located in Utah, receives on a daily basis a detailed performance report on every outlet throughout the world. In addition to providing operational measures of performance, the system also has the capability to conduct initial interviews with prospective workers.

Wal-Mart provides another good example of how technology can provide a firm with the ability to have rapid growth while maintaining consistency across all locations. Through advances in technology, Wal-Mart has installed in its headquarters in Arkansas a satellite hookup with all of its retail operations. With this new system, the president of Wal-Mart can now have weekly meetings with all of his store managers. With this satellite system, all company news is quickly disseminated to all its employees, thereby eliminating rumors. Since all employees are receiving the same message at the same time, possible sources of miscommunication and unnecessary delays are also eliminated.

**Improve Performance**   Service managers must recognize that the decision to adopt technology is often driven by the need to increase the existing performance of their current operations rather than only to increase productivity. Often, however, with the proper technology, both performance and productivity can be improved to create a win-win situation for the firm. Performance here can be defined as (*a*) faster service, (*b*) improved knowledge about their customers and (*c*) increased customization.

For example, to provide faster service, many hotels now provide their guests with an in-room checkout option. Guests who want to take advantage of this option simply follow the menu-driven instructions on the television in their rooms, leave their room keys in the rooms, and never have to wait in line at the front desk to check out.

Databases are now available that can provide managers with detailed information on their customers' purchasing characteristics. As part of their focus on attention to personal detail, for example, the Ritz-Carlton hotel chain, with its management information system, can track individual guest preferences including the type of bed they like to sleep in (such as a queen or king-size bed) and the type of wine they prefer. Any previous incidents involving the customer, particularly complaints, are also recorded in the database to assure that similar incidents do not occur again. Another method of using technology for obtaining data on individual customers is through membership cards. Many retail operations now require membership cards or provide discount incentives to encourage the use of these cards. For example, BJ's Wholesale Club, Costco, and Sam's Club all require their customers to have membership cards.

Technology also allows service managers to provide their customers with a wider variety of options than they could offer previously. The terms **micro-niching** and **mass customization** have evolved, in part, as a direct result of advances in technology that permit firms to identify and provide customized goods and services to individual customers. As an example, Levi Strauss now provides customers in its retail stores with the option of buying jeans that are made to the customer's exact size. The customer's measurements are entered into the computer and a few weeks later the jeans are delivered to the customer's home. Additional pairs can be ordered with only a telephone call, thereby eliminating the need to visit the store.

**micro-niching**
Dividing the market into very small segments that often comprise only one customer.

**mass customization**
Ability to provide customized products to a large group of customers.

**Increased Efficiency**     Another goal in using technology in services is to reduce operating costs. Just as capital equipment is often used to reduce costs in a manufacturing company, technology can be similarly applied in a service environment. The two primary ways in which the efficiency or productivity of the operation can be increased are through (*a*) economies of scale and (*b*) reduced direct labor costs, recognizing that there is some overlap between the two.

In making the decision to adopt new technologies for their operations, service managers must recognize the fact that these technologies require a significant amount of training and support in order for both workers and customers to reap the full benefits. The lack of proper training and support, in many instances, will not only fail to yield the expected improvements in performance and/or productivity, but could also prove disastrous financially as frustrated workers quit and customers defect.

It is also critical that managers, when investing in technology, review the long-term goals of the firm to ensure that compatibility in the form of strategic alignment exists between the technology being adopted and these goals. For example, the customers of a five-star hotel chain want personalized, individual attention (and are willing to pay for it) will probably be turned off by an automated, menu-driven room reservation system that is very time consuming (from the customer's perspective).

## CONCLUSION

It is becoming more and more apparent that successful firms are not simply a collection of vaguely related activities acting independently. Rather, the successful companies of today and tomorrow are well-integrated and well-disciplined organizations. Just like a physical machine, each part of the firm—labor, equipment and management—has an important role to play in achieving that success. The choice of process is also a contributing factor. Goods and services can be produced by several different types of processes, each of which has its own distinctive characteristics. It is important for management to identify these process characteristics in selecting a process to ensure that the goods and services being delivered meet the needs of the firm's customers. In other words, to succeed in the marketplace, a company's processes should be compatible with the customer requirements of the specific market niche that it is trying to serve.

The understanding of how to better manage services clearly lags behind manufacturing. In fact, many of the concepts that have been successfully developed in manufacturing have been adopted by service operations. Nevertheless, services are different from manufacturing, and managers must recognize these differences (the prime difference being the interaction of the customer with the service delivery process). Although service design was once considered an art form, specific logical approaches to better design and management of service systems are slowly emerging.

It is also apparent that advances in technology will continue to alter the ways in which goods and services are designed, produced and delivered. How much of an impact such innovations will have is one of the most intriguing questions to be answered in the coming years. We do know, however, that product life cycles and delivery times will continue to decrease and that customer demand for more customized products will continue to grow. Both of these factors will only increase the pressure on organizations to maintain state-of-the-art technologies in their processes.

At the same time, there also appears to be a blurring between what we typically think of as manufacturing firms and what we think of as service firms. For example, companies such as Bally Manufacturing, Turner Construction, and Exxon Pipeline, which started out as manufacturing firms, are now listed among the Fortune 500 service companies. IBM, which is considered to be a manufacturer, derives a major portion of its revenues and profits from various services that it provides. We anticipate that this "blurring" between manufacturing and services will continue. The key to success in the future will be dependent on the ability of firms to properly integrate their manufacturing and services elements so that the customer perceives it as a seamless, total entity rather than as independent and separate components.

## KEY TERMS

break-even analysis   p. 59
computer-aided (or -assisted) design
   (CAD)   p. 64
computer-aided design and manufacturing
   system (CAD/CAM)   p. 64
computer-integrated manufacturing
   (CIM)   p. 64
concurrent engineering   p. 50
facilities-based services   p. 60
field-based services   p. 60
flexible manufacturing system (FMS)   p. 64
industrial robots   p. 63
islands of automation   p. 65
least-cost envelope   p. 60

levels of customer interaction in
   services   p. 51
   high degree of customer contact   p. 51
   low degree of customer contact   p. 51
machining centers   p.63
mass customization   p. 68
micro-niching   p. 68
numerically controlled machines (NC)   p. 63
product's specifications   p. 48
service-system design matrix   p. 54
types of processes   p. 55
   project   p. 56
   intermittent   p. 56
   line-flow   p. 56

## REVIEW AND DISCUSSION QUESTIONS

1. What factors have contributed to the increased emphasis on faster product development and introduction?

2. Discuss the product design phases of design for manufacturability and customer service support. Which do you think is the more important?

3. Discuss the "ready, fire, aim" philosophy of many Japanese companies with respect to new product introduction. How does it compare with that of the typical U.S. company?

4. Why is daily contact between engineering and production groups so important in making early involvement effective?

5. What are the three major categories of processes, and how do they differ in terms of operational characteristics?

6. What is the product-process matrix telling us? How does automation change its basic premise?

7. Assume that a firm would like to manufacture a new product. What are the areas of responsibility for each of the functional business areas (marketing, finance, accounting, human resources, operations)?

8. Why is it important that managers understand the relationship between the various stages of a product's life cycle and the different types of processes that are available for manufacturing that product?

9. Is it possible for a service firm to use either a production line approach or a self-serve design approach and still keep a high customer focus (personal attention)? Explain and support your answer with examples.

10. Identify the high-contact and low-contact operations that exist in the following services:
    *a.* A dental office.
    *b.* An airline.
    *c.* An accounting office.
    *d.* An automobile agency.

11. Some suggest that customer expectation is the key to service success. Give an example from your own experience to support or refute this assertion.

12. Where would you place a drive-in church, a campus food vending machine, and a bar's automatic mixed drink machine on the service-system design matrix?

13. Using Schmenner's classification scheme that is shown in Exhibit 3.6, identify different segments within a broad service industry (e.g., food service, health care, transportation, etc.) that meet the characteristics found in at least two of the four quadrants, and discuss the key managerial issues in each segment.

14. What are the different ways in which technology can impact an operation? Use examples in both manufacturing and service operations.

 # INTERNET UPDATE

Conduct a search on the Internet to locate companies where specific products are identified and the various types of processes that are required to make them are described. Suggested key words to assist you in this search include: OPERATIONS, MANUFACTURING, SERVICES, and PRO-CESSES.

# PROBLEMS

1. *a.* List specific products that you especially like. What do you like most about them?
   *b.* Create a list of products that you dislike or are unhappy with. What don't you like about them?
   *c.* Are there some common reasons for your lists? For example, is it more important for products that you don't see or see very little to be functional rather than attractive (e.g., the furnace or air conditioning in the house, the transmission or engine in the car)? Is it more important for things to be well designed that other people see and relate to you such as your car, your clothes, or your apartment or home furnishings?
   Can you formulate some general design guidelines based on your answers?

2. Pick a product and make a list of issues that need to be considered in its design and manufacture. The product can be something like a stereo, a telephone, a desk, a kitchen appliance, etc. Consider the functional and aesthetic aspects of design as well as the important concerns for manufacturing.

3. Place the following functions of a department store on the service-system design matrix: Mail order (i.e., catalog), phone order, hardware, stationery, apparel, cosmetics, customer service (i.e., complaints).

4. Place the following functions of a hospital on the service-design system matrix: Physician/patient, nurse/patient, billing, medical records, lab tests, admissions, diagnostic tests (e.g., X-rays).

5. The first step in studying a production process is to develop a description of that process. Once the process is described, we are better able to determine why it works well or poorly and to recommend production-related improvements. Since we are all familiar with fast-food restaurants, try your hand at describing the production process employed at, say, a McDonald's. In doing so, answer the following questions:

   *a.* What are the important aspects of the service package?

   *b.* Which skills and attitudes are needed by the service personnel?

   *c.* How can customer demand be altered?

   *d.* Can the customer/provider interface be changed to include more technology? More self-serve?

   *e.* How does it measure up on the seven characteristics of a well-designed service?

## CASE: THE BEST ENGINEERED PART IS NO PART

Putting together NCR Corp.'s new 2760 electronic cash register is a snap. In fact, William R. Sprague can do it in less than two minutes—blindfolded. To get that kind of easy assembly, Sprague, a senior manufacturing engineer at NCR, insisted that the point-of-sale terminal be designed so that its parts fit together with no screws or bolts.

The entire terminal consists of just 15 vendor-produced components. That's 85 percent fewer parts, from 65 percent fewer suppliers, than in the company's previous low-end model, the 2160. And the terminal takes only 25 percent as much time to assemble. Installation and maintenance are also a breeze, says Sprague. "The simplicity flows through to all of the downstream activities, including field service."

The new NCR product is one of the best examples to date of the payoffs possible from a new engineering approach called "design for manufacturability," mercifully shortened to DFM. Other DFM enthusiasts include Ford, General Motors, IBM, Motorola, Perkin-Elmer, and Whirlpool. Since 1981, General Electric Co. has used DFM in more than 100 development programs, from major appliances to gearboxes for jet engines. GE figures that the concept has netted $200 million in benefits, either from cost savings or from increased market shares.

### NUTS TO SCREWS

One U.S. champion of DFM is Geoffrey Boothroyd, a professor of industrial and manufacturing engineering at the University of Rhode Island and the co-founder of Boothroyd Dewhurst Inc. This tiny Wakefield (R.I.) company has developed several computer programs that analyze designs for ease of manufacturing.

The biggest gains, notes Boothroyd, come from eliminating screws and other fasteners. On a supplier's invoice, screws and bolts may run mere pennies apiece, and collectively they account for only about 5 percent of a typical product's bill of materials. But tack on all of the associated costs, such as the time needed to align components while screws are inserted and tightened, and the price of using those mundane parts can pile up to 75 percent of total assembly costs. "Fasteners should be the first thing to design out of a product," he says.

Had screws been included in the design of NCR's 2760, calculates Sprague, the total cost over the lifetime of the model would have been $12,500—per screw. "The huge impact of little things like screws, primarily on overhead costs, just gets lost," he says. That's understandable, he admits, because for new-product development projects "the overriding factor is hitting the market window. It's better to be on time and over budget than on budget but late."

But NCR got its simplified terminal to market in record time without overlooking the little details. The product was formally introduced last January, just 24 months after development began. Design was a paperless, interdepartmental effort from the very start. The product remained a computer model until all members of the team—from design engineering, manufacturing, purchasing, customer service, and key suppliers—were satisfied.

That way, the printed-circuit boards, the molds for its plastic housing, and other elements could all be developed simultaneously. This eliminated the usual lag after designers throw a new product "over the wall" to manufacturing, which then must figure out how to make it. "Breaking down the walls between design and manufacturing to facilitate simultaneous engineering," Sprague declares, "was the real breakthrough."

The design process began with a mechanical computer-aided engineering program that allowed the team to fashion three-dimensional models of each part on a computer screen. The software also analyzed the overall product and its various elements for performance and durability. Then the simulated components were assembled on a computer workstation's screen to assure that they would fit together properly. As the design evolved, it was checked periodically with Boothroyd Dewhurst's DFM software. This prompted several changes that trimmed the parts count from an initial 28 to the final 15.

## NO MOCK-UP

After everyone on the team gave their thumbs-up, the data for the parts were electronically transferred directly into computer-aided manufacturing systems at the various suppliers. The NCR designers were so confident everything would work as intended that they didn't bother making a mock-up.

DFM can be a powerful weapon against foreign competition. Several years ago, IBM used Boothroyd Dewhurst's software to analyze dot-matrix printers it was sourcing from Japan—and found it could do substantially better. Its Proprinter had 65 percent fewer parts and slashed assembly time by 90 percent. "Almost anything made in Japan," insists Professor Boothroyd, "can be improved upon with DFM—often impressively."

## QUESTION

What development problems has the NCR approach overcome?

Source: Otis Port, "The Best-Engineered Part Is No Part at All," *Business Week,* May 8, 1989, p. 150.

# CASE: KINKO'S COPIER STORES

"We're not your average printer," says Annie Odell, Kinko's regional manager for Louisiana. She's right. She may have the only printshops in town where customers come as much for the company as for the copies. It's a free-wheeling, high-tech operation that marches to the beat of a different drum machine. It looks chaotic; it is chaotic. Yet it produces profit as well as fun.

Odell's copy shop empire has grown from one to seven in six years, including five in the greater New Orleans area.

Kinko's keeps its sales figures a secret, but Odell estimates her New Orleans stores make about 40 million copies a year. At the firm's advertised 4 1/2 cents-per-copy price, that would mean around $1.8 million a year in sales, or an average of over $300,000 per shop. The New Orleans operations rank among Kinko's top 25 percent nationally, reports Becky Barieau of Kinko's of Georgia.

Sales in New Orleans have climbed even while the marketplace has been sinking. At the Carrollton store, revenues increased 10 percent over last year, an excellent showing considering the 4½ cents-per-copy rate has not budged since 1980.

"Depression seems to generate more need for copies," says Wallis Windsor, manager of the Carrollton store, "There are bankruptcies, legal documents and resumes—hundreds of people who want 50 copies of their resumes on specialty paper."

## PRINTERS SNEER

Kinko's is unique. For one thing, it doesn't do a lick of offset printing. It makes copies, copies, and almost nothing but copies. On the side it binds, folds, staples, collates, makes pads, and takes passport photos.

Kinko's is also unique among quick printing chains in that it doesn't franchise. All 300 or so Kinko's stores are divided among a few closely held corporations, and founder Paul Orfalea holds a piece of virtually all of them. Odell explains that the company avoids franchising to ensure tight control over quality at its outlets.

Others attribute the structure to a desire to avoid the legal restrictions and paperwork demanded by setting up franchises in different states. How it's been kept together is a management feat in itself.

Even the name sticks out. The Yellow Pages list dozens of quick printers with some reference to speed in their names, often intentionally misspelled. "Kinko's" denotes a place that's . . . well, a little kinky. For the record, Orfalea, who plugged in his first photocopier when he was in college, was nicknamed by classmates as "Kinko" for his curly head of hair.

## BROADWAY AND BENIHANA

Kinko's management style draws on both the restaurant business and the stage. Fast copies are like fast food, say the managers. It's not just that every Big Mac is a copy of every other one. Images of eating come up again and again as they try to explain what keeps their customers coming back.

"Making copies is addictive," says Windsor, and points to her clientele of "regulars," who "have made this their office. They will spend four or five hours here although they don't spend more than $5 or $6. People have suggested we open a bar in here."

"Instant gratification is what Kinko's is offering," says another manager.

The last time managers from around the country huddled in Santa Barbara for the company "picnic," they studied looseleaf binders crammed full of floor plans for McDonald's and Benihana of Tokyo—a variation on the acclaimed art of Japanese management.

"You'd find it hard to believe," says Odell, "but Benihana is a lot like Kinko's. They're masters of efficiency. We'll try to set up the floor to get one person operating two copiers, just like Benihana puts one cook between two tables. Our paper is centrally located, just as they have all the chopping prepared ahead of time. Then there's the floater, who floats around and pops in wherever he's needed."

Both Kinko's and Benihana's use theater to attract clients, charging their employees with putting on a good show as well as putting out good service. At the Japanese restaurant, the show is the cook, who sizzles a sukiyaki right in front of your table. At Kinko's, it's the clatter of copy machines and the Charlie Chaplinlike spectacle of operators running back and forth between them.

"They do it right in front of you and you get instant quality control," says Odell, "There's no way you're going to drop that document with the customer watching you."

She deliberately displays all her machines and personnel in one big room. "We work out with the public. That's why it's fun," says Odell, "The other guys are behind closed doors."

Windsor enjoys working in a fishbowl. "My personality changes," she says. "I'll be a little more dramatic and louder than I would be in a closed group. I walk quickly. I'll wad up and throw papers a lot."

She believes customers unconsciously get into the act. "Some of the mildest-mannered people get aggressive in here. I've seen a little old lady elbow her way in ahead of people, where if she were in a bank she'd stand in line neatly."

Kinko's does no broadcast and little print advertising, counting on price and word-of-mouth to draw customers, and ambience doesn't hurt. Each Kinko's has its "regulars," who get friendly with particular operators and who favor particular machines. The area in front of the counter is strewn with typewriters, lettering machines and light tables, all the better to hook people into making themselves comfortable and coming back.

A recent addition to that melange is the customer comment form. The customer mails the postage-paid form straight to headquarters in Santa Barbara, where senior management review it and send a thank-you note to the author before routing it back to the shop manager for action. Odell has several inches of forms on file, along with notes on the follow-up calls she made to the customers.

"We don't choose our market so much as our market chooses us," she says. Each shop keeps a different mix of machines, depending on the needs of its patrons. An operator learns quickly that the Xerox 1000 series picks up blue but not yellow, while the 9000 series picks up yellow and black but not blue. Thus, the store adjoining the Tulane campus does not have a 9000 because students tend to bring in notes and books highlighted with yellow markers.

Another adaptation to the market is "Professor Publishing," a service which lets professors excerpt chapters from several books and print them up together as a single textbook. During the first two weeks of every semester, the Broadway office works virtually around-the-clock on this specialty.

Odell maintains that her managers clear all material with publishers before printing a professor's anthology. Indeed, Kinko's says it is one of the most scrupulous of the copy chains about observing copyright laws.

## PRINTING IN A FISHBOWL

If working at the Kinko's shops in New Orleans is like working in a fishbowl, it's a two-way fishbowl where the fish are always peering back at their audience. The crazy-quilt mix of customers provides endless entertainment and a fund of oddball stories to exchange over beers. A sampling:

- One woman insisted that the manager throw away the ribbon on the self-service typewriter she'd just used, fearing that someone might try to use it to recreate her document. Another customer wanted several confidential pages typed, and asked, "Can you get me a typist who won't read them?"

- Some artists enjoy using the photocopiers for the oddest things. One woman brings in stuffed dead birds for reproduction. Another brought in a box of pecans purported to be from the backyard of a house where Tennessee Williams once lived.

- A tipsy woman, about 25 years of age, meandered in from a Mardi Gras parade, curled up next to a window, and fell asleep. There she remained for four hours, while the copiers and binding machines pounded and rattled. Manager Raynell Murphy called the home office. "What should I do?" she asked.

"Get a picture," came the word from California, "We can use it as a promotion, you know, to show what a relaxed atmosphere we have at Kinko's."

Finally, a hulking woman who had just bought some copies walked over to the sleeper, kicked her a couple of times, and asked, "Are you ready yet?" The sleeper arose and groggily headed out the door.

### QUESTIONS

1. Can general operational standards be developed and implemented in all or a majority of Kinko's shops?

2. Discuss the idea of grouping copiers in machine centers so that certain copiers are available for specific tasks.

3. How do the different services offered (private copying versus copying services provided) present separate types of problems for management?

4. Kinko's Professor Publishing apparently did not pan out. What might have been the cause?

Source: Mark Ballard, "Working in a Fishbowl," *Quick Printing,* May 1987, pp. 30–32. Reprinted by permission.

## SELECTED BIBLIOGRAPHY

Adler, Paul S.; Henry E. Riggs; and Steven C. Wheelwright. "Product Development Know-How: Trading Tactics for Strategy." *Sloan Management Review,* Fall 1989, pp. 7–17.

Albrecht, Karl, and Ron Zemke. *Service America! Doing Business in the New Economy* (Homewood, IL: Dow Jones-Irwin, 1985).

Bitran, Gabriel R., and Johannes Hoech. "The Humanization of Service: Respect at the Moment of Truth." *Sloan Management Review,* Winter 1990, pp. 89–96.

Bolwijn, P. T., and T. Kumpe. "Manufacturing in the 1990s— Productivity, Flexibility, and Innovation." *Long Range Planning* 23, no. 4 (1990), pp. 44–57.

Chase, R. B. "The Customer Contact Approach to Services: Theoretical Bases and Practical Extensions." *Operations Research* 21, no. 4 (1981), pp. 698–705.

Cohen, Morris A., and Hau L. Lee. "Out of Touch with Customer Needs?" *Sloan Management Review,* Winter 1990, pp. 55–66.

Collier, D. A. *Service Management: The Automation of Services.* Reston, VA: Reston Publishing, 1986.

Davis, Mark M., and Paul L. Tumolo. *Operations Management in Manufacturing.* Watertown, MA: American Management Association, 1994, pp. 29–31.

Davidow, William H., and Bro Uttal. "Service Companies: Focus or Falter," *Harvard Business Review* 67, no. 4 (July–August 1989), pp. 77–85.

Dixon, John R., and Michael R. Duffy. "The Neglect of Engineering Design." *California Management Review,* Winter 1990, pp. 9–23.

Drucker, Peter F. "The Emerging Theory of Manufacturing." *Harvard Business Review,* May–June 1990, pp. 94–102.

Edmondson, Harold E., and Steven C. Wheelwright. "Outstanding Manufacturing in the Coming Decade." *California Management Review,* Summer 1989, pp. 70–90.

Eisenhardt, K. M., and S. L. Brown, "Time Pacing: Competing in Markets That Won't Stand Still," *Harvard Business Reivew,* March–April 1998, pp. 59–69.

Fitzsimmons, James A., and Mona J. Fitzsimmons. *Service Management: Operations, Strategy, and Information Technology.* 2nd ed. New York: McGraw-Hill, 1998.

Galsworth, G. D. *Smart, Simple Design.* Essex Junction, VT: Oliver Wight Productions, 1994.

Hackett, Gregory P. "Investment in Technology: The Service Sector Sinkhole?" *Sloan Management Review,* Winter 1990, pp. 97–103.

Heskett, James L. *Managing in the Service Economy.* Cambridge, MA: Harvard University Press, 1986.

_____. "Lessons from the Service Sector." *Harvard Business Review,* March–April 1987, pp. 118–26.

Huthwaite, Bart. "Managing at the Starting Line: How to Design Competitive Products." Presented at a Workshop at the University of Southern California, Los Angeles, CA, January 14, 1991.

Levitt, Theodore. "Production-Line Approach to Service." *Harvard Business Review* 50, no. 5 (September–October 1972), pp. 41–52.

Lieber, Ronald B. "Storytelling: A New Way to Get Close to Your Customer." *Fortune,* February 4, 1997, pp. 102–10.

Lovelock, C. H., and R. F. Young. "Look to Customers to Increase Productivity." *Harvard Business Review* 57, no. 3 (May–June 1979), pp. 168–78.

Machlis, Sharon. "Three Shortcuts to Better Design," *Design News,* November 19, 1990, pp. 89–91.

Main, Jeremy. "Manufacturing the Right Way." *Fortune,* May 21, 1990, pp. 54–64.

Meyers, Christopher. *Fast Cycle Time: How to Align Purpose, Strategy and Structure for Speed.* New York: Free Press, 1993.

Nussbaum, Bruce. "Hot Products: Smart Design Is the Common Thread." *Business Week,* June 7, 1993.

Nussbaum, Bruce, and Robert Neff. "I Can't Work This Thing!" *Business Week,* April 29, 1991, pp. 58–66.

Pare, Terence P. "Why Some Do It the Wrong Way." *Fortune,* May 21, 1990, pp. 75–76.

Peavey, Dennis E. "It's Time for a Change." *Management Accounting,* February 1990, pp. 31–35.

Peters, Tom. *Quality!* Palo Alto, CA: TPG Communications, 1986.

Port, Otis. "The Best Engineered Part Is No Part at All." *Business Week,* May 8, 1989, p. 150.

Quinn, J. B., and M. N. Bailey. "Information Technology: Increasing Productivity in Services." *Academy of Management Executive* 8, no. 3, 1994.

Rao, Ashok, et al. *Total Quality Management: A Cross Functional Perspective.* New York: John Wiley and Sons, 1996.

Roach, S. S. "Services Under Siege—The Restructuring Imperative." *Harvard Business Review,* September–October 1991, pp. 82–91.

Roehm, Harper A.; Donald Klein; and Joseph F. Castellano. "Springing to World-Class Manufacturing." *Management Accounting,* March 1991, pp. 40–44.

Sakai, Kuniyasu. "The Feudal World of Japanese Manufacturing." *Harvard Business Review,* November–December 1990, pp. 38–49.

Sanderson, Susan Walsh, and Vic Uzumeri. "Strategies for New Product Development and Renewal: Design-Based Incrementalism." Center for Science and Technology Policy, School of Management, Rensselaer Polytechnic Institute, May 1990.

Schmenner, Roger W. "How Can Service Businesses Survive and Prosper?" *Sloan Management Review* 27, no. 3 (Spring 1986), pp. 21–32.

Schmenner, Roger. *Service Operations Management.* Englewood Cliffs, NJ: Prentice Hall, 1995.

Shina, Sammy G. *Concurrent Engineering and Design for Manufacture of Electronic Products.* New York: Van Nostrand Reinhold, 1991.

Shunk, Dan L. *Integrated Process Design and Development.* Homewood, IL: Business One Irwin, 1992.

Spenser, William J. "Research to Product: A Major U.S. Change." *California Management Review,* Winter 1990, pp. 45–53.

Stalk, George, Jr. "Time—The Next Source of Competitive Advantage." *Harvard Business Review,* July–August 1988, pp. 41–51.

Wheelwright, Steven C., and W. Earl Sasser, Jr. "The New Product Development Map," *Harvard Business Review,* May–June 1989, pp. 112–27.

Ziemke, M. Carl, and Mary S. Spann. "Warning: Don't Be Half-Hearted in Your Efforts to Employ Concurrent Engineering." *Industrial Engineering,* February 1991, pp. 45–49.

# FINANCIAL ANALYSIS IN OPERATIONS MANAGEMENT

3

## *Supplement Outline*

## *Supplement Objectives*

- Introduce various cost definitions and demonstrate how they are applied in operations management.

- Demonstrate how break-even analysis is used within an operations management context.

- Demonstrate how the concepts of obsolescence, depreciation, and taxes impact the decision-making process within an operations management context.

- Introduce and demonstrate how the time value of money can be used as a financial tool in the decision-making process with respect to various types of operations management issues.

same time taking into consideration the expected return on investment of the owners of the firm.

# ACTIVITY-BASED COSTING

In order to determine the total costs involved with making a certain product or delivering a service, some method of allocating overhead costs must be applied. The traditional approach has been to allocate overhead costs to products on the basis of direct labor dollars or hours. The overhead rate can be established by dividing the total estimated overhead costs by total budgeted direct labor hours. The problem with this approach is that direct labor as a percentage of total costs has fallen dramatically over the past decade, especially in manufacturing companies. For example, the introduction of advanced manufacturing technology and other productivity improvements has driven direct labor to less than 10 percent of total manufacturing costs in many industries. As a result, overhead rates of 600 percent or even 1,000 percent are found in some highly automated plants.[1]

This traditional accounting practice of allocating overhead to direct labor can lead to questionable investment decisions; for example, automated processes may be chosen over labor-intensive processes based on a comparison of projected costs. Unfortunately, overhead does not disappear when the equipment is installed and overall costs may actually be lower with the labor-intensive process. It can also lead to wasted effort since an inordinate amount of time is spent tracking direct labor hours. For example, one plant spent 65 percent of its computer costs tracking information about direct labor transactions even though direct labor accounted for only 4 percent of total production costs.[2]

**activity-based costing**
Accounting technique that allocates overhead costs in actual proportion to the overhead consumed by the production activity.

**Activity-based costing** techniques have been developed to alleviate these problems by refining the overhead allocation process to more directly reflect actual proportions of overhead consumed by the production activity. Causal factors, known as cost drivers, are identified and used as the means for allocating overhead. These factors might include machine hours, beds occupied, computer time, flight hours, or miles driven. The accuracy of overhead allocation, of course, depends on the selection of the appropriate cost drivers.

Activity-based costing involves a two-stage allocation process with the first stage assigning overhead costs to cost activity pools. These pools represent activities such as performing machine setups, issuing purchase orders, and inspecting parts. In the second stage, costs are assigned from these pools to activities based on the number or amount of pool-related activity required in their completion. Exhibit 3S.2 shows a comparison of traditional cost accounting and activity-based costing.

Consider the example of activity-based costing in Exhibit 3S.3. Two products, A and B, are produced using the same number of labor hours. Applying traditional cost accounting methods, identical overhead costs (usually expressed as a percentage of direct labor costs) would be charged to each product. For example, in Exhibit 3S.3, the $875,000 would be divided by the total labor costs required to make products A and B in order to obtain an overhead rate. By applying activity-based costing, traceable costs are assigned to specific activities. Because each product requires a different amount of transactions, different overhead amounts, expressed here as $s per transaction, are allocated to these products from the pools.

---

[1]Matthew J. Libertore. *Selection and Evaluation of Advanced Manufacturing Technologies* (New York: Springer-Verlag, 1990), pp. 231–56.

[2]Thomas Johnson and Robert Kaplan, *Relevance Lost: The Rise and Fall of Management Accounting* (Boston: Harvard Business School Press, 1987), p. 188.

**EXHIBIT 3S.2**

Traditional and Activity-Based Costing

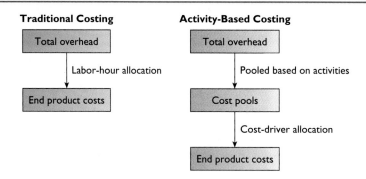

**Traditional Costing**

Total overhead

↓ Labor-hour allocation

End product costs

**Activity-Based Costing**

Total overhead

↓ Pooled based on activities

Cost pools

↓ Cost-driver allocation

End product costs

**EXHIBIT 3S.3**

Overhead Allocations by an Activity Approach

**Basic Data**

| Activity | Traceable Costs | Events or Transactions Total | Product A | Product B |
|---|---|---|---|---|
| Machine setups | $230,000 | 5,000 | 3,000 | 2,000 |
| Quality inspections | 160,000 | 8,000 | 5,000 | 3,000 |
| Production orders | 81,000 | 600 | 200 | 400 |
| Machine-hours worked | 314,000 | 40,000 | 12,000 | 28,000 |
| Material receipts | 90,000 | 750 | 150 | 600 |
| | $875,000 | | | |

**Overhead Rates by Activity**

| | (a) Traceable Costs | (b) Total Events or Transactions | (a) ÷ (b) Rate per Event or Transaction |
|---|---|---|---|
| Machine setups | $230,000 | 5,000 | $46/setup |
| Quality inspections | 160,000 | 8,000 | $20/inspection |
| Productuon orders | 81,000 | 600 | $135/order |
| Machine-hours worked | 314,000 | 40,000 | $7.85/hour |
| Material receipts | 90,000 | 750 | $120/receipt |

**Overhead Cost per Unit of Product**

| | Product A Events or Transactions | Product A Amount | Product B Events or Transactions | Product B Amount |
|---|---|---|---|---|
| Machine setups, at $46/setup | 3,000 | $138,000 | 2,000 | $ 92,000 |
| Quality inspections, at $20/inspection | 5,000 | 100,000 | 3,000 | 60,000 |
| Production orders at $135/order | 200 | 27,000 | 400 | 54,000 |
| Machine-hours worked, at $7.85/hour | 12,000 | 94,200 | 28,000 | 219,800 |
| Material receipts, at $120/receipt | 150 | 18,000 | 600 | 72,000 |
| Total overhead cost assigned (a) | | $377,200 | | $497,800 |
| Number of units produced (b) | | 5,000 | | 20,000 |
| Overhead cost per unit, (a) ÷ (b) | | $75.44 | | $24.89 |

Source: Ray Garrison, *Managerial Accounting,* 6th ed. (Homewood, IL: Richard D. Irwin, 1991), p. 94.

As stated earlier, activity-based costing overcomes the problem of cost distortion by creating a cost pool for each activity or transaction that can be identified as a cost driver, and by assigning overhead costs to products or jobs on the basis of the number of separate activities required for their completion. Thus, in the previous situation, the low-volume product would be assigned the bulk of the costs for machine setup, purchase orders, and quality inspections, thereby showing it to have high unit costs compared to the other product.

Finally, activity-based costing is sometimes referred to as *transactions costing.* This transactions focus gives rise to another major advantage over other costing methods; that is, it improves the traceability of overhead costs and thus results in more accurate *unit* cost data for management.

# BREAK-EVEN ANALYSIS

**break-even analysis**
Determination of product volume where revenues equal total costs or costs associated with two alternative processes are the same.

**Break-even analysis,** as we define it here, can be viewed from two perspectives. From the overall view of the company, break-even analysis usually refers to determining how much volume of business the company must do in order to break-even, that is, to have neither profits nor losses. The *break-even point,* in this case is where total revenues equal total costs. Break-even analysis from a purely operational perspective usually focuses on the choice of processes. Here, break-even implies that the two processes have equal costs for a specific level of volume, which is again referred to as the break-even point. We will address both of these types of break-even analysis. In each case we apply a simple linear model that uses only fixed costs and variable costs.

## Revenues versus Costs

As stated above, the objective here is to determine how much volume of business a company has to do to break-even. The volume can be stated in either monetary units or product units, although the latter is usually easier to conceptualize from an operational perspective.

The underlying assumptions in this linear model are:

- *The selling price per unit is constant.* In other words, there is one selling price for a unit, with no allowances for quantity discounts or special terms for major customers.
- *Variable costs per unit remain constant.* Here, the cost to produce each unit remains the same over the range of volume that we are concerned with. (Consequently, there are no allowances for economies of scale.) Since variable costs refer to the material and direct labor that go into making each unit, additional unit costs such as overtime, second shift premiums or subcontracting are, therefore, excluded from consideration.
- *Fixed costs remain constant.* Over the range of volume that we are concerned with, the fixed costs of the operation do not change regardless of the volume produced. As defined earlier, these fixed costs usually include rent, insurance and taxes on the facility, senior management salaries, and other overhead expenses.

Example

The West Pacific Toy Company, a small manufacturing firm located in Manila, Philippines, produces cloth dolls for export to the United States. The company sells these dolls to major retail chains for US$3.00 each, which does not include shipping costs of US$0.50 per doll. (These dolls are then marked up to a retail selling price in the United

States of US$14.95 per doll.) The workers in the factory are paid, on the average, the equivalent of US$8.00 per day, and it is estimated that the average daily output per worker is 50 dolls. The cost of the material is estimated at US$1.25 per doll. Fixed costs for this operation are estimated to be US$160,000 per year.

a. What is the break-even point for this company, in terms of the number of dolls per year?

b. If the company sold 135,000 dolls last year, how much profit (loss) did it have for the year?

**Solution**

a. As seen in Exhibit 3S.4, the break-even point is that point on the graph where the total sales line intersects with the total cost line. This point can be calculated as follows:

Selling price $= SP =$ US$3.00 per doll

Variable cost $= VC =$ Material cost + Labor cost

$\qquad = 1.25 + 8.00/50$

$\qquad =$ US$1.41 per doll

Fixed costs $= FC =$ US$160,000 per year

$X =$ Number of dolls sold per year

As seen in Exhibit 3S.4, total annual sales

$$= TS = (SP)(X)$$

Total annual costs equals fixed costs plus variable costs

$$= TC = FC + (VC)(X)$$

The point at which the total sales line and the total costs line intersect is the break-even point, which is where they are equal to each other.

Thus

$$TS = TC$$
$$(SP)(X) = FC + (VC)(X)$$

Solving for $X$ we have

$$X = \frac{FC}{(SP - VC)}$$

Substituting the values for $SP$, $VC$, and $FC$ we have

$$X = \frac{160,000}{(3.00 - 1.41)}$$

$$X = 100,629 \text{ dolls per year}$$

b. Profits $= P =$ Total sales − Total costs

$$P = TS - TC$$
$$P = (SP)(X) - [FC + (VC)(X)]$$

$$P = (3.00)(135,000) - [160,000 + (1.41)(135,000)]$$
$$P = 405,000 - [160,000 + 190,350]$$
$$P = 405,000 - 350,350$$
$$\text{Profits for the year} = US\$54,650$$

**EXHIBIT 3S.4**

Break-Even Analysis for Revenues versus Costs

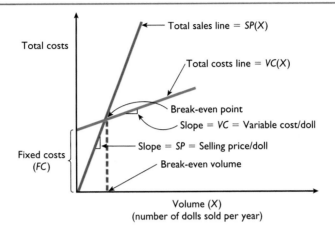

Volume (X)
(number of dolls sold per year)

## Choice of Processes

Break-even analysis can also be used to choose from among alternative processes a company can use. Again, we assume that both the variable costs per unit and the fixed costs over the range of volumes being evaluated remain constant. Sales are not considered in this analysis, in terms of identifying the break-even points. (Although the forecasted level of sales is definitely a factor in selecting the process to be used.) Here, we define the break-even point as that volume where we are indifferent with respect to the costs of the two alternative processes.

Example

Allison and Jon, to earn extra money while they are in high school, have a small catering business. They provide a variety of freshly made sandwiches in the evenings to college students. Currently, they prepare the sandwiches at their home which is about 15 miles away. The average cost per sandwich, including the transportation, material and direct labor is approximately $2.55. The school has recently offered to lease them a small kitchen on campus. The rent for this kitchen is $360.00 per month for each of the nine months that the school is open full time. (The building in which the kitchen is located is closed for the other three months, so the kitchen is also closed.) Allison and Jon estimate that they will be able to produce the sandwiches at this new location at an average cost of $1.80 per sandwich. (The savings are attributed to working more efficiently in a professional kitchen.)

a. How many sandwiches a month do Allison and Jon have to sell in order to be indifferent to the costs of working at home versus working in the kitchen on campus?

*b.* The parents of Allison and Jon have decided that they are going to charge them $120.00 per month because of the additional out-of-pocket costs involved with preparing the sandwiches at home (electricity, cleaning supplies, etc.). What is the new break-even point under these circumstances between working at home and working on campus?

**Solution**

*a. Alternative 1: Working at Home*

Total costs $= TC_1 = VC_1X$

where

$VC_1$ = Variable costs per sandwich of $2.55

$X$ = Number of sandwiches sold

or

$TC_1 = 2.55X$

*Alternative 2: Working on Campus*

Total costs $= TC_2 = FC_2 + VC_2X$

where

$FC_2$ = Fixed costs of $360.00 per month

$VC_2$ = Variable cost per sandwich of $1.80

As seen in Exhibit 3S.5, the break-even point between these two alternatives is where the two total costs lines intersect.

The break-even point is calculated as follows:

$$TC_1 = TC_2$$

Substituting for $TC_1$ and $TC_2$ from above, we have

$$VC_1X = FC_2 + VC_2X$$
$$2.55X = 360 + 1.80X$$
$$0.75X = 360$$
$$X = 480 \text{ Sandwiches a month.}$$

Note that when we analyze process alternatives, we do not need to know the selling price per unit. The decision here is based upon the forecasted volume to be sold, with the goal being to select that process which has the lowest total costs at the forecasted volume. In this example, if the forecast per month is greater than 480 sandwiches, then they should rent the kitchen on campus, otherwise they should continue working at home.

*b. Alternative 1: Working at Home*

Total costs $= TC_1 = FC_1 + VC_1X$

where

$FC_1$ = Fixed costs of $120.00 per month

$VC_1$ = Variable cost per sandwich of $2.55

$X$ = Number of sandwiches sold

or

$TC_1 = 120 + 2.55X$

*Alternative 2: Working on Campus*

Total costs $= TC_2 = FC_2 + VC_2X$

where

$FC_2$ = Fixed costs of \$360.00 per month

$VC_2$ = Variable cost per sandwich of \$1.80

As seen in Exhibit 3S.6, the new break-even point between these two alternatives is again where the two total costs lines intersect. Under these conditions, the break-even point is calculated as follows:

$$TC_1 = TC_2$$
$$FC_1 + VC_1X = FC_2 + VC_2X$$
$$120 + 2.55X = 360 + 1.80X$$
$$.75X = 240$$
$$X = 320 \text{ Sandwiches a month.}$$

Here, if the forecast is more than 320 sandwiches a month, they should use the kitchen at school, if it is less, they should continue working at home.

---

**EXHIBIT 3S.5**

Break-Even Analysis for Alternative Types of Processes

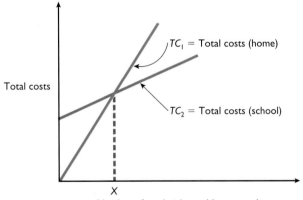

---

**EXHIBIT 3S.6**

Break-Even Analysis for Alternative Types of Processes

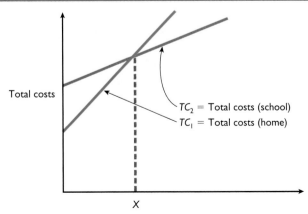

# Obsolescence, Depreciation, and Taxes

## Economic Life and Obsolescence

**obsolete**
Status of an asset when it has worn out or been surpassed by a superior performing asset.

When a firm invests in an income-producing asset, the economic life of the asset is estimated. For accounting purposes, the asset is depreciated over this period. It is assumed that the asset will perform its function during this time and then be considered **obsolete** or worn out, and replacement will be required. However, this view of asset life rarely coincides with reality.

To illustrate this, assume that a machine with an expected productive life of 10 years is purchased. If at any time during the ensuing 10 years a new machine is developed that can perform the same task more efficiently or economically, the old machine is considered to be obsolete. Whether it is "worn out" or not is irrelevant.

**economic life**
Useful life of an asset in which it provides the best method of operation to an organization.

The **economic life** of a piece of equipment is the period over which it provides the best method for performing its task. When a new, superior method is developed, the actual value of the existing equipment is usually significantly less than the stated *book value* of a machine (that is, the "official" remaining value).

## Types of Depreciation

**depreciation**
Method for allocating capital equipment costs over more than one time period.

**Depreciation** is a method for allocating the costs of capital equipment over more than one time period (for discussion here, we will use years). The value of any capital asset—buildings, machinery, and so forth—decreases as its useful life is expended. *Amortization* and *depreciation* are often used interchangeably. Through convention, however, *depreciation* refers to the allocation of costs due to the physical or functional deterioration of *tangible* (physical) assets, such as buildings or equipment, while *amortization* refers to the allocation of costs over the useful life of *intangible* assets, such as patents, leases, franchises, or goodwill.

Depreciation procedures may not reflect an asset's true value at any point in its life because obsolescence at any time may result in a large difference between the true value and book value of the asset. Also, since depreciation rates significantly affect taxes, a firm may choose a particular depreciation method from the several alternatives that are available, giving more consideration to its effect on taxes than its ability to make the book value of an asset reflect the true resale value.

We describe five commonly used methods of depreciation:

**1.** *Straight-line method.*   With this method, an asset's value is reduced in uniform annual amounts over its estimated useful life. The general straight-line depreciation formula is:

$$\text{Annual amount to be depreciated} = \frac{\text{Cost} - \text{Salvage value}}{\text{Estimated useful life}}$$

For example, a machine costing $10,000, with an estimated salvage value of $0 and an estimated life of 10 years, would be depreciated at the rate of $1,000 per year for each of the 10 years. If its estimated salvage value at the end of the 10 years is $1,000, the annual depreciation then becomes:

$$\frac{\$10,000 - \$1,000}{10} = \$900 \text{ per year}$$

**2.** *Sum-of-the-years'-digits (SYD) method.*   The purpose of the SYD method is to reduce the book value of an asset rapidly in the early years of its life and at a lower rate in its later years. This is done both for tax purposes and to more accurately reflect the true value of an asset.

To illustrate this, suppose that the estimated useful life of a piece of equipment is five years. Here, the sum of the years' digits is $1 + 2 + 3 + 4 + 5 = 15$. Therefore, the asset is depreciated by $5 \div 15$ (or 33 percent) after the first year, $4 \div 15$ (or 26.7 percent) after the second year, and so on, down to $1 \div 15$ (or 6.7 percent) in the last year. (We are assuming here that the salvage value at the end of the fifth year is zero.)

**3.** *Declining-balance method.* This method also provides for an accelerated depreciation. The asset's value is decreased each year by reducing its book value by a constant percentage each year. The percentage rate selected is often the one that just reduces book value to salvage value at the end of the asset's estimated life. In any case, the asset should never be reduced below estimated salvage value. Use of the declining-balance method and allowable rates is controlled by Internal Revenue Service regulations. As a simplified illustration, the example in the next table uses an arbitrarily selected rate of 40 percent. (Salvage value after five years is estimated at $2,000.) Depreciation with this method is based on full cost, *not* cost minus salvage value.

| Year | Depreciation Rate | Beginning Book Value | Depreciation Charge | Accumulated Depreciation | Ending Book Value |
|---|---|---|---|---|---|
| 1 | 0.40 | $17,000 | $6,800 | $ 6,800 | $10,200 |
| 2 | 0.40 | 10,200 | 4,080 | 10,880 | 6,120 |
| 3 | 0.40 | 6,120 | 2,448 | 13,328 | 3,672 |
| 4 | 0.40 | 3,672 | 1,469 | 14,797 | 2,203 |
| 5 | | 2,203 | 203 | 15,000 | 2,000 |

Note that in the fifth year, reducing book value by 40 percent would have caused it to drop below salvage value. Consequently, the asset was depreciated by only $203, which decreased book value to salvage value.

**4.** *Double-declining-balance method.* Again, for tax advantages, the double-declining-balance method offers higher depreciation early in the economic life of the asset. The double-declining-balance method uses a percentage that is equal to twice the straight line rate over the life of the item but applies this rate to the undepreciated original cost. The method is the same as the declining-balance method, but the term *double-declining balance* means double the straight-line rate. Thus, equipment with a 10-year lifespan would have a straight line depreciation rate of 10 percent per year and a double-declining-balance rate (applied to the undepreciated amount) of 20 percent per year. (At some point, usually near the end of the equipment's life span, one switches to straight-line depreciation.)

**5.** *Depreciation-by-use method.* The purpose of this method is to depreciate a capital investment in proportion to its use. It is applicable, for example, to a machine that performs the same operation many times. The life of the machine is not estimated in years but rather it is estimated in the total number of operations it may reasonably be expected to perform before wearing out. Suppose that a metal-stamping press has an estimated life of 1 million stampings and costs $100,000. The charge for depreciation per stamping is then $100,000 \div 1,000,000$, or $0.10. Assuming a $0 salvage value, the depreciation charges are as shown:

| Year | Total Yearly Stampings | Cost per Stamping | Yearly Depreciation Charge | Accumulated Depreciation | Ending Book Value |
|---|---|---|---|---|---|
| 1 | 150,000 | 0.10 | $15,000 | $15,000 | $85,000 |
| 2 | 300,000 | 0.10 | 30,000 | 45,000 | 55,000 |
| 3 | 200,000 | 0.10 | 20,000 | 65,000 | 35,000 |
| 4 | 200,000 | 0.10 | 20,000 | 85,000 | 15,000 |
| 5 | 100,000 | 0.10 | 10,000 | 95,000 | 5,000 |
| 6 | 50,000 | 0.10 | 5,000 | 100,000 | 0 |

The depreciation-by-use method is an attempt to allocate depreciation charges in proportion to actual use and thereby coordinate expense charges with productive output more accurately. Also, since a machine's resale value is related to its remaining productive life, it is expected that with this method the book value will more closely approximate the resale value.

### The Effects of Taxes

Tax rates and the methods of applying them occasionally change. When analysts evaluate investment proposals, tax considerations often prove to be the deciding factor since depreciation expenses directly affect taxable income and, therefore, profit. The ability to write off depreciation in early years provides an added source of funds for investment.

## TYPES OF ECONOMIC DECISIONS

The capital investment decision has become highly rationalized, as evidenced by the variety of techniques that are now available. In contrast to pricing or marketing decisions, the capital investment decision can usually be made with a higher degree of confidence because the variables affecting the decision are relatively well known and can be quantified with a relatively high degree of accuracy.

Investment decisions may be grouped into six general categories:

1. Purchase of new equipment or facilities.
2. Replacement of existing equipment or facilities.
3. Make-or-buy decisions.
4. Lease-or-buy decisions.
5. Temporary shutdown or plant-abandonment decisions.
6. Addition or elimination of a product or product line.

Investment decisions are usually made with regard to the *lowest acceptable rate of return* on investment. This is often referred to as the "threshold" rate of return. As a starting point, the threshold rate of return may be considered to be the cost of investment capital needed to underwrite the expenditure. Certainly an investment will not be made if it does not return at least the cost of capital.

Investments are generally ranked according to the return they yield in excess of their cost of capital. In this way a business with only limited investment funds can select investment alternatives that yield the highest *net returns*. (*Net return* is the earnings an investment yields after gross earnings have been reduced by the cost of the funds used to finance the investment.) In general, investments should not be made unless the return in funds exceeds the *marginal* cost of investment capital (*marginal cost* is the incremental cost of each new acquisition of funds from outside sources).

## FINANCIAL DEFINITIONS

There are two basic methods to account for the effects of interest accumulation. One is to compute the total amount accumulated over the time period into the future as the *compound value*. The other is to remove the interest rate effect over time by reducing all future sums to present-day dollars, or the *present value*.

## Compound Value of a Single Amount

Albert Einstein was once quoted as saying that compound interest is the eighth wonder of the world. After reviewing this section, with its dramatic growth effects during a longer term of years, you might wish to propose a new government regulation: on the birth of a child, the parents must put, say, $1,000 into a retirement fund for that child at age 65. This might be one way to reduce the pressure on Social Security and other state and federal pension plans. While inflation will decrease the value significantly, there is still a lot left over. At 14 percent interest, our $1,000 increased to $500,000 after subtracting the $4.5 million for inflation (assuming that inflation erodes 90 percent of the gain!). That's still 500 times larger than the original $1,000.

Most calculators make such computation easy. However, many people still refer to tables for compound values. Using Appendix A, Table 1 (compound sum of $1), for example, we see that the value of $1 at 10 percent interest after three years is $1.331. (Note: Tables 1 through 4 are in Appendix A.)

## Compound Value of an Annuity

An *annuity* is the receipt of a constant sum each year for a specified number of years. Usually an annuity is received at the end of a period and does not earn interest during that period. Therefore, an annuity of $10 for three years would bring in $10 at the end of the first year (allowing the $10 to earn interest if invested for the remaining two years), $10 at the end of the second year (allowing the $10 to earn interest for the remaining one year), and $10 at the end of the third year (with no time to earn interest). If the annuity receipts were placed in a bank savings account at 5 percent interest, the total or compound value of the $10 at 5 percent for the three years would be:

| Year | Receipt at End of Year | Compound Interest Factor $(1 + i)^n$ | Value at End of Third Year |
|------|------------------------|--------------------------------------|----------------------------|
| 1 | $10.00 × | $(1 + 0.05)^2 =$ | $11.02 |
| 2 | 10.00 × | $(1 + 0.05)^1 =$ | 10.50 |
| 3 | 10.00 × | $(1 + 0.05)^0 =$ | 10.00 |
| | | | $31.52 |

The general formula for finding the compound value of any annuity is

$$S_n = R[(1 + i)^{n-1} + (1 + i)^{n-2} + \cdots + (1 + i)^1 + 1]$$

where

$S_n$ = Compound value of an annuity

$R$ = Periodic receipts in dollars

$n$ = Length of the annuity in years

Applying this formula to the above example, we get

$$S_n = R[(1 + i)^2 + (1 + i) + 1]$$
$$= \$10[(1 + 0.05)^2 + (1 + 0.05) + 1]$$
$$= \$31.52$$

Appendix A, Table 2 lists the compound value factor of $1 for 5 percent after three years as 3.152. Multiplying this factor by $10 yields $31.52.

Consider the beneficial effects of investing $2,000 each year, starting at the age of 21. Assume investments in AAA-rated bonds are available today yielding 9 percent. From Table 2 in Appendix A, after 30 years (age 51) the investment is worth 136.3 times $2,000, or $272,600. Fourteen years later (age 65) this would be worth $962,993 (using a hand calculator, since the table only goes up to 30 years, and assuming the $2,000 is deposited at the end of each year)! But what 21-year-old thinks about retirement?

## Present Value of a Future Single Payment

Compound values are used to determine the future value of a stream of cash flows after a specified period has elapsed; present-value (PV) procedures accomplish just the reverse. They are used to determine the current value of a sum or stream of receipts expected to be received in the future. Most investment decision techniques use present-value concepts rather than compound values. Since decisions affecting the future are made in the present, it makes more sense to convert future returns into their present value at the time the decision is being made. In this way, investment alternatives are viewed from a better perspective in terms of current dollars.

**Example**

If a rich uncle offers to make you a gift of $100 today or $250 after 10 years, which should you choose? You must determine whether $250 in 10 years will be worth more than the $100 now. Suppose that you base your decision on the rate of inflation in the economy and believe that inflation will be 10 percent per year. But deflating the $250, you can compare its relative purchasing power with $100 received today. Procedurally, this is accomplished by solving the compound formula for the present sum, $P$, where $V$ is the future amount of $250 in 10 years at 10 percent.

**Solution**

The general formula for compound value is

$$V_n = P(1 + i)^n$$

where

$V_n$ = Value of principal at the end of year $n$

$n$ = Length of the compounding period in years

$P$ = Present value of principal

$i$ = Interest rate

Dividing both sides by $(1 + i)^n$ gives:

$$P = \frac{V_n}{(1 + i)^n}$$

$$= \frac{250}{(1 + 0.10)^{10}}$$

$$= \$96.39$$

This shows that, at a 10 percent inflation rate, $250 in 10 years will be worth $93.39 today. The rational choice is to take the $100 now based on a belief that inflation will remain constant at 10 percent per year for the next 10 years.

The use of tables is also standard practice in solving present-value problems. With reference to Appendix A, Table 3, the present-value factor for $1 received 10 years hence is 0.386. Multiplying this factor by $250 yields $96.50.

## Present Value of an Annuity

The present value of an annuity is the value of an annual amount to be received over a future period expressed in terms of the present. To find the value of an annuity of $100 for three years at 10 percent, find the factor in the present-value table that applies to 10 percent in *each* of the three years in which the amount is received and multiply each receipt by this factor. Then sum the resulting figures. Remember that annuities are usually received at the end of each period.

| Year | Amount Received at End of Year | | Present-Value Factor at 10% | | Present Value |
|------|-------------------------------|---|----------------------------|---|--------------|
| 1 | $100 | × | 0.909 | = | $ 90.90 |
| 2 | 100 | × | 0.826 | = | 82.60 |
| 3 | 100 | × | 0.751 | = | 75.10 |
| Total receipt | $300 | | Total present value | = | $248.60 |

The general formula used to derive the present value of an annuity is

$$A_n = R \left[ \frac{1}{(1+i)} + \frac{1}{(1+i)^2} + \cdots + \frac{1}{(1+i)^n} \right]$$

where

$A_n$ = Present value of annuity of $n$ years

$R$ = Periodic receipts

$n$ = Length of the annuity in years

Applying the formula to the above example gives

$$A_n = \$100 \left[ \frac{1}{(1+0.10)} + \frac{1}{(1+0.10)^2} + \frac{1}{(1+0.10)^3} \right]$$

$$= \$100 \, (2.488)$$

$$= \$248.80$$

Appendix A, Table 4 contains present values of an annuity for varying maturities. The present-value factor for an annuity of $1 for three years at 10 percent (from Appendix A, Table 4) is 2.487. Since our sum is $100 rather than $1, we multiply this factor by $100 to arrive at $248.70. The slight variance from the previous answers results from rounded figures in the table.

When the stream of future receipts is uneven, the present value of each annual receipt must be calculated. The present values of the receipts for all years are then summed to determine the total present value. This process can sometimes be tedious, if done manually. Fortunately, today's software programs can accomplish this easily.

## Discounted Cash Flow

The term *discounted cash flow,* or DCF, refers to the total stream of payments that an asset will generate in the future discounted to the present time. This is simply present value analysis that includes all flows: single payments, annuities, and all others.

# METHODS FOR EVALUATING INVESTMENT ALTERNATIVES

## Net Present Value

**net present value**
Present cash value of a stream of future cash flows.

The **net present value** method is commonly used in business. With this method, decisions are based on the amount by which the present value of a projected income stream exceeds the cost of an investment.

**Example**

A firm is considering two alternative investments: the first, Alternative A, costs $30,000 and the second, Alternative B, costs $50,000. The expected yearly cash income streams for each of the two alternatives are shown in the next table.

|  | Cash Inflow | |
| --- | --- | --- |
| Year | Alternative A | Alternative B |
| 1 | $10,000 | $15,000 |
| 2 | 10,000 | 15,000 |
| 3 | 10,000 | 15,000 |
| 4 | 10,000 | 15,000 |
| 5 | 10,000 | 15,000 |

To decide which of the two alternatives is better, we need to determine which has the highest net present value. (For this calculation we need the cost of capital; let's assume it is 8 percent.)

**Solution**

*Alernative A*

$$3.993 \text{ (PV factor)} \times \$10,000 = \$39,930$$
$$\text{Less cost of investment} = \underline{\ \ 30,000}$$
$$\text{Net present value} = \$\ \ 9,930$$

*Alternative B*

$$3.993 \text{ (PV factor)} \times \$15,000 = \$59,895$$
$$\text{Less cost of investment} = \underline{\ \ 50,000}$$
$$\text{Net present value} = \$\ \ 9,895$$

Based purely on economic criteria, management would prefer Alternative A because its net present value exceeds that of Alternative B by $35 ($9,930 − $9,895 = $35).

## Payback Period

**payback period**
Time necessary for the firm to recover its initial investment.

The **payback period** method ranks investments according to the time required for each investment to return earnings equal to the cost of the investment. The rationale is that the sooner the investment capital can be recovered, the sooner it can be reinvested in new revenue-producing projects. Thus, supposedly, a firm will be able to get the most benefit from its available investment funds.

Consider two alternatives, each requiring a $1,000 investment. The first will earn $200 per year for six years; the second will earn $300 per year for the first three years and $100 per year for the next three years.

If the first alternative is selected, the initial investment of $1,000 will be recovered at the end of the fifth year. The income produced by the second alternative will total $1,000 after only four years. The second alternative will permit reinvestment of the full $1,000 in new revenue-producing projects one year sooner than the first.

Although the payback period method is declining in popularity as the sole measure for evaluating investments, it is still frequently used in conjunction with other methods to give an indication of the time commitment of funds. The major problems with the payback period method are that it does not consider income beyond the payback period and it ignores the time value of money. Any method that ignores the time value of money must be considered questionable.

## Internal Rate of Return

**internal rate of return**
Interest rate which equates present value of future cash flows with cost of an investment.

The **internal rate of return** (IRR) can be defined as the interest rate that equates the present value of an income stream with the cost of an investment. There is no procedure or formula that may be used directly to compute the internal rate of return—it must be found by interpolation or iterative calculation (in other words, trial and error which can be performed quite easily with a computer).

Example

Suppose we wish to find the internal rate of return for an investment costing $12,000 that will yield a cash inflow of $4,000 per year for four years.

Solution

We see that the present value factor sought is

$$\text{PV factor} = \frac{\$12,000}{\$4,000} = 3.000$$

and we seek the interest rate that will provide this factor over a four-year period. The interest rate must lie between 12 percent and 14 percent because 3.000 lies between 3.037 and 2.914 (in the fourth row of Appendix A, Table 4). Linear interpolation between these two values, according to the following equation

$$i = 12 + (14 - 12)\frac{(3.037 - 3.000)}{(3.037 - 2.914)}$$

$$= 12 + 0.602 = 12.602\%$$

provides us with a good approximation to the actual internal rate of return.

When the income stream is discounted at 12.6 percent, the resulting present value closely approximates the cost of the investment. Thus, the internal rate of return for this investment is 12.6 percent. The cost of capital can be compared with the internal rate of return to determine the net rate of return on the investment. If, in this example, the cost of capital were 8 percent, the net rate of return on the investment would be 4.6 percent.

The net present value and internal rate of return methods involve procedures that are essentially the same. They differ in that the net present value method enables investment alternatives to be compared in terms of the dollar value in excess of cost, whereas the internal rate of return method permits a comparison of rates of return on alternative investments. Moreover, the internal rate of return method occasionally encounters problems in calculation, as multiple rates frequently appear in the computation.

### Ranking Investments with Uneven Lives

When proposed investments have the same life expectancy, comparison among them using the preceding methods will give a reasonable picture of their relative value. When lives are unequal, however, there is the question of how to relate the two different time periods. Should replacements be considered the same as the original? Should productivity for the shorter-term unit that will be replaced earlier be considered to have higher productivity? How should the cost of future units be estimated?

No estimate dealing with investments unforeseen at the time of decision can be expected to reflect a high degree of accuracy. Still, the problem must be dealt with, and some assumptions must be made in order to determine a ranking. The following section presents several different examples of how different methods can be applied to OM-related investment decisions.

## SAMPLE PROBLEMS ON INVESTMENT DECISIONS

### An Expansion Decision

Example

William J. Wilson Ceramic Products, Inc., leases plant facilities in which firebrick is manufactured. Because of rising demand, Wilson could increase sales by investing in new equipment to expand output. The selling price of $2.50 per brick will remain unchanged if output and sales increase. Based on engineering and cost estimates, the accounting department provides management with the following cost estimates based on an annual increased output of 400,000 bricks:

| | |
|---|---|
| Cost of new equipment having an expected life of five years | $500,000 |
| Equipment installation cost | 20,000 |
| Expected salvage value | 0 |
| New operation's share of annual lease expense | 40,000 |
| Annual increase in utility expenses | 40,000 |
| Annual increase in labor costs | 160,000 |
| Annual additional cost for raw materials | 400,000 |

The sum-of-the-years'-digits method of depreciation will be used, and taxes are paid at a rate of 40 percent. Wilson's policy is not to invest capital in projects earning less than a 20 percent rate of return. Should the proposed expansion be undertaken?

Solution

Compute cost of investment:

| | |
|---|---|
| Acquisition cost of equipment | $500,000 |
| Equipment installation costs | 20,000 |
| Total cost of investment | $520,000 |

Determine yearly cash flows throughout the life of the investment.

The lease expense is a sunk cost. It will be incurred whether or not the investment is made and is therefore irrelevant to the decision and should be disregarded. Annual production expenses to be considered are utility, labor, and raw materials. These total $600,000 per year.

Annual sales revenues are $2.50 × 400,000 units of output, or $1,000,000. Yearly income before depreciation and taxes is thus $1,000,000 gross revenues, less $600,000 expenses, or $400,000.

Next, determine the depreciation charges to be deducted from the $400,000 income each year using the SYD method (sum-of-years'-digits = 1 + 2 + 3 + 4 + 5 = 15):

| Year | Proportion of $500,000 to Be Depreciated | | Depreciation Charge |
|------|------------------------------------------|---|---------------------|
| 1 | 5/15 × $500,000 | = | $166,667 |
| 2 | 4/15 × 500,000 | = | 133,333 |
| 3 | 3/15 × 500,000 | = | 100,000 |
| 4 | 2/15 × 500,000 | = | 66,667 |
| 5 | 1/15 × 500,000 | = | 33,333 |
| Accumulated depreciation | | | $500,000 |

Find each year's cash flow when taxes are 40 percent. Cash flow for only the first year is illustrated:

| | |
|---|---|
| Earnings before depreciation and taxes | $400,000 |
| Less depreciation | −$167,667 |
| Earnings before taxes | $233,333 |
| Less federal taxes (40%) | −93,333 |
| Net earnings | $140,000 |
| Net cash flow = Net earnings + Depreciation | $306,667 |
| (first year) | |

Determine present value of the cash flow. Since Wilson demands at least a 20 percent rate of return on investments, multiply the cash flows by the 20 percent present-value factor for each year. The factor for each respective year must be used because the cash flows are not an annuity.

| Year | Present Value Factor (20%) | | Cash Flow | | Present Value |
|------|----------------------------|---|-----------|---|---------------|
| 1 | 0.833 | × | $306,667 | = | $255,454 |
| 2 | 0.694 | × | 293,333 | = | 203,573 |
| 3 | 0.579 | × | 280,000 | = | 162,120 |
| 4 | 0.482 | × | 266,667 | = | 128,533 |
| 5 | 0.402 | × | 253,334 | = | 101,840 |
| Total present value of cash flows (discounted at 20%) | | | | = | $851,520 |

Now find whether net present value is positive or negative:

| | |
|---|---|
| Total present value of cash flows | $851,520 |
| Total cost of investment | 520,000 |
| Net present value | $331,520 |

The net present value is positive when returns are discounted at 20 percent. Wilson will earn an amount in excess of 20 percent on the investment and the proposed expansion should be undertaken.

## A Replacement Decision

Example

For five years Bennie's Brewery has been using a machine that attaches labels to bottles. The machine was purchased for $4,000 and is being depreciated over 10 years to a $0 salvage value using straight-line depreciation. The machine can be sold now for $2,000. Bennie can buy a new labeling machine for $6,000 that will have a useful life of five years and cut labor costs by $1,200 annually. The old machine will require a major overhaul in the next few months at an estimated cost of $300. If purchased, the new machine will be depreciated over five years to a $500 salvage value using the straight-line method. The company will invest in any project earning more than the 12 percent cost of capital. The tax rate is 40 percent. Should Bennie's Brewery invest in the new machine?

**Solution**

Determine the cost of investment:

| | | |
|---|---:|---:|
| Price of new machine | | $6,000 |
| Less: Sale of old machine | $2,000 | |
| Avoidable overhaul costs | 300 | 2,300 |
| Effective net cost of investment | | $3,700 |

Determine the increase in cash flow resulting from investment in the new machine:

Yearly cost savings = $1,200

Differential depreciation:

Annual depreciation on old machines: $\dfrac{\text{Cost} - \text{Salvage}}{\text{Expected life}} = \dfrac{\$4,000 - \$0}{10} = \$400$

Annual depreciation on new machines: $\dfrac{\text{Cost} - \text{Salvage}}{\text{Expected life}} = \dfrac{\$6,000 - \$500}{5} = \$1,100$

Differential depreciation = $1,100 − $400 = $700

Yearly net increase in cash flow into the firm:

| | | |
|---|---:|---:|
| Cost savings | | $1,200 |
| Deduct: Taxes at 40% | $480 | |
| Add: Advantage of increase in depreciation (0.4 × 700) | 280 | 200 |
| Yearly increase in cash flow | | $1,000 |

Determine the total present value of the investment:

The five-year cash flow of $1,000 per year is an annuity.

Discounted at 12 percent, the cost of capital, the present value is 3.605 × $1,000 = $3,605

The present value of the new machine, if sold at its salvage value of $500 at the end of the fifth year, is 0.567 × $500 = $284

Total present value of the expected cash flows: $3,605 + $284 = $3,889

Determine whether the net present value is positive:

| | |
|---|---:|
| Total present value | $3,889 |
| Cost of investment | 3,700 |
| Net present value | $ 189 |

Bennie's Brewery should make the purchase because the investment will return slightly more than the cost of capital.

*Note:* The importance of depreciation has been shown in this example. The present value of the yearly cash flow resulting from operation is only

$$\underset{(\$1,200 - \$480)}{(\text{Cost savings} - \text{Taxes})} \times \underset{(3.605)}{(\text{Present value factor})} = \$2,596$$

This figure is $1,104 less than the $3,700 cost of the investment. Only a very large depreciation advantage makes this investment worthwhile. The total present value of the advantage is $1,009:

$$\underset{(0.4 \times \$700)}{(\text{Tax rate} \times \text{Differential depreciation})} \times \underset{3.605}{(\text{P.V. factor})} = \$1,009$$

## A Make-or-Buy Decision

Example

The Triple X Company manufactures and sells refrigerators. It makes some of the parts for the refrigerators and purchases others. The engineering department believes it might be possible to cut costs by manufacturing one of the parts currently being purchased for $8.25 each. (It is assumed that there is an unlimited supply of these parts at this price.) The firm uses 100,000 of these parts each year, and the accounting department compiles the following list of costs based on engineering estimates.

Fixed costs will increase by $50,000.

Labor costs will increase by $125,000.

Factory overhead, currently running $500,000 per year, may be expected to increase 12 percent.

Raw materials used to make the part will cost $600,000.

Given these estimates, should Triple X make the part or continue to buy it?

Solution

Find total cost incurred if the part were manufactured:

| | |
|---|---:|
| Additional fixed costs | $ 50,000 |
| Additional labor costs | 125,000 |
| Raw materials cost | 600,000 |
| Additional overhead costs = 0.12 × $500,000 | 60,000 |
| Total cost to manufacture | $835,000 |

Find cost per unit to manufacture:

$$\frac{\$835,000}{100,000} = \$8.35 \text{ per unit}$$

Triple X should continue to buy the part. Manufacturing costs exceed the present cost to purchase by $0.10 per unit.

## An Example Using Excel

Example

It is July 1, 1990, and you are currently operating a re-export business in Hong Kong. Your warehouse where you store the products you receive from Ghuangzhou in the People's Republic of China is old and very poorly laid out. Consequently, your operating expenses are very high.

You have just been approached by a developer who has an empty warehouse that he built for a client that went bankrupt. He offers to sell you the warehouse for HK$8,250,000. However, the warehouse is located on land that is leased from the government, and the lease expires on June 30, 1997, when Hong Kong becomes part of the People's Republic of China. As a result, you do not anticipate that you will be able to renew this lease.

Your current annual operating expenses is HK$3,200,000. You hire a consultant to conduct an analysis of the new warehouse. The consultant estimates that because of its efficiencies your annual operating expenses in the new warehouse will be HK$1,750,000. In addition, the developer has told you that he can sell your current warehouse for HK$2,600,000.

a. If your current cost of capital is 15 percent, what is the net present value of purchasing this new warehouse?

b. What is the internal rate on return of this investment?

c. Should you buy this new warehouse?

**Solution**

a. Using Excel, set up a worksheet showing the net cost of the warehouse and the projected savings for the next seven years, as shown in Exhibit 3S.7. Using the Net Present Value (NPV) function, as shown in Exhibit 3S.7, determine the net present value of the project, which is HK$1,060,000. Since the NPV is positive, this means that the overall return on this investment exceeds your cost of capital of 15 percent.

b. Again using the same Excel worksheet, use the Internal Rate of Return (IRR) function, as shown in Exhibit 3S.7, to determine the internal rate of return for this investment which is 22 percent. (Note: the .15 in the IRR function is an estimate that is needed to start the IRR calculation.)

c. Inasmuch as the project has a 22 percent return on investment that exceeds your minimum requirement of 15 percent, you should buy the new warehouse, even though the lease expires in seven years.

**EXHIBIT 3S.7**

Application of Excel to Determining Net Present Value and Internal Rate of Return

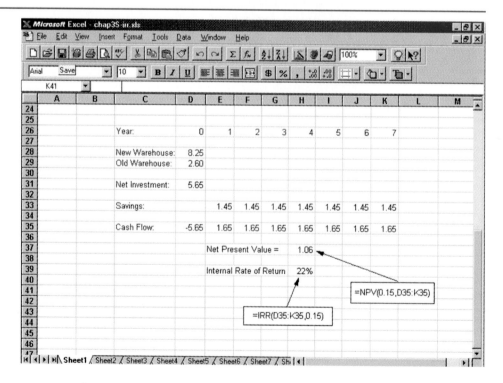

# KEY FORMULAS

**Compound value of an annuity**

$$S_n = R[(1+i)^{n-1} + (1+i)^{n-2} + \cdots + (1+i)^1 + 1]$$

where

$S_n$ = Compound value of an annuity

$R$ = Periodic receipts in dollars

$n$ = Length of the annuity in years

**Present value of a future single payment**

$$V_n = P(1+i)^n$$

where

$V_n$ = Value of principal at the end of year $n$

$n$ = Length of the compounding period in years

$P$ = Present value of principal

$i$ = Interest rate

**Present value of an annuity**

$$A_n = R\left[\frac{1}{(1+i)} + \frac{1}{(1+i)^2} + \cdots + \frac{1}{(1+i)^n}\right]$$

where

$A_n$ = Present value of annuity of $n$ years

$R$ = Periodic receipts

$n$ = Length of the annuity in years

# KEY TERMS

activity-based costing   p. 79
avoidable costs   p. 78
break-even analysis   p. 81
cost of capital   p. 78
depreciation   p. 86
economic life   p. 86
fixed costs   p. 77
internal rate of return   p. 93

net present value   p. 92
obsolete   p. 86
opportunity costs   p. 78
out-of-pocket costs   p. 78
payback period   p. 92
sunk costs   p. 77
variable costs   p. 77

# REVIEW AND DISCUSSION QUESTIONS

1.  List three examples of capital investments in operations management.
2.  Define the following terms: *fixed, variable, opportunity, and avoidable costs; obsolescence* and *depreciation.*
3.  What are the goals of the two types of break-even analysis?

4. What are the main advantages of activity-based costing techniques?

5. How do taxes affect profits? Why?

6. How does depreciation affect capital investment? Why?

7. If a firm is short of capital, what action might it take to conserve the capital it has and to obtain more?

8. What are the reasons for using present-value analysis rather than "future-value" analysis?

9. Why might a decision maker like to use the payback period method as well as the rate of return and the net present value?

10. Discuss why the comparison of alternative investment decisions is especially difficult when the investment choices have different life lengths.

11. Compare the advantages and disadvantages of the following depreciation methods: straight-line, sum-of-the years' digits, double-declining balance.

# PROBLEMS

1. Jana and Marla, two recent business school graduates, have decided to open their own copy-service business on a part-time basis. They estimate that their annual fixed costs are $32,000 and their average variable cost for each copy sold at $.03. They expect their selling price to average $.07 per copy.

   a. Draw the break-even chart for their business, and indicate all of the relevant costs.

   b. What is their break-even point in dollars? In number of copies?

   c. After their first year of operations, in which they generated $84,000 in revenues, Jana and Marla decide to pay themselves each $5,000 per year in salaries. What do their annual sales have to be in the second year if they want to make the same amount of profit as they did in their first year?

2. Peter McWalters is president of Transformonics, a firm that produces power transformers for personal computer manufacturers. Peter's analysis of the various methods by which a new model of transformer can be built has been narrowed down to one of three alternatives. Because of the rapidly changing technology in the industry, Peter estimates the product life of the transformer to be one year. Marketing has estimated that it can sell 5,000 of these new transformers within that time period. The three alternative processes are:

   • Use existing equipment and fixtures, and hire high-skilled machinists and technicians at $16.00 per hour (including benefits). With this method, each transformer will require two (2) labor-hours to assemble.

   • Use existing equipment, but invest $30,000 in new fixtures and instruction manuals to simplify some of the more complicated operations. Semiskilled workers could be employed at $12.00 per hour (including benefits), with each transformer requiring one (1) labor-hour to complete.

   • Invest $75,000 in new equipment, fixtures, and instruction manuals. This approach would eliminate all of the complicated procedures, thereby requiring only unskilled labor, which could be hired at $6.00 per hour (including benefits). With this method, each transformer would require only 20 labor-minutes to complete.

   a. Draw a break-even chart using total cost versus volume for the above processes.

   b. Calculate the two break-even volumes (i.e., those volumes at which you shift from one process to another).

c.  Which alternative would you recommend, and why?

3.  Marisa Strauss, a financial analyst for Green Garden Salads, Inc., is currently evaluating three different sites for locating its plant in the greater San Francisco area. This plant will produce prepackaged tossed salads in five and ten pound bags. The three locations are: (a) Oakland, (b) Petaluma and (c) San Jose. Marisa estimates that the fixed costs and variable unit costs associated with each site are as follows:

| Location | Fixed Costs per Year | Variable Costs per Unit |
| --- | --- | --- |
| Oakland | $250,000 | $10.00/100 lb. |
| Petaluma | $100,000 | $30.00/100 lb. |
| San Jose | $150,000 | $20.00/100 lb. |

a.  Plot the total costs curves for each of these locations on a single graph and identify the range of outputs for which each alternative site is the most economical.

b.  If the vice-president of marketing has estimated that the demand for prepackaged salads to be 500,000 lb per year, which location would you pick and why?

4.  What is the depreciation expense for the third year, using the sum-of-the-years'-digits method, for the following cost of a new machine?

| | |
| --- | --- |
| Cost of machine | $35,000 |
| Estimated life | 6 years |
| Estimated salvage value | $5,000 |

5.  Disregarding tax considerations, is it cheaper to buy or to lease a piece of equipment with the following costs for a five-year term? (Assume the cost of capital is 10 percent.)

| | To Buy | To Lease |
| --- | --- | --- |
| Purchase (or lease) cost | $50,000 | $10,000/yr. |
| Annual operating cost | 4,000/yr. | 4,000/yr. |
| Maintenance cost | 2,000/yr. | 0 |
| Salvage value at end of 5 years | $20,000 | 0 |

6.  A new piece of office equipment must be purchased, and the choice has been narrowed down to two styles, each capable of meeting the intended needs. With a 10-year horizon and an interest rate of 8 percent, which piece of equipment should be purchased?

| | Equipment A | Equipment B |
| --- | --- | --- |
| Initial cost | $10,000 | $7,000 |
| Salvage value (10 years hence) | 4,000 | 2,000 |
| Estimated annual operation and maintenance cost | 1,000 | 1,500 |

7.  The local university is accepting bids for the hot dog and cold drink concession at the new stadium. The contract is for a five-year period, and it is your feeling that a bid of $40,000 will win the contract. A preliminary analysis indicates that annual operating costs will be $35,000 and average annual sales will be $50,000. The contract can be written off during the five

years. Taxes are at the 40 percent rate, and your goal is to make a 20 percent return on your investment.

   *a.* Will you meet your goal if you use straight-line depreciation?

   *b.* Would you meet your goal using sum-of-the-years'-digits depreciation?

8. In adding a new product line, a firm needs a new piece of machinery. An investigation of suitable equipment for the production process has narrowed the choice to the two machines listed.

| | Machine A | Machine B |
|---|---|---|
| Type of equipment | General purpose | Special purpose |
| Installed cost | $8,000 | $13,000 |
| Salvage value | 800 | 3,000 |
| Annual labor cost | 6,000 | 3,600 |
| Estimated life (years) | 10 | 5 |

Assume that at the end of five years, a comparable replacement for Machine B will be available. Using present-value analysis with a 10 percent interest rate, which machine would you choose?

9. ABC's business has been going so well that the firm decides to diversify with a sideline business. Ballard, a partner and an experienced cabinetmaker, has a great deal of know-how in making cabinets for kitchens and vanities for bathrooms. (Countertops would be subcontracted because of the specialized equipment needed for molding and pressing.) The company is anticipating putting out a standard line of cabinets available in birch, walnut, mahogany, or oak veneer at no extra charge.

   Three manufacturing methods are feasible for producing the cabinets. The first is largely manual, the second uses some semiautomated equipment, and the third is largely automatic. The semiautomatic equipment requires an investment of $45,000. ABC expects this equipment to generate incremental after-tax cash flows of $15,000 for each of the next four years. What is the net present value for this equipment? What is the payback period? What should ABC do?

10. Matt Koslow, having just graduated from business school, has decided to open his own brewery, which he named JoJo Brewery in honor of his grandparents, Joe and Joan. He purchases the necessary brewing and fermenting equipment to get started for $60,000, and locates his brewery in an old brick building that was previously a textile mill. His annual fixed costs are estimated to be $45,000. In addition, the variable costs are estimated to be $14.00 per barrel of beer. Initially, to save money, he will produce only kegs of beer, which he will sell to local bars and restaurants. Based on a market survey that he had conducted, Matt forecasts his sales for the first five years to be as follows:

| Year: | 1 | 2 | 3 | 4 | 5 |
|---|---|---|---|---|---|
| Barrels: | 3,000 | 4,400 | 6,200 | 7,000 | 7,800 |

Currently, the cost of money is 15 percent and the tax rate is 35 percent. The average selling price per barrel is estimated to be $35.00.

   Using a spreadsheet software program, answer the following questions:

   *a.* If Matt uses straight-line depreciation and a five-year life on the equipment with no salvage value, what is the net present value (NPV) of his investment? If he uses sum-of-the-years' digits method of depreciation, what is his NPV?

   *b.* What is the internal rate of return (IRR) on this investment with the current tax rate of 35 percent? If the tax rate was increased to 42 percent?

   *c.* What is the NPV at the current cost of money (15 percent) and tax rate (35 percent) if sales each year are 20 percent lower than his original forecast?

# Selected Bibliography

Brigham, Eugene F. *Fundamentals of Financial Management,* 7th ed. Fort Worth, TX: The Dryden Press, 1995.

Gitman, Lawrence. *Principles of Managerial Finance,* 7th ed. New York: HarperCollins, 1994.

Hodder, James E., and Henry E. Riggs. "Pitfalls in Evaluating Risky Projects." *Harvard Business Review,* January–February 1985, pp. 128–35.

Johnson, Thomas, and Robert Kaplan. *Relevance Lost: The Rise and Fall of Management Accounting.* Boston: Harvard Business School Press, 1987, p. 188.

Libertore, Matthew J. *Selection and Evaluation of Advanced Manufacturing Technologies.* New York: Springer-Verlag, 1990, pp. 231–56.

Pringle, John J., and Robert S. Harris. *Essentials of Managerial Finance,* Glenview, IL: Scott Foresman, 1984.

Ross, Stephen A.; Randolph W. Westerfield; and Jeffrey Jaffe. *Corporate Finance.* Burr Ridge, IL: Irwin/McGraw-Hill, 1996.

Van Horne, James C. *Financial Management and Policy,* 9th ed. Englewood Cliffs, NJ: Prentice Hall, 1992.

Welsch, Glenn A., and Robert N. Anthony. *Fundamentals of Financial Accounting.* Burr Ridge, IL: Richard D. Irwin, 1984.

# PROCESS MEASUREMENT AND ANALYSIS

## Chapter Outline

## Chapter Objectives

- Identify the different measures of performance that can be used to evaluate a process.

- Introduce the concept of benchmarking and demonstrate why it is an important tool for those companies that want to have world class operations.

- Demonstrate how process analysis can provide management with an in-depth understanding of a process and explain the difference between demand and the capacity of a process.

- Introduce the concept of service blueprinting and illustrate how it is used to evaluate service operations.

- Introduce the concept of business process reengineering and show how it is changing the way in which managers view their operations.

P rior to the fast food era, hamburgers, like any other sandwich in a restaurant, were made to order. To begin the process the cook, upon receipt of the order, reached into the refrigerator for a raw hamburger patty and placed it on the grill. The customer could specify the degree of doneness (e.g., rare, medium, or well done) and request certain condiments. The roll could be toasted or not. However, the quality of the hamburger produced in this fashion was highly dependent on the skill of the cook, and consequently the quality could vary significantly between cooks, even within the same restaurant. In addition, hamburgers prepared using this method took a relatively long time to deliver, as they were cooked only after the order was received (see Exhibit 4.1A).

The arrival of Burger King and McDonald's in the 1950s, and later Wendy's totally changed the way in which hamburgers were cooked and delivered to the customer. Unlike most

restaurants at that time, which offered a wide variety of food items, Burger King and McDonald's were highly focused operations with very limited menus. In addition, both firms offered low-cost products that were delivered quickly. However, each has taken a different approach in the type of process they have adopted to cook and deliver hamburgers and the particular markets that they serve. This chapter focuses on processes and how they contribute to the overall success of the firm. ▪

# PROCESS ANALYSIS

An analysis of the methods used by various food service operations to prepare and deliver hamburgers provides us with some insight into the trade-offs that managers face when selecting one particular process over another. This type of analysis also allows us to identify the strengths and weaknesses of each process, which can then be related to the specific market segments that each firm is focusing on.

To continue the chapter opener, McDonald's cooks its hamburgers on grills in batches, with 12 hamburgers per batch. The rolls are similarly toasted or caramelized in batches of 12. After cooking, the hamburgers are assembled (that is, placed on rolls with condiments, etc.) and wrapped, also in batch sizes of 12. The finished products are then stored in holding bins for immediate delivery to the customer. This low-cost, highly efficient, make-to-stock process produces highly standardized products that can be delivered quickly to the customer (see Exhibit 4.1B). As a result, a major market for McDonald's is families with small children for whom speed of delivery is important. Thus, fast service is emphasized in many of McDonald's advertisements.

Burger King, on the other hand, cooks its hamburgers with a conveyor-broiler, which is a highly specialized piece of equipment. Using this method, a worker places raw hamburgers on one end of a moving conveyor which proceeds under a broiler where they are cooked from both the top and bottom. Ninety seconds later the hamburgers emerge from the other end of the conveyor, cooked to the desired degree. The rolls also are toasted in the conveyor-broiler. The use of this highly focused process ensures consistency of product quality with minimum dependence on worker skill; however, the process is very limited in terms of flexibility. Because all hamburgers are cooked in 90 seconds, the thickness of the patty cannot vary. Consequently, when Burger King came out with the Whopper, the only way it could make the bigger burger was to make it wider because the thickness had to remain the same as that of the regular-sized patties.

Once cooked, the hamburgers at Burger King are placed on rolls and stored in a steam cabinet. This work-in-process (WIP) inventory is then used to replenish standard items in the holding bins (or finished goods inventory). It is also used as the starting point for assembling hamburgers to meet individual customer requests. The WIP inventory of cooked hamburgers allows Burger King to custom assemble hamburgers in a relatively short time (as compared to cooking them from the raw state) while simultaneously reducing the level of finished goods inventory in holding bins (as compared to McDonald's) because replenishment time is shorter (see Exhibit 4.1C). The strength of Burger King's process lies in its ability to quickly deliver assembled-to-order products; therefore, it tries to attract individuals who "want it their way."

Wendy's has adopted still a different approach. Here hamburgers are cooked on a grill, awaiting individual customer orders. Upon receipt of the order, the hamburger is taken off the grill and placed on a bun with the specific condiments requested, all within view of the customer. Customers perceive this assemble-to-order process as higher quality in comparison to that at McDonald's or Burger King, due, in part, to the fact that everything is done in front of the customer. The trade-off here is that an average hamburger takes longer to prepare than a special request at Burger King because the order begins farther upstream in the process (see Exhibit 4.1D).

As we have noted, each of these operations has its strengths and weaknesses. All three fast food chains are successful because they recognize their strengths and focus advertising and promotional efforts on attracting those segments of the market that value their particular process characteristics.

## EXHIBIT 4.1

Process Flowcharts for Making Hamburgers

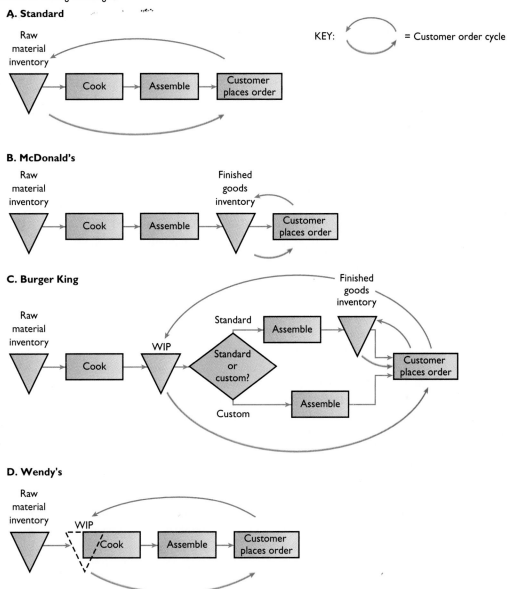

### A. Standard

### B. McDonald's

### C. Burger King

### D. Wendy's

## PROCESS MEASUREMENT

A key factor in the success of every organization is its ability to measure performance. Such feedback on a continuous basis provides management with data to determine if established goals or standards are being met. As Peter Drucker, a well-known management guru has said, "If you can't measure it, you can't manage it." Without proper measures of performance, managers could not assess how well their organizations do or compare their performance with that of their competitors. Managers would be like ships' captains, adrift on the ocean with no land in sight and no compass or other navigational instruments to guide them.

However, with a growing number of performance measures available, managers must be selective in choosing only those measures that are critical to their firm's success. Depending on the specific industry and market niche within that industry, some measures of performance are more important to management than others. For example, in a fast food outlet, a key performance indicator is the speed with which food is delivered to the customer. In an upscale restaurant, on the other hand, key performance measures may be the variety of items offered on the menu and the quality of food served.

Today, in the information age, management, like everyone else, is swamped with reams of reports containing data on all aspects of a company's performance. It is, therefore, essential for management to identify those key indicators that measure those parameters that are critical to the success of their firms.

## Types of Performance Measures

**productivity**
Efficiency of a process.

**Productivity**    The efficiency with which inputs are transformed into outputs is a measure of the process's **productivity.** In other words, productivity measures how well we convert inputs into outputs. In its broadest sense, productivity is defined as:

$$\text{Productivity} = \frac{\text{Outputs}}{\text{Inputs}}$$

Ideally, we would like to measure the total productivity of a process, which would be the total outputs divided by the total inputs. Unfortunately, the inputs come in various forms. For example, labor is measured in hours, a building is measured in square feet, raw material is measured in pounds, units, and so forth. It would therefore be impossible to obtain a measure for the total inputs into a process unless we converted all of the inputs to a common denominator like money. However, in doing so, the operations manager loses an understanding of how the process is performing. Consequently, management will adopt one or more partial measures of productivity, which is the output of the process (in either revenues or units) divided by a single input. Some commonly used partial measures of productivity are presented in Exhibit 4.2. Such measures give managers the necessary information in familiar units, thereby allowing the manager to more easily relate to the actual performance of the operation.

Productivity is what we call a *relative measure.* In other words, to be meaningful it needs to be compared with something else. For example, what can we learn from the fact that we operate a restaurant, and that its productivity last week was 8.4 customers/labor hour? (Nothing!)

Productivity comparisons can be made in two ways. First, a company can compare itself with similar operations within its industry, or can use industry data when it is available (e.g., comparing productivity among the different stores in a franchise).

**EXHIBIT 4.2**
Partial Measures of Productivity

| Type of Business | Productivity Measure (Output/Input) |
| --- | --- |
| Restaurant | Customers (meals)/labor hour |
| Retail store | Sales/square foot |
| Chicken farm | Pounds of meat/pound of feed |
| Utility plant | Kilowatts/ton of coal |
| Paper mill | Tons of paper/cord of wood |

Another approach is to measure productivity over time within the same operation. Here we would compare our productivity in one time period with that of the next.

**capacity**
Output of a process in a given time period.

**Capacity** The output capability of a process is referred to as the **capacity** of the process. This performance measure is typically presented in units of output per unit of time, although, as we shall see later in the section, this is not always practical. Examples of measures of capacity are shown in Exhibit 4.3.

As noted by these examples, measures of capacity exist for both manufacturing and services. The major difference between manufacturing and services, in terms of measuring capacity, is that with service operations the measures of capacity usually include the customer, since the customer is typically an integral part of the process. (Because customers very often participate in the service delivery process, they can be viewed as both an input and an output.)

*Design capacity* is defined as the ideal output rate at which a firm would like to produce under normal circumstances and for which the system was designed. Depending on the product or process and goals of the company, design capacity could even be established using a five-day-a-week, single-shift operation. *Maximum capacity* is used to define the maximum potential output rate that could be achieved when productive resources are used to their maximum. Typically, most firms can operate effectively at maximum capacity for only short periods of time. Operating at maximum capacity, for example, results in higher energy costs, the need for overtime wage premiums, and increased machine breakdowns due to the lack of time to conduct scheduled preventive maintenance. Worker fatigue resulting from extended hours on the job can also cause an increase in defective products as well as a decrease in labor productivity.

**capacity utilization**
Percentage of available capacity that is actually used.

The degree to which a firm utilizes its productive capacity is referred to as **capacity utilization,** which is defined as follows:

$$\text{Capacity utilization} = \frac{\text{Actual output}}{\text{Design capacity}}$$

For example, if an automobile assembly plant had a design capacity of 3,600 cars per week, and actually produced only 2,700 cars in one week, then its capacity utilization for that week would be:

$$\text{Capacity utilization} = \frac{2,700}{3,600} = 75\%$$

With this definition of capacity utilization, it is possible to have utilization rates that are in excess of 100 percent, which should be a warning to management that excessive production costs are being incurred.

So far, we have measured capacity in terms of units of output per unit of time, which is appropriate as long as the output is relatively homogeneous (e.g., cars, stereos, etc.). However,

---

**EXHIBIT 4.3**

Measures of Capacity

| Type of Operation | Measure of Capacity |
|---|---|
| Fast-food restaurant | Customers per hour |
| Brewery | Barrels of beer per year |
| Hotel reservation call center | Telephone calls per hour |
| Automobile assembly plant | Cars per hour |
| Paper mill | Tons of paper per year |

when the output units are highly variable, especially in terms of process requirements, a more meaningful measure of capacity is often expressed in terms of one of the inputs. Consider, for example, a flexible machining center that can make parts that take anywhere from five minutes to two hours to produce. The capacity of the center, in terms of units produced per week, could vary significantly depending on which particular units were being produced. In this case, a better measure of capacity utilization would be:

$$\text{Capacity utilization} = \frac{\text{Actual machine hours used}}{\text{Total machine hours available}}$$

 Such measures of capacity utilization will become more popular as the flexibility of processes increases to permit wider varieties of products to be made. This approach to measuring capacity utilization is also more applicable to many service operations that have a very high labor content and also require that labor to perform a wide variety of tasks. Examples here include medical doctors, whose tasks can vary from performing surgical operations to having office visits and attending required meetings. College professors provide another good example. In addition to teaching students, they are also required to conduct research and be of service to the college and the community. In both these instances, capacity as measured in terms of available hours per week is clearly the appropriate measure.

**Quality**    The quality of a process is usually measured by the defect rate of the products produced. Defects include those products that are identified as nonconforming, both internally (prior to shipping the product to the customer) as well as externally (i.e., products whose defects are found by the customer). The topic of process quality measurement and control is presented in greater detail in Chapter 5 and its supplement.

There are additional measures of a process's overall quality. With increasing awareness and concern for the environment, for example, the amount of toxic waste generated is also a measure of a process's quality. Similarly, the amount of scrap and waste material produced is another process quality indicator.

**Speed of Delivery**    Many companies are experiencing increased pressure with respect to speed of delivery. Firms that once took weeks and months to deliver a product are now delivering those products in hours and days. (See the OM in Practice on MBNA.)

Speed of delivery has two dimensions to measure. The first is the amount of time from when the product is ordered to when it is shipped to the customer, which is known as a product's *lead time*. Companies that produce standard products significantly reduce lead times by producing products for finished goods inventory. For such situations, orders are immediately filled from existing inventories, thereby eliminating any lead times. Companies that produce customized products, however, do not have the luxury of a finished goods inventory. Firms producing such products typically require a significant lead time before the finished product can be shipped.

The other dimension in measuring speed of delivery is the variability in delivery time. In many cases, this dimension is more critical than the estimated lead time itself. In other words, customers, whether they be other companies or end users, do not like uncertainty. Uncertainty affects work scheduling, capacity utilization, and so forth, which negatively affects the overall efficiency of the process. Thus, the less variability in delivery times, the better.

**Flexibility**    Currently, the competitive advantage for many companies lies in their ability to produce customized products to meet individual customer needs. The capability of a

# Operations Management in Practice

## MBNA IS TRULY A SPEED FREAK

Credit card issuer MBNA sets up scoreboards in its various offices to keep employees up to speed on how quickly they're serving customers.

"MBNA, the Wilmington, Delaware, credit card company, has developed a very loyal customer base due, in large part, to its ability to provide outstanding service. To accomplish this, MBNA has developed 15 different measures of performance, many of which pertain directly to speed. For example, customer address changes must be processed within one day; telephones must be answered within two rings; switchboard calls must be transferred to the appropriate individual within 21 seconds. State-of-the-art technology allows MBNA to monitor performance on a continuous basis.

At any given moment it is possible to obtain a performance measurement that shows, for example, that employees are achieving "two-ring pick-up" 99.7 percent of the time, as shown in the picture. The current standard for the minimum level of service that is acceptable for each of the 15 performance measures is 98.5 percent, which was increased recently from 98.0 percent and is significantly up from 10 years ago when it was 90 percent.

Source: Martin, J. and J. E. Davis, "Are You As Good As You Think?" *Fortune*, September 30, 1996.

---

**agile manufacturing**
Ability of a manufacturing process to respond quickly to the demands of the customer.

company to provide such customized products in a timely manner is often referred to as **agile manufacturing.** Flexibility is the measure of how readily the company's transformation process can adjust to meet the ever-changing demands of its customers.

There are three dimensions of flexibility. The first type of flexibility indicates how quickly a process can convert from producing one product or family of product(s) to another. For example, many U.S. automobile assembly plants still require a minimum of several weeks shutdown annually in order to convert from one model year to the next, indicating a degree of inflexibility in this area.

Another measure of a process's flexibility is its ability to react to changes in volume. Those processes that can accommodate large fluctuations in volume are said to be more flexible than those that cannot. Most service operations need to be very flexible in this dimension because of their inability to inventory demand. (For example, customers wanting to eat at a restaurant on Saturday night will not wait until Monday morning.) Thus, service operations such as retail stores, restaurants, and health clinics can adjust to meet the demand from a few customers per hour to several hundred customers per hour. The typical assembly line operation in a manufacturing facility cannot similarly adjust. The volume of output from an assembly line is fixed, and consequently companies with this type of process must resort to other means of balancing supply and demand. For example, appliance makers and automobile companies offer discounts and low-cost financing to encourage consumer buying during slow periods of demand, due in part to their inability to adjust the outputs of their manufacturing facilities without shutting them down entirely.

The third dimension of flexibility is the ability of the process to produce more than one product simultaneously. Thus, the more products that a process can produce at a time, the more flexible it is said to be.

**process velocity**
Ratio of total throughput time for a product to the value-added time.

**Process Velocity**    A relatively new measure of performance is **process velocity.** Also referred to as *manufacturing velocity,* process velocity is the ratio of the actual throughput time that it takes for a product to go through the process divided by the value-added time required to complete the product or service.

For example, if the throughput time for a product is six weeks, and the actual value-added time to complete the product is four hours, then the process velocity of this product is:

$$\text{Process velocity} = \frac{\text{Total throughput time}}{\text{Value-added time}}$$

$$\text{Process velocity} = \frac{6 \text{ weeks} \times 5 \text{ days per week} \times 8 \text{ hours per day}}{4 \text{ hours}} = 60$$

A process velocity of 60, in this case, means that it takes 60 times as long to complete the product as it does to do the actual work on the product itself. In other words, process velocity is like a golf score, the lower it is, the better.

Process velocities in excess of 100 are not uncommon. For example, University Microfilms, Inc. (UMI), the largest publisher of dissertations in the United States, took 150 days to process a manuscript, although only two hours were actually spent adding value to the manuscript. For UMI, the process velocity for a manuscript was therefore:

$$\text{Process velocity} = \frac{150 \text{ days per manuscript} \times 8 \text{ hours per day}}{2 \text{ hours}} = 600$$

UMI was able to reduce the throughput time to 60 days, thereby lowering its process velocity to 240.[1]

As noted by the above example, the concept of process velocity is equally applicable to manufacturing and services. Process velocity can also be applied to any particular segment of the process, or to the overall process. For example, a firm may want to focus only on its manufacturing velocity, in which case it would look at the throughput time from when the product is first begun to when it is completed and ready to ship. A broader perspective may measure process velocity from the time when the customer first places the order for the product to when payment is finally received and the check has cleared.

In the past, especially in the United States, companies have focused solely on increasing the efficiency of the value-added time, which often constitutes only a very small portion of a product's overall time in the process.

---

[1]A. Bernstein, "Quality Is Becoming Job One in the Office, Too," *Business Week,* April 29, 1991.

# BENCHMARKING[2]

**benchmarking**
Comparison of a company's measures of performance with those of firms that are considered to be world class.

**Benchmarking** is simply a comparison of a company's performance in certain areas with the performance of other firms in its industry and/or with those firms that are identified as world-class competitors in specific functions and operations. Benchmarking can cut across traditional industry lines, providing opportunities for new and innovative ways to increase performance. For example, Xerox, in its desire to deliver products quickly, studied how L.L. Bean of Freeport, Maine, a mail order company well-known for fast accurate service, accomplished this.

Firms that want to compete as world-class organizations in the highly competitive global arena must attain "best of breed" status in those performance parameters that are critical for success in their respective industries and market segments. This can be accomplished only through measuring and comparing their performance with that of others, and then instituting the necessary actions for improvement. Companies like AT&T, Du Pont, Ford Motor, IBM, Eastman Kodak, Milliken, Motorola, Xerox, and other industry leaders, in an attempt to increase both quality and productivity now use benchmarking as a standard management tool.

David T. Kearns, CEO of Xerox Corporation, defines benchmarking as follows:

> Benchmarking is the continuous process of measuring products, services, and practices against the toughest competitors or those companies recognized as industry leaders.[3]

Several key elements in this definition should be emphasized. Continuous measuring implies that benchmarking is an iterative process with no end. With competition constantly "raising the bar," accepted levels of performance yesterday will not be tolerated by the customer tomorrow. Only through constant monitoring of our performance and that of our competitors will we be able to know where we stand at any point in time.

Benchmarking means measurement. This can be accomplished internally within the organization as well as externally with competitors and world-class firms. It is important for management to be cognizant that benchmarking is not limited only to manufacturing, but can also be applied to all of the other functional areas in an organization. This means that it can be used for products, services, and processes/practices.

Benchmarking should not be limited only to direct competitors. Rather it should focus on those firms or business functions or operations within firms that have achieved recognition as world-class operations. In other words, as Robert Camp states in the title of his book, "benchmarking is the search for best practices that leads to superior performance."[4]

## What Should We Benchmark?

Benchmarking can be applied to many areas within an organization. Robert Camp identifies three of these: (*a*) goods and services, (*b*) business processes, and (*c*) performance measures.

**Goods and Services**   Benchmarking identifies the features and functions of the goods and services that are desired by the firm's customers. This information is incorporated into

---

[2]This section has drawn heavily on the following two books: Robert C. Camp, *Benchmarking: The Search for Industry Best Practices That Lead to Superior Performance* (Milwaukee, WI: ASQC Quality Press, 1989) and Robert C. Camp, *Business Process Benchmarking: Finding and Implementing Best Practices* (Milwaukee, WI: ASQC Quality Press, 1995).

[3]Robert C. Camp, *Benchmarking: The Search for Industry Best Practices That Lead to Superior Performance,* p. 10.

[4]Ibid.

product planning, design, and development in the form of product goals and technology design practices.

**Business Processes**   Benchmarking in this area provides the basis for business process improvement and reengineering. These changes should be an integral part of the continuous quality improvement initiative.

**Performance Measures**   The end result of benchmarking goods, services, and processes is to establish and validate objectives for the vital few performance measures that have been identified as critical to the success of the organization.

## Key Steps in Benchmarking

Robert Camp, based on his experience with Xerox Corporation, has identified five phases that are necessary for successfully implementing benchmarking within an organization. These phases are planning, analysis, integration, action, and maturity. (These five phases and the various steps within each phase are summarized in Exhibit 4.4.)

**Planning**   This phase of benchmarking identifies the areas that we should benchmark, the specific organizations against which we should be benchmarking, the types of data we should collect, and the ways we should collect that data.

**Analysis**   The analysis phase focuses on obtaining an in-depth understanding of our firm's existing practices and processes as well as those of the organizations against which we will be benchmarking.

**Integration**   Here we use the findings from the first two phases to define those target areas that we want to change. As part of this phase, we need to ensure that benchmarking concepts are implemented in the corporate planning process, and that benchmarking is accepted by all levels of management.

**Action**   The benchmarking findings and associated goals must be translated into action. Those individuals who actually perform the tasks should determine how the findings can best be incorporated into the existing process.

**Maturity**   An organization reaches maturity when the best business practices that have been identified have been incorporated into all of the relevant business processes, thereby ensuring superior performance for the organization as a whole.

## Types of Benchmarking

There are four general categories of benchmarking: (*a*) internal, (*b*) competitive, (*c*) functional, and (*d*) generic.

MARKETING
MANAGEMENT
ACCOUNTING
FINANCE

**Internal Benchmarking**   This type of benchmarking provides for a comparison among similar operations or processes within a firm's own organization. It is often the starting point for identifying best practices that currently exist with the company. Internal benchmarking also provides the first step to documenting processes, which is necessary for identifying future areas for improvement. Internal benchmarking is especially appropriate for organizations (both manufacturing and services) with multiple locations.

**Competitive Benchmarking**   This provides a comparison between an organization's performance and that of its best direct competitors. The relative information obtained here will show how the company compares to other firms in its industry. Benchmarking within an

**EXHIBIT 4.4**

Benchmarking Process Steps

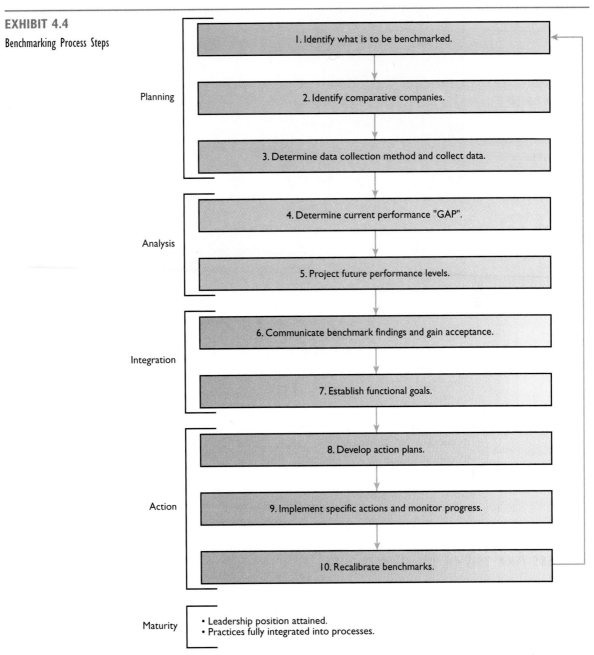

Planning

1. Identify what is to be benchmarked.

2. Identify comparative companies.

3. Determine data collection method and collect data.

Analysis

4. Determine current performance "GAP".

5. Project future performance levels.

Integration

6. Communicate benchmark findings and gain acceptance.

7. Establish functional goals.

Action

8. Develop action plans.

9. Implement specific actions and monitor progress.

10. Recalibrate benchmarks.

Maturity
- Leadership position attained.
- Practices fully integrated into processes.

Source: Robert C. Camp, *Benchmarking: The Search for Industry Best Practices That Lead to Superior Performance*, (Milwaukee, WI: ASQC Quality Press, 1989).

industry is often difficult because of the natural unwillingness of competitors to share critical information.

 **Functional Benchmarking** This type of benchmarking addresses performance comparisons with the best functional areas, regardless of the industry in which they are located. The benefits to this are several. First, a firm may have less difficulty in obtaining benchmarking partners in other industries which are not direct competitors. In addition, it is often

Technology has allowed John Deere, the farm equipment manufacturer, to be more responsive to the needs of its customers. Dealers, through satellites and CD-ROM technology, can now directly communicate electronically with John Deere warehouses. Farmers, through their own computers, also have ready access to Deere parts and other equipment.

easy to identify those firms that are considered to be the "best of breed" in performing a specific function. The L.L. Bean example presented at the beginning of this section provides a good example of functional benchmarking. Other examples of leaders in specific functional areas include General Electric (information systems), John Deere (service parts logistics, see photo) and Ford (assembly automation).

 **Generic Benchmarking**   Here performance measures are concerned with specific work processes that are virtually the same for all industries that use these processes. Generic benchmarking can easily identify those firms that have adopted innovative processes, thereby providing targets that can be more readily acceptable by members of the organization. Examples of leaders in generic benchmarking include the Federal Reserve Bank (bill scanning) and Citicorp (document processing).

## PROCESS ANALYSIS IN MANUFACTURING

### Definitions

As a first step in understanding the important characteristics of processes, we have defined some of the more commonly used terms.

**multistage process**
Process that consists of more than one step.

**hybrid process**
Multistage process that consists of more than one type of process.

**Hybrid Process**   Most of the processes that we encounter consist of more than one stage or step to produce the required goods or services. These are often referred to as **multistage processes.** Within a multistage process a different type of process can exist at each stage. When this occurs, these multistage processes are frequently referred to as **hybrid processes.** For example, in making potato chips at Cape Cod Potato Chips in Hyannis, Massachusetts, the potatoes are first washed in a continuous process, cooked in a batch process, and then packaged in an assembly line type of operation. Within a given industry, different firms may adopt different types of processes to produce the same or similar products. As an example, some potato chip manufacturers cook their potatoes with a continuous process instead of a batch process. To further illustrate, at McDonald's, the hamburgers are both cooked and assembled in batches. This approach produces a highly standardized product. Burger King, on the other hand, cooks its hamburgers on a continuous flow broiler, but assembles them individually to meet specific customer requests.

**Make-to-Stock versus Make-to-Order**  Which type of process is chosen for each stage is dependent on the firm's operations strategy and the type of product being manufactured. A **make-to-stock system** is compatible with producing a highly standardized product that can be stored in a finished goods inventory for quick delivery to the customer. As a result, these products are usually forecasted in anticipation of future customer orders. In contrast, a **make-to-order system** focuses on producing customized items which have already been ordered by the customer. It is important to note here that a make-to-order system requires more flexibility than a make-to-stock system, and as a result tends to be slower and more inefficient and, therefore, more expensive.

However, the choice of a make-to-stock system tends to limit the number of product variations to a few highly standardized items. In order to achieve maximum process efficiency while at the same time increase product variety, firms will delay the customization step until the last possible moment. A good example of this application is the mixing of custom colored paints at home improvement centers while the customers wait.

**Modularization**  Another approach that attempts to combine process efficiency with some degree of customization is called **modularization.** With this approach, the end product is designed so it can be assembled from several individual components that are considered to be standard items. The concept of modularization is used extensively throughout the computer industry. As an illustration, suppose a computer firm produces four different types of central processors, three different kinds of input/output devices, and two varieties of printers. From a customer's perspective, this firm offers a choice of 24 different computer configurations ($4 \times 3 \times 2$), although manufacturing has to produce only nine standard products ($4 + 3 + 2$). The final assembly of automobiles provides another good example. Here standard components are delivered to the automobile assembly plant and the selection of a particular combination of these components produces a "custom-made" car. Modularization also has application in services. For example, an Italian restaurant can offer its customers a choice of 60 different dishes by combining four types of pasta, three types of sauces and five varieties of meat ($4 \times 3 \times 5$).

Exhibit 4.5 shows a comparison of the process flow charts for make-to-stock, make-to-order, and modularized production processes.

**Tightness and Dependence**  The relationship between the various stages in a process is frequently referred to as the degree of *tightness* in the process. Processes that are considered very tight, like assembly lines, have a great deal of *dependence* between stages. In other words, if production stops due to a machine breakdown at an early stage in the process, work ceases almost immediately at all of the subsequent operations. This high degree of dependence among the stages is caused by a lack of buffer inventories between adjacent stages. The greater the buffer inventories, the greater the independence between stages and the "looser" the process. Batch processes typically exhibit a high degree of independence between stages as shown by the large amounts of buffer inventories in the form of work-in-process (WIP). With these types of processes, a failure at one stage in the process does not impact any other stages until the WIP between them is depleted.

**Bottlenecks**  The capacity of each stage in a multistage process often varies for several reasons, including dissimilar output rates of the different pieces of equipment that comprise

---

**make-to-stock system**
Process for making highly standardized products for finished goods inventory.

**make-to-order system**
Process for making customized products to meet individual customer requirements.

**modularization**
Use of standard components and subassemblies to produce customized products.

**EXHIBIT 4.5**

A Comparison of Make-to-Stock, Make-to-Order, and Modularized Processes

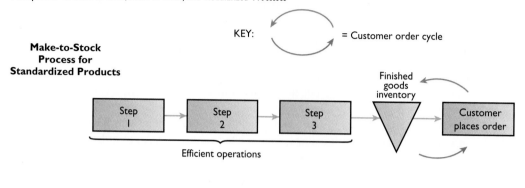

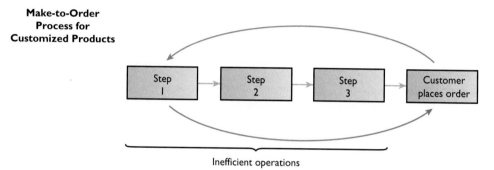

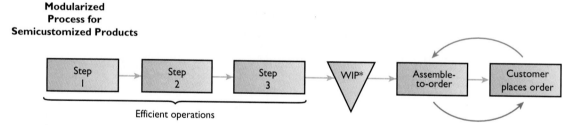

\* WIP consists of standardized components and subassemblies.

the overall process. In these situations, the stage of the process with the lowest capacity is referred to as the **bottleneck** in the process. Adding additional capacity to alleviate the bottleneck at one stage in the process will shift the bottleneck to another stage. When this occurs, the full capacity potential of the additional equipment may not be realized.

**bottleneck**
Stage or stages that limits the total output of a process.

Example

A commercial bread bakery wants to evaluate its capacity, in terms of how many pounds of bread it can produce per hour. A simplified version of the process is shown below:

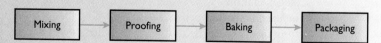

In the mixing stage, all of the ingredients are combined to form the dough. The dough must then rise in a controlled environment called a proofing box or proofing oven, which monitors humidity and temperature. Following the proofing, the bread is then formed into loaves and baked. In the final stage, the bread is packaged prior to distribution to retail outlets. The bakery currently has the following equipment:

| Stage | Capacity (Lb/Hr/Machine) | Number of Machines |
|---|---|---|
| Mixing | 60 | 3 |
| Proofing | 25 | 6 |
| Baking | 40 | 4 |
| Packaging | 75 | 3 |

a. What is the current capacity of the bakery in pounds of bread per hour?
b. Where is the bottleneck in the process?
c. If an additional piece of equipment is purchased to increase the capacity of the bottleneck, what is the new capacity of the bakery?

**Solution**

a. The total capacity of the bakery is determined by calculating the total capacity at each stage of the process as follows:

| Stage | Equipment Capacity (Lb/Hr/Machine) | Number of Machines | Total Capacity (Lb/Hr/Machine) |
|---|---|---|---|
| Mixing | 60 | 3 | 180 |
| Proofing | 25 | 6 | 150 |
| Baking | 40 | 4 | 160 |
| Packaging | 75 | 3 | 225 |

The overall capacity of the bakery is 150 pounds per hour, as determined by the proofing operation, which is that stage with the smallest capacity.

b. Currently, the bottleneck is at the proofing stage because that has the smallest hourly capacity.

c. If another proofing oven is purchased, the capacity of the proofing stage is now 175 pounds per hour. However, with the addition of the new proofing oven, the bottleneck in the process now shifts to the baking stage because that has the lowest capacity of 160 pounds per hour. Thus the new overall capacity of the bakery with the addition of another proofing oven is only 160 pounds per hour.

## Capacity versus Demand

In the above example, we have focused entirely on the available capacity of the process without considering the demand for the bread. It is important when analyzing the capacity requirements for a process that we do not confuse the capacity of the process with the demand for the firm's products. For example, if the demand for a product is less than the capacity of the smallest stage, then no bottleneck really exists (In the bakery example, if demand was less than 150 pounds per hour, there would not be any bottleneck). As a result no additional equipment is needed. Only when demand exceeds the capacity at one or more stages do we have to address the problem of a bottleneck and consider installing additional equipment.

## Process Flowcharts

**process flowchart**
Schematic diagram for describing a process.

A **process flowchart** provides management with an opportunity to view the entire process step by step. The traditional symbols used in drawing a process flowchart are presented in Exhibit 4.6.

**EXHIBIT 4.6**

Elements in a Process Flowchart

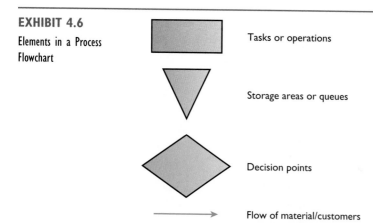

Tasks or operations

Storage areas or queues

Decision points

Flow of material/customers

**Example**

A potato chip manufacturer in Hawaii produces "Maui-style, kettle-cooked" potato chips for distribution throughout the Hawaiian Islands to retail outlets as well as to hotels and resort areas. The process of making potato chips is relatively simple. Raw potatoes, which are delivered once a week to the factory, are first washed and peeled. After a visual inspection to ensure all of the peel and eyes are removed, the potatoes are then sliced and immediately fried in a large kettle. (The peeling and frying operations are done in batches while the slicing is a continuous operation.) After frying, the cooked chips are inspected and any burnt ones are removed. The chips are then salted and stored in large cartons. This first phase of the process is done on two shifts of eight hours each. In contrast, the packaging operation is run only eight hours a day because of the large capacity of the equipment. The cooked chips are packaged in either one-ounce or eight-ounce packages. The last step in the process places the packages in cartons for delivery. (There are 24 one-ounce packages to a carton and 12 eight-ounce packages to a carton.

Draw the process flowchart for this operation.

**Solution**

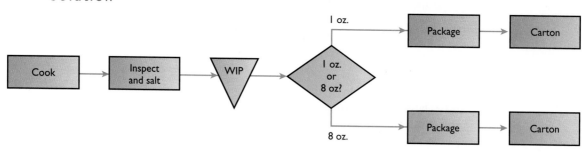

**Example**

To continue with a more in-depth analysis of the potato chip company, the following information is given about the capacities of the different stages in the operation.

| Stage | Capacity per Machine | Number of Machines |
|---|---|---|
| Peeling | 600 lb./hr. | 2 |
| Slicing | 1,500 lb./hr. | 1 |
| Cooking | 250 lb./hr. | 2 |
| Packaging (1 oz.) | 120 pkgs./min. | 2 |

3. How much of your own and your roommate's valuable time will it take to fill each order?

4. Because your baking trays can hold exactly one dozen cookies, you will produce and sell cookies by the dozen. Should you give any discount for people who order two dozen cookies, three dozen cookies, or more? If so, how much? Will it take you any longer to fill a two-dozen cookie order than a one-dozen cookie order?

5. How many food processors and baking trays will you need?

6. Are there any changes you can make in your production plans that will allow you to make better cookies or more cookies in less time or at lower cost? For example, is there a bottleneck operation in your production process that you can expand cheaply? What is the effect of adding another oven? How much would you be willing to pay to rent an additional oven?

### Problems for Further Thought

1. What happens if you are trying to do this by yourself without a roommate?

2. Should you offer special rates for rush orders? Sup-

pose you have just put a tray of cookies into the oven and someone calls up with a "crash priority" order for a dozen cookies of a different flavor. Can you fill the priority order while still fulfilling the order for the cookies that are already in the oven? If not, how much of a premium should you charge for filling the rush order?

3. When should you promise delivery? How can you look quickly at your order board (list of pending orders) and tell a caller when his or her order will be ready? How much of a safety margin for timing should you allow?

4. What other factors should you consider at this stage of planning your business?

5. Your product must be made to order because each order is potentially unique. If you decide to sell standard cookies instead, how should you change the production system? The order-taking process?

## SELECTED BIBLIOGRAPHY

Albrecht, Karl, and Ron Zemke. *Service America! Doing Business in the New Economy.* Homewood, IL: Dow Jones-Irwin, 1985.

Bernstein, A. "Quality Is Becoming Job One in the Office, Too." *Business Week,* April 29, 1991.

Bitran, Gabriel R., and Johannes Hoech. "The Humanization of Service: Respect at the Moment of Truth." *Sloan Management Review,* Winter 1990, pp. 89–96.

Camp, Robert C. *Benchmarking: The Search for Industry Best Practices That Lead to Superior Performance.* Milwaukee, WI: American Society for Quality Control, Quality Press, 1989.

Camp, Robert C. *Business Process Benchmarking: Findings and Implementing Best Practices.* Milwaukee, WI: ASQC Quality Press, 1995.

Chase, R. B. "The Customer Contact Approach to Services: Theoretical Bases and Practical Extensions." *Operations Research* 21, no. 4 (1981), pp. 698–705.

Fitzsimmons, James A., and Mona J. Fitzsimmons. *Service Management: Operations, Strategy, and Information Technology.* 2nd edition. Burr Ridge, IL: Irwin/McGraw-Hill, 1998.

Hall, Gene; Jim Rosenthal; and Judy Wade. "How to Make Reengineering Really Work." *Harvard Business Review,* November–December 1993.

Hammer, Michael. "Reengineering Work: Don't Automate, Obliterate." *Harvard Business Review,* July–August 1990, pp. 104–12.

Hammer, Michael, and James Champy. *Reengineering the Corporation.* New York: HarperCollins Books, 1993.

Levitt, Theodore. "Production-Line Approach to Service." *Harvard Business Review* 50, no. 5 (September–October 1972), pp. 41–52.

Lipin, Steven. "A New Vision." *The Wall Street Journal,* June 25, 1993.

Main, Jeremy. "How to Steal the Best Ideas Around." *Fortune,* October 19, 1992.

Manganelli, Raymond L., and Steven P. Raspa. "Why Reengineering Has Failed." *Management Review,* July 1995, pp. 39–43.

Port, Otis, and Geoffrey Smith. "Beg, Borrow and Benchmark." *Business Week,* November 30, 1992.

Roehm, Harper A.; Donald Klein; and Joseph F. Castellano. "Springing to World-Class Manufacturing." *Management Accounting,* March 1991, pp. 40–44.

Shostack, G. Lynn. "Designing Services That Deliver." *Harvard Business Review* 62, no. 1 (January–February 1984), pp. 133–39.

Stoddard, Donna; B. Sirkka; L. Jarvenpaa; and Michael Littlejohn. "The Reality of Business Reengineering: Pacific Bell's Centrex Provisioning Process." *California Management Review* 38, no. 3 (Spring 1996), pp. 57–76.

Rikert, David C. *Burger King.* Harvard Business School Case No. 681–045. Boston: Harvard Business School, 1980.

Rikert, David C. *McDonald's Corporation.* Harvard Business School Case No. 681–044. Boston: Harvard Business School, 1980.

# QUALITY MANAGEMENT

## Chapter Outline

## Chapter Objectives

- Identify the different dimensions of quality in both goods and services and show how they relate to a firm's overall strategy.

- Present a framework for the development of Total Quality Management (TQM) within an organization.

- Define the various elements that comprise the cost of quality.

- Identify the various tools that can be used to assess and improve the quality of a process.

- Introduce the Malcolm Baldrige National Quality Award and its criteria for evaluating companies.

- Introduce the ISO 9000 standards and describe the steps a company must take to obtain certification.

BM Rochester, 1990 winner of the Malcolm Baldrige National Quality Award, manufactures intermediate computer systems and has more than 400,000 systems installed worldwide. The concept of quality at IBM Rochester is linked directly to its customers, who are involved in every step of the process from product design to delivery. As a result of this focus on quality, productivity increased 30 percent between 1986 and 1989. Product development time for new mid-range computer systems has been reduced by more than 50 percent, while the manufacturing cycle has been trimmed by more than 60 percent. Customers have benefited from a threefold increase in product reliability; an increase from 3 to 12 months in the product warranty period; and a cost of ownership that is among the lowest in the industry.

IBM Rochester strengthened its strategic quality initiatives by formulating improvement plans that are based upon six critical success factors: (a) improved product and service requirements definition, (b) an enhanced product strategy, (c) a six-sigma defect elimination strategy, (d) further cycle time reductions, (e) improved employee education and (f) increased employee involvement and ownership. Each senior manager "owns" one of these six factors and assumes responsibility for its plans and implementation.

Quality at IBM Rochester is viewed as continuous journey where the objective is always excellence in customer satisfaction.  ■

In today's highly competitive markets, managers are recognizing the value of customer loyalty. To maintain customer loyalty it is not sufficient for a firm to satisfy its customers. Now goods and services must "delight" customers in order to retain them, and this is achieved by providing only the highest quality goods and services.

The quality movement can trace its roots back to Walter Shewhart's development of the first process control chart in the 1920s, while he was employed as a statistician at Bell Labs. During World War II, the use of statistics to monitor the quality of wartime production increased out of necessity, due in part to both the vast quantities of material being produced and the shortage of labor on the home front. After the war, demand for consumer goods in the United States was high. As a result, the quality emphasis that was so important during the war gave way to a focus on production volume. Meanwhile, W. Edwards Deming and Joseph Juran were teaching managers in Japan how to lower costs and improve quality by "doing it right the first time." As a result of their efforts, Japanese goods, by the 1970s, were considered to be among the best in the world.

In the United States, the importance of quality as a key element in the success of an organization didn't begin to be recognized until the late 1970s. In 1980, NBC presented a documentary entitled "If Japan Can, Why Can't We?" which highlighted Deming's significant contribution to improving the quality of Japanese products. Only after this documentary was aired was Deming asked to assist U.S. companies in improving the quality of their products. The shift in focus of U.S. companies to quality has not gone unnoticed. Consumers have recognized significant improvements in the quality of U.S. products. The Ford Taurus, for example, is now the best-selling car in the United States, a distinction previously held for many years by the Honda Accord.

**total quality management (TQM)**
Approach for integrating quality at all levels of an organization.

In this chapter we introduce some of the basic concepts of **total quality management (TQM),** which are critical elements in the successful implementation of quality programs not only in Japan, but around the world. As part of this discussion, we present traditional as well as emerging topics relating to quality with which all managers should be familiar. While we emphasize the technical aspects that are required for a successful quality effort, we also recognize the importance of providing proper leadership and the need for worker involvement as integral parts of the quality improvement process. To quote Tom Peters, "Most quality programs fail for one of two reasons: They have system without passion, or passion without system."[1]

## THE STRATEGIC ROLE OF QUALITY

For many years following World War II, quality was viewed primarily as a defensive function rather than as a competitive weapon for use in developing new markets and increasing market share. In this role, the quality emphasis was on quality control (QC): reducing the number of customer complaints that were received. As a result, there was a heavy reliance on inspection (sorting the good from the bad) rather than on prevention. Identifying defective output and either fixing it (rework) or disposing of it (scrap) incurred costs. It was therefore believed that higher quality must be more costly. Quality control managers often reported to manufacturing managers, who were measured primarily on output; consequently they had little or no power to either halt production or delay the shipment of faulty products.

Today, however, more and more companies recognize the value of using quality as an offensive, strategic weapon. In adopting this approach, these firms are able to both identify new market niches as well as increase their market share in existing ones. However, in

---

[1]Tom Peters, *Thriving on Chaos* (New York: Knopf, 1987), p. 74.

**quality dimensions**
Recognition that quality can be defined in many ways and that companies can use quality as a competitive advantage.

taking the offensive with quality, managers must realize that there is more than one facet or dimension on which it can focus, and, in fact, some of these may even be in conflict. David Garvin[2] has identified eight different **quality dimensions** on which a company can compete. These are: (1) performance, (2) features, (3) reliability, (4) conformance, (5) durability, (6) serviceability, (7) aesthetics, and (8) perceived quality.

## Quality in Goods

**Performance**    Performance is a measure of a product's primary operating characteristics. Since performance can usually be measured in specific quantitative terms, a product's performance characteristics are often compared and ranked with those of the competition. With an automobile, for example, performance characteristics would include how fast it can accelerate from 0 to 60 mph and its fuel efficiency in terms of miles per gallon. For a personal computer, performance characteristics would include operating speed and random access memory capacity.

**Features**    Features are the "bells and whistles" that are offered with a product. While features are not the primary operating characteristics of a product, they may, nonetheless, be very important to the customer. For example, a moon roof and stereo system may be the deciding factors for a new car buyer while a specific type of refrigerator may appeal to a customer because it offers an icemaker and water dispenser.

**Reliability**    The reliability of a product relates to the probability that the product will fail within a specified time. Reliability is often measured as the mean time between failures (MTBF) or the failure rate per unit of time or other measure of usage. High product reliability is important in such products as airplanes, computers, and copying machines. Stratus Computers, for example, has successfully carved out a niche for itself in the highly competitive computer industry by offering "fault-free" computer systems. The bored Maytag repairman with no service calls offers another good example of product reliability.

**Durability**    The durability dimension of quality relates to the expected operational life of a product. In some instances, like with a light bulb, the filament eventually burns out and the entire product must be replaced. In other cases, such as with an automobile, the consumer must evaluate the trade-off between replacing the product entirely versus spending money on repairs for the existing one.

**Conformance**    A product's conformance to design specifications is primarily process oriented, in that it reflects how well the product and its individual components meet the established standards.

**Serviceability**    Serviceability is concerned with how readily a product can be repaired and the speed, competence, and courtesy associated with that repair. This dimension of quality is sometimes overlooked in the design stage. For example, Chevrolet in the 1970s designed a car in which one of the spark plugs could not be removed without pulling out the entire engine. The speed of the repair is also important, in that it affects the overall number of products needed in those circumstances where constant coverage is required. Using a city's paramedic service as an example, the frequency and the amount of time a paramedic vehicle requires repair and maintenance impacts directly on the total number of vehicles needed to provide the proper level of coverage.

---

[2]David Garvin, "Competing on the Eight Dimensions of Quality," *Harvard Business Review* (November–December 1987), pp. 101–9.

**poka-yoke**
Simple devices, such as automatic shutoff valves or fixtures to orient parts, which prevent defects from being produced.

quality of the product that is delivered to the customer. One of the ways kaizen is achieved is through the use of **poka-yoke** or foolproofing in the methods that are used to make the products. United Electric Controls in Watertown, Massachusetts, a winner of the Shingo Prize in Manufacturing, attributes much of its quality improvements to introducing poka-yoke into its manufacturing processes. In manufacturing, poka-yoke often requires that a part be redesigned so that it can fit only one way. A good example of poka-yoke in services is the bathroom onboard an airplane. Here the light will not go on until the door is locked, ensuring privacy. Also, height bars at amusement parks, as shown in the photo, ensure proper height for the rides.

### Customer Focus

 MARKETING

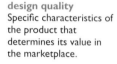

The customer's perception of quality must be taken into account in setting acceptable quality levels. In other words, a product isn't reliable unless the customer says it's reliable and a service isn't fast unless the customer says it's fast. Translating customer quality demands into specifications requires marketing (or product development) to accurately determine what the customer wants and product designers to develop a product (or service) that can be produced to consistently achieve that desired level of quality. This, in turn, requires that we have an operational definition of quality, an understanding of its various dimensions, and a process for including the voice of the customer in those specifications. The quality of a product or service may be defined by the quality of its design (product quality) and the quality of its conformance to that design (process quality). **Design quality** refers to the inherent value of the product in the marketplace and is thus a strategic decision for the firm, as discussed earlier.

**design quality**
Specific characteristics of the product that determines its value in the marketplace.

**conformance quality**
Defines how well the product is made with respect to its design specifications.

**Conformance quality** refers to the degree to which the product or service meets design specifications. It, too, has strategic implications, but the execution of the activities involved in achieving conformance are of a tactical day-to-day nature. It should be evident that a product or service can have high design quality but low conformance quality, and vice versa.

The operations function and the quality organization within the firm are primarily concerned with quality of conformance. Achieving all the quality specifications is typically the responsibility of manufacturing management (for products) and branch operations management (for services).

Both design quality and conformance quality should provide products that meet the customer's objectives for those products. This is often termed the product's *fitness for use,* and it entails identifying those dimensions of the product (or service) that the customer wants and developing a quality control program to ensure that these dimensions are met.

## THE GURUS OF QUALITY MANAGEMENT

**quality gurus**
Individuals who have been identified as making a significant contribution to improving the quality of goods and services.

Over the years there have been many individuals involved in the quality revolution. Several have been recognized as **quality gurus** for their valuable contributions and forward thinking. They are Walter A. Shewhart, W. Edwards Deming, Joseph M. Juran, Armand Feigenbaum, Philip Crosby, and Genichi Taguchi. While they share much in common in terms of how they view quality, each has left his own unique stamp on the quality movement. Consequently, their philosophical approaches to quality are significantly different. A comparison of the philosophies of three of the more prominent quality gurus is presented in Exhibit 5.2.

## Walter A. Shewhart

Walter A. Shewhart as mentioned earlier was a statistician at Bell Laboratories who studied randomness in industrial processes. He developed a system that permitted workers to determine whether the variability of a process was truly random or due to assignable causes. If a process exhibited only random variation, it was considered to be "in control." If a process exhibited nonrandom variation, the cause for the variation had to be identified and addressed in order for the process to be brought back into control. In addition to

**EXHIBIT 5.2**

Three of the Quality Gurus Compared

| | Crosby | Deming | Juran |
|---|---|---|---|
| Definition of quality | Conformance to requirements | A predictable degree of uniformity and dependability at low cost and suited to the market | Fitness for use |
| Degree of senior management responsibility | Responsible for quality | Responsible for 85% of quality problems | Less than 20% of quality problems are due to workers |
| Performance standard/ motivation | Zero defects | Quality has many "scales": use statistics to measure performance in all areas; critical of zero defects | Avoid campaigns to do perfect work |
| General approach | Prevention, not inspection | Reduce variability by continuous improvement; cease mass inspection | General management approach to quality, especially human elements |
| Structure | 14 steps to quality improvement | 14 points for management | 10 steps to quality improvement |
| Statistical process control (SPC) | Rejects statistically acceptable levels of quality | Statistical methods of quality control must be used | Recommends SPC but warns that it can lead to tool-driven approach |
| Improvement basis | A process, not a program; improvement goals | Continuous to reduce variation; eliminate goals without methods | Project-by-project team approach; set goals |
| Teamwork | Quality improvement teams; quality councils | Employee participation in decision making; break down barriers between departments | Team and quality circle approach |
| Costs of quality | Cost of nonconformance; quality is free | No optimum, continuous improvement | Quality is not free, there is an optimum |
| Purchasing and goods received | State requirements; supplier is extension of business; most faults due to purchasers themselves | Inspection too late; allows defects to enter system through AQLs; statistical evidence and control charts required | Problems are complex; carry out formal surveys |
| Vendor rating | Yes and buyers; quality audits useless | No, critical of most systems | Yes, but help supplier improve |
| Single sourcing of supply | | Yes | No, can neglect to sharpen competitive edge |

Source: Modified from John S. Oakland, *Total Quality Management* (London: Heinemann Professional Publishing Ltd., 1989), pp. 291–92.

**EXHIBIT 5.3**

Shewhart's Plan-Do-Check-Act (PDCA) Cycle

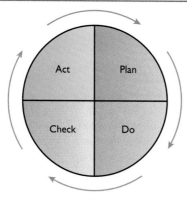

Source: Mary Walton, *Deming Management at Work* (New York: Perigree Books, 1991), p. 22.

developing the foundations for modern statistical process control, Shewhart also developed the "plan-do-check-act" (PDCA) cycle shown in Exhibit 5.3. Prior to the PDCA cycle, organizations typically managed activities as though they had identifiable beginning and end points. The PDCA cycle uses a circular model to emphasize the need for continuous improvement. Shewhart's pioneering work in statistical process control had a strong influence on both Deming and Juran.

### W. Edwards Deming

**statistical process control (SPC)**
Methods, such as control charts, which signal shifts in a process that will likely lead to products and/or services not meeting customer requirements.

A thorough understanding of **statistical process control (SPC)** is the basic cornerstone of Deming's approach to quality. In fact, the Japanese were so impressed with his knowledge of SPC that they invited him back to teach the subject to Japanese managers and workers. Deming emphasized the importance of having an overall organizational approach for quality management. He therefore insisted that top managers attend his lectures, knowing that the QC staff by itself could not support and sustain an ongoing organizationwide quality effort. The Japanese have recognized Deming's tremendous contribution to the success of their companies by naming their highest award for industrial excellence after him—the Deming Prize. (Another indicator that U.S. companies are making significant progress toward improving quality is that Florida Power & Light, a non-Japanese company, was awarded the Deming Prize.)

One of Deming's major contributions focused on disproving the fallacy that it costs more to make better-quality products. He demonstrated that just the opposite is true: a high-quality process is, in fact, less costly than a low-quality one. When products are made properly the first time, substantial savings accrue from the elimination of unnecessary labor for rework and repairs and the cost to scrap nonconforming material.

Deming also introduced the plan-do-check-act (PDCA) cycle to the Japanese.

According to Deming, 85 percent of the quality problems generated by a company can be attributed to management, because they have the power to make the decisions that impact on the current systems and practices. His extensive consulting experiences with such companies as Ford, Nashua Corp., and Florida Power & Light have supported this claim. Over the years, Deming identified 14 points that he believed to be critical for improving quality. These 14 points are presented in Exhibit 5.4.

### Joseph M. Juran

Like Deming, Juran also visited Japan shortly after the end of World War II to assist in rebuilding its industrial base. Also like Deming, Juran emphasized the importance of

**EXHIBIT 5.4**

Deming's 14-Point Program
for Improving Quality

1. Create constancy of purpose for improvement of product and service.
2. Adopt the new philosophy.
3. Cease dependence on mass inspection.
4. End the practice of awarding business on the price tag alone.
5. Improve constantly and forever the system of production and training.
6. Institute training.
7. Institute leadership.
8. Drive out fear.
9. Break down barriers between staff areas.
10. Eliminate slogans, exhortations, and targets for the workforce.
11. Eliminate numerical quotas.
12. Remove barriers to pride in workmanship.
13. Institute a vigorous program of education and retraining.
14. Take action to accomplish the program.

Source: Mary Walton, *Deming Management at Work* (New York: Perigree Books, 1991),
pp. 17–18.

producing quality products, and thus directed his efforts while in Japan toward teaching quality concepts and their application to the factory floor. Based on his experiences with Japanese companies, Juran developed an approach to quality that focuses primarily on three areas: (*a*) quality planning, (*b*) quality control, and (*c*) quality improvement.

According to Juran, the quality of a product is defined as fitness for use, as viewed by the customer. Juran further defines fitness for use as consisting of five components: (*a*) quality of design, (*b*) quality of conformance, (*c*) availability, (*d*) safety, and (*e*) field use. In evaluating a product's fitness for use, Juran takes into account the total life cycle of the product.

Juran uses the cost of quality as his framework for introducing his approach to quality. In doing so, he divides the cost of quality into three major categories: (*a*) cost of prevention, (*b*) cost of detection/appraisal, and (*c*) cost of failure, all of which are presented in greater detail later in this chapter.

### Armand Feigenbaum

In 1956, Armand Feigenbaum proposed the concept of "total quality control," which begins with the recognition that quality is the responsibility of everyone in the organization. He stressed interdepartmental communication, particularly with respect to product design control, incoming material control, and production control. Like Juran, he believed in the power of the cost-of-quality framework, and emphasized careful measurement and reporting of these costs. Also like Juran, he believed that a new type of quality professional was needed, the quality control engineer, who would oversee cross-functional elements. The application of statistics by itself was no longer enough. The Japanese embraced this concept and expanded it to "companywide quality control." In recognition of his contribution to improving quality, The Massachusetts Quality Award is named in honor of Armand Feigenbaum.

### Philip Crosby

Unlike Deming and Juran, both of whom were trained initially as statisticians, Crosby was educated as an engineer and began his career in manufacturing. After working for several large companies, primarily in quality-related positions, he founded his own "Quality College" in Florida in 1979.

Crosby's philosophy, which is similar in some respects to Deming's, states that any organization can reduce its total overall costs by improving the quality of its processes. In one of his first books, Crosby preached that "quality is free." According to Crosby, the cost of providing poor-quality goods and services is significant. He estimated that the cost of producing poor quality can run as high as 25 percent of revenues for manufacturing companies and 40 percent of operating expenses in service operations. Crosby also claims that companies that have successfully implemented quality programs can expect to reduce their costs of quality to less than 2.5 percent of sales.[5]

## Genichi Taguchi

Genichi Taguchi has contributed importantly to both the refinement of quality management philosophy and the development of quality tools. Taguchi takes an engineering approach to design quality, focusing on the design of experiments to improve both the yield and performance quality of products. He emphasizes the minimization of variation, which is also the cornerstone of his philosophical approach. While Juran emphasized the cost of quality to the firm, Taguchi is also concerned with the cost of quality to society as a whole. He takes Juran's concept of external failure much further, including not only the cost to the firm that ships the defective product, but also the cost to the firm that accepts it, the customer that buys and uses it, and so on. His dual engineering-philosophical perspective shows how much is lost when products fail to meet specifications, which "ups the stakes" for managers concerned with the quality of their products and services.

# THE COST OF QUALITY

**cost of quality**
Framework for identifying quality components that are related to producing both high quality products and low quality products, with the goal of minimizing the total cost of quality.

Following Juran's model, we divide the **cost of quality** into three major categories: (*a*) cost of prevention, (*b*) cost of detection/appraisal, and (*c*) cost of failure. The third category, the cost of failure, is further subdivided into internal failure costs and external failure costs.

The total cost of quality is the sum of the costs in all three categories. The typical percentages of total quality costs that are estimated for each of the three categories are shown in Exhibit 5.5.

## Cost of Prevention

**cost of prevention**
Costs associated with the development of programs to prevent defectives from occurring in the first place.

**Costs of prevention,** by definition, are those costs incurred by an organization in its effort to prevent defective goods and services from being produced. Included in this category are investments in machinery, technology, and education programs that are designed to reduce the number of defects that the process produces. Also included in this category are the costs to administer the firm's quality program, data collection and analysis, and vendor certification. All of the quality gurus strongly support investments in this category because the returns are so high, including the benefits gained from increasing customer satisfaction and reducing scrap losses and rework expenses.

[5]Philip B. Crosby, *Quality Is Free* (New York: New America Library, 1979), p. 15.

**EXHIBIT 5.5**

Typical Quality Cost Ratios

| Category | Feigenbaum | Juran and Gryna |
|---|---|---|
| Prevention costs | 5%–10% | 0.5%–5% |
| Detection/appraisal costs | 20%–25% | 10%–50% |
| Failure costs | 65%–70% | Internal : 25%–40% |
| | | External: 20%–40% |
| Total cost of quality | 100% | 100% |

Source: A.V. Feigenbaum, *Total Quality Control*, 3rd ed. (New York: McGraw-Hill, 1983), p. 112; and Joseph M. Juran, and F. M. Gryna, *Quality Planning and Analysis* (New York: McGraw-Hill, 1970), p. 60.

## Cost of Detection/Appraisal

**cost of detection/appraisal**
Costs associated with the test and inspection of subassemblies and products after they have been made.

**Costs of detection or appraisal** are those costs associated with evaluating the quality of the product. Costs included in this category are: incoming material inspection, tests and inspection throughout the transformation process, test equipment maintenance, and products destroyed during destructive testing.

## Cost of Failure

**cost of failure**
Costs associated with the failure of a defective product.

**Costs of failure** pertain to nonconforming and nonperforming products. Also included in this category are the costs associated with the evaluation and disposition of customer complaints. As stated earlier, we further subdivide failure costs into internal and external failure costs.

**internal failure costs**
Costs associated with producing defective products that are identified prior to shipment.

**Internal failure costs** are identified as those costs that are eliminated when no defects are produced within the system. They include only those costs attributed to defects that are found before the products are delivered to the customer. Examples of internal failure costs include: scrap, rework/repair, retesting of reworked/repaired products, downtime, yield losses due to process variability, and the disposition of the defective items.

**external failure costs**
Costs associated with producing defective products that are delivered to the customer.

**External failure costs** are those costs that are incurred after the product has been delivered to the customer. Included in this category are: the cost of returned material, warranty charges, field survey costs, legal expenses from lawsuits, customer dissatisfaction, loss of revenues due to downgrading products as seconds, and costs of allowances/concessions made to customers.

It is generally now recognized that increased spending on prevention provides significant returns in the form of reductions in detection/appraisal and failure costs—and in the overall cost of quality. Thus the old adage, "An ounce of prevention is worth a pound of cure" is also most appropriate for quality.

At the same time, Deming suggested that total quality costs can be decreased by improving the process itself. An improved process reduces both the number of defects produced and the costs of prevention and appraisal. A comparison of Deming's model with the previously traditional view toward quality is presented in Exhibit 5.6.

When defective products or services are eliminated, there are two direct effects. First, there are more good units produced (and capacity is therefore increased) and second, each unit produced costs less because the cost of the failures is both reduced and also spread over a larger number of nondefective goods or services. For example, if a plastic injection molding process scraps 15 defective pen barrels out of every 100 that are produced, the cost to produce the 15 scrapped units must be spread over the remaining 85 units—and there are only 85 units available to sell. If the quality of the process is improved and only five units are scrapped per 100 produced, then there are 95 units that are available for sale, and the cost of only the five scrapped units is now spread over the 95 good units rather than 85 as was previously the case.

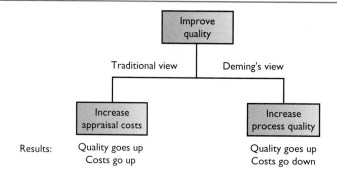

Results:

A bank, for example, that set out to improve quality and reduce its costs found that it had also boosted productivity. The bank developed this productivity measure for the loan processing area: the number of tickets processed divided by the resources required (labor cost, computer time, ticket forms). Before the quality improvement program, the productivity index was 0.2660 [2,080/($11.23 × 640 hours + $0.05 × 2,600 forms + $500 for systems costs)]. After the quality improvement project was completed, labor time fell to 546 hours and the number of forms processed increased to 2,100 for a change in the index to 0.3088, or an increase in productivity of 16 percent.

## THE SEVEN BASIC QUALITY CONTROL TOOLS

**seven basic quality control tools**
Quantitative techniques that can assist a manager in collecting, grouping, presenting and analyzing data that is process-generated.

Within the quality literature, seven basic tools have been identified that can assist managers in organizing, displaying, and analyzing process-generated data. These **seven basic quality control (QC) tools** are (*a*) process flowcharts (or diagrams), (*b*) run (or trend) charts, (*c*) checksheets, (*d*) scatter plots (or diagrams), (*e*) cause and effect diagrams (or fishbone charts), (*f*) Pareto charts, and (*g*) histograms. These different quality control tools are shown in Exhibit 5.7.

### Process Flowcharts

Process flowcharts or diagrams show each of the steps that are required to produce either a good or a service. As stated previously in Chapter 4, actions are usually depicted as rectangles, waits or inventories are shown as inverted triangles, and decision points as diamonds. Arrows connecting these activities show the direction of flow in the process. In service operations, this procedure is often referred to as "blue-printing" the process, as discussed in detail in the previous chapter.

### Checksheets

Checksheets are used to record the frequency of occurrence of problems and/or errors.

### Run Charts

Run charts show data that is plotted over time, for example, hamburgers sold per hour throughout a day or patients seen per day over a month. The visual representation of the data in a run chart makes it easy to identify unusual points or patterns that might have managerial significance. (As an illustration, Exhibit 5.8 shows a run chart of on-time departures for an airline.)

**EXHIBIT 5.7**

The Seven Basic Quality Control Tools

**Process Flow Diagram**

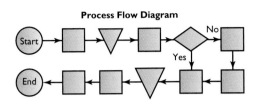

**Run Chart**

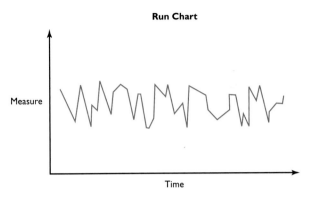

**Checksheet**

| Problem | Occurrence |
|---------|------------|
| A | ⫽⫽⫽ ⫽⫽⫽ ⫽⫽⫽ ‖ |
| B | ⫽⫽⫽ ⫽⫽⫽ ‖‖‖ |
| C | ⫽⫽⫽ ‖ |
| D | ‖‖ |

**Histogram**

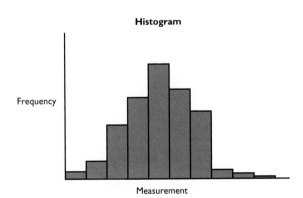

**Scatter Plot**

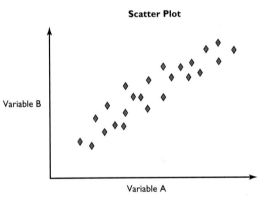

**Pareto Chart**

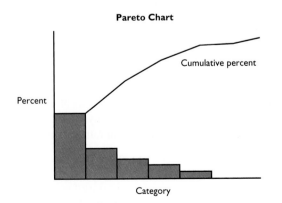

**Cause-and-Effect Diagram**

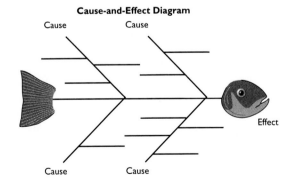

**EXHIBIT 5.8**

Run Chart of Midway
Airlines On-Time Departures

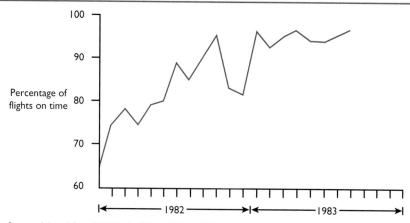

Source: Adapted from D. D. Wychoff, "New Tools for Achieving Service Quality," *Cornell Hotel and Restaurant Administration Quarterly* (November 1984), p. 246.

For example, if a hotel manager plotted complaints on a run chart by the day of the week, she might notice that complaints are unusually high on Wednesdays in comparison to other days of the week. The manager could then investigate the cause for this difference—perhaps low staffing or inexperienced personnel—and take the appropriate action to correct the situation.

Statistical process control (SPC) charts are a specialized version of run charts which incorporate statistics which show the mean and measures of variation in a process. Supplement 5S which follows this chapter addresses SPC in detail.

## Scatter Diagrams

Scatter diagrams or scatter plots are used to determine whether or not a relationship exists between two variables or product characteristics. For example, a restaurant manager might look at the relationship between customer satisfaction values on a survey and the length of wait prior to being seated at a table.

## Cause-and-Effect Diagrams

Cause-and-effect diagrams, first introduced by Kaoru Ishikawa, are also referred to as fishbone diagrams because of their shape. They attempt to identify all of the potential causes for a recurring defect or failure.

First the major causes are identified. Then, for each cause, "Why?" is asked until the root cause for that category can be identified. Consider the example in Exhibit 5.9, a cause-and-effect diagram for customer complaints in a restaurant. If customers complain about the rudeness of the waitstaff, the cause of the rudeness must first be identified before the manager can take the appropriate action. In this example, the servers are rude because they are rushed, and they are rushed because they have been assigned too many tables. Thus the table assignment process should be the focus of the manager's action rather than admonishing the servers to be more polite.

## Histograms and Bar Charts

Histograms and bar charts visually display data variation. A bar chart is used to graph nominal data (also referred to as "categorical" or "attribute" data), which are data that can be counted rather than measured. For example, one can count the number of people in a room with brown, blue, or hazel eyes. Similarly, a manufacturing company can count the number

**EXHIBIT 5.9**

Cause-and-Effect Diagram
for Restaurant Customer
Complaints

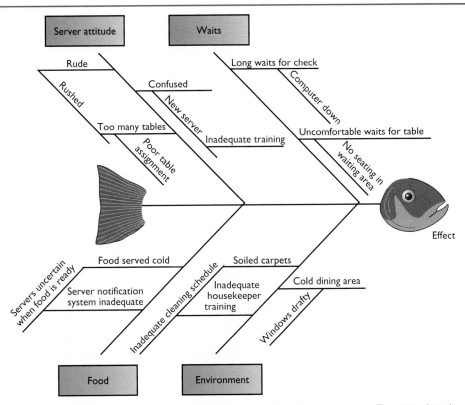

This cause-and-effect diagram demonstrates the search for root causes of complaints in a restaurant. The reason why each cause exists is assessed until the root cause is identified.

 of customers it has in various countries. An example of a bar chart is shown in Exhibit 5.10 which shows the train service regularity for different lines of the London Underground subway system.

Histograms are used to display continuous data: data that can be measured. For example, one can weigh the ounces in different boxes of cereal. The scale for ounces is continuous. Therefore, if we want to show the variation in weight of a number of cereal boxes, we would first have to determine how to divide the ounces scale into appropriate intervals. We could use intervals of one-half ounce, one ounce, or five ounces, depending on how much detail we wanted to show and how much variation in weight there was in our sample. It is important to note here that the histogram interval, once chosen, must remain constant and must not overlap.

## Pareto Charts

 Pareto charts are specialized bar charts. The frequency of occurrence of items is sorted in descending order and a cumulative percent line is usually added to make it easy to determine how the categories add up. Pareto charts can help to establish priorities for managerial action, focusing attention on those categories of variables that occur most frequently. Exhibit 5.11 shows a Pareto chart in a hotel in the People's Republic of China.

 There are times when frequency of occurrence, however, does not determine the importance of a factor. For example, when making a bar chart of student complaints about the food served at a university, it might be known that complaints about waiting in line are twice as common as complaints about food availability, but that students consider food availability to be five times more important than waiting. The Pareto diagram can weight

**EXHIBIT 5.10**

Bar Chart Showing Performance of Different Subway Lines in London

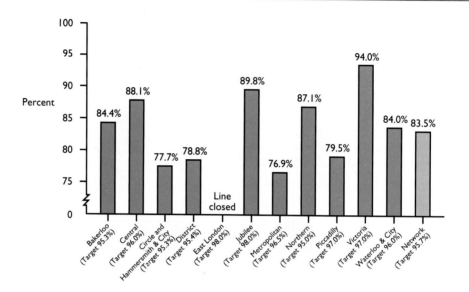

| **Train Service Regularity** |
| **4 weeks ending Friday 19 July 1996** |

This graph shows how each Underground line and the Underground as a whole performed against its target for service regularity. We measure this by timing the intervals between a sample of the trains we run each weekday. If the time between trains is twice the scheduled interval, this counts as a failure to meet the target.

Information is expressed in percentage terms for comparison, and the Hammersmith & City and Circle line figures are unified because the intervals between trains are measured at the same location.

the factors being considered, which will enable managers to take action on those items that most need attention.

## SERVICE GUARANTEES

Warrantees are common for products such as automobiles, washing machines, and televisions. Such warrantees guarantee that these products will work throughout a stated period of time or else they will either be repaired or replaced free of charge. Less common are guarantees for services. Nevertheless, Christopher Hart has suggested that the service guarantee can be a powerful tool for obtaining feedback from customers on how your operations are performing.

In order for a service guarantee to be effective it must contain the following elements: It must be (a) unconditional, (b) easy to understand and communicate, (c) meaningful, (d) easy and painless to invoke, and (e) easy and quick to collect on. For example, at FedEx, the service guarantee is simple, if your package is not delivered on time, then there is no charge. At L. L. Bean, a leading mail order firm located in Freeport, Maine, the guarantee is "100 percent satisfaction in every way." If you buy an L. L. Bean product and are not satisfied with it, you can return it for an exchange or a refund, regardless of how long you have owned it.

From a quality standpoint, the unconditional service guarantee provides management with continuous customer feedback. If it is easy to invoke and collect on, then customers will use the service guarantee to voice their complaints rather than just taking their business elsewhere. (See OM in Practice on a Guarantee of Service Excellence.)

**EXHIBIT 5.11**

Examples of a Cause-and-Effect Diagram and a Histogram in a Hotel in Guangzhou, People's Republic of China

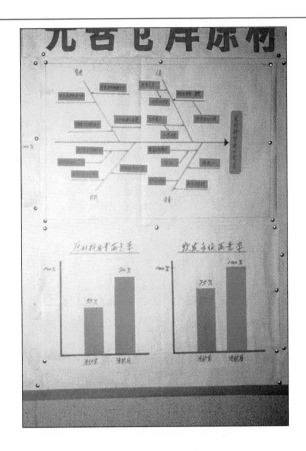

# THE MALCOLM BALDRIGE NATIONAL QUALITY AWARD

### Background

On August 20, 1987, President Ronald Reagan affixed his signature to Public Law 100–107. This groundbreaking legislation, known commonly as the Malcolm Baldrige National Quality Improvement Act, established the nation's annual award to recognize total quality management in American industry. The Malcolm Baldrige National Quality Award (MBNQA) named after Malcolm Baldrige, who served as secretary of commerce from 1981 until his death in 1987, represents the United States government's endorsement of quality as an essential part of successful business strategy.

# Operations Management in Practice

## A GUARANTEE OF SERVICE EXCELLENCE (GOSE) PLAYS A MAJOR ROLE IN THE SUCCESS OF NORTHEAST DELTA DENTAL

Northeast Delta Dental, a nonprofit dental insurance company located in Concord, New Hampshire, attributes much of its growth and success in recent years to its Guarantee of Service Excellence (GOSE).

According to Tom Raffio, President of Northeast Delta Dental, having a service guarantee is "... like putting water through a hose. You turn on the pressure and you find out where all the holes are. An unconditional service guarantee like GOSE, when properly designed and implemented, quickly identifies all of the flaws that exist in the current system."

The Guarantee of Service Excellence Program at Northeast Delta Dental consists of the following seven elements:

1. Smooth implementation to Northeast Delta Dental.
2. Exceptional customer service.
3. Quick processing of claims.
4. No inappropriate billing by participating dentists.
5. Accurate and quick turnaround of identification cards.
6. Timely employee booklets.
7. Marketing service contacts.

With each element, the guarantee is clearly explained and the customer is refunded a stated amount when the service in that element is not provided—no hassles, no questions asked!

Source: Special thanks to Tom Raffio, President of Northeast Delta Dental.

By establishing a national quality improvement act, Congress sought to encourage greater U.S. competitiveness in global markets through the recognition and commendation of exceptional quality in American business. As an instrument of the U.S. government, the Baldrige Award seeks to improve quality and productivity by:

1. Helping to stimulate American companies to improve quality and productivity for the pride of recognition while obtaining a competitive advantage through decreased costs and increased profits.
2. Establishing guidelines and criteria that can be used by business, industrial, governmental, and other organizations in evaluating their quality improvement efforts.
3. Recognizing the achievements of those companies that improve the quality of their goods and services and thereby provide an example to others.
4. Providing specific guidance for other American organizations that wish to learn how to manage for high quality by making available detailed information on how winning organizations were able to change their cultures and achieve quality eminence.

Without question, the MBNQA and its comprehensive criteria for evaluating total quality in an organization have had considerable impact. Some observers have begun referring to the award as the Nobel Prize for business. As seen in Exhibit 5.12, the MBNQA is awarded in three categories: manufacturing, services, and small business. Beginning in 1995, two additional categories, health care and education, have been undergoing evaluation through a pilot program.

## The Baldrige Criteria

To evaluate and recognize effective quality systems, Baldrige administrators created a comprehensive process and set of quality criteria based on the comments and observations

**EXHIBIT 5.12**

Baldrige Award Winners,
by Category

| Manufacturing | Service | Small Business |
|---|---|---|
| Motorola Inc. (1988) | Federal Express (1990) | Globe Metallurgical Inc.(1988) |
| Westinghouse Commercial Nuclear Fuel Division (1989) | AT&T Universal Card Services (1992) | Wallace Co. (1990) |
| Milliken & Co. (1989) | The Ritz-Carlton Hotel (1992) | Marlow Industries (1991) |
| Xerox Business Products (1989) | AT&T Consumer Communications Services (1994) | Granite Rock Co. (1992) |
| Cadillac (1990) | GTE Directories Corp. (1994) | Ames Rubber Co. (1993) |
| IBM Rochester (1990) | Dana Commercial Credit Corp. (1996) | Wainwright Industries (1994) |
| Solectron (1991) | Merrill Lynch Credit Corp. (1997) | Custom Research, Inc. (1996) |
| Zytec Corp. (1991) | Xerox Business Services (1997) | Trident Precision Manufacturing, Inc. (1996) |
| AT&T Network Systems Group (1992) | | |
| Texas Instruments, Inc. (1992) | | |
| Eastman Chemical Company (1993) | | |
| Armstrong Building Products Operation (1995) | | |
| Corning Telecommunication Products Division (1995) | | |
| ADAC Laboratories (1996) | | |
| 3M Dental Products Division (1997) | | |
| Solectron (1997) | | |

**Baldrige criteria**
Process for assessing the
overall quality of an
organization and for
determining the
winner(s) of the Malcolm
Baldrige National Quality
Award.

of experts from throughout the country. The **Baldrige criteria** consequently reflects the combined experience and wisdom of many people. As a set of principles, it is nondenominational in the sense that it does not favor any one system. Instead, the Baldrige criteria are designed to be flexible, evaluating quality on three broad dimensions: (*a*) the soundness of the approach or systems; (*b*) the deployment or integration of those systems throughout the entire organization; and (*c*) the results generated by those systems (see Exhibit 5.13).

The Baldrige quality criteria focuses on seven broad topical areas that are dynamically related, as seen in Exhibit 5.14 which provides an integrated framework for the Baldrige criteria.

In short, the Baldrige criteria create an integrated set of indicators of excellence and continuity that describes total quality. In the Baldrige view, total quality is a value system. It is a way of life, an approach to doing business that affects every corporate decision and permeates the entire organization.

When a company applies for the Baldrige Award or uses the Baldrige criteria internally to evaluate its quality program, its organization must address 20 subcategories that fall under the seven broad topical areas. Each topical area and subcategory are weighted according to general importance (see Exhibit 5.15).

For evaluation purposes, a maximum of 1,000 points are allocated for the seven Baldrige quality categories. Just as the Japanese stress the importance of both the means and ends when considering quality, the Baldrige criteria tie approximately half their points to the quality process (methods and means) and half to the results (ends and trends). The means or process is a leading indicator of the ends that will be attained. In turn, the results verify that the appropriate process is in place and being used effectively.

**EXHIBIT 5.13**

Scoring Guidelines for the Malcolm Baldrige National Quality Award

| Score | Approach/Deployment |
|---|---|
| 0% | ■ No systematic approach evident; anecdotal information |
| 10% to 30% | ■ Beginning of a systematic approach to the primary purposes of the item<br>■ Early stages of a transition from reacting to problems to a general improvement orientation<br>■ Major gaps exist in deployment that would inhibit progress in achieving the primary purposes of the item |
| 40% to 60% | ■ A sound, systematic approach, responsive to the primary purposes of the item<br>■ A fact-based improvement process in place in key areas; more emphasis is placed on improvement than on reaction to problems<br>■ No major gaps in deployment, though some areas or work units may be in very early stages of deployment |
| 70% to 90% | ■ A sound, systematic approach, responsive to the overall purposes of the item<br>■ A fact-based improvement process is a key management tool; clear evidence of refinement and improved integration as a result of improvement cycles and analysis<br>■ Approach is well-deployed, with no major gaps; deployment may vary in some areas or work units |
| 100% | ■ A sound, systematic approach, fully responsive to all the requirements of the item<br>■ A very strong, fact-based improvement process is a key management tool; strong refinement and integration—backed by excellent analysis<br>■ Approach is fully deployed without any significant weaknesses or gaps in any areas or work units |

| Score | Results |
|---|---|
| 0% | ■ No results or poor results in areas reported |
| 10% to 30% | ■ Early stages of developing trends; some improvements *and/or* early good performance levels in a few areas<br>■ Results not reported for many to most areas of importance to the applicant's key business requirements |
| 40% to 60% | ■ Improvement trends *and/or* good performance levels reported for many to most areas of importance to the applicant's key business requirements<br>■ No pattern of adverse trends *and/or* poor performance levels in areas of importance to the applicant's key business requirements<br>■ Some trends *and/or* current performance levels—evaluated against relevant comparisons *and/or* benchmarks—show areas of strength *and/or* good to very good relative performance levels |
| 70% to 90% | ■ Current performance is good to excellent in most areas of importance to the applicant's key business requirements<br>■ Most improvement trends *and/or* performance levels are sustained<br>■ Many to most trends *and/or* current performance levels—evaluated against relevant comparisons and/or benchmarks—show areas of leadership and very good relative performance levels |
| 100% | ■ Current performance is excellent in most areas of importance to the applicant's key business requirements<br>■ Excellent improvement trends *and/or* sustained excellent performance levels in most areas<br>■ Strong evidence of industry and benchmark leadership demonstrated in many areas |

Source: *1997 Criteria for Performance Excellence*, U.S. Dept. of Commerce, National Institute of Standards and Technology.

**EXHIBIT 5.14**

The Integrated Framework
of the Baldrige Award
Criteria

**BALDRIGE AWARD CRITERIA FRAMEWORK**
A Systems Perspective

Customer and market focused
strategy and action plans

| | | | |
|---|---|---|---|
| | 2 Strategic planning | 5 Human resource development and management | |
| 1 Leadership | | | 7 Business results |
| | 3 Customer and market focus | 6 Process management | |

4 Information and analysis

Source: *1997 Criteria for Performance Excellence*, U.S. Dept. of Commerce, National Institute of Standards and Technology.

**EXHIBIT 5.15**

1997 Award Criteria—Item
Listing

| Categories/Items | Points Values |
|---|---|
| **1.0 Leadership** | **110** |
| 1.1 Leadership system | 80 |
| 1.2 Company responsibility and citizenship | 30 |
| **2.0 Strategic planning** | **80** |
| 2.1 Strategy development process | 40 |
| 2.2 Company strategy | 40 |
| **3.0 Customer and market focus** | **80** |
| 3.1 Customer and market knowledge | 40 |
| 3.2 Customer satisfaction and relationship enhancement | 40 |
| **4.0 Information and analysis** | **80** |
| 4.1 Selection and use of information and data | 25 |
| 4.2 Selection and use of comparative information and data | 15 |
| 4.3 Analysis and review of company performance | 40 |
| **5.0 Human resource development and management** | **100** |
| 5.1 Work systems | 40 |
| 5.2 Employee education, training, and development | 30 |
| 5.3 Employee well-being and satisfaction | 30 |
| **6.0 Process management** | **100** |
| 6.1 Management of product and service processes | 60 |
| 6.2 Management of support processes | 20 |
| 6.3 Management of supplier and partnering processes | 20 |
| **7.0 Business results** | **450** |
| 7.1 Customer satisfaction results | 130 |
| 7.2 Financial and market results | 130 |
| 7.3 Human resource results | 35 |
| 7.4 Supplier and partner results | 25 |
| 7.5 Company-specific results | 130 |
| **Total Points** | **1,000** |

Source: *1997 Criteria for Performance Excellence*, U.S. Dept. of Commerce, National Institute of Standards and Technology.

## Application of the Baldrige Quality Criteria

For companies using them, the Baldrige criteria serve many purposes. Indeed, part of the Baldrige criteria's power lies in the fact that they can be applied in many different ways to organizations whose quality improvement programs are of different maturities.

As a practical tool for assessing operations, the Baldrige guidelines can be used:

1. To help define and design a total quality system.
2. To evaluate ongoing internal relationships among departments, divisions, and functional units within an organization.
3. To assess and assist outside suppliers of goods and services to a company.
4. To assess customer satisfaction.

Early-stage companies can literally use the Baldrige guidelines as a checklist or blueprint to help them design their overall quality programs. Middle-stage companies can use them as a road map to guide them down the road to continued quality improvement. Finally, advanced-stage companies can use them as an evaluative tool to help fine-tune their quality programs and benchmark them against other industry and world leaders.

 The Baldrige guidelines also provide a common language for discussing quality across companies, functional areas, industries, and disciplines. By providing a broad, flexible approach to assessing total quality, the Baldrige system fosters improved information sharing and overall communications. These activities, in turn, lead employees and management to develop a shared meaning of total quality that can be built into the organization's goals and policies. From such shared meaning develops an organizational value system that is customer-focused, quality-driven, and central to the culture of the company. So deeply does Motorola believe in the value of total quality control that the company has ordered all 3,500 of its suppliers to apply for the Baldrige Award, as tangible evidence of their commitment to total quality management, or lose Motorola's business.

The role of the Baldrige Award as an instructor of quality is also rapidly growing. The application process compels management and employees:

1. To recognize the far-reaching importance of quality.
2. To examine the organization's total quality progress and current standing.
3. To exchange information between departments, divisions, and organizational levels.

Assimilating the Baldrige view of total quality can also lead to actions with profound long-term consequences. At Baldrige winners such as Globe, Motorola, and Westinghouse's CNFD, quality planning has been elevated to the same level as strategic planning and integrated with it. Indeed, all these organizations have wrought significant cultural and organizational changes to support companywide total quality. (See OM in Practice on Quality Pays.)

## Award Process

The Baldrige applications are scored by quality experts from business, consulting, and academia. Of the 1,000 points that can possibly be awarded on the overall application, none of the applicants received more than 751 points in 1994. A good company usually falls in the 500 range on the Baldrige scoring.

Only about 10 percent of the applicants become Baldrige finalists and receive site visits from a team of examiners. From this group of finalists, the Baldrige winners are chosen. All companies applying for the award receive from the examiners written feedback reports summarizing the examiners' findings of the company's organizational strengths and weaknesses.

customer firms can be more confident that supplier firms will produce the goods and services that will satisfy their needs.

## CONCLUSION

The production and delivery of high-quality goods and services are critical elements in determining the success of an organization. No longer is quality relegated to a passive, defensive role; rather, quality now contributes offensively as a strategic weapon in defining market niches. Total quality management (TQM) consists of four integral components, all of which are necessary for a TQM program to succeed. High quality is not more expensive; in fact, just the reverse is true. High quality is cost effective, especially when emphasis is placed on preventing defects from occurring in the first place.

**EXHIBIT 5.17**

Three Schools of Total Quality Management Programs

| | Total Quality Harangue | Total Quality Tools | Total Quality Integration |
|---|---|---|---|
| Noticeable characteristics | Exhortation, lots of talk about quality; generally a marketing campaign intended to create buying signals without incurring the expense of fundamental changes | Introduction of specific tools; viz, statistical process control, employee involvement programs, and/or quality circles | Serious review of all elements of the organization; efforts to involve suppliers and customers |
| Rationale | Management may believe that quality is better than generally known or may be creating a smoke screen; viz, "everybody's doing it," "it's the thing to do these days" | Valued customers insist on implementation of a team program; or competitors have introduced successful programs creating a "bandwagon" effect | Systematic effort to improve earnings through differentiation based on quality |
| Responsibility for quality | Unchanged; specific function within organization assigned responsibility for quality | Lower-level members of organization regardless of function | Shared responsibility, senior management accepts responsibility to create an environment encouraging quality |
| Structural changes | None; the organization remains unchanged | Incremental changes within functional areas or processes | Dramatic changes integrating functions within the organization and involving customers and suppliers in the total production process |
| Representative employee attitudes and behaviors | Total quality is just a fad, "this too shall pass"; smart employees learn to keep their heads down, they talk about quality when expected to but know that business continues as usual | "It's a nice idea, too bad management isn't really serious about quality"; clever employees participate in seminars and use appropriate tools to fix obvious flaws in their areas of responsibility, but are careful not to rock the boat | "At last, we've got a chance to do it right"; committed employees study the total quality vision, actively search for opportunities to improve performance across the organization, challenge conventional assumptions, and seek to involve customers and suppliers |
| Role of the quality professional | Police officer, watchdog | Resident expert, advisor | Strategic leaders, change agent |

Source: Eric W. Skopec, Strategic Visions Inc. (used by permission).

Thus, quality management as a strategic issue should not be approached with an off-the-shelf program devised by others. Quality must be integrated internally and externally (see Exhibit 5.17). Managers are paid to use new concepts, but more important, to lead customization and integration of these concepts into their organizations.

## KEY TERMS

Baldrige criteria   p. 153
conformance quality   p. 140
continuous improvement   p. 139
cost of quality   p. 144
cost of prevention   p. 144
cost of detection/appraisal   p. 145
cost of failure   p. 145
   internal failure costs   p. 145
   external failure costs   p. 145
design quality   p. 140

house of quality   p. 137
ISO 9000 series quality standards   p. 158
poka-yoke   p. 140
quality dimensions   p. 135
quality function deployment (QFD)   p. 137
quality gurus   p. 140
seven basic quality control tools   p. 146
statistical process control (SPC)   p. 142
total quality management (TQM)   p. 134
voice of the customer   p. 137

## REVIEW AND DISCUSSION QUESTIONS

1. Is quality free? Debate!
2. Identify the quality dimensions for each of the following:
   a. IBM personal computer
   b. School registration process
   c. Steakhouse
   d. University
   e. Travel agency
   f. Television
3. An agreement is made between a supplier and a customer such that the supplier must ensure that all parts are within tolerance before shipment to the customer. What is the effect on the cost of quality to the customer?
4. In the situation described in Question 3, what would be the effect on the cost of quality to the supplier?
5. If line employees are required to assume the quality control function, their productivity will decrease. Discuss this.
6. "You don't inspect quality into a product; you have to build it in." Discuss the implications of this statement.
7. How could you apply the Baldrige Award criteria to your college or university?
8. How is the Baldrige award process beneficial to companies who do not win?
9. What is the major contribution of the ISO 9000 standards?
10. Compare the ISO certification process with the Malcolm Baldrige National Quality Award criteria. What are the main differences?

## INTERNET UPDATE

a. Conduct a search on the Web to identify the various ways in which companies are applying TQM to improve the quality of the products that they make. Suggested key words are MANUFACTURING and TQM.
b. Referring to Exhibit 5.12, which lists the annual winners of the Malcolm Baldrige National Quality Award (MBNQA), find the homepage of at least one winner and describe in detail its operations.

*c.* Using ISO 9000 and CERTIFICATION as key words, identify two firms that provide ISO 9000 certification and describe their certification process in detail.

## PROBLEMS

1. A company currently using an inspection process in its material receiving department is trying to install an overall cost reduction program. One possible reduction is the elimination of one of the inspection positions. This position tests material that has a defect rate on the average of 4 percent. By inspecting all items, the inspector is able to remove all defects. The inspector can inspect 50 units per hour. The hourly rate, including fringe benefits, for this position is $9. If the inspection position is eliminated, defects will go into product assembly and will have to be replaced later at a cost of $10 each when they are detected in final product testing.

   *a.* Should this inspection position be eliminated?

   *b.* What is the cost to inspect each unit?

   *c.* Is there benefit (or loss) from the current inspection process? How much?

2. You have just returned from a trip to New York City where you stayed at a first-class hotel. After spending $250 per night for the room plus an additional $35 per night to park your car, you are very unhappy with the level of service you received during your stay at this hotel.

   *a.* Draw a fishbone diagram identifying the major causes for your dissatisfaction and possible secondary causes within each of these categories (do not include price).

   *b.* You call the hotel to voice your complaint and the manager asks you if you would be willing to collect some data for her so she can get at the root cause of the problem. You collect the following data on 100 complaints:

   | Cause (Select from part *a*) | Frequency |
   |---|---|
   | 1. _____ | 16 |
   | 2. _____ | 11 |
   | 3. _____ | 27 |
   | 4. _____ | 42 |
   | 5. _____ | 4 |

   *c.* Draw a Pareto diagram for the above data, labeling the axes appropriately. How does this information assist the manager in improving the service quality of her operation?

3. You have just returned from an airline trip to California and are very unhappy with your onboard experience.

   *a.* Draw a fishbone diagram identifying the different possible primary causes (within each of these categories) for your dissatisfaction with your trip. Also identify several possible secondary causes.

   *b.* You call the airline to voice your complaint and the manager asks you if you will collect some data for him so that he can get at the root cause of the problem. You collect the following data on 100 complaints:

   | Cause (Select from part *a*) | Frequency |
   |---|---|
   | 1. _____ | 6 |
   | 2. _____ | 22 |
   | 3. _____ | 14 |
   | 4. _____ | 43 |
   | 5. _____ | 10 |
   | 6. _____ | 5 |

    *c.* Draw a Pareto diagram for the above data, labeling the axes appropriately. How does this information assist the manager in improving the service quality of his operation?

4. The following is a partial house of quality for a golf facility. Provide an importance weighting from your perspective (or that of a golfing friend) in the unshaded areas. If you can, compare it to a club where you or your friend plays using the QFD approach.

**WHATs versus HOWs**
Strong relationship: ●
Medium relationship: ○
Weak relationship: △

| WHATs \ HOWs | Physical aspects | Course location | Ground maintenance | Landscaping | Pin placement | Course tuning | Tee placement | Service facilities | Customer-trained attendants | Top quality food | Highly rated chefs | Attractive restaurant | Tournament activities | Calloway handicapping | Exciting door prizes | Perception issues | Invitation only | Types of guests | Income level | Celebrity |
|---|---|---|---|---|---|---|---|---|---|---|---|---|---|---|---|---|---|---|---|---|
| Physical aspects | | | | | | | | | | | | | | | | | | | | |
| Manicured grounds | | | | | | | | | | | | | | | | | | | | |
| Easy access | | | | | | | | | | | | | | | | | | | | |
| Challenging | | | | | | | | | | | | | | | | | | | | |
| Service facilities | | | | | | | | | | | | | | | | | | | | |
| Restaurant facilities | | | | | | | | | | | | | | | | | | | | |
| Good food | | | | | | | | | | | | | | | | | | | | |
| Good service | | | | | | | | | | | | | | | | | | | | |
| Good layout | | | | | | | | | | | | | | | | | | | | |
| Plush locker room | | | | | | | | | | | | | | | | | | | | |
| Helpful service attendant | | | | | | | | | | | | | | | | | | | | |
| Tournament facilities | | | | | | | | | | | | | | | | | | | | |
| Good tournament prize | | | | | | | | | | | | | | | | | | | | |
| Types of players | | | | | | | | | | | | | | | | | | | | |
| Fair handicapping system | | | | | | | | | | | | | | | | | | | | |
| Perception issues | | | | | | | | | | | | | | | | | | | | |
| Prestigious | | | | | | | | | | | | | | | | | | | | |

# CASE: SHORTENING CUSTOMERS' TELEPHONE WAITING TIME

This case illustrates how a bank applied some of the basic seven quality tools shown in Exhibit 5.7 and storyboard concepts to improve customer service. It is the story of a QC program implemented in the main office of a large bank. An average of 500 customers call this office every day. Surveys indicated that callers tended to become irritated if the phone rang more than five times before it was answered, and often would not call the company again. In contrast, a prompt answer after just two rings reassured the customers and made them feel more comfortable doing business by phone.

### Selection of a Theme
Telephone reception was chosen as a QC theme for the following reasons: (*a*) Telephone reception is the first impression a customer receives from the company, (*b*) this theme coincided with the company's telephone reception slogan, "Don't make customers wait, and avoid needless switching from extension to extension," and (*c*) it also coincided with a companywide campaign being promoted at that time which advocated being friendly to everyone one met.

First, the staff discussed why the present method of answering calls made callers wait. Case Exhibit C5.1 illustrates a frequent situation, where a call from customer B comes in while the operator is talking with customer A. Let's see why the customer has to wait.

At (1), the operator receives a call from the customer but, due to lack of experience, does not know where to connect the call. At (2), the receiving party cannot answer the phone quickly, perhaps because he or she is unavailable, and no one else can take the call. The result is that the operator must transfer the call to another extension while apologizing for the delay.

### Cause-and-Effect Diagram and Situation Analysis

To fully understand the situation, the quality circle members decided to conduct a survey regarding callers who waited for more than five rings. Circle members itemized factors at a brainstorming discussion and arranged them in a cause-and-effect diagram. (See Exhibit C5.2.) Operators then kept checksheets on several points to tally the results spanning 12 days from June 4 to 16. (See Exhibit C5.3A.)

### Results of the Checksheet Situation Analysis

The data recorded on the checksheets unexpectedly revealed that "one operator (partner out of the office)" topped the list by a big margin, occurring a total of 172 times. In this case, the operator on duty had to deal with large numbers of calls when the phones were busy. Customers who had to wait a long time averaged 29.2 daily, which accounted for 6 percent of the calls received every day. (See Exhibits C5.3B and C5.3C.)

### Setting the Target

After an intense but productive discussion, the staff decided to set a QC program goal of reducing the number of waiting callers to zero. That is to say that all incoming calls would be handled promptly, without inconveniencing the customer.

### Measures and Execution

(*a*) Taking Lunches on Three Different Shifts, Leaving at Least Two Operators on the Job at All Times: Up until this resolution was made, a two-shift lunch system had been employed, leaving only one operator on the job while the other was taking a lunch break. However, since the survey revealed that this was a major cause of customers waiting on the line, the company brought in a helper operator from the clerical section.

(*b*) Asking All Employees to Leave Messages When Leaving Their Desks: The objective of this rule was to simplify the operator's chores when the receiving party was not at his desk. The new program was explained at the employees' regular morning meetings, and companywide support was requested. To help implement this practice, posters were placed around the office to publicize the new measures.

(*c*) Compiling a Directory Listing the Personnel and Their Respective Jobs: The notebook was specially designed to aid the operators, who could not be expected to know the details of every employee's job or where to connect her incoming calls.

### Confirming the Results

Although the waiting calls could not be reduced to zero, all items presented showed a marked improvement as shown in Exhibits C5.4A and C5.4B. The major cause of delays, "one operator (partner out of the office)," plummeted from 172 incidents during the control period to 15 in the follow-up survey.

Source: From "The Quest for Higher Quality—the Deming Prize and Quality Control," Ricoh Company, Ltd., in Masaaki Imai, *Kaizen: The Key to Japan's Competitive Success* (New York: The McGraw-Hill Companies, 1986), pp. 54–58.

---

**EXHIBIT C5.1**

Why Customers Had to Wait

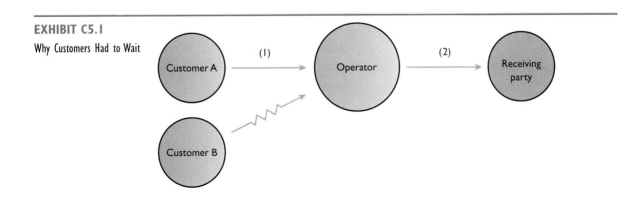

**EXHIBIT C5.2**

Cause-and-Effect Diagram

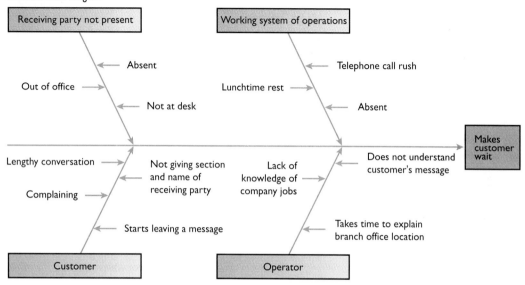

**EXHIBIT C5.3**

Causes of Callers' Waits

**A. Checksheet—Designed to Identify the Problems**

| Reason<br><br>Date | No one present in the section receiving the call | Receiving party not present | Only one operator (partner out of the office) | Total |
|---|---|---|---|---|
| June 4 | \\\\\ | ⅡⅢⅠ | ⅡⅢ ⅡⅢ Ⅰ | 24 |
| June 5 | ⅡⅢ | ⅡⅢ \\\ | ⅡⅢ ⅡⅢ \\\\\ | 32 |
| June 6 | ⅡⅢ \ | \\\\\ | ⅡⅢ ⅡⅢ \\ | 28 |
| June 15 | ⅡⅢ | ⅡⅢ | ⅡⅢ \\\ | 25 |

**B. Reasons Why Callers Had to Wait**

|  |  | Daily average | Total number |
|---|---|---|---|
| A | One operator (partner out of the office) | 14.3 | 172 |
| B | Receiving party not present | 6.1 | 73 |
| C | No one present in the section receiving the call | 5.1 | 61 |
| D | Section and name of receiving party not given | 1.6 | 19 |
| E | Inquiry about branch office locations | 1.3 | 16 |
| F | Other reasons | 0.8 | 10 |
| | Total | 29.2 | 351 |

Period: 12 days from June 4 to 16, 1980

**C. Reasons Why Callers Had to Wait (Pareto Diagram)**

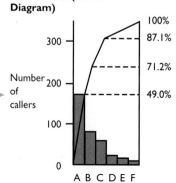

**EXHIBIT C5.4**

Effects of QC

**A. Effects of QC (Comparison Before and After QC)**

| | Reasons why callers had to wait | Total number | | Daily average | |
|---|---|---|---|---|---|
| | | Before | After | Before | After |
| A | One operator (partner out of the office) | 172 | 15 | 14.3 | 1.2 |
| B | Receiving party not present | 73 | 17 | 6.1 | 1.4 |
| C | No one present in the section receiving the call | 61 | 20 | 5.1 | 1.7 |
| D | Section and name of receiving not given | 19 | 4 | 1.6 | 0.3 |
| E | Inquiry about branch office locations | 16 | 3 | 1.3 | 0.2 |
| F | Others | 10 | 0 | 0.8 | 0 |
| | Total | 351 | 59 | 29.2 | 4.8 |

Period: 12 days from Aug. 17 to 30.

Problems are classified according to cause and presented in order of the amount of time consumed. They are illustrated in a bar graph. 100% indicates the total number of time-consuming calls.

**B. Effects of QC (Pareto Diagram)**

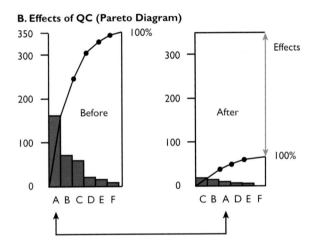

# Selected Bibliography

Berry, L. L.; V. A. Zeithaml; and A. Parasuraman. "Five Imperatives for Improving Service Quality." *Sloan Management Review,* no. 29 (Summer 1990), pp. 29–38.

Bounds, Greg; Lyle Yorks; Mel Adams; and Gipsie Rannet. *Total Quality Management: Towards the Emerging Paradigm.* New York: McGraw-Hill, Inc., 1994.

Crosby, Philip B. *Quality Is Free.* New York: McGraw-Hill, Inc., 1979.

Crosby, Philip B. *Quality Without Tears.* New York: McGraw-Hill, Inc., 1984.

Deming, W. Edwards. *Quality, Productivity and Competitive Position.* Cambridge, MA: MIT Center for Advanced Engineering Study, 1982.

Feigenbaum, A. V. *Total Quality Control.* 3rd ed. New York: McGraw-Hill, 1983.

Garvin, David. "Competing on the Eight Dimensions of Quality." *Harvard Business Review,* November–December 1987, pp. 101–109.

Gitlow, Howard; Allan Oppenheim; and Rosa Oppenheim. *Quality Management: Tools and Methods for Improvement.* 2nd ed. Burr Ridge, IL: Irwin/McGraw-Hill, 1995.

Goetsch, David L., and Stanley B. Davis. *Introduction to Total Quality: Quality Management for Production, Processes and Services.* 2nd ed. Upper Saddle River, NJ: Prentice Hall, 1997.

Hart, Christopher W. L. "The Power of Unconditional Service Guarantees." *Harvard Business Review,* July–August 1988, pp. 54–62.

Huyink, David S., and Craig Westover. *ISO 9000: Motivating the People; Mastering the Process; Achieving Registration!* Burr Ridge, IL: Irwin Professional Publishing, 1994.

Ishikawa, Kaoru. Translated by David J. Lu. *What Is Total Quality Control?—The Japanese Way.* Englewood Cliffs, NJ: Prentice Hall, 1985.

Juran, Joseph M. *Juran on Quality by Design: The New Steps for Planning Quality in Goods and Services.* New York: The Free Press, 1992.

March, A. "A Note on Quality: The Views of Deming, Juran and Crosby." Note No. 9-687-011. ICCH, Harvard Business School, Cambridge, MA, 1986.

Oakland, John S. *Total Quality Control.* London: Heinemann, 1989.

Parasuraman, A.; L. L. Berry; and V. A. Zeithaml. "SERVQUAL: A Multiple-Item Scale for Measuring Consumer Perceptions of Service Quality." Marketing Science Institute, Cambridge, MA, 1986.

Parasuraman, A; L. L. Berry; and V. A. Zeithaml. "Understanding, Measuring, and Improving Service Quality: Findings From a Multiphase Research Program." *Service Breakthroughs: Changing the Rules of the Game.* New York: The Free Press, 1989.

Peters, Tom. *Thriving on Chaos.* New York: Knopf, 1987.

————. and Robert H. Waterman, Jr. *In Search of Excellence.* New York: Harper and Row, 1982.

Rabbitt, John T., and Peter A. Bergh. *The ISO 9000 Book: A Global Competitor's Guide to Compliance and Certification.* 2nd ed. White Plains, NY: Quality Resources, a Division of The Kraus Organization Limited, 1994.

Reichhold, F. F., and W. E. Sasser. "Zero Defections: Quality Comes to Services." *Harvard Business Review* 68, no. 5 (September–October 1990), pp. 105–11.

Rao, Ashok; L. P. Carr et al. *Total Quality Management: A Cross Functional Perspective.* New York: John Wiley & Sons, Inc., 1996.

Ross, Joel E. *Total Quality Management: Text, Cases and Readings.* Delray Beach, FL: St. Lucie Press, 1993.

Taguchi, G. *On-Line Quality Control During Production.* Tokyo: Japanese Standards Association, 1987.

Tenner, A. R., and I. J. DeToro. *Total Quality Management.* Reading, MA: Addison-Wesley, 1992.

Turner, Joseph. "Is an Out-of-Spec Product Really Out of Spec?" *Quality Progress.* December 1990, pp. 57–59.

Walton, Mary. *Deming Management at Work,* New York: Perigree Books, 1991.

Zeithaml, V. A.; L. L. Berry; and A. Parasuraman. "Communication and Control Processes in the Delivery of Service Quality." *Journal of Marketing* 52, (April 1988), pp. 35–48.

# STATISTICAL QUALITY CONTROL METHODS

5

*Supplement Objectives*

- Provide a brief history of the introduction of statistical methods into companies for the purpose of monitoring and improving the quality of goods and services.

- Define the two different types of sampling errors that can occur when statistical sampling is used.

- Distinguish between attributes and variables with respect to statistical quality control.

- Introduce the concept of acceptance sampling and how it is applied in industry.

- Introduce the concept of statistical process control and how it is applied in industry.

- Discuss Taguchi methods and how they are different from traditional statistical quality control methods.

There are two major reasons why we use statistical quality methods. As discovered during World War II, testing and/or inspecting a sample rather than the entire population of items is both faster and more economical because it requires significantly less labor. In addition, for certain products and for certain types of tests, the product must be destroyed when it is tested. Examples of products that fall into this category include bullets and flashbulbs. An example of destructive testing is the crash testing of automobiles to assess the damage to the passenger compartment. In both of these situations it would never make sense to conduct 100 percent testing.

Statistical quality methods can be divided into two broad categories: (*a*) acceptance sampling which assesses the quality of products that have already been produced and (*b*) statistical process control which assesses whether or not a process is performing within established limits. The mathematical calculations are the same for each category. The interpretation of the results, however, varies as we shall see later in this chapter.

## ATTRIBUTES AND VARIABLES

**types of data:**
**attribute data**
Data which count items, such as the number of defective items on a sample.

**variable data**
Data which measure a particular product characteristic such as length or weight.

The application of statistical quality control methods can be further divided into two additional categories: the first approach uses **attribute data** (that is, data which are counted, such as the number of defective parts produced or the number of dissatisfied customers); the second approach uses **variable data** (that is, data which are measured, such as the length of a wire or the weight of a package of cereal). Each approach can be used in either acceptance sampling or in statistical process control, as shown in Exhibit S5.1.

---

**EXHIBIT S5.1**

Statistical Quality Control Methods

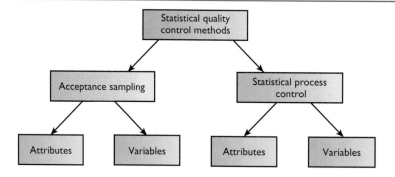

---

**EXHIBIT S5.2**

Types of Sampling Errors

|  |  | The population or process is actually: | |
|---|---|---|---|
|  |  | Good or in control | Bad or out of control |
| The sample says that the population or process is: | Good or in control | In agreement | $\beta$ or Type II error |
|  | Bad or out of control | $\alpha$ or Type I error | In agreement |

# SAMPLING ERRORS

**types of sampling errors:**

$\alpha$ **error, Type I error, or producer's risk** Occurs when a sample says parts are bad or the process is out of control when the opposite is true.

$\beta$ **error, Type II error, or consumer's risk** Occurs when a sample says parts are good or the process is in control when just the reverse is true.

When we use a sample from a larger population or from the output generated by a process instead of monitoring the entire population or output, there is the possibility that the sample results are not representative of the actual population or process. When this occurs, we have a sampling error. There are two types of sampling errors that can occur, as shown in Exhibit S5.2. The first occurs when the population is considered bad or the process is considered out of control, when neither is the case. This type of error is referred to as an **$\alpha$ error, Type I error, or producer's risk.** The second type of sampling error occurs when the population is considered good or the process is considered in control, when they really are not. This type of error is referred to as a **$\beta$ error, Type II error, or consumer's risk.** Balancing the risk of occurrence between the Type I and Type II errors is a major consideration in determining the sample size and the control limits.

# ACCEPTANCE SAMPLING

## Designing a Sampling Plan for Attributes

Acceptance sampling, as previously stated, is performed on goods that already exist to determine if they conform to specifications. These products may be items received from another company and evaluated by the receiving department or they may be components that have passed through a processing step and are evaluated by company personnel either in production or later in the warehousing function. Whether inspection should be done at all is addressed in the following example.

Acceptance sampling is executed through a sampling plan. In this section, we illustrate the planning procedures, with respect to attributes, for a single sampling plan—that is, a plan in which the quality is determined from the evaluation of one sample. (Other plans may be developed using two or more samples. See J. M. Juran and F. M. Gryna's *Quality Planning and Analysis* for a discussion of these plans.)

An employee inspects the manufacture of Reese's peanut butter cups. This is the last stage of full quality control where defective cups are removed.

**Costs to Justify Inspection**    Total or 100 percent inspection is justified when the cost of a loss incurred by not inspecting is greater than the cost of inspection. For example, suppose a faulty item results in a $10 loss. If the average percentage of defective items in a lot is 3 percent, the expected cost of faulty items is $0.03 \times \$10$, or $0.30 each. Therefore, if the cost of inspecting each item is less than $0.30, the economic decision is to perform 100 percent inspection. Not all defective items will be removed, however, since inspectors will pass some bad items and reject some good ones.

The purposes of a sampling plan are to test the lot to either (*a*) find its quality or (*b*) ensure that the quality is what it is supposed to be. Thus, if a quality control supervisor already knows the quality (such as the 0.03 given in the example), he or she does not sample for defects. Either all of the items must be inspected to remove the defects or none of them should be inspected, and the rejects pass into the process. The choice simply depends on the cost to inspect and the cost incurred by passing a reject.

A single sampling plan when we are looking at attributes is defined by *n* and *c*, where *n* is the number of units in the sample and *c* is the acceptance number. The size of *n* may vary from one to all the items in the lot (usually denoted as *N*) from which it is drawn. The acceptance number *c* denotes the maximum number of defective items that can be found in the sample before the lot is rejected. Values for *n* and *c* are determined by the interaction of four factors (AQL, $\alpha$, LTPD, and $\beta$) that quantify the objectives of the product's producer and its consumer. The objective of the producer is to ensure that the sampling plan has a low probability of rejecting good lots. Lots are defined as good if they contain no more than a specified level of defectives, termed the **acceptable quality level (AQL)**.[1] The objective of the consumer is to ensure that the sampling plan has a low probability of accepting bad lots. Lots are defined as bad if the percentage of defectives is greater than a specified amount, termed *lot tolerance percent defective* (LTPD). As presented earlier, the probability associated with rejecting a good lot is denoted by the Greek letter alpha ($\alpha$) and is termed the *producer's risk*. The probability associated with accepting a bad lot is denoted by the Greek letter beta ($\beta$) and is termed the *consumer's risk*. The selection of particular values for AQL, $\alpha$, LTPD, and $\beta$) is an economic decision based on a cost trade-off or, more typically, on company policy or contractual requirements.

There is a humorous story supposedly about Hewlett-Packard during its first dealings with Japanese vendors, who place great emphasis on high-quality production. HP had insisted on 2 percent AQL in a purchase of 100 cables. During the purchase agreement some heated discussion took place wherein the Japanese vendor did not want this AQL specification; HP insisted that they would not budge from the 2 percent AQL. The Japanese vendor finally agreed. Later, when the box arrived, there were two packages inside. One contained 100 good cables. The other package had 2 cables with a note stating: "We have sent you 100 good cables. Since you insisted on 2 percent AQL, we have enclosed 2 defective cables in this package, though we do not understand why you want them."

The following example, using an excerpt from a standard acceptance sampling table, illustrates how the four parameters—AQL, $\alpha$, LTPD, and $\beta$—are used in developing a sampling plan.

**acceptable quality level (AQL)**
Maximum percentage of defects that a company is willing to accept.

---

[1]There is some controversy surrounding AQLs, based on the argument that specifying some acceptable percent of defectives is inconsistent with the philosophical goal of zero defects. In practice, even in the best companies, there is an acceptable quality level. The difference is that it may be stated in parts per million rather than in parts per hundred. This is the case in Motorola's six-sigma quality standard which holds that no more than 3.4 defects per million parts are acceptable.

**EXHIBIT S5.3**

Excerpt from a Sampling Plan Table for $\alpha = 0.05$, $\beta = 0.10$

| c | LTPD ÷ AQL | n • AQL | c | LTPD ÷ AQL | n • AQL |
|---|---|---|---|---|---|
| 0 | 44.890 | 0.052 | 5 | 3.549 | 2.613 |
| 1 | 10.946 | 0.355 | 6 | 3.206 | 3.286 |
| 2 | 6.509 | 0.818 | 7 | 2.957 | 3.981 |
| 3 | 4.890 | 1.366 | 8 | 2.768 | 4.695 |
| 4 | 4.057 | 1.970 | 9 | 2.618 | 5.426 |

**Example**

*Values of n and c:* Hi-Tech Industries manufactures Z-Band radar scanners used to detect speed traps. The printed circuit boards in the scanners are purchased from an outside vendor. The vendor produces the boards to an AQL of 2 percent defectives and is willing to run a 5 percent risk ($\alpha$) of having lots of this level or fewer defectives rejected. Hi-Tech considers lots of 8 percent or more defectives (LTPD) unacceptable and wants to ensure that it will accept such poor-quality lots no more than 10 percent of the time ($\beta$). A large shipment has just been delivered. What values of n and c should be selected to determine the quality of this lot?

**Solution**

The parameters of the problem are AQL = 0.02, $\alpha = 0.05$, LTPD = 0.08, and $\beta = 0.10$. We can use Exhibit S5.3 to find c and n.

First divide LTPD by AQL ($0.08 \div 0.02 = 4$). Then find the ratio in column 2 that is equal to or just greater than that amount (i.e., 4). This value is 4.057, which is associated with c = 4.

Finally, find the value in column 3 that is in the same row as c = 4 and divide that quantity by AQL to obtain n ($1.970 \div 0.02 = 98.5$).

The appropriate sampling plan is c = 4, n = 99.

## Operating Characteristic Curves

operating characteristic (OC) curves
Curves which show the probability of accepting lots that contain different percent defectives.

While a sampling plan such as the one just described meets our requirements for the extreme values of good and bad quality, we cannot readily determine how well the plan discriminates between good and bad lots at intermediate values. For this reason, sampling plans are generally displayed graphically through the use of **operating characteristic (OC) curves**. These curves, which are unique for each combination of n and c, simply illustrate the probability of accepting lots with varying percent defectives. The procedure we have followed in developing the plan, in fact, specifies two points on an OC curve—one point defined by AQL and $1 - \alpha$, and the other point defined by LTPD and $\beta$. Curves for common values of n and c can be computed or obtained from available tables.[2] (See Exhibit S5.4.)

A sampling plan discriminating perfectly between good and bad lots has an infinite slope (vertical) at the selected value of AQL. In Exhibit S5.4, percent defectives to the left of 2 percent would always be accepted and to the right, always rejected. However, such a curve is possible only with complete inspection of all units and thus is not a possibility with a true sampling plan.

---

[2]See, for example, H. F. Dodge and H. G. Romig, *Sampling Inspection Tables—Single and Double Sampling* (New York: John Wiley & Sons, 1959), and *Military Standard Sampling Procedures and Tables for Inspection by Attributes* (MIL-STD-105D) (Washington, DC: U.S. Government Printing Office, 1983).

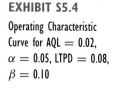

**EXHIBIT S5.4**

Operating Characteristic
Curve for AQL = 0.02,
$\alpha = 0.05$, LTPD = 0.08,
$\beta = 0.10$

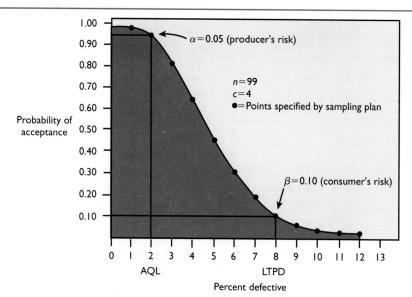

An OC curve should be steep in the region of most interest (between the AQL and the LTPD), which is accomplished by varying $n$ and $c$. If $c$ remains constant, increasing the sample size $n$ causes the OC curve to be more vertical. While holding $n$ constant, decreasing $c$ (the maximum number of defective units) also makes the slope more vertical, moving closer to the origin.

The size of the lot that the sample is taken from has relatively little effect on the quality of protection. Consider, for example, that samples—all of the same size of 20 units—are taken from different lots ranging from a lot size of 200 units to a lot size of infinity. If each lot is known to have 5 percent defectives, the probability of accepting the lot based on the sample of 20 units ranges from about 0.34 to about 0.36. This means that so long as the lot size is several times the sample size, it makes little difference how large the lot is. It seems a bit difficult to accept, but statistically (on the average in the long run) whether we have a carload or box full, we'll get about the same answer. It just seems that a carload should have a larger sample size.

## Designing a Sampling Plan for Variables

When we use variables to determine if we should accept an entire lot, we again take a sample of the items. However, instead of counting the number of defectives in the sample, we measure the variable of interest for each item in the sample and compute the mean for the sample. We then compare the mean of the sample with **control limits** that have been previously established to determine whether or not we accept the entire lot.

There are three factors that must be taken into consideration in designing a sampling plan for an item where variables are used as the criterion for acceptance. These are: (*a*) the probability of rejecting a lot that is actually good (that is, committing an $\alpha$ error), (*b*) the probability of accepting a lot that is actually bad (that is, committing a $\beta$ error), and (*c*) the sample size, $n$.

**control limits**
Points on an acceptance sampling chart that distinguish the accept and reject region(s). Also, points on a process control chart that distinguish between a process being in and out of control.

Example

ABC Electronics Company buys a 50-ohm resistor from an outside vendor. (A resistor is an electrical component used in electrical circuits to retard current. An ohm is the measure of how much a resistor retards the current.) From historical data, the standard deviation for this resistor is 3 ohms. Determine the appropriate control limits if we use a sample size of $n = 100$ and we want to be 95 percent confident that the sample results are truly representative of the total population. (In other words, the probability of committing an $\alpha$ error is $1 - 0.95$ or 5 percent.)

Solution    The equation for determining the control limits (CL) is:

$$CL = \mu \pm z_{\alpha/2} \frac{\sigma}{\sqrt{n}} \tag{S5.1}$$

where

$\mu$ = The desired mean of the population.

$z_{\alpha/2}$ = The number of standard deviations from the mean that corresponds to the given level of $\alpha$. ($\alpha/2$ indicates that this is a two-tail test and that the $\alpha$ error is equally divided between the two tails of the distribution.) The value of $z$ is obtained from the normal distribution table in Appendix B or C at the end of this book. (As noted in the table, the $z$-value for a two-tailed test with 95 percent confidence is 1.96.)

$\sigma$ = The value of the population's standard deviation.

Substituting we have:

$$CL = 50 \pm 1.96 \frac{(3)}{\sqrt{100}}$$

$$= 50 \pm 0.588$$

The lower control limit (LCL) is therefore 49.412 and the upper control limit (UCL) is 50.588, as shown in Exhibit S5.5.

The inspection procedure for this resistor therefore is to (*a*) take a random sample of 100 resistors, (*b*) measure the number of ohms in each resistor in the sample, (*c*) compute the mean of the sample, and finally (*d*) compare the sample mean with the established control limits; in other words, if the sample mean falls within the range of 49.412–50.588, then the lot is accepted, otherwise the lot is rejected.

---

**EXHIBIT S5.5**

Establishing Control Limits for Acceptance Sampling Using Variables

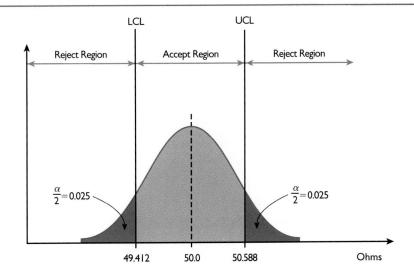

Example        Continuing with the resistor problem, we can tolerate some variation in the number of
               ohms in each resistor. However, if the number of ohms falls below 49, then we would
               have a serious problem in our electrical circuit. What is the probability of us accepting
               a lot when the average resistance is 49 ohms or less?

Solution       This situation is depicted in Exhibit S5.6. It is important to note that the control limits
               that were previously established do not change. The probability of accepting a bad lot or
               committing a $\beta$ error is defined by that percentage of the area under the curve with a
               mean of 49 that falls within the acceptance range. (Note that this is a one-tailed test be-
               cause the $\beta$ error occurs only in the right tail under the curve.)
                   The probability of committing this error is determined as follows:

$$\text{LCL} = \mu + z_\beta \frac{\sigma}{\sqrt{n}}$$

where

   $z_\beta$ = The number of standard deviations from the mean that corresponds to the given
             level of $\beta$.

Substituting, we have:

$$49.412 = 49 + z_\beta \frac{(3)}{\sqrt{100}}$$

$$0.412 = (z_\beta)0.3$$

$$z_\beta = 1.373$$

Again, using the normal distribution table at the end of this book, we look up the
value of $z = 1.373$ and find the corresponding area under the curve of 0.0853. Thus the
probability of committing a $\beta$ error under these conditions is 8.53 percent.

**EXHIBIT S5.6**

Determining the Probability
of Committing a $\beta$ Error

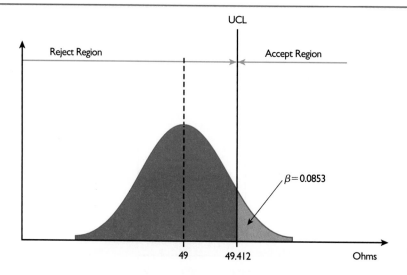

**exponential
smoothing**
Time series forecasting
technique that does not
require large amounts of
historical data.

the new forecast is calculated. In many applications (perhaps even in most), the most recent data points tend to be more indicative of the future than those in the distant past. If this premise is valid—that the importance of data diminishes as the past becomes more distant—then **exponential smoothing** may be the most logical and easiest method to use.

The reason this is called "exponential smoothing" is because each increment in the past is decreased by $(1 - \alpha)$, or

|                                                         | Weighting at $\alpha = 0.05$ |
| ------------------------------------------------------- | :--------------------------: |
| Most recent weighting $= \alpha(1 - \alpha)^0$          | 0.0500                       |
| Data 1 time period older $= \alpha(1 - \alpha)^1$       | 0.0475                       |
| Data 2 time periods older $= \alpha(1 - \alpha)^2$      | 0.0451                       |
| Data 3 time periods older $= \alpha(1 - \alpha)^3$      | 0.0429                       |

Therefore, the exponents 0, 1, 2, 3 … , etc. give this method its name.

Exponential smoothing is the most used of all forecasting techniques. It is an integral part of virtually all computerized forecasting programs, and is widely used for ordering inventory in retail firms, wholesale companies, and other service operations.

Exponential smoothing accomplishes virtually everything that can be done with moving average forecasts, but requires significantly less data. The **exponential smoothing constant alpha ($\alpha$)** is a value between 0 and 1. If the actual demand tends to be relatively stable over time, we would choose a relatively small value for $\alpha$ to decrease the effects of short-term or random fluctuations, which is similar to having a moving average that involves a large number of periods. If the actual demand tends to fluctuate rapidly, we would choose a relatively large value for $\alpha$ to keep up with these changes. This is similar to using a moving average with a small number of periods.

The major reasons that exponential smoothing techniques have become so well accepted are:

**exponential
smoothing
constant alpha ($\alpha$)**
Value between 0 and 1
that is used in
exponential smoothing
to minimize the error
between historical
demand and respective
forecasts.

1. Exponential models are surprisingly accurate.
2. Formulating an exponential model is relatively easy.
3. The user can readily understand how the model works.
4. There is very little computation required to use the model.
5. Computer storage requirements are small because of the limited use of historical data.
6. Tests for accuracy as to how well the model is performing are easy to compute.

In the exponential smoothing method, only three pieces of data are needed to forecast the future: the most recent forecast, the actual demand that occurred for that forecast period, and a smoothing constant alpha ($\alpha$). This smoothing constant determines the level of smoothing and the speed of reaction to differences between forecasts and actual occurrences. The value for the constant is arbitrary and is determined both by the nature of the product and the manager's sense of what constitutes a good response rate. However, error measuring techniques, such as MAD (which is discussed later in this chapter) can be used to evaluate different values for $\alpha$ until that value is found which minimizes the historical error. For example, if a firm produced a standard item with relatively stable demand, the reaction rate to differences between actual and forecast demand would tend to be small, perhaps just a few percentage points. However, if the firm were experiencing growth, it would be desirable to have a higher reaction rate, to give greater importance to recent growth experience. The more rapid the growth, the higher the reaction rate should be. Sometimes users of the simple moving average switch to exponential smoothing but like to keep the forecasts about the same as the simple moving average. In this case, $\alpha$ is approximated by $2 \div (n + 1)$ where $n$ was the number of time periods that were used in the moving average.

The equation for an exponential smoothing forecast is:

$$F_t = (1 - \alpha)F_{t-1} + \alpha A_{t-1}$$

or rewritten as

$$F_t = F_{t-1} + \alpha(A_{t-1} - F_{t-1}) \qquad (6.3)$$

where

$F_t$ = Exponentially smoothed forecast for period $t$

$F_{t-1}$ = Exponentially smoothed forecast made for the prior period

$A_{t-1}$ = Actual demand in the prior period

$\alpha$ = Desired response rate, or smoothing constant

This equation states that the new forecast is equal to the old forecast plus a portion of the error (the difference between the previous forecast and what actually occurred).[1]

When exponential smoothing is first introduced, the initial forecast or starting point may be obtained by using a simple estimate or an average of preceding periods. If no historical forecast data are available, then the forecast for the previous period (that is, last month) is set equal to the demand for that period.

Example

To demonstrate the exponential smoothing method, assume that the long-run demand for the product under study is relatively stable and a smoothing constant ($\alpha$) of 0.05 is considered appropriate. If the exponential smoothing method were used as a continuing policy, a forecast would have been made for last month. Assume that last month's forecast ($F_{t-1}$) was 1,050 units, and 1,000 were actually demanded, rather than 1,050.

Solution

The forecast for this month would then be calculated as follows:

$$\begin{aligned}
F_t &= F_{t-1} + \alpha(A_{t-1} - F_{t-1}) \\
&= 1,050 + 0.05(1,000 - 1,050) \\
&= 1,050 + 0.05(-50) \\
&= 1,047.5 \text{ units}
\end{aligned}$$

Because the smoothing coefficient is relatively small, the reaction of the new forecast to an error of 50 units is to decrease the next month's forecast by only 2.5 units.

Example

Kevin Alexander owns a small restaurant that is open seven days a week. Until just recently he forecasted the number of customers using his "gut feel." However, he wants to open another restaurant and recognizes the need to adopt a more formal method of forecasting that can be used in both locations. He decided to compare a three-week moving average, and exponential smoothing with $\alpha = .7$ and $\alpha = .3$. The actual sales for the past three weeks are shown below, along with his forecast for last week.

---

[1]Some writers prefer to call $F_t$ a smoothed average.

| | Customers per Day | | | | | | |
|---|---|---|---|---|---|---|---|
| **Week** | **Sun** | **Mon** | **Tue** | **Wed** | **Thu** | **Fri** | **Sat** |
| Actual: | | | | | | | |
| 3 weeks ago | 138 | 183 | 182 | 188 | 207 | 277 | 388 |
| 2 weeks ago | 143 | 194 | 191 | 200 | 213 | 292 | 401 |
| Last week | 157 | 196 | 204 | 193 | 226 | 313 | 408 |
| Forecast: | | | | | | | |
| Last week | 155 | 191 | 192 | 198 | 204 | 286 | 396 |

*a.* Forecast sales for each day of the next week using:

- A three-week moving average
- Exponential smoothing with $\alpha = .7$
- Exponential smoothing with $\alpha = .3$

*b.* The actual sales for the next week were as follows:

| | Customers per Day | | | | | | |
|---|---|---|---|---|---|---|---|
| **Week** | **Sun** | **Mon** | **Tue** | **Wed** | **Thu** | **Fri** | **Sat** |
| Actual: | 160 | 204 | 197 | 210 | 215 | 300 | 421 |

Evaluate each of the three forecasting techniques based on the one week's data. Which technique would you recommend to Kevin?

**Solution**   *a.* The forecasts for each of the three methods is presented below.

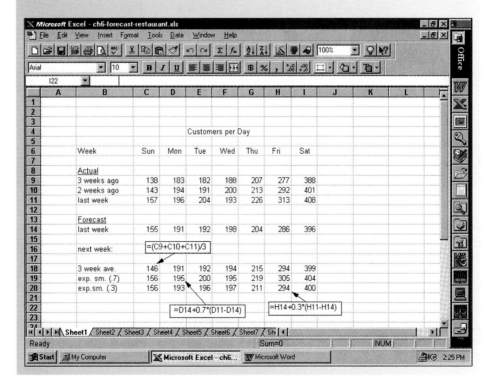

*b.*

| | B | C | D | E | F | G | H | I | J |
|---|---|---|---|---|---|---|---|---|---|
| 13 | Forecast | | | | | | | | |
| 14 | last week | 155 | 191 | 192 | 198 | 204 | 286 | 396 | |
| 16 | next week: | | | | | | | | |
| 18 | 3 week ave. | 146 | 191 | 192 | 194 | 215 | 294 | 399 | |
| 19 | exp. sm. (.7) | 156 | 195 | 200 | 195 | 219 | 305 | 404 | |
| 20 | exp.sm. (.3) | 156 | 193 | 196 | 197 | 211 | 294 | 400 | |
| 25 | Actual: | | | | | | | | |
| 27 | next week: | 160 | 204 | 197 | 210 | 215 | 300 | 421 | |
| 28 | | | | | | | | | Average |
| 29 | MAD (3 wk): | 14 | 13 | 5 | 16 | 0 | 6 | 22 | 10.90 |
| 30 | MAD (alpha =.7): | 4 | 10 | 3 | 16 | 4 | 5 | 17 | 8.27 |
| 31 | MAD (alpha =.3): | 4 | 12 | 1 | 14 | 4 | 6 | 21 | 8.93 |

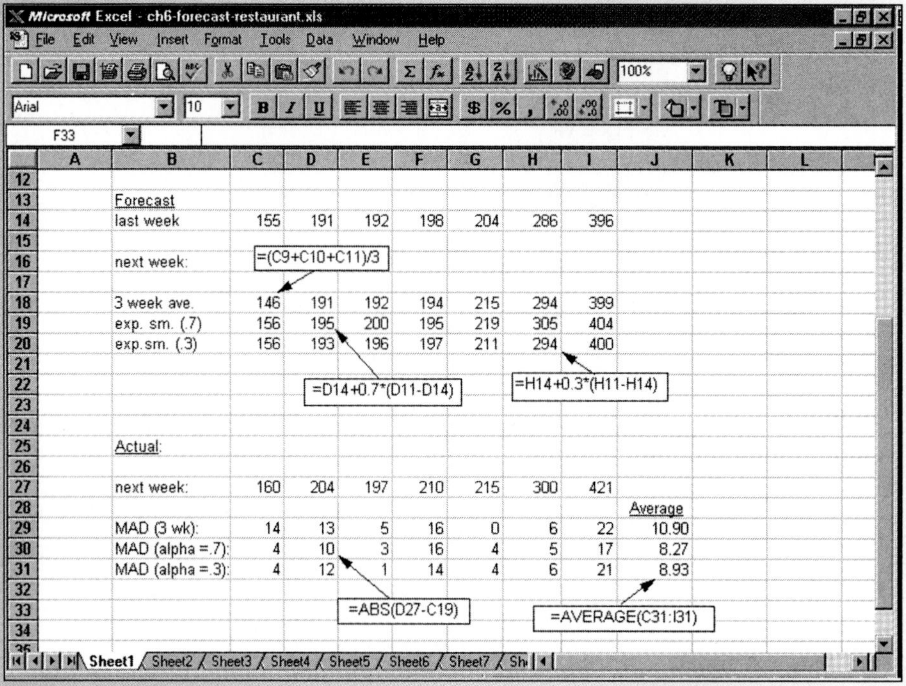

Using the average MAD as a criterion, Kevin should use the exponential smoothing method with $\alpha = .7$, as that method has the lowest average MAD of 8.27.

As discussed above, exponential smoothing has the shortcoming of lagging changes in demand. Exhibit 6.7 shows actual data plotted as a smooth curve to show the lagging effects of the exponential forecasts. The forecast lags the actual demand during an increase or decrease, but overshoots actual demand when a change in the direction occurs. Note that the higher the value of alpha, the more closely the forecast follows the actual. In order to more closely track actual demand, a trend factor may be added. What also helps is the ability to adjust the value of alpha. This is termed *adaptive forecasting.* Both trend effects and adaptive forecasting are briefly explained in the following sections.

**Trend Effects in Exponential Smoothing** As stated earlier, an upward or downward trend in data collected over a sequence of time periods causes the exponential forecast to always lag behind (that is, to be above or below) the actual occurrence. Exponentially smoothed forecasts can be corrected somewhat by including a trend adjustment. To correct for the trend, we now need two smoothing constants. In addition to the smoothing constant $\alpha$, the trend equation also requires a **trend smoothing constant delta ($\delta$).** Like alpha, delta is limited to values between 0 and 1. The delta reduces the impact of the error which occurs between the actual and the forecast. If both alpha and delta are not included, the trend would overreact to errors.

**trend smoothing constant delta ($\delta$)** Value between 0 and 1 that is used in exponential smoothing when there is a trend.

To initiate the trend equation, the trend value must be entered manually. This first trend value can be an educated guess or a computation based on observed past data.

**EXHIBIT 6.7**

Exponential Forecasts versus
Actual Demands for Units of
a Product over Time
Showing the Forecast Lag

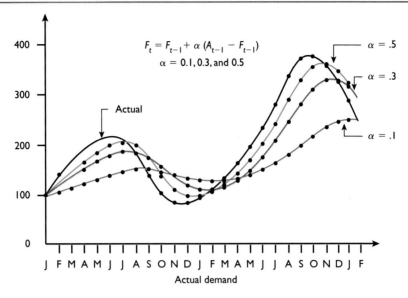

The equation to compute the forecast including trend (FIT) is:

$$\text{FIT}_t = F_t + T_t \tag{6.4}$$

where

$$F_t = \text{FIT}_{t-1} + \alpha(A_{t-1} - \text{FIT}_{t-1}) \tag{6.5}$$

$$T_t = T_{t-1} + \alpha\delta(A_{t-1} - \text{FIT}_{t-1}) \tag{6.6}$$

Example

Assume an initial starting point for $F_t$ of 100 units, a trend of 10 units, an alpha of .20, and a delta of .30. If the actual demand turned out to be 115 rather than the forecast 100, calculate the forecast for the next period.

Solution

Adding the starting forecast and the trend, we have:

$$\text{FIT}_{t-1} = F_{t-1} + T_{t-1} = 100 + 10 = 110$$

The actual $A_{t-1}$ is given as 115. Therefore,

$$F_t = \text{FIT}_{t-1} + \alpha(A_{t-1} - \text{FIT}_{t-1})$$
$$= 110 + .2(115 - 110) = 111.0$$
$$T_t = T_{t-1} + \alpha\delta(A_{t-1} - \text{FIT}_{t-1})$$
$$= 10 + (.2)(.3)(115 - 110) = 10.3$$
$$\text{FIT}_t = F_t + T_t = 111.0 + 10.3 = 121.3$$

If, instead of 121.3, the actual turned out to be 120, the sequence would be repeated and the forecast for the next period would be:

$$F_{t+1} = 121.3 + .2(120 - 121.3) = 121.04$$
$$T_{t+1} = 10.3 + (.2)(.3)(120 - 121.3) = 10.22$$
$$\text{FIT}_{t+1} = 121.04 + 10.22 = 131.26$$

**Adaptive Forecasting**    There are two approaches for adjusting the value of alpha. One uses various values of alpha and the other uses a tracking signal.

**1.** *Two or more predetermined values of alpha.* The amount of error between the forecast and the actual demand is measured. Depending on the degree of error, different values of alpha are used. For example, if the error is large, alpha is 0.8; if the error is small, alpha is 0.2.

**2.** *Computed values of alpha.* A tracking signal computes whether the forecast is keeping pace with genuine upward or downward changes in demand (as opposed to random changes). The tracking signal is defined here as the exponentially smoothed actual error divided by the exponentially smoothed absolute error. Alpha is set equal to this tracking signal and therefore changes from period to period within the possible range of 0 to 1.

In logic, computing alpha seems simple. In practice, however, it is quite prone to error. There are three exponential equations—one for the single exponentially smoothed forecast as done in the previous section of this chapter, one to compute an exponentially smoothed actual error, and the third to compute the exponentially smoothed absolute error. Thus, the user must keep three equations running in sequence for each period. Further, assumptions must be made during the initial time periods until the technique has had a chance to start computing values. For example, alpha must be given a value for the first two periods until actual data are available. Also, the user must select a second smoothing constant, in addition to alpha, which is used in the actual and absolute error equations. Clearly, those who use adaptive forecasting on a regular basis rely on technology for the calculations.

# FORECASTING ERRORS

When we use the word *error,* we are referring to the difference between the forecast value and what actually occurred. So long as the forecast value is within the confidence limits, as we discuss below in "Measurement of Error," this is not really an error. However, common usage refers to the difference as an error.

Demand for a product is generated through the interaction of a number of factors which are too complex to describe accurately in a model. Therefore, all forecasts contain some degree of error. In discussing forecast errors, it is convenient to distinguish between *sources of error* and the *measurement of error.*

## Sources of Error

Errors can come from a variety of sources. One common source that many forecasters are unaware of is caused by the projection of past trends into the future. For example, when we talk about statistical errors in regression analysis, we are referring to the deviations of observations from our regression line. It is common to attach a confidence band to the regression line to reduce the unexplained error. However, when we then use this regression line as a forecasting device by projecting it into the future, the error may not be correctly defined by the projected confidence band. This is because the confidence interval is based on past data; consequently it may or may not be totally valid for projected data points and therefore cannot be used with the same confidence. In fact, experience has shown that the actual errors tend to be greater than those predicted from forecasting models.

Errors can be classified as either bias or random. *Bias errors* occur when a consistent mistake is made, that is, the forecast is always too high. Sources of bias include: (*a*) failing to include the right variables, (*b*) using the wrong relationships among variables, (*c*) employing the wrong trend line, (*d*) mistakenly shifting the seasonal demand from where it normally occurs, and (*e*) the existence of some undetected secular trend. *Random errors* can be defined simply as those that cannot be explained by the forecast model being used. These random errors are often referred to as "noise" in the model.

## Measurement of Error

Several of the common terms used to describe the degree of error associated with forecasting are *standard error, mean squared error* (or *variance*), and *mean absolute deviation.* In addition, *tracking signals* may be used to indicate the existence of any positive or negative bias in the forecast.

Standard error is discussed in the section on linear regression later in the chapter. Since the standard error is the square root of a function, it is often more convenient to use the function itself. This is called the *mean square error,* or variance.

**mean absolute deviation (MAD)** Average forecasting error based upon the absolute value between the forecast and actual demand.

The **mean absolute deviation (MAD)** was at one time very much in vogue but subsequently was ignored in favor of the standard deviation and standard error measures. In recent years, however, MAD has made a comeback because of its simplicity and usefulness in obtaining tracking signals. MAD is the average error in the forecasts, using absolute values. It is valuable because MAD, like the standard deviation, measures the dispersion (or variation) of observed values around some expected value.

MAD is computed using the differences between the actual demand and the forecast demand without regard to whether it is negative or positive. It is therefore equal to the sum of the absolute deviations divided by the number of data points, or, stated in equation form:

$$\text{MAD} = \frac{\sum_{t=1}^{n} |A_t - F_t|}{n} \quad (6.7)$$

where

$t$ = Period number

$A_t$ = Actual demand for period $t$

$F_t$ = Forecast demand for period $t$

$n$ = Total number of periods

$|\ |$ = A symbol used to indicate the absolute value of a number and thus disregarding positive and negative signs

When the errors that occur in the forecast are normally distributed (which is assumed to be the usual case), the mean absolute deviation relates to the standard deviation as

$$1 \text{ standard deviation} = \sqrt{\frac{\pi}{2}} \times \text{MAD, or approximately 1.25 MAD.}$$

Conversely,

$$1 \text{ MAD} \approx 0.8 \text{ standard deviation}$$

The standard deviation is the larger measure. If the MAD for a set of points was found to be 60 units, then the standard deviation would be 75 units. And, in the usual statistical manner, if control limits were set at $\pm 3$ standard deviations (or $\pm 3.75$ MADs), then 99.7 percent of the points would fall within these limits. (See Exhibit 6.8.)

**tracking signal** Measure of error to determine if the forecast is staying within specified limits of the actual demand.

A **tracking signal** is a measurement that indicates whether the forecast average is keeping pace with any genuine upward or downward changes in demand. As used in forecasting, the tracking signal is the *number* of mean absolute deviations that the forecast value is above or below the actual occurrence. Exhibit 6.8 shows a normal distribution with a mean of zero and a MAD equal to one. Thus, if we compute a tracking signal and find it equal to $-2$, we

**EXHIBIT 6.8**

A Normal Distribution
with a Mean = 0 and
a MAD = 1

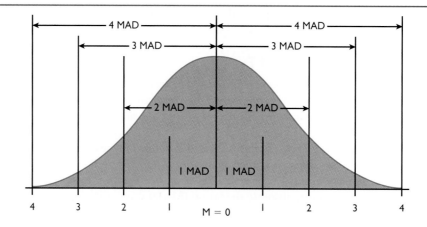

**EXHIBIT 6.9**

Computing the Mean
Absolute Deviation (MAD),
the Running Sum of
Forecast Errors (RSFE), and
the Tracking Signal from
Forecast and Actual Data

| Month | Demand Forecast | Actual | Deviation | (RSFE) | Abs Dev | Sum of Abs Dev | MAD* | TS = RSFE/MAD |
|---|---|---|---|---|---|---|---|---|
| 1 | 1,000 | 950 | −50 | −50 | 50 | 50 | 50 | −1.00 |
| 2 | 1,000 | 1,070 | +70 | +20 | 70 | 120 | 60 | .33 |
| 3 | 1,000 | 1,100 | +100 | +120 | 100 | 220 | 73.3 | 1.64 |
| 4 | 1,000 | 960 | −40 | +80 | 40 | 260 | 65 | 1.23 |
| 5 | 1,000 | 1,090 | +90 | +170 | 90 | 350 | 70 | 2.43 |
| 6 | 1,000 | 1,050 | +50 | +220 | 50 | 400 | 66.7 | 3.31 |

*Mean absolute deviation (MAD). For Month 6, MAD = 400 ÷ 6 = 66.7.

† Tracking signal = $\frac{\text{RSFE}}{\text{MAD}}$. For Month 6. TS = $\frac{\text{RSFE}}{\text{MAD}}$ = $\frac{220}{66.7}$ = 3.3 MADs.

can conclude that the forecast model is providing forecasts that are quite a bit above the mean of the actual occurrences.

A tracking signal can be calculated using the arithmetic sum of forecast deviations divided by the mean absolute deviation, or

$$TS = \frac{RSFE}{MAD} \tag{6.8}$$

where

   RSFE = Running sum of forecast errors

   MAD = Mean absolute deviation

Exhibit 6.9 illustrates the procedure for computing MAD and the tracking signal for a six-month period where the forecast had been set at a constant 1,000 and the actual demands that occurred are as shown. In this example, the forecast, on the average, was off by 66.7 units and the tracking signal was equal to 3.3 mean absolute deviations.

We can obtain a better interpretation of the MAD and tracking signal by plotting the points on a graph. While not completely legitimate from a sample size standpoint, we plotted each month in Exhibit 6.10 to show the drifting of the tracking signal. Note that it

**EXHIBIT 6.10**

A Plot of the Tracking Signals Calculated in Exhibit 6.9

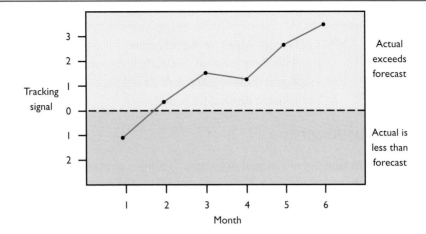

**EXHIBIT 6.11**

The Percentages of Points Included within the Control Limits for a Range of 0 to 4 MADs

| Control Limits | | |
|---|---|---|
| **Number of MADs** | **Related Number of Standard Deviations** | **Percentage of Points Lying within Control Limits** |
| =1 | 0.798 | 57.048 |
| =2 | 1.596 | 88.946 |
| =3 | 2.394 | 98.334 |
| =4 | 3.192 | 99.856 |

drifted from minus 1 MAD to $+3.3$ MADs. This occurred because the actual demand was greater than the forecast in four of the six periods. If the actual demand doesn't fall below the forecast to offset the continual positive RSFE, the tracking signal would continue to rise and we would conclude that assuming a demand of 1,000 is a bad forecast. When the tracking signal exceeds a pre-established limit (for example, $\pm 2.0$ or $\pm 3.0$), the manager should consider changing the forecast model or the value of $\alpha$.

Acceptable limits for the tracking signal depend on the size of the demand being forecast (high-volume or high-revenue items should be monitored frequently) and the amount of personnel time available (narrower acceptable limits cause more forecasts to be out of limits and therefore require more time to investigate). Exhibit 6.11 shows the area within the control limits for a range of zero to four MADs.

In a perfect forecasting model, the sum of the actual forecast errors would be zero; that is, the errors that result in overestimates should offset errors that are underestimates. The tracking signal would then also be zero, indicating an unbiased model, neither leading nor lagging the actual demands.

Often, MAD is used to forecast errors. It might then be desirable to make the MAD more sensitive to recent data. A useful technique to do this is to compute an exponentially smoothed MAD (often identified as $MAD_t$) to forecast the next period's error range. The procedure is similar to single exponential smoothing, which was presented earlier in this chapter. The value of the $MAD_t$ forecast is to provide a range of errors; in the case of inventory control, this is useful in establishing safety stock levels.

$$\text{MAD}_t = \alpha |A_{t-1} - F_{t-1}| + (1 - \alpha)\text{MAD}_{t-1} \qquad (6.9)$$

where

$\text{MAD}_t$ = Forecast MAD for the $t$th period

$\alpha$ = Smoothing constant (normally in the range of 0.05 to 0.20)

$A_{t-1}$ = Actual demand in the period $t - 1$

$F_{t-1}$ = Forecast demand for period $t - 1$

## LINEAR REGRESSION ANALYSIS

**linear regression analysis**
Type of forecasting technique which assumes that the relationship between the dependent and independent variables is a straight line.

**Linear regression analysis** is used to define a functional relationship between two or more correlated variables. The relationship is usually developed from observed data where one parameter (the independent variable) is used to predict another (the dependent variable). Linear regression refers to a special class of regression where the relationship between the variables is assumed to be represented by a straight line. The equation for simple linear regression includes only one independent variable and takes the form:

$$Y = a + bX \qquad (6.10)$$

where

$Y$ = Dependent variable we are solving for

$a$ = $Y$ intercept

$b$ = Slope

$X$ = Independent variable (in time series analysis, $X$ represents units of time)

This forecasting method is useful for long-term forecasting of major occurrences and aggregate planning. For example, linear regression would be very useful to forecast demands for product families. Even though demand for individual products within a family may vary widely during a time period, demand for the total product family is surprisingly smooth.

The major restriction in using linear regression forecasting is, as the name implies, that past data and future projections are assumed to fall around a straight line. While this does limit its application, sometimes, if we use a shorter period of time, linear regression analysis can still be used.

Linear regression is used for both time series forecasting and for causal relationship forecasting. When the dependent variable (which is usually represented on the vertical axis of a graph) changes as a result of time (which is plotted on the horizontal axis), it is referred to as time series analysis. If the dependent variable changes due to the change in the independent variable, then it is a causal relationship (such as the number of deaths from lung cancer increasing with the number of people who smoke).

The following example illustrates time series analysis using the least squares method for obtaining the linear regression equation that forecasts sales for future quarters.

**Example**

A firm's sales for a product line during the 12 quarters of the previous three years were as follows:

| Quarter | Sales | Quarter | Sales |
|---------|-------|---------|-------|
| 1 | 600 | 7 | 2,600 |
| 2 | 1,550 | 8 | 2,900 |
| 3 | 1,500 | 9 | 3,800 |
| 4 | 1,500 | 10 | 4,500 |
| 5 | 2,400 | 11 | 4,000 |
| 6 | 3,100 | 12 | 4,900 |

**Solution**    The firm wants to forecast each quarter of the fourth year, that is, quarters 13, 14, 15, and 16. The least squares equation for linear regression is:

$$\hat{y} = a + bX$$

where

$\hat{y}$ = Dependent variable computed by the equation (sales in this example)

$y$ = Dependent variable data point (see below)

$a$ = Y intercept

$b$ = Slope of the line

$X$ = Independent variable (time period in this example)

The least squares method identifies that line which *minimizes the sum of the squares of the vertical distances* between each data point ($y$) and its corresponding point on the line ($y$). If a straight line is drawn through the general area of the points, the difference between the point and the line is ($y - \hat{y}$). Exhibit 6.12 shows these differences. The sum of the squares of the differences between the plotted data points and the line points is:

$$(y_1 - \hat{y}_1)^2 + (y_2 - \hat{y}_2)^2 + \cdots + (y_{12} - \hat{y}_{12})^2$$

The best line to use is the one that minimizes this total.

In the least squares method, the equations for solving for $a$ and $b$ are obtained using calculus and are:

$$a = \bar{Y} - b\bar{X}$$

$$b = \frac{\sum XY - n\bar{X}\bar{Y}}{\sum X^2 - n\bar{X}^2}$$

where

$a$ = Y intercept

$b$ = Slope of the line

$\bar{Y}$ = Arithmetic mean of all $Y$s

$\bar{X}$ = Arithmetic mean of all $X$s

$X$ = X value at each data point

$Y$ = Y value at each data point

$n$ = Number of data points

$\hat{y}_i$ = Value of the dependent variable computed with the regression equation

Exhibit 6.13 shows these computations carried out for the 12 data points. Note that the final equation for $Y$ shows an intercept of 441.6 and a slope of 359.6. The slope shows that for every unit change in $X$, $Y$ changes by 359.6.

Using this linear regression equation, the forecasts for periods 13 through 16 would be

$Y_{13} = 441.6 + 359.6(13) = 5,116.4$

$Y_{14} = 441.6 + 359.6(14) = 5,476.0$

$Y_{15} = 441.6 + 359.6(15) = 5,835.6$

$Y_{16} = 441.6 + 359.6(16) = 6,195.2$

**EXHIBIT 6.12**

Least Squares Regression Line

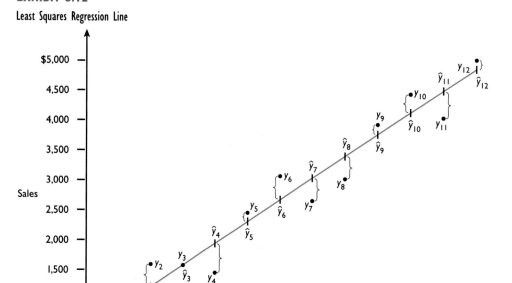

**EXHIBIT 6.13**

Least Squares Regression
Analysis

| (1) X | (2) Y | (3) XY | (4) $X^2$ | (5) $Y^2$ | (6) $\hat{y}$ |
|---|---|---|---|---|---|
| 1 | 600 | 600 | 1 | 360,000 | 801.3 |
| 2 | 1,550 | 3,100 | 4 | 2,402,500 | 1,160.9 |
| 3 | 1,500 | 4,500 | 9 | 2,250,000 | 1,520.5 |
| 4 | 1,500 | 6,000 | 16 | 2,250,000 | 1,880.1 |
| 5 | 2,400 | 12,000 | 25 | 5,760,000 | 2,239.7 |
| 6 | 3,100 | 18,600 | 36 | 9,610,000 | 2,599.4 |
| 7 | 2,600 | 18,200 | 49 | 6,760,000 | 2,959.0 |
| 8 | 2,900 | 23,200 | 64 | 8,410,000 | 3,318.6 |
| 9 | 3,800 | 34,200 | 81 | 14,440,000 | 3,678.2 |
| 10 | 4,500 | 45,000 | 100 | 20,250,000 | 4,037.8 |
| 11 | 4,000 | 44,000 | 121 | 16,000,000 | 4,397.4 |
| 12 | 4,900 | 58,800 | 144 | 24,010,000 | 4,757.1 |
| 78 | 33,350 | 268,200 | 650 | 112,502,500 | |

$\overline{X} = 6.5$

$\overline{Y} = 2,779.17$

$b = 359.6153$

$a = 441.6666$

Therefore:     $Y = 441.66 + 359.6 X$

$S_{YX} = 363.9$ which is the standard error of the estimate

The success of most retail operations, especially restaurants and other food service outlets, has often been attributed to three factors: location, location, and location. Major chains now view site location as a two-stage process: the first involves locating the actual retail operations, the second focuses on locating a central commissary where the initial food preparation takes place.

Bruegger's Bagels, for example, mixes the dough and forms the bagels in its regional commissaries and then ships them to retail outlets where they are boiled and baked in front of customers. On the other hand, Au Bon Pain, a cafe and bakery chain that offers a variety of French breads, croissants, muffins, and other pastries, has decided to use a single central facility to support its approximately 250 Au Bon Pain and Saint Louis Bread locations throughout the United States. Its goods are mixed and formed at the central location and then frozen, to be baked at the retail operations.

The site selection criteria are significantly different for each of the two stages of the site location process. For the retail site the criteria are determined by customer demographics such as average household income, average family size, population density, and automobile and/or pedestrian traffic counts; at the central production facility, the criteria are determined by labor costs, building costs, and distribution costs. ∎

# LOCATING MANUFACTURING FACILITIES

With the continued development of the global marketplace, businesses must take a more international perspective in determining where to locate their manufacturing operations. However, the complexity of the decision-making process increases several fold when a firm decides to shift from a national to an international site location strategy. Typically, with manufacturing, the facility location decision needs to include the location of both the manufacturing operations and the warehouse or distribution facilities. As a general rule, products that decrease in weight and volume during the transformation process tend to be located near sources of raw material. An example of this would be a lumber mill located near a forest. On the other hand, products that increase in weight and volume during the transformation process are usually located near points of consumption. An example of this would be a soft drink bottler located near a city.

In weighing the advantages and disadvantages of alternative sites, the analysis should include an evaluation of both qualitative and quantitative factors.[1]

## Qualitative Factors

The qualitative factors include: (*a*) local infrastructure, (*b*) worker education and skills, (*c*) product content requirements, and (*d*) political/economic stability.

**Local Infrastructure**   The local infrastructure that is necessary to support a manufacturing operation can be divided into two broad categories: institutional and transportational. With manufacturing operations becoming more flexible and responsive to customer requirements, there is a growing dependence on local institutions or suppliers to be more flexible and responsive. In addition the local transportation network that links the suppliers to the manufacturer must be efficient and reliable. For example, a lack of adequate transportation infrastructure in the Former Soviet Union (FSU) or the People's Republic of China would preclude a firm that uses just-in-time (JIT) concepts from locating in these areas.

**Worker Education and Skills**   The increased sophistication of today's manufacturing processes requires that the workforce be highly educated and equipped with a wide variety of skills. Increased emphasis on automation requires specific worker skills to operate and maintain equipment. Modern manufacturing processes like just-in-time (JIT) also require a well-educated workforce. As an illustration, the significant growth of business in Singapore in recent years can be attributed, in large part, to the investment of its government in educating and training its population.

**content requirements**
Requirement that a percentage of a product must be made within a country for it to be sold there.

**Product Content Requirements**   **Content requirements** state that a minimum percentage of a product must be produced within the borders of a country in order for that product to be sold in that country. This assures jobs in the local economy while reducing the difference between imports and exports. For example, for a car to be sold in the Philippines, it must be assembled there. Consequently, each of the major car manufacturers that wants to sell cars in the Philippines has an assembly plant there even though demand for cars in that country is sufficiently small to suggest that importing them would be more economical.

**Political/Economic Stability**   The stability of a region refers to the number and intensity of economic and political fluctuations that might occur there. The dissolution of the Former

---

[1]Alan D. MacCormack, Lawrence J. Newmann, III, and Donald B. Rosenfeld, "The New Dynamics of Global Manufacturing Site Location, *Sloan Management Review*, Summer 1994.

Soviet Union provide ample evidence of the problems associated with locating a business in unstable economies.

## Quantitative Factors

The quantitative factors include: (*a*) labor costs, (*b*) distribution costs, (*c*) facility costs, and (*d*) exchange rates.

 **Labor Costs**   Labor costs can vary dramatically, depending on location. In Western Europe, the United States, and Japan, the cost of labor can exceed US$20.00 per hour in comparison to countries in Asia where the cost can be as low as three or four U.S. dollars per day (see Exhibit 7.1). An important factor that must be considered is the skill requirements of the worker. Although the cost of labor in many areas is very cheap, the workers in these very same regions often lack adequate education and skills.

**Distribution Costs**   As we become more global, distribution and transportation costs take on added importance. In addition to the cost of transportation, the time required to deliver the products must also be taken into consideration. Consequently, in many cases the low costs associated with manufacturing products in Asia are offset by the long lead times and the high cost of delivery to markets in North America and Europe.

**Facility Costs**   Undeveloped or third-world countries often offer incentives in the form of low-cost manufacturing facilities to attract companies. For example, within the People's Republic of China (PRC) many **special economic zones (SEZ)** have been established that are exempt from tariffs and duties—provided that the products made there are sold outside the PRC. In some countries, the local government will enter into a partnership with a firm, with the government providing the land, the building, and perhaps the training of the workforce.

**special economic zones**
Duty-free areas in a country established to attract foreign investment in the form of manufacturing facilities.

**Exchange Rates**   The volatility of the exchange rates between countries can have a significant impact on sales and profits. For example, the change in rates between the Japanese

**EXHIBIT 7.1**

Comparison of 1995 Hourly Wages for Manufacturing Workers

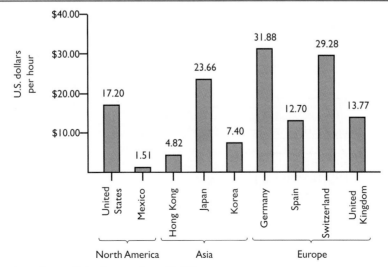

Source: Bureau of Labor Statistics, August 23, 1996.

yen and the U.S. dollar from below 90 yen per dollar to more than 120 yen per dollar between 1996 and 1997 increased the price competitiveness of Japanese products in the United States while decreasing the ability of U.S. products to compete in Japan.

## Plant Location Methods

"If the boss likes Bakersfield, I like Bakersfield." The decisions that a company must make in choosing a location for a manufacturing facility are summarized in Exhibit 7.2. While the exhibit implies a step-by-step process, virtually all activities listed take place simultaneously. As suggested by the preceding vote for Bakersfield, political decisions may occasionally override systematic analysis.

**center of gravity method**
Quantitative approach for determining the location of facilities by minimizing transportation costs.

**factor-rating systems**
Qualitative approach for evaluating site locations.

The evaluation of alternative regions, subregions, and communities is commonly termed *macro analysis,* while the evaluation of specific sites in the selected community is often termed *micro analysis.* One technique used in macro analyses is the **center of gravity method.** This method provides a quantitative approach for determining where to locate a facility based upon minimizing the total transportation costs between where the goods are produced and where they are consumed. A more qualitative technique is **factor-rating systems,** which is described in detail below. A detailed cost analysis would accompany each of these methods.

**EXHIBIT 7.2**

Plant Search: Company XYZ

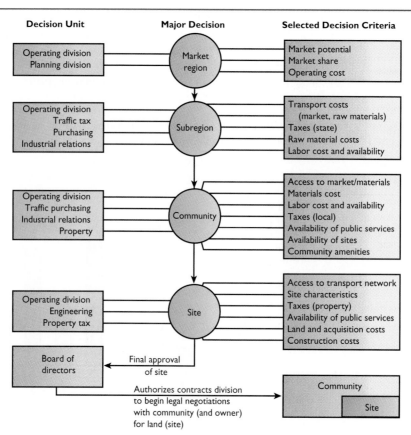

Source: Thomas M. Carroll and Robert D. Dean, "A Bayesian Approach to Plant-Location Decisions," *Decision Sciences* 11, no. 1 (January 1980), p. 87.

**Factor-Rating Systems** Factor-rating systems are perhaps the most widely used of the general location techniques because they provide a mechanism to combine diverse factors in an easy-to-understand format.

By way of example, a refinery assigned the following range of point values to major factors affecting a set of possible sites.

|  | Range |
|---|---|
| Fuels in region | 0 to 330 |
| Power availability and reliability | 0 to 200 |
| Labor climate | 0 to 100 |
| Living conditions | 0 to 100 |
| Transportation | 0 to 50 |
| Water supply | 0 to 10 |
| Climate | 0 to 50 |
| Supplies | 0 to 60 |
| Tax policies and laws | 0 to 20 |

Each site was then rated against each factor, and a point value was selected from its assigned range. The sums of assigned points for each site were then compared, and the site with the maximum number of points was selected.

One of the major problems with simple point-rating schemes is that they do not account for the wide range of costs that may occur within each factor. For example, there may be only a few hundred dollars' difference between the best and worst locations on one factor and several thousands of dollars' difference between the best and the worst on another. The first factor may have the most points available to it, but it provides little help in making the location decision; the latter factor may have few points available but potentially shows a real difference in the value of locations.

Another problem with this approach is that often the values for some of the factors included in the decision analysis are highly subjective, such as the quality of the public education system and the quality of life in a certain location being good examples.

# LOCATING SERVICE OPERATIONS

Within service organizations, the selection of the proper site is also a critical factor. However, unlike manufacturing operations where low production costs are an important consideration in selecting a location, services must focus primarily on customer-driven factors. As stated previously, these factors can include: (*a*) average family income, (*b*) average family size, (*c*) population density, and (*d*) pedestrian and automobile traffic. A manufacturing firm can expand its capacity by just building a larger facility at its current location. In contrast, because services must be located near the customer, the growth of a service business usually requires multiple locations, each focusing on serving a particular geographic market.

Many of the issues manufacturing companies have to address when expanding their operations internationally also must be addressed by service operations. (See the OM in Practice on Toys "R" Us in Japan.) For example, when McDonald's opened its first restaurant in Moscow, the lack of an existing institutional infrastructure to support its operation required that it build a central commissary. This commissary prepared everything for the retail outlet from hamburger patties to rolls and french fries. In addition, the Russian farmers had to be shown how to grow vegetables, such as potatoes and lettuce, that would meet

# Operations Management in Practice

## TOYS "R" US IN JAPAN

Toys "R" Us has successfully entered the Japanese toy market through private-sector help—in this case, with the help of Nintendo.

On December 20, 1991, Toys "R" Us—the world's largest toy retailer—opened its first retail store in Japan. What may now sound like an American success story in Japan traveled a difficult road for two years. The retailer had established locations in Canada, the United Kingdom, Germany, France, Singapore, Hong Kong, Malaysia, and Taiwan well before it attempted to enter the Japanese market.

In January 1990, Toys "R" Us formally applied to open its first (large) toy store in Niigata, Japan. This caused local toy retailers to proclaim their opposition by invoking provisions contained in the Large-Scale Retail Store Act. Then they organized a lobbying group to mobilize support against the American firm. Toys "R" Us appealed for help directly through the U.S. trade representative and other channels. Sustained American political pressure and widespread publicity finally forced MITI to confront the local lobby and limit to 18 months the application process under the restrictive retail law. It was April 1990, and Toys "R" Us had overcome its first major hurdle.

But there was another hurdle to cross. Toys "R" Us succeeds in large part by selling below suggested retail price. It accomplishes this mainly through exploiting economies it obtains through volume purchases. Anticipating the threat posed by that strategy to their own profit margins, Japanese toy manufacturers banded together and vowed not to sell their wares to Toys "R" Us. But Nintendo depends heavily on Toys "R" Us for the distribution of its products in the United States and other major markets. Nintendo's defection triggered an ultimate end to this boycott.

Private sector countermeasures consciously adopted by numerous major Japanese corporations are replacing the falling barriers to entry of public sector regulation.

Source: Mark Mason, "United States Direct Investment in Japan: Trends and Prospects," Copyright © 1992 by The Regents at the University of California. Reprinted from the California Management Review, vol. 35, no. 1 by permission of The Regents.

McDonald's high-quality product specifications. In contrast, the opening of a McDonald's in the United States or Western Europe would only require a call to established, local suppliers.

## Location Strategies

In an effort to better serve customers, service operations have adopted a variety of location strategies, depending on the particular customer requirements they are trying to address. Exhibit 7.3 presents several approaches to satisfying these customer needs.

**EXHIBIT 7.3**

Customer Requirements and Location Strategies for Service Operations

| Customer Requirements | Strategy |
|---|---|
| Customers are hungry because airlines no longer serve food on short flights. | Locate "real" restaurants in airports (Legal Seafoods, Logan Airport, Boston, MA; Sam Adams Atlanta Brewhouse, Hartsfield International Airport, Atlanta, GA). |
| Customers want more convenient locations to save time. | Combine previously separate service operations into one location (Dunkin' Donuts in 7-Eleven; convenience stores with gas stations). |
| Customers are reluctant to shop frequently in large megastores because they are time consuming. | Add other services to increase convenience such as fast food and banking (McDonald's in Wal-Mart; Bank of Boston, and Barnes and Noble Bookstores at Super Stop & Shop Supermarkets). |

Source: Adapted from Hal Reid, "Retailers Seek the Unique," *Business Geographics* 5, no. 2, February 1997, pp. 32–35.

Geographic Information Systems (GIS), shown here from MapInfo, are used by retailers, financial services groups, insurance companies, and utilities in the site selection process. Mapping relevant information on potential sites such as demographics, customers buying patterns, trade areas, competitors, and drive times allows this information to be seen in a single, comprehensive view for more informed and precise decision making.

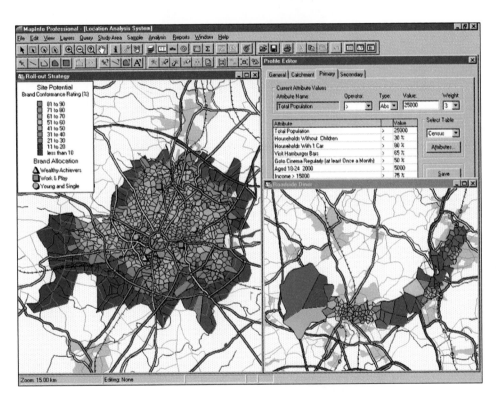

## Computer Programs for Site Selection

**Geographic Information Systems (GIS)**
Computer tool that assesses alternative locations for service operations.

With the growth in **Geographic Information Systems (GIS),** service operations are able to conduct location analysis more quickly and with greater accuracy than was previously possible. GIS allows large databases to be displayed graphically, thereby providing the service manager with a "bird's eye view" of a particular region of interest. These regional maps can display a wide variety of demographic data, depending on the needs of the service manager. (See OM in Practice on Using GIS to Locate Retail Operations.) Exhibit 7.4A, for example, shows the location of housing loans for a bank, including a

**EXHIBIT 7.4**

A. Distribution of a Bank's Housing Loans in an Area

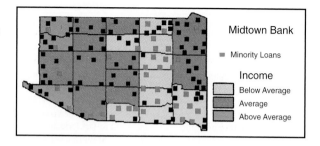

B. Distribution of Sales for a Regional Mall by Area

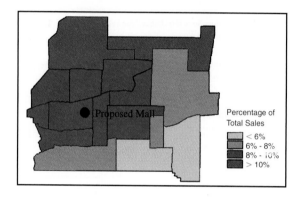

C. Demand for Healthcare in a Region and the Services That Are Available

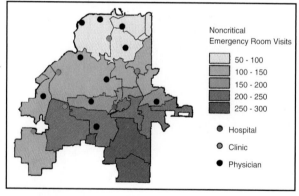

Source: *Getting to Know ArcView GIS* (Redlands, CA: Environmental Systems Research Institute, Inc., 1997).

breakdown by income of the different areas served by the bank. Exhibit 7.4B analyzes the percentage of total sales that would be generated from different areas if a regional mall were to be built. Exhibit 7.4C identifies the gap between the demand for noncritical emergency room visits and the availability of clinics and physicians to meet that demand.

In addition to GIS, there are many nongraphic computer programs available to assist the service manager in evaluating alternative site locations. Many of these models incorporate forecasting techniques like regression analysis which were introduced in the previous chapter.

# Operations Management in Practice

## USING GEOGRAPHICAL INFORMATION SYSTEMS (GIS) TO LOCATE RETAIL OPERATIONS

An analysis of Santa Clara County, California, using a computer-based geographical information system (GIS), indicated that retail operations specializing in child-related merchandise could take advantage of the area's growth in both the short and long term—provided they could obtain retail locations that would follow the path of new housing scheduled to be built to support expansion in Silicon Valley business. Using GIS, the analysis identified specific areas within the county where above average sales in children's toys and apparel are anticipated.

Source: Adapted from Len Strazewski, "Silicon Valley Holds Fertile Kids' Market," *Franchise Times*, February 1997.

---

**EXHIBIT 7.5**

Summary of the Variables That Correlated with Operating Margin in 1983 and 1986

| Variable | 1983 | 1986 |
|----------|------|------|
| ACCESS | .20 | |
| AGE | .29 | .49 |
| COLLEGE | | .25 |
| DISTCBD | | −.22 |
| EMPLYPCT | −.22 | −.22 |
| INCOME | | −.23 |
| MILTOT | | .22 |
| NEAREST | −.51 | |
| OFCCBD | .30 | |
| POPULACE | .30 | .35 |
| PRICE | .38 | .58 |
| RATE | | .27 |
| STATE | −.32 | −.33 |
| SIGNVIS | .25 | |
| TRAFFIC | .32 | |
| URBAN | −.22 | −.26 |

Source: Reprinted by permission of Sheryl E. Kimes and James A. Fitzsimmons, "Selecting Profitable Hotel Sites at La Quinta Motor Inns," *Interfaces* 20 (March–April 1990). Copyright 1990 The Institute of Management Sciences, 290 Westminster Street, Providence, Rhode Island 02903 USA.

## Screening Location Sites at La Quinta Motor Inns

Selecting good sites plays a crucial role in the success of a service operation such as a hotel chain. Of the four major marketing considerations—price, product, promotion, and location—location and product have been shown to be the most important for multisite firms. As a result, hotel chain owners who can pick good sites quickly have a distinct competitive advantage.

Thirty-five variables were identified for inclusion in a study to assist La Quinta Motor Inns in screening potential locations for its new hotels.[2] Data were collected on 57 existing La Quinta Inns. A technique known as *exploratory data analysis* identified 16 variables that correlated with operating profit in 1983 and 1986 (see Exhibit 7.5).

[2]Sheryl E. Kimes and James A. Fitzsimmons, "Selecting Profitable Hotel Sites at La Quinta Motor Inns," *Interfaces* 20 (March–April 1990), pp. 12–20.

A multiple regression model was then constructed and in its final form appears as follows:

Profitability = 39.05 − 5.41 × State population per inn (1,000)
+ 5.86 × Price of the inn
− 3.91 × Square root of the median income of the area (1,000)
+ 1.75 × College students within four miles.

The model shows that profitability is negatively affected by market penetration, positively affected by price, negatively affected by higher incomes (the inns do better in lower median income areas), and positively affected by colleges nearby.

La Quinta implemented the model on a Lotus 1-2-3 spreadsheet and routinely uses the spreadsheet to screen potential real estate acquisitions. The founder and president of La Quinta has accepted the model's validity and no longer feels obligated to personally select the sites.

This example shows how a specific model can be developed from the requirements of a service organization and then be used to identify those features that are most important in making the right site selection. The OM in Practice discusses the expansion criteria and strategies of AM/PM International, a chain of convenience stores.

# CAPACITY DECISIONS

HUMAN RESOURCES
MARKETING

The capacity of the production system defines the firm's competitive boundaries. Specifically, it sets the firm's response rate to the market, its cost structure, its workforce composition, its level of technology, its management and staff support requirements, and its general inventory strategy. If capacity is inadequate, a company may lose customers through slow service or by allowing competitors to enter the market. If capacity is excessive, a company may have to reduce its prices to stimulate demand, underutilize its workforce, carry excess inventory, or seek additional, less profitable products to stay in business.

**Factors Affecting Capacity**   Capacity is affected by both external and internal factors. The external factors include: (a) government regulations (working hours, safety, pollution), (b) union agreements, and (c) supplier capabilities. The internal factors include: (a) product and service design, (b) personnel and jobs (worker training, motivation, learning, job content, and methods), (c) plant layout and process flow, (d) equipment capabilities and maintenance, (e) materials management, (f) quality control systems, and (g) management capabilities.

## Important Capacity Concepts

In service operations we often distinguish between *maximum capacity* and *optimum capacity* because of the customer's direct interaction with the service facility. Christopher Lovelock has identified four different situations that the service manager may encounter in trying to match customer demand with the existing capacity of the operation. These situations, illustrated in Exhibit 7.6, are: (a) demand exceeds maximum capacity causing customers to be turned away, (b) demand exceeds optimum capacity resulting in customers who receive poor service, (c) demand equals optimum capacity, and (d) demand is less than optimum capacity, resulting in idle capacity.

**Best Operating Level**   The *best operating level* is that capacity for which the average unit cost is at a minimum. This is depicted in Exhibit 7.7. Note that as we move down the unit

Green, Timothy J., and Randall P. Sadowski. "A Review of Cellular Manufacturing Assumptions, Advantages and Design Techniques." *Journal of Operations Management* 4, no. 2 (February 1984), pp. 85–97.

Hayes, Robert H., and Steven C. Wheelwright. *Restoring Our Competitive Edge.* New York: John Wiley & Sons, 1984.

Heskett, J. L.; W. E. Sasser, Jr.; and C. W. L. Hart. *Service Breakthroughs: Changing the Rules of the Game.* New York: Free Press, 1990.

Hyer, Nancy Lea. "The Potential of Group Technology for U.S. Manufacturing." *Journal of Operations Management* 4, no. 3 (May 1984), pp. 183–202.

Kimes, Sheryl E., and James A. Fitzsimmons. "Selecting Profitable Hotel Sites at La Quinta Motor Inns." *Interfaces,* March–April 1990, pp. 12–20.

Lovelock, Christopher. "Strategies for Managing Capacity-Constrained Services." *Managing Services: Marketing, Operations Management and Human Resources.* 2nd ed. Englewood Cliffs, NJ: Prentice Hall, 1992.

MacCormack, Alan D.; Lawrence J. Newman, III; and Donald B. Rosenfeld. "The New Dynamics of Global Manufacturing Site Location." *Sloan Management Review,* Summer 1994, pp. 69–80.

Manivannan, S., and Dipak Chudhuri. "Computer-Aided Facility Layout Algorithm Generates Alternatives to Increase Firm's Productivity." *Industrial Engineering,* May 1984.

Mason, Mark. "United States Direct Investment in Japan: Trends and Prospects." *California Management Review,* Fall 1992, pp. 98–115.

Mondon, Yasuhiro, *Toyota Production System, Practical Approach to Production Management.* Atlanta, GA: Industrial Engineering and Management Press, 1983.

Moutinho, Luiz; Bruce Curry; and Fiona Davies. "Comparative Computer Approaches to Multi-Outlet Retail Site Location Decisions." *The Service Industries Journal* 13, no. 4 (October 1993), pp. 201–20.

Reid, Hal. "Retailers Seek the Unique." *Business Geographics* 5, no. 2 (February 1997), pp. 32–35.

Schonberger, Richard J. "The Rationalization of Production." *Proceedings of the 50th Anniversary of the Academy of Management.* Chicago: Academy of Management, 1986, pp. 64–70.

Strazewski, Len. "Silicon Valley Holds Fertile Kids' Market," *Franchise Times,* February 1997.

Tayman, Jeff, and Louis Pol. "Retail Site Selection and Geographic Information Systems." *Journal of Applied Business Research* 11, no. 2, pp. 46–54.

Vannelli, Anthony, and K. Ravi Kumar. "A Method for Finding Minimal Bottleneck Cells for Grouping Part-Machine Families." *International Journal of Production Research* 24, no. 2 (1986), pp. 387–400.

Wheelwright, Steven C., ed. *Capacity Planning and Facilities Choice: Course Module.* Boston: Harvard Business School, 1979.

# WAITING LINE MANAGEMENT

## Chapter Outline

## Chapter Objectives

- Emphasize the importance of providing fast service as a competitive advantage to companies.

- Show the relationship between customer expectations, customer perceptions, and customer satisfaction as they pertain to waiting time.

- Identify the various factors that can affect customer satisfaction with waiting time and provide a framework for showing managers which of these factors are under their control.

- Demonstrate how service managers can design their operations and train their employees to provide faster service without incurring any additional costs.

- Illustrate how technology can assist companies in providing faster service to their customers.

You drive your car into the Hertz rental lot at the West Palm Beach, Florida, airport. As you begin to remove your luggage from the car, a service attendant greets you and asks for a copy of your rental car contract. The attendant quickly enters the contract number into a hand-held terminal, which prints a receipt before you have removed all of your luggage. Without further ado, you board the Hertz bus which takes you to your airline terminal.

At the Marriott Hotel in Newton, Massachusetts, guests who have preregistered can go directly to a self-service key rack to pick up their room keys and then can proceed directly to their rooms without the aggravation of waiting in line at the check-in desk. Guests who want to avoid the hassle of waiting in line to check out at Bally's Hotel in Las Vegas can take advantage of the express check-out feature available on the television in each room. A guest simply follows menu-driven options on the television screen. The final bill is then totaled and charged to the proper credit card. The guest simply deposits the room key in a box on the way out.

These examples illustrate a growing trend among companies in general, and service firms in particular, to provide continually faster service, and in some cases, as noted above, even totally eliminating customer waiting time.  ■

Every day we encounter waiting lines in one form or another. These include the checkout line at the supermarket where we shop or the line in the bank where we conduct our financial transactions. Other examples include the hotel or airline reservation line we wait in when we are placed on hold on the telephone.

Service managers need to properly manage these customer waiting times to ensure both efficiency and that customers are not so negatively affected by the wait that they take their future business elsewhere. To accomplish this, managers need to recognize that good waiting line management consists of two major components: the **actual waiting time** itself and the customer's **perceived waiting time.**

**actual waiting time**
Time, as measured by a stopwatch, of how long a customer has waited prior to receiving service.

**perceived waiting time**
Amount of time customers believe they have waited prior to receiving service.

The determination of actual waiting times is presented in the supplement to this chapter; this supplement focuses on queuing theory and mathematical waiting line models for a variety of service delivery system configurations. The use of these models provides the manager with a framework for managing actual waiting times.

Providing improved levels of customer satisfaction through the management of the customer's perceived waiting time is the primary focus of this chapter. Understanding how customer satisfaction can be improved for a given waiting time provides service managers with an opportunity for managing their operations more effectively.

## THE IMPORTANCE OF GOOD SERVICE

As stated previously in Chapter 2, those companies in both manufacturing and service operations that provide outstanding service to their customers can achieve a competitive advantage in the marketplace in the 1990s. And good service begins when the customer first comes in contact with an organization and waits in some type of line or queue prior to being served. There are many factors that contribute to good service, such as the friendliness and knowledge of workers, but customers' experiences with waiting lines, which are often their initial encounter with a firm, can significantly affect their overall level of satisfaction with the organization.

Providing ever-faster service, with the ultimate goal of having zero customer waiting time, has recently received managerial attention for several reasons. First, in the more highly developed countries, where standards of living are rising, time becomes more valuable as a commodity and, consequently, customers are less willing to wait for service. As a result, customers in many cases, are willing to pay a premium price to those firms that minimize their waiting time. (See OM in Practice Box on Time Is Money at Disney's Theme Parks.)

Another reason for this increased emphasis on providing fast and efficient service to customers is the realization by organizations that how they treat their customers today significantly impacts on whether or not they will remain loyal customers tomorrow. This differs from the past, when the treatment of customers in the present was viewed to be independent of any potential future sales. This attitude by management has persisted because the impact of future customer behavior does not appear anywhere on the firm's financial statements.

Finally, advances in technology, especially in information technology, have provided firms with the ability to provide faster service than was previously possible. Fax machines, e-mail, and satellite communications provide firms with this new capability to respond faster to the customer.

In providing fast service, however, the real goal of service managers should not be to ensure that customers are served within a specified time (e.g., a stated number of minutes), but rather to ensure that customers are sufficiently satisfied with the level of service provided so that they will want to return in the future.

What causes waiting lines in the first place? Whenever there is more than one user of a limited resource, a waiting line or queue forms. This delay phenomenon occurs in a wide range of activities affecting many types of users and resources.

In this supplement we discuss the basic elements of waiting line problems and provide standard steady-state formulas for solving them. These formulas, arrived at in the course of developing queuing theory, enable planners to analyze service requirements and establish service facilities appropriate to stated conditions. Queuing theory is broad enough to cover such dissimilar delays as those encountered by customers in a shopping mall or by aircraft awaiting landing slots.

Queuing theory is used extensively in both manufacturing and service environments, and is a standard tool of operations management in areas such as, service delivery system design, scheduling, and machine loading.

# WAITING LINE CHARACTERISTICS

 The waiting line (or queuing) phenomenon consists essentially of six major components: (*a*) the source population, (*b*) the way customers arrive at the service facility, (*c*) the physical line itself, (*d*) the way customers are selected from the line, (*e*) the characteristics of the service facility itself (such as how the customers flow through the system and how much time it takes to serve each customer), and (*f*) the condition of the customers exiting the system (back to the source population or not?). These six elements, shown in Exhibit S8.1, are discussed separately in the following sections.

## Population Source

Arrivals at a service system may be drawn from either a *finite* or an *infinite* population. The distinction is important because the analyses are based on different premises and require different equations for their solution.

**Finite Population**   A *finite population* refers to the limited size of the customer pool which is the source that will use the service, and at times form a line.The reason this finite classification is important is because when a customer leaves his/her position as a member of the population of users, the size of the user group is reduced by one, which reduces the probability of a customer requiring service. Conversely, when a customer is serviced and returns to the user group, the population increases and the probability of a user requiring service also increases. This finite class of problems requires a separate set of formulas from that of the infinite population case.

**EXHIBIT S8.1**

Framework for Viewing Waiting Line Situations

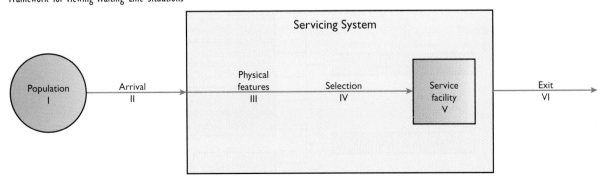

**Infinite Population**    An infinite population is one that is sufficiently large in relation to the service system, that any changes in the population size caused by subtractions or additions to the population (e.g., a customer needing service or a serviced customer returning to the population) does not significantly affect the system probabilities. If, for example, there were 100 machines that were maintained by one repairperson, and one or two machines broke down and required service, the probabilities for the next breakdowns would not be very different and the assumption could be made without a great deal of error that the population, for all practical purposes, was infinite. Nor would the formulas for "infinite" queuing problems cause much error if applied to a physician who has 1,000 patients, or a department store that has 10,000 customers.

 ## Arrival Characteristics

Another determinant in the analysis of waiting line problems is the *arrival characteristics* of the queue members. As shown in Exhibit S8.2, there are four main descriptors of arrivals: the *pattern of arrivals* (whether arrivals are controllable or uncontrollable); the *size of arrival units* (whether they arrive one at a time or in batches); the *distribution pattern* (whether the time between arrivals is constant or follows a statistical distribution such as a Poisson, exponential, or Erlang); and the *degree of patience* (whether the arrival stays in line or leaves). We describe each of these in more detail.

**Arrival Patterns**    The arrivals at a system are far more *controllable* than is generally recognized. Barbers may decrease their Saturday arrival rate (and hopefully shift it to other days of the week) by charging an extra $1 for adult haircuts or charging adult prices for children's haircuts. Department stores run sales during the off season or one-day-only sales in part for purposes of control. Airlines offer excursion and off-season rates for similar reasons. The simplest of all arrival-control devices is the posting of business hours.

Some service demands are clearly *uncontrollable,* such as emergency medical demands on a city's hospital facilities. However, even in these situations, the arrivals at emergency rooms in specific hospitals are controllable to some extent by, say, keeping ambulance drivers in the service region informed of the status of their respective host hospitals.

**Size of Arrival Units**    A *single arrival* may be thought of as one unit (a unit is the smallest number handled). A single arrival on the floor of the New York Stock Exchange (NYSE)

**EXHIBIT S8.2**

Arrival Characteristics in Queues

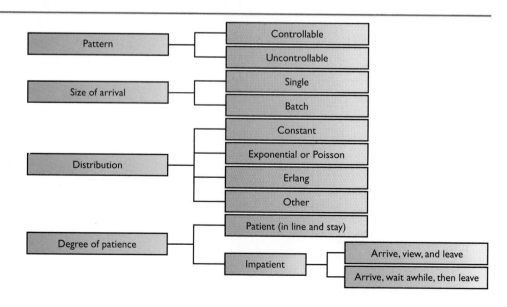

is 100 shares of stock; a single arrival at an egg-processing plant might be a dozen eggs or a flat of two and a half dozen.

A *batch arrival* is some multiple of the unit, as a block of 1,000 shares on the NYSE, a case of eggs at the processing plant, or a party of five at a restaurant.

**arrival rate**
Rate at which customers arrive into a service delivery system, usually expressed in terms of customers per hour.

**Distribution of Arrivals**   Waiting line formulas generally require an **arrival rate,** or the average number of customers or units per time period (e.g., 10 per hour). The time between arrivals is the interarrival time (such as an average of one every six minutes). A *constant* arrival distribution is periodic, with exactly the same time period between successive arrivals. In production processes, probably the only arrivals that truly approach a constant interarrival period are those that are subject to machine control. Much more common are *variable* random arrival distributions. The variable or random distribution patterns that occur most frequently in system models are described by the *negative exponential, Poisson,* or *Erlang* distributions.

**Degree of Patience**   A *patient* arrival is one who waits as long as necessary until the service facility is ready to serve him or her. (Even if arrivals grumble and behave impatiently, the fact that they wait is sufficient to label them as patient arrivals for purposes of waiting line theory.)

There are two classes of *impatient* arrivals. Members of the first class arrive, survey both the service facility and the length of the line, and then decide to leave. Those in the second class arrive, view the situation, and join the waiting line, and then, after some period of time, depart. The behavior of the first type is termed *balking,* and the second is termed *reneging.*

 ## Physical Features of Lines

**Length**   In a practical sense, an infinite line is very long in terms of the capacity of the service system. Examples of *infinite potential length* are a line of vehicles backed up for miles at a bridge crossing and customers who must form a line around the block as they wait to purchase tickets at a theater.

Gas stations, loading docks, and parking lots have *limited line capacity* caused by legal restrictions or physical space characteristics. This complicates the waiting line problem not only in service system utilization and waiting line computations but also in the shape of the actual arrival distribution as well. The arrival denied entry into the line because of lack of space may rejoin the population at a later time or may seek service elsewhere. Either action makes an obvious difference in the finite population case.

**Number of Lines**   A *single line* or single file is, of course, one line only. The term *multiple lines* refers either to the single lines that form in front of two or more servers or to single lines that converge at some central redistribution point.

### Customer Selection

**Queuing Discipline**   A queuing discipline is a priority rule, or set of rules (some of which are listed in Exhibit S8.3), for determining the order of service to customers in a waiting line. The rules selected can have a dramatic effect on the system's overall performance. The number of customers in line, the average waiting time, the range of variability in waiting time, and the efficiency of the service facility are just a few of the factors affected by the choice of priority rules.

Probably the most common priority rule, particularly in service operations, is *first come, first served* (FCFS), also known as first in, first out (FIFO). This rule states that the customers in line are served on the basis of their chronological arrival; no other characteristics have any bearing on the selection process. This is popularly accepted as the fairest rule, even though in practice, it discriminates against the arrival requiring a short service time.

**EXHIBIT S8.3**

Factors in a Queuing Discipline

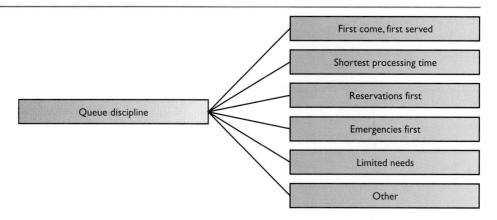

*Reservations first, emergencies first, highest-profit customer first, largest orders first, best customers first, longest waiting time in line,* and *soonest promised date* are other examples of priority rules. Each has its advantages as well as its shortcomings.

Directives such as "single transactions only" (as in a bank) or "cash only" express lanes (as in a supermarket) seem similar to priority rules, but in reality they are methodologies for structuring the line itself. Such lines are formed to serve a specific class of customers with similar characteristics. Within each line, however, priority rules still apply (as before) to the method of selecting the next customer to be served. A classic case of line structuring is the supermarket with the fast checkout line for customers with 12 items or less.

 ## Service Facility Structure

Several types of service facility structures are presented in Exhibit S8.4, four of which are discussed in detail in the following sections. The physical flow of items or customers to be serviced may go through a single line, multiple lines, or some combination of the two. The choice of format depends partly on the volume of customers served, partly on physical constraints, and partly on the restrictions imposed by sequential requirements governing the order in which the service must be performed.

**Single Channel, Single Phase**   This is the simplest type of waiting line structure, and straightforward formulas are available to solve the problem for standard distribution patterns of arrival and service. When the distributions are nonstandard, the problem is easily solved by computer simulation. A typical example of a single-channel, single-phase situation is the one-person barbershop.

**Single Channel, Multiphase**   A car wash is an illustration for a series of services—vacuuming, wetting, washing, rinsing, drying, window cleaning, and parking—performed in a fairly uniform sequence. A critical factor in the single-channel case with service in series is the amount of buildup of items allowed in front of each service, which in turn constitutes separate waiting lines.

Because of the inherent variability in service times, the optimal situation in maximizing the use of the service station is to allow an infinite waiting line to build in front of each station. The worst situation is that in which no line is permitted and only one customer at a time is allowed. When no sublines are allowed to build up in front of each station, as in a car wash, the use of the overall service facility is governed by the probability that a long service time will be required by any one of the servers in the system. This problem is common in most product-oriented systems, such as assembly lines.

**Multichannel, Single Phase**   Tellers' windows in a bank and checkout counters in supermarkets and high-volume department stores exemplify this type of structure. The difficulty

**EXHIBIT S8.4**

A Service Facility's Structure

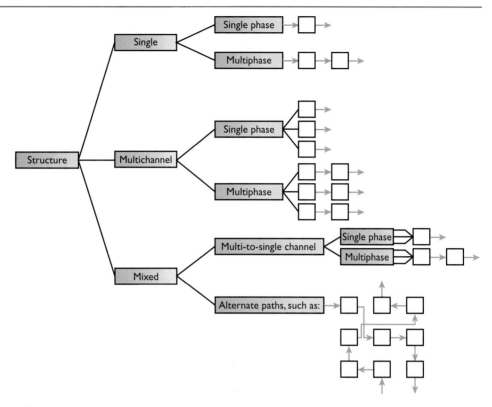

with this format is that the uneven service time given each customer results in unequal speed or flow among the lines. This results in some customers being served before others who arrived earlier as well as in some degree of line shifting. Varying this structure to assure the servicing of arrivals in chronological order would require forming a single line, from which, as a server becomes available, the next customer in the queue is assigned. This type of line structure is now commonly used at airport ticket counters and banks.

**Multichannel, Multiphase**    This case is similar to the preceding one except that two or more services are performed in sequence. The admission of patients in a hospital follows this pattern because a specific sequence of steps is usually followed: initial contact at the admissions desk, filling out forms, making identification tags, obtaining a room assignment, escorting the patient to the room, and so forth. Since several servers are usually available for this procedure, more than one patient at a time may be processed.

**service rate**
Capacity of a service station, usually expressed in terms of customers per hour. The reciprocal of the service rate is the average time to serve a customer.

**Service Rate**    Waiting line formulas generally define **service rate** as the capacity of the server in number of units per time period (such as 12 completions per hour) and *not* as service time, which might average five minutes each. A *constant* service time rule states that each service takes exactly the same time. As in constant arrivals, this characteristic is generally limited to machine-controlled operations. As with arrival rates, Erlang and hyperexponential distributions represent variable service times.

A frequently used illustration of the *Erlang* distribution employs a single-channel, multiservice situation. However, the conditions that must be met for the Erlang approximation are so severe that practical application is rare.

The *exponential* distribution is frequently used to approximate the actual service distribution. This practice, however, may lead to incorrect results; few service situations are exactly represented by the exponential function since the service facility must be able to perform services much shorter than the average time of service.

Most other services also have some practical minimum time. A clerk in a checkout line may have a three-minute average service time but a one-minute minimum time. This is particularly true where another checkout aisle provides a quick service. Likewise in a barbershop, while the average service time may be 20 minutes, a barber rarely cuts hair or gives a shave in fewer than 10 or more than 45 minutes. Hence, these and similar types of services that have strong time dependency are poorly characterized by the exponential curve.

**capacity utilization**
Percentage of time a service station is busy serving a customer.

**Capacity Utilization**    The percentage of time that a service station is busy attending to the needs of a customer is referred to as the **capacity utilization** of that station. This is the percentage of time that the station is busy. The remainder of the time there are no customers to be waited on and the station is, therefore, considered to be idle. In single channel service systems, the capacity utilization is simply the ratio of the arrival rate to the service rate. For example, if customers arrive into a system at the rate of eight per hour and the service rate is 12 customers per hour, then the capacity utilization of this service station is 8/12 or 66.7 percent. It is important to note that in determining the capacity utilization for a station both the arrival rate and the service rate must be expressed in the same units.

## Exit

Once a customer is served, two exit scenarios are possible: (*a*) the customer may return to the source population and immediately become a competing candidate for service again or (*b*) there may be a low probability of reservice. The first case can be illustrated by a machine that has been routinely repaired and returned to duty but may break down again; the second can be illustrated by a machine that has been overhauled or modified and has a low probability of reservice over the near future. We might refer to the first as the "recurring-common-cold case" and to the second as the "appendectomy-only-once case."

It should be apparent that when the population source is finite, any change in the service performed on customers who return to the population modifies the arrival rate at the service facility. This, of course, alters the characteristics of the waiting line under study and necessitates reanalysis of the problem.

---

**EXHIBIT S8.5**

Properties of Some Specific Waiting Line Models

| Model | Layout | Service Phase | Source Population | Arrival Pattern | Queue Discipline | Service Pattern | Permissible Queue Length | Typical Example |
|---|---|---|---|---|---|---|---|---|
| 1 | Single channel | Single | Infinite | Poisson | FCFS | Exponential | Unlimited | Drive-in teller at bank, one-lane toll bridge |
| 2 | Single channel | Single | Infinite | Poisson | FCFS | Constant | Unlimited | Roller coaster rides in amusement park |
| 3 | Single channel | Single | Infinite | Poisson | FCFS | Exponential | Limited | Ice cream stand, cashier in a restaurant |
| 4 | Single channel | Single | Infinite | Poisson | FCFS | Discrete distribution | Unlimited | Empirically derived distribution of flight time for a transcontinental flight |
| 5 | Single channel | Single | Infinite | Poisson | FCFS | Erlang | Unlimited | One-person barbershop |
| 6 | Multi-channel | Single | infinite | Poisson | FCFS | Exponential | Unlimited | Parts counter in auto agency, two-lane toll bridge |

$120 per day. Unit II, a larger unit, can wash cars at the rate of one every four minutes but costs $160 per day. Unit III, the largest, cost $220 per day and can wash a car in three minutes.

The franchisee estimates that customers will not wait in line more than five minutes for a car wash. A longer time will cause Robot to lose both gasoline sales and car wash sales.

If the estimate of customer arrivals resulting in washes is 10 per hour, which wash unit should be selected?

**Solution**  Using Unit I, calculate the average waiting time of customers in the wash line ($\mu$ for Unit I = 12 per hour). From the Model 2 equations (Exhibit S8.6),

$$\bar{t}_l = \frac{\lambda}{2\mu(\mu - \lambda)} = \frac{10}{2(12)(12 - 10)} = 0.208 \text{ hour, or } 12\tfrac{1}{2} \text{ minutes}$$

For Unit II at 15 per hour,

$$\bar{t}_l = \frac{10}{2(15)(15 - 10)} = 0.067 \text{ hour, or 4 minutes}$$

If waiting time is the only criterion, Unit II should be purchased. However, before we make the final decision, we must look at the profit differential between both units.

With Unit I, some customers would balk or renege because of the 12½-minute wait. And although this greatly complicates the mathematical analysis, we can gain some estimate of lost sales with Unit I by inserting $\bar{t}_l = 5$ minutes or $\tfrac{1}{12}$ hour (the average length of time customers will wait) and solving for $\lambda$. This would be the effective arrival rate of customers:

$$\bar{t}_l = \frac{\lambda}{2\mu(\mu - \lambda)}$$

$$\lambda = \frac{2\bar{t}_l\mu^2}{1 + 2\bar{t}_l\mu}$$

$$\lambda = \frac{2(1/12)(12)^2}{1 + 2(1/12)(12)} = 8 \text{ per hour}$$

Therefore, since the original estimate of $\lambda$ was 10 per hour, an estimated two customers per hour will be lost. Lost profit of two customers per hour × 14 hours × ½ ($7.00 fill-up profit + $4.00 wash profit) = $154.00 per day.

Because the additional cost of Unit II over Unit I is only $40 per day, the loss of $154.00 profit obviously warrants the installation of Unit II.

The original constraint of a five-minute maximum wait is satisfied by Unit II. Therefore, Unit III is not considered unless the arrival rate is expected to increase in the future.

# COMPUTER SIMULATION OF WAITING LINES

Some waiting line problems that seem very simple on first impression turn out to be extremely difficult or impossible to solve. Throughout this chapter we have been treating waiting line situations that are independent; that is, either the entire system consists of a single phase, or else each service that is performed in a series is independent. (This could happen if the output of one service location is allowed to build up in front of the next one so that this, in essence, becomes a calling population for the next service.) When a series of services is performed in sequence where the output rate of one becomes the input rate of the next, we can no longer use the simple formulas. This is also true for any problem where conditions do not meet the conditions of the equations, as specified in Exhibit S8.7. The analytical technique best suited for solving this type of problem is computer simulation.

## CONCLUSION

Waiting line problems present both a challenge and a frustration to those who try to solve them. One of the main concerns in dealing with waiting line problems is what procedure or priority rule to use in selecting the next product or customer to be served.

Many queuing problems appear simple until an attempt is made to solve them. This supplement has dealt with the simpler problems. When the situation becomes more complex, such as when there are multiple phases and/or where services are performed only in a particular sequence, computer simulation is usually necessary to obtain the optimal solution.

## KEY TERMS

arrival rate   p. 293                                    service rate   p. 295
capacity utilization   p. 296

## REVIEW AND DISCUSSION QUESTIONS

1. How many waiting lines did you encounter during your last airline flight?
2. Distinguish between a *channel* and a *phase.*
3. Which assumptions are necessary to employ the formulas given for Model 1?
4. In what way might the first-come, first-served rule be unfair to the customers waiting for service in a bank or hospital?
5. Identify the various types of waiting lines you encounter in a "normal" day.

## SOLVED PROBLEMS

### Problem 1

Quick Lube, Inc. operates a fast lube and oil change garage. On a typical day, customers arrive at the rate of three per hour, and lube jobs are performed at an average rate of one every 15 minutes. The mechanics operate as a team on one car at a time.

Assuming Poisson arrivals and exponential service, determine the:

*a.* Utilization of the lube team.

*b.* Average number of cars in line.

*c.* Average time a car waits before it is lubed.

*d.* Total time it takes a car to go through the sytem (i.e., waiting in line plus lube time).

*Solution*

$\lambda = 3$, $\mu = 4$

*a.* Utilization $(\rho) = \dfrac{\lambda}{\mu} = \dfrac{3}{4} = 75\%$.

*b.* $\bar{n}_1 = \dfrac{\lambda^2}{\mu(\mu - \lambda)} = \dfrac{3^2}{4(4 - 3)} = \dfrac{9}{4} = 2.25$ cars in line.

c. $\bar{t}_l = \dfrac{\lambda}{\mu(\mu - \lambda)} = \dfrac{3}{4(4-3)} = \dfrac{3}{4} = .75$ hour $= 45$ minutes in line.

d. $\bar{t}_s = \dfrac{1}{\mu - \lambda} = \dfrac{1}{1} = 1$ hour (waiting $+$ lube).

### Problem 2

American Vending Inc. (AVI) supplies vended food to a large university. Because students kick the machines at every opportunity out of anger and frustration, management has a constant repair problem. The machines break down on an average of three per hour, and the breakdowns are distributed in a Poisson manner. Downtime costs the company $25/hour per machine, and each maintenance worker gets $4 per hour. One worker can service machines at an average rate of five per hour, distributed exponentially; two workers, working together, can service seven per hour, distributed exponentially; and a team of three workers can do eight per hour, distributed exponentially.

What is the optimum maintenance crew size for servicing the machines?

*Solution*

American Vending Inc.

*Case I: One worker.*

$$\lambda = 3/\text{hour Poisson}, \mu = 5/\text{hour exponential}$$

The average number of machines (either broken down or being repaired) in the system is:

$$\bar{n}_s = \frac{\lambda}{\mu - \lambda} = \frac{3}{5 - 3} = \frac{3}{2} = 1\frac{1}{2} \text{ machines}$$

Downtime cost is $25 \times 1.5 = \$37.50$ per hour; repair cost is $4.00 per hour; and total cost per hour for 1 worker is $37.50 + \$4.00 = \$41.50$.

$$\text{Downtime } (1.5 \times \$25) = \$37.50$$
$$\text{Labor } (1 \text{ worker} \times \$4) = \underline{\phantom{00}4.00}$$
$$\$41.50$$

*Case II: Two workers.*

$$\lambda = 3, \mu = 7$$

$$\bar{n}_s = \frac{\lambda}{\mu - \lambda} = \frac{3}{7 - 3} = 0.75 \text{ machines}$$

$$\text{Downtime } (0.75 \times \$25) \quad = \$18.75$$
$$\text{Labor } (2 \text{ workers} \times \$4.00) = \underline{\phantom{0}8.00}$$
$$\$26.75$$

*Case III: Three workers.*

$$\lambda = 3, \mu = 8$$

$$\bar{n}_s = \frac{\lambda}{\mu - \lambda} = \frac{3}{8 - 3} = \frac{3}{5} = 0.60 \text{ machines}$$

$$\text{Downtime } (0.60 \times \$25) \quad = \$15.00$$
$$\text{Labor } (3 \text{ workers} \times \$4.00) = \underline{12.00}$$
$$\$27.00$$

Comparing the costs for one, two, or three workers, we see that Case II with two workers is the optimal decision.

## PROBLEMS

1. Burrito King is a new fast-food franchise that is opening up nationwide. Burrito King has been successful in automating burrito production for its drive-up fast-food establishments. The Burro-Master 9000 requires a constant 45 seconds to produce a burrito (with any of the standard fillings). It has been estimated that customers will arrive at the drive-up window according to a Poisson distribution at an average of 1 every 50 seconds.

    a. What is the expected average time in the system?

    b. To help determine the amount of space (in terms of number of cars) needed for the line at the drive-up window, Burrito King would like to know the average line length (in cars) and the average number of cars in the system (both in line and at the window).

2. Big Jack's drive-through hamburger service is planning to build another stand at a new location and must decide how much land to lease to optimize returns. Leased space for cars will cost $1,000 per year per space. Big Jack is aware of the highly competitive nature of the quick-food service industry and knows that if his drive-through is full, customers will go elsewhere. The location under consideration has a potential customer arrival rate of 30 per hour (Poisson). Customers' orders are filled at the rate of 40 per hour (exponential) since Big Jack prepares food ahead of time. The average profit on each arrival is $0.60, and the stand is open from noon to midnight every day. How many spaces for cars should be leased?

3. To support National Heart Week, the Heart Association plans to install a free blood pressure testing booth in El Con Mall for the week. Previous experience indicates that, on the average, 10 persons per hour request a test. Assume arrivals are Poisson from an infinite population. Blood pressure measurements can be made at a constant time of five minutes each. Assume the queue length can be infinite with FCFS discipline.

    a. What is the average number of persons that can be expected to be in line?

    b. What is the average number of persons that can be expected to be in the system?

    c. What is the average amount of time that a person can expect to spend in line?

    d. On the average, how much time will it take to measure a person's blood pressure, including waiting time?

    e. On weekends, the arrival rate can be expected to increase to nearly 12 per hour. What effect will this have on the number in the waiting line?

4. A cafeteria serving line has a coffee urn from which customers serve themselves. Arrivals at the urn follow a Poisson distribution at the rate of three per minute. In serving themselves, customers take about 15 seconds, exponentially distributed.

    a. How many customers would you expect to see on the averge at the coffee urn?

    b. How long would you expect it to take to get a cup of coffee?

    c. What percentage of time is the urn being used?

    d. What is the probability that there would be three or more people in the cafeteria?

    If the cafeteria installs an automatic vendor that dispenses a cup of coffee at a constant time of 15 seconds, how does this change your answers to *a* and *b*?

5. L. Winston Martin is an allergist in Tuscon who has an excellent system for handling his regular patients who come in just for allergy injections. Patients arrive for an injection and fill out a name slip, which is then placed in an open slot that passes into another room staffed by one or two nurses. The specific injections for a patient are prepared and the patient is called through a speaker system into the room to receive the injection. At certain times during the day, the patient load drops and only one nurse is needed to administer the injections.

    Let's focus on the simpler case, when there is one nurse. Also assume that patients arrive in a Poisson fashion and the service rate of the nurse is exponentially distributed. During this slower period, patients arrive with an interarrival time of approximately three minutes. It takes the nurse an average of two minutes to prepare the patients' serum and administer the injection.

*a.* What is the average number you would expect to see in Dr. Martin's facilities?

*b.* How long would it take for a patient to arrive, get an injection, and leave?

*c.* What is the probability that there will be three or more patients on the premises?

*d.* What is the utilization of the nurse?

6. The NOL Income Tax Service is analyzing its customer service operations during the month prior to the April 15 filing deadline. On the basis of past data it has been estimated that customers arrive according to a Poisson process with an average interarrival time of 12 minutes. The time to complete a return for a customer is exponentially distributed with a mean of 10 minutes. Based on this information, answer the following questions.

*a.* If you went to NOL, how much time would you allow for getting your return done?

*b.* On average, how much room should be allowed for the waiting area?

*c.* If the NOL service were operating 12 hours per day, how many hours on average, per day, would the office be busy?

*d.* What is the probability that the system is idle?

*e.* If the arrival rate remained unchanged but the average time in the system must be 45 minutes or less, what would need to be changed?

*f.* A robotic replacement has been developed for preparing the new "simplified" tax forms. If the service time became a constant nine minutes, what would total time in the system become?

7. The law firm of Larry, Darryl and Darryl (L,D & D) specialize in the practice of waste disposal law. They are interested in analyzing their caseload. Data were collected on the number of cases they received in a year and the times to complete each case. They consider themselves a dedicated firm and will only take on one case at a time. Calls for their services apparently follow a Poisson process with a mean of one case every 30 days. Given the fact that L,D & D are outstanding in their field, clients will wait for their turn and are served on a first come, first served basis. The data on the number of days to complete each case for the last 10 cases are 27, 26, 26, 25, 27, 24, 27, 23, 22, and 23.

Determine the average time for L,D & D to complete a case, the average number of clients waiting, and the average wait for each client.

## SELECTED BIBLIOGRAPHY

Bartfai, P., and J. Tomko. *Point Processes Queuing Problems.* New York: Elsevier-North Holland Publishing, 1981.

Bruell, Steven C. *Computational Algorithms for Closed Queuing Networks.* New York: Elsevier-North Holland Publishing, 1980.

Cooper, Robert B. *Introduction to Queuing Theory.* 2nd ed. New York: Elsevier-North Holland Publishing, 1980.

Gorney, Leonard. *Queuing Theory: A Solving Approach.* Princeton, NJ: Petrocelli, 1981.

Griffin, Walter C. *Queuing: Basic Theory and Application.* Columbus, OH: Grid, 1978.

Hillier, Frederick S., et al. *Queuing Tables and Graphs.* New York: Elsevier-North Holland Publishing, 1981.

Newell, Gordon F. *Applications of Queuing Theory.* New York: Chapman and Hall, 1982.

_____. *Approximate Behavior of Tandem Queues.* New York: Springer-Verlag, 1980.

Solomon, Susan L. *Simulation of Waiting Lines.* Englewood Cliffs, NJ: Prentice Hall, 1983.

Srivastava, H. M., and B. R. Kashyap. *Special Functions in Queuing Theory: And Related Stochastic Processes.* New York: Academic Press, 1982.

Vinrod, B., and T. Altiok. "Approximating Unreliable Queuing Networks under the Assumption of Exponentiality." *Journal of the Operational Research Society* (March 1986), pp. 309–16.

# HUMAN RESOURCES ISSUES IN OPERATIONS MANAGEMENT

## Chapter Objectives

- Explain the role of an organization's human resources in providing high-quality goods and services and in maintaining a competitive advantage in the marketplace.

- Describe the changing role of the manager from command and control to team leader and coach, and the critical skills required for this emerging role.

- Define the concept of employee empowerment and demonstrate its impact on management and the organization.

- Distinguish between traditional work groups, self-managed teams, and cross-functional teams.

- Introduce behavioral and physical factors that should be taken into consideration when designing jobs.

**"W**e Are Ladies and Gentlemen Serving Ladies and Gentlemen" is the motto of The Ritz-Carlton Hotel Company, L.L.C. which won the Malcolm Baldrige National Quality Award in 1992. In order to provide superior service to its hotel guests, Ritz-Carlton starts with a recruitment process that identifies those potential employees that have the personal characteristics necessary to succeed. Upon being selected, each employee goes through an in-depth orientation, followed by extensive on-the-job training and job certification. Every employee receives a card with the company's credo on it and is expected to learn the credo and practice it daily on the job. The values of Ritz-Carlton are continuously reinforced on a daily basis through "line-ups," frequent employee recognition for extraordinary achievement, and a performance appraisal based on specific expectations. To ensure that problems are resolved quickly, workers are required to act at the first notice of a customer complaint, regardless of the type of problem. *Every* employee is empowered to take whatever action is necessary when a guest is dissatisfied. Consequently, much of the responsibility for ensuring high-quality guest services and accommodations rests with employees. ▪

> *"We Are Ladies and Gentlemen Serving Ladies and Gentlemen"*

THE RITZ-CARLTON

**CREDO**

The Ritz-Carlton Hotel is a place where the genuine care and comfort of our guests is our highest mission.

We pledge to provide the finest personal service and facilities for our guests who will always enjoy a warm, relaxed yet refined ambience.

The Ritz-Carlton experience enlivens the senses, instills well-being, and fulfills even the unexpressed wishes and needs of our guests.

Source: Adapted from "Profiles of Winners of the Malcolm Baldrige National Quality Award." Photo: 1992 The Ritz-Carlton Hotel Company. All rights reserved. Reprinted with permission of The Ritz-Carlton Hotel Company, L. L. C.

As suggested by how the Ritz-Carlton treats its employees and the direct impact this treatment has on the high level of service provided to its guests, the role of workers has changed dramatically in recent years. This trend is expected to continue into the foreseeable future. In fact, both manufacturing and service operations today face more rapid and radical organizational changes than they have at any time since World War II. In order to remain competitive, today's organizations, as we previously discussed, must simultaneously focus on a wide range of issues to better meet the increasing demands of their customers. These issues include increasing quality, decreasing delivery time, and customizing products. Organizations must introduce new technologies, concentrate on process improvements and reengineering, increase efficiency, and create new organizational structures to succeed in an increasingly competitive and global marketplace. However, an organization's ability to first attain and then maintain world-class status in the manufacture of goods and the delivery of services depends on more than the introduction of new technologies and processes. It also depends on the activities of a trained and motivated workforce. In fact, the ability of managers to effectively manage the workforce has been shown to be three times more powerful than all other factors combined in accounting for the financial success of a firm when measured over a five-year period.[1]

The effective management of an organization's human resources is a very broad topic that cannot be covered adequately in one textbook, let alone one chapter. The purpose of this chapter, therefore, is to introduce you to several issues and emerging trends that organizations and managers must consider with respect to today's workforce and the ever changing, competitive environment that currently exists. These issues include the new managerial role, the growing emphasis on groups and teams to accomplish organizational tasks, and the new approaches to work design.

## THE NEW MANAGERIAL ROLE

Managers in today's organizations face a rapidly changing and often unpredictable environment. Large-scale corporate restructuring, layoffs (or "downsizing"), and mergers and acquisitions mean that today's managers must identify new ways to produce more with fewer workers and fewer organizational layers. Attempts to create more profitable, "lean and mean" organizations have resulted in an unexpected byproduct: a sharp decline in perceptions of loyalty between the employee and the organization. In 1993, for example, 77 percent of workers surveyed said that companies were less loyal to employees than five years before. In addition, sixty percent of these workers judged that employees were less loyal to the organization.[2] As a consequence, today's managers are challenged to motivate employees who may feel less commitment to their organizations than was previously the norm.

The processes and technologies used to accomplish work are also changing, requiring managers to change with them. Total Quality Management, for example, emphasizes employee involvement. It also requires managers to assist workers in learning how to take responsibility for their work, and it requires managers to view workers from a new perspective, that of partners in the decision-making process rather than subordinates. No

[1]Gary Hanson, "Determinants of Firm Performance: An Integration of Economic and Organizational Factors" (Ph.D. diss., University of Michigan) cited in David A. Cameron and Kim S. Whetten, *Developing Manager Skills,* 3rd ed. (New York, Harper Collins, 1995).

[2]B. B. Moskal, "Company Loyalty Dies, a Victim of Neglect," *Industry Week,* March 1, 1993.

# KEY TERMS

cross-functional work teams    p. 314                self-managed work teams    p. 313
job design    p. 316                                 specialization of labor    p. 318
job enlargement    p. 319                            worker empowerment    p. 315
job enrichment    p. 319

# REVIEW AND DISCUSSION QUESTIONS

1.  Think of three examples of ways in which an organization has changed to become more competitive. What impact do you think these changes have on the employees of the organization?

2.  Which of the eight managerial roles do you practice in your role as a student, . . . in activities in which you participate, . . . in your job? Which of Cameron and Whetten's ten skills do you use in these roles?

3.  What problems might arise from empowering employees? What are some of the hurdles that managers must overcome in empowering employees? What could the organization do to address these issues?

4.  Would you prefer to work in a traditional work group or in a self-managed work team? Why?

5.  This chapter mentioned some of benefits of and the difficulties in implementing cross-functional and self-managed work teams. What other difficulties can you predict? What other benefits do you see?

6.  Is there any inconsistency when a company requires precise time standards and, at the time, encourages job enlargement?

7.  The study team from one American car manufacturer observed that the Japanese used techniques such as job rotation, making workers responsible for quality control, minimal work classifications, and indirect employee participation in management. What gains can be made with this approach, in contrast to the job specialization approach? If the Japanese approach were to be adopted in a specialized job environment, what changes would have to take place for it to be successfully implemented?

# CASE: AT&T CREDIT CORP.

Millions of clerical employees toil in the back offices of financial companies, processing applications, claims, and customer accounts on what amounts to electronic assembly lines. The jobs are dull and repetitive and efficiency gains minuscule—when they come at all.

That was the case with AT&T Credit Corp. (ATTCC) when it opened shop in 1985 as a newly created subsidiary of American Telephone & Telegraph Corp. Based in Morristown, New Jersey, ATTCC provides financing for customers who lease equipment from AT&T and other companies. A bank initially retained by ATTCC to process lease applications couldn't keep up with the volume of new business.

ATTCC President Thomas C. Wajnert saw that the fault lay in the bank's method of dividing labor into narrow tasks and organizing work by function. One department

handled applications and checked the customer's credit standing, a second drew up contracts, and a third collected payments. So no one person or group had responsibility for providing full service to a customer. "The employees had no sense of how their jobs contributed to the final solution for the customer," Wajnert says.

## UNEXPECTED BONUS

Wajnert decided to hire his own employees and give them "ownership and accountability." His first concern was to increase efficiency, not to provide more rewarding jobs. But in the end, he did both.

In 1986, ATTCC set up 11 teams of 10 to 15 newly hired workers in a high-volume division serving small businesses. The three major lease-processing functions were combined in each team. No longer were calls from customers shunted from department to department. The company also divided its national staff of field agents into seven regions and assigned two or three teams to handle business from each region. That way, the same teams always worked with the same sales staff, establishing a personal relationship with them and their customers. Above all, team members took responsibility for solving customers' problems. ATTCC's new slogan: "Whoever gets the call owns the problem."

The teams largely manage themselves. Members make most decisions on how to deal with customers, schedule their own time off, reassign work when people are absent, and interview prospective new employees. The only supervisors are seven regional managers who advise the team members, rather than give orders. The result: The teams process up to 800 lease applications a day versus 400 under the old system. Instead of taking several days to give a final yes or no, the teams do it in 24 to 48 hours. As a result, ATTCC is growing at a 40 percent to 50 percent compound annual rate, Wajnert says.

### Extra Cash

The teams also have economic incentives for providing good service. A bonus plan tied to each team's costs and profits can produce extra cash. The employees, most of whom are young college graduates, can add $1,500 a year to average salaries of $28,000, and pay rises as employees learn new skills. "It's a phenomenal learning opportunity," says 24-year-old team member Michael LoCastro.

But LoCastro and others complain that promotions are rare because there are few managerial positions. And everyone comes under intense pressure from co-workers to produce more. The annual turnover rate is high: Some 20 percent of ATTCC employees either quit or transfer to other parts of AT&T. Still, the team experiment has been so successful that ATTCC is involving employees in planning to extend the concept throughout the company. "They will probably come up with as good an organizational design as management could," Wajnert says, "and it will work a lot better because the employees will take ownership for it."

### Question

1. Besides few opportunities for promotion and intense peer pressure, what other factors might contribute to the high employee turnover rate?

2. What would you do to reduce the employee turnover rate at ATTCC?

Source: John Hoerr, "The Payoff from Teamwork" (July 10, 1989), p. 59, issue of *Business Week* by special permission © 1989 by The McGraw-Hill Companies.

## Selected Bibliography

Bowen, David E., and Edward E. Lawler. "The Empowerment of Service Workers: What, Why, How and When." *Sloan Management Review,* Spring 1991, pp. 31–39.

Carlisle, Brian. "Job Design Implications for Operations Managers." *International Journal of Production and Operations Management* 3, no. 3 (1983), pp. 40–48.

Cusumano, Michael. *Japan's Software Factories: A Challenge to U.S. Management.* New York: Oxford University Press, 1991.

Hanson, Gary. "Determinants of Firm Performance: An Integration of Economic and Organizational Factors." Ph.D. dissertation, University of Michigan. Cited in Cameron, David A., and Kim S. Whetten. *Developing Manager Skills.* 3rd ed. New York: Harper Collins, 1995.

Hoerr, John. "The Payoff from Teamwork." *Business Week,* July 10, 1989, p. 59.

Hoojberg, Robert, and Robert Quinn. "Behavioral Complexity and the Development of Effective Managers." In *Strategic Leadership: A Multiorganizational-Level Perspective,* eds. R. Phillips and J. Hunt. Westport, CT: Quorum Publishing, 1992.

Katzenbach, Jon R., and Douglas K. Smith. *The Wisdom of Teams: Creating the High Performance Organization.* Boston: Harvard Business School Press, 1993.

Konz, Stephan. *Work Design: Industrial Ergonomics.* 2nd ed. New York: John Wiley & Sons, 1983.

Lipin, Steven. "A New Vision." *The Wall Street Journal,* June 25, 1993.

Main, J. "Betting on the 21st Century Jet." *Fortune,* April 20, 1992, pp. 102–17.

Manz, Charles C., and Henry P. Sims, Jr. *Business Without Bosses.* New York: John Wiley and Sons, 1995.

Manz, Charles C., and Henry P. Sims, Jr. "Super-Leadership: Beyond the Myth of Heroic Leadership." *Organizational Dynamics* 19, no. 4 (1991), pp. 18–35.

Mondy, R. Wayne, and Robert N. Noe. *Human Resource Management.* Upper Saddle River, NJ: Prentice-Hall, 1996.

Moskal, B. B. "Company Loyalty Dies, A Victim of Neglect." *Industry Week,* March 1, 1993.

Orsburn J. D.; L. Moran; E. Mussselwhite; and J. H. Zenger. *Self-Directed Work Teams: The New American Challenge.* Homewood, IL: Business One Irwin, 1990.

Peters, Tom. "Prometheus Barely Unbound," *The Executive* IV, no. 4 (November 1990), pp. 79–83.

Quinn, R. E.; S. R. Faerman; M. P. Thompson; and M. R. McGrath. *Becoming a Master Manager: A Competency Framework.* New York: John Wiley and Sons, 1996, p. 23.

Sasser, W. Earl, and William E. Fullmer. "Creating Personalized Service Delivery Systems," in D. Bowen, R. Chase, and T. Cummings (eds.), *Service Management Effectiveness.* San Francisco: Jossey-Bass, 1990, pp. 213–33.

Schrage Michael. "Big Brother May Be Coming to the Workplace." *The Washington Post*, June 9, 1984.

Scott, Gerald. "A Look at the Goings-on inside Chrysler's Plant That Builds Viper and Prowler, Tour de Force." *Chicago Tribune*, March 8, 1998.

Songer, N. B. "Work Force Diversity." *Business and Economic Review,* April–June 1991.

Teitelbaum, Richard. "How to Harness Gray Matter." *Fortune,* June 9, 1997, p. 168.

Wellins, R.; W. Byham; and J. Wilson. *Empowered Teams.* San Francisco: Jossey-Bass, 1991.

Wetten, Kim, and David Cameron. *Developing Management Skills.* New York: Harper Collins, 1995.

Woodruff, D. "Chrysler's Neon." *Business Week,* May 3, 1993, pp. 116–26.

Yang, D. J. "When the Going Gets Tough, Boeing Gets Touchy-Feely." *Business Week,* January 17, 1994, pp. 65–68.

## Supplement Outline

## Supplement Objectives

- Introduce the basic elements involved in job design.

- Understand the fundamental issues involved in developing work measurements.

- Determine how to design a work sampling study and apply it to an actual operation.

- Recognize that there are many different methods to compensate employees including reward structures for good performance.

A fundamental building block in most organizations, whether manufacturing or service, is the proper design of work tasks and the measurement of how long it takes to accomplish these tasks. In the early part of this century, beginning with Frederick W. Taylor and continuing with Frank and Lillian Gilbreth, work measurements were done almost exclusively in manufacturing companies. The purpose of conducting these measurements was to determine the most efficient way to accomplish a specific task. In addition, management was able to compare worker performance to a set of established standards. These work standards, which stated how long it should take to complete a given set of tasks, also provided a basis for determining the labor costs associated with manufacturing.

While the specific methodology associated with work measurement has basically not changed since its inception with Taylor, the manner in which work measurements are conducted has changed significantly (See OM in Practice: Work Measurement Then and Now). In addition, with the development of sophisticated computerized worker scheduling systems for service operations, the length of time it takes service workers to complete various tasks is a critical element in determining how many workers to schedule to meet a forecasted level of customer demand in a given time period.

## WORK METHODS

An integral part in the development of operational processes is the definition of the tasks that must be performed by the workers. But how should these tasks be done? Years ago, production workers were craftspeople who had their own (and sometimes secret) methods for doing things. However, over time products have become more complicated, as mechanization of a higher order was introduced, and output rates have increased. As a result, the responsibilities for work methods have been transferred to management. It was no longer logical or economically feasible to allow individual workers to produce the same product by different methods. Work specialization brought much of the concept of craftwork to an end, as less-skilled workers were employed to do the simpler tasks.

While in some large companies, the responsibility for developing work methods is typically assigned to either a staff department designated *methods analysis* or an industrial engineering department, in small firms this activity is often performed by consulting firms that specialize in work methods design. However, as illustrated in the NUMMI example (see OM in Practice), a growing number of firms are allowing their workers to design their own jobs and also to determine how long they should take.

The principal approach to the study of work methods is the construction of charts, such as operations charts, worker-machine charts, simo (simultaneous motion) charts, and activity charts, in conjunction with time study or standard time data. The choice of which charting method to use depends on the activity level of the task; that is, whether the focus is on (*a*) the overall operation, (*b*) the worker at a fixed workplace, (*c*) a worker interacting with equipment, or (*d*) a worker interacting with other workers (see Exhibit S9.1).

### Overall Operation

The objective in studying the overall production system is to identify delays, transport distances, processes, and processing time requirements, in order to simplify the entire operation. The underlying philosophy is to eliminate any step in the process that does not add value to the product. The approach used here is to develop a process flowchart and then ask

# Operations Management in Practice

## WORK MEASUREMENT THEN AND NOW

### JOB DESIGN THEN . . .

Frederick W. Taylor recounts his "motivation" of his trusty worker, Schmidt (in *Principles of Scientific Management*, 1910):

"Schmidt, are you a high-priced man?"

"Vell, I don't know vat you mean."

"Oh yes you do. What I want to know is whether you are a high-priced man or not. . . . What I want to find out is whether you want to earn $1.85 a day or whether you are satisfied with $1.15, just the same as all those cheap fellows are getting?"

"Vell, yes I vas a high-priced man."

"Now come over here. You see that pile of pig iron?"

"Yes."

"You see that car?"

"Yes."

"Well, if you are a high-priced man, you will load that pig iron on that car tomorrow for $1.85."

"You see that man over there? . . . Well, if you are a high-priced man, you will do exactly as this man tells you tomorrow, from morning till night. When he tells you to pick up a pig and walk, you pick it up and you walk, and when he tells you to sit down and rest, you sit down. You do that straight through the day. And what's more, no back talk."

### AND NOW . . .

Researcher Paul S. Adler describes job design at New United Motor Manufacturing Inc.'s (NUMMI) Fremont, California, plant. NUMMI is a joint venture between General Motors and Toyota.

Team members hold the stopwatch and design their own jobs. Team members begin by timing one another, seeking the most efficient way to do each task at a sustainable pace. They pick the best performance, break it down into its component parts, and then look for ways of improving each element. The team then takes the resulting methods, compares them with those used by teams working on the other shift at the same workstation, and writes detailed specifications that become the standard work definition for everyone on both teams.

Source: Discussions with Paul S. Adler; Paul S. Adler, "Time and Motion Regained," *Harvard Business Review* 71, no. 1 (January–February 1993), pp. 97–110; and "Return of the Stopwatch," *The Economist*, January 23, 1993, p. 69.

---

**EXHIBIT S9.1**

Work Methods and Design Aids

| Activity | Objective of Study | Study Techniques |
|---|---|---|
| Overall production system | Eliminate or combine steps; shorten transport distance; identify delays | Flow diagram, service blueprint, process chart |
| Worker at fixed workplace | Simplify method; minimize motions | Operations charts, simo charts; apply principles of motion economy |
| Worker interacts with equipment | Minimize idle time; find number or combination of machines to balance cost of worker and machine idle time | Activity chart, worker-machine charts |
| Worker interacts with other workers | Maximize productivity, minimize interference | Activity charts, gang process charts |

the following questions:

What is done? Must it be done? What would happen if it were not done?

Where is the task done? Must it be done at that location or could it be done somewhere else?

When is the task done? Is it critical that it be done then or is there flexibility in time and sequence? Could it be done in combination with some other step in the process?

How is the task done? Why is it done this way? Is there another way?

Who does the task? Can someone else do it? Should the worker be of a higher or lower skill level?

These types of questions usually help to eliminate much unnecessary work, as well as to simplify the remaining work, by combining a number of processing steps and changing the order of performance.

Use of the process chart is valuable in studying an overall operation, though care must be taken to follow the same item throughout the process. The subject may be a product being manufactured, a service being created, or a person performing a sequence of activities. An example of a process chart (and flow diagram) for a clerical operation is shown in Exhibit S9.2. Common notation in process charting is given in Exhibit S9.3.

## Worker at a Fixed Workplace

There are many jobs that require workers to remain at a specified workstation in order to complete their assigned tasks. When the nature of the work is primarily manual (such as sorting, inspecting, making entries, or assembly operations), the focus of work design is on simplifying the work method and making the required operator motions as few and as simple as possible.

There are two basic ways to determine the best method when a method analyst studies a single worker performing an essentially manual task. The first is to search among the various workers performing a given task and find that one who performs the job best. That person's method is then accepted as the standard, and the other workers are trained to perform it in the same way. This was basically F. W. Taylor's approach. The second method is to observe the performance of a number of workers, analyze in detail each step of their work, and pick out the superior features of each worker's performance. This results in a composite method that combines the best elements of the group studied. This was the procedure used by Frank Gilbreth, the father of motion study, to determine the "one best way" to perform a work task.

**therbligs**
Basic units of measurement used in micromotion analysis.

Taylor observed actual performance to find the best method; Frank Gilbreth and his wife Lillian relied on movie film. Through micromotion analysis—observing the filmed work performance frame by frame—the Gilbreths studied work very closely and defined its basic elements, which was termed **therbligs** ("Gilbreth" spelled backward, with the *t* and *h* transposed). They also used the motion model—a wire representation of the path of a motion. Their study led to the rules or principles of motion economy listed in Exhibit S9.4.

Once the various motions for performing a task have been identified, an *operations chart* is then developed, listing the individual operations and their sequence of performance. For greater detail, a *simo* (simultaneous motion) *chart* may be constructed, listing not only the operations but also the times for both left and right hands. This chart may be assembled from the data collected with a stopwatch, from analysis of a film of the operation, or from predetermined motion-time data (discussed later in the chapter). Many aspects of poor design become immediately obvious with this technique—a hand being used as a holding device (rather than a jig or fixture), an idle hand, or an exceptionally long time for positioning.

**EXHIBIT S9.2**

Flow Diagram and Process
Chart of an Office
Procedure—Present
Method*

Superintendent

Purchasing
agent

Secretary

**Research Laboratory**

Offices

Supervisor's office

| | | | **PROCESS CHART** |
|---|---|---|---|
| Present Method ☒ | | | |
| Proposed Method ☐ | | | |

SUBJECT CHARTED  Requisition for small tools          DATE _____

  Chart begins at supervisor's desk and ends at      CHART BY  J.C.H.

   typist's desk in purchasing department            CHART NO.  R136

DEPARTMENT  Research laboratory                       SHEET NO.  1  OF  1

| DIST. IN FEET | TIME IN MINS. | CHART SYMBOLS | PROCESS DESCRIPTION |
|---|---|---|---|
| | | ●⇨☐D▽ | Requisitions written by supervisor (one copy) |
| | | O⇨☐D▽ | On supervisor's desk (awaiting messenger) |
| 65 | | O➡☐D▽ | By messenger to superintendent's secretary |
| | | O⇨☐D▽ | On secretary's desk (awaiting typing) |
| | | ●⇨☐D▽ | Requisition typed (original requisition copied) |
| 15 | | O➡☐D▽ | By secretary to superintendent |
| | | O⇨☐D▽ | On superintendent's desk (awaiting messenger) |
| | | O⇨◪D▽ | Examined and approved |
| | | O⇨☐D▽ | On superintendent's desk (awaiting messenger) |
| 20 | | O➡☐D▽ | To purchasing department |
| | | O⇨☐D▽ | On purchasing agent's desk (awaiting approval) |
| | | O⇨◪D▽ | Examined and approved |
| | | O⇨☐D▽ | On purchasing agent's desk (awaiting messenger) |
| 5 | | O➡☐D▽ | To typist's desk |
| | | O⇨☐D▽ | On typist's desk (awaiting typing of purchase order) |
| | | ●⇨☐D▽ | Purchase order typed |
| | | O⇨☐D▽ | On typist's desk (awaiting transfer to main office) |
| | | O⇨☐D▽ | |
| | | | |
| 105 | | 3  4  2  8 | Total |

*Requisition is written by supervisor, typed by secretary, approved by superintendent, and approved by purchasing agent; then a purchase order is prepared by a stenographer.

Source: Ralph M. Barnes, *Motion and Time Study,* 8th ed. (New York: Wiley & Sons, 1980), pp. 76–79. Reprinted by permission of John Wiley & Sons, Inc.

**EXHIBIT S9.7**

Types of Work Measurement
Applied to Different Tasks

| Type of Work | Major Methods of Determining Task Time |
|---|---|
| Very short interval, highly repetitive | Videotape analysis |
| Short interval, repetitive | Stopwatch time study: predetermined motion-time data |
| Task in conjunction with machinery or other fixed-processing-time equipment | Elemental data |
| Infrequent work or work of a long cycle time | Work sampling |

the collected times are averaged. (The standard deviation may be computed to give a measure of variance in the performance times.) The averaged times for each element are then added together, and the result is the performance time for the operator. However, to make this operator's time usable for all workers, a measure of speed, which is expressed as a *performance rating* and which reflects how hard the observed operator is working, must also be included to "normalize" the job. The application of a rating factor gives what is called *normal time.*

**Example**

An industrial engineer conducts a time study on an operator and determines that a specific task takes about two minutes to complete. The engineer estimates that the particular operator that she is observing is working about 20 percent faster than normal. The company has an allowance factor of 15 percent of job time for personal needs, delays, and fatigue. Calculate the standard time for this task.

**Solution**

$$\text{Normal time} = \text{observed performance time per unit} \times \text{Performance rating}$$

In this example, denoting normal time by $NT$,

$$NT = 2(1.2) = 2.4 \text{ minutes}$$

When an operator is observed over a long period of time, the number of units produced during this time, along with the performance rating, gives the normal time as

$$NT = \frac{\text{Total time observed}}{\text{Number of units produced}} \times \text{Performance rating}$$

*Standard time* is derived by adding allowances to normal time. These allowances include personal needs (washroom and coffee breaks, and so forth), unavoidable work delays (equipment breakdown, lack of materials, and so forth), and worker fatigue (physical or mental). There are two equations for calculating standard time:

$$\text{Standard time} = \text{Normal Time} + (\text{Allowances} \times \text{Normal time})$$

or

$$ST = NT\,(1 + \text{Allowances}) \tag{S9.1}$$

and

$$ST = \frac{NT}{1 - \text{Allowances}} \tag{S9.2}$$

Equation (S9.1) is most often used in practice. Here the allowances are stated as a percentage of the "job time." In other words, the allowance factor is added to the job time in order to obtain the standard time. However, if the allowances are stated as a percentage of the total "work time," then equation (S9.2) is the correct one to use.

In this example, the normal time to perform a task is 2.4 minutes and the allowances for personal needs, delays, and fatigue total 15 percent of the job time; then by equation (1),

$$ST = 2.4(1 + 0.15) = 2.76 \text{ minutes}$$

In an eight-hour day, a worker would produce $8 \times 60 / 2.76 = 174$ units. This implies $174 \times 2.4$ minutes per unit (normal time) $= 417.6$ minutes working and $480 - 417.6 = 62.4$ minutes for allowances.

However, if the allowance factor is stated as a percentage of the total work time, then we would use equation (S9.2):

$$ST = \frac{2.4}{1 - 0.15} = 2.82 \text{ minutes}$$

In the same eight-hour day, using equation (2), $8 \times 60 / 2.82$ (or 170) units are produced with 408 working minutes and 72 minutes for allowances. Depending on how the allowance factor is specified, there is a difference of 4 units produced and also approximately 10 minutes in the daily allowance time.

Before a time study is conducted, each task is broken down into elements or parts. Some general rules for this breakdown are:

1. Define each work element to be short in duration but sufficiently long enough so that each can be timed with a stopwatch and the time can be written down.
2. If the operator works with equipment that runs separately—the operator performs a task and the equipment runs independently—separate the actions of the operator and that of the equipment into different elements.
3. Define any delays by the operator or equipment into separate elements.

How many observations are enough? Time study is really a sampling process; that is, we take a relatively small number of observations as being representative of many subsequent cycles to be performed by the worker. A great deal of analysis and experience indicates that the number of observations is a function of cycle length and the number of repetitions of the job over a one-year planning period.

**Elemental Standard-Time Data**    Elemental standard-time data is obtained from previous time studies and codified in tables in a handbook or in a computer data bank. Such data are used to develop time standards for new jobs or to make time adjustments to reflect changes in existing jobs. They are more correctly viewed as *normal-time data,* because tabled values have been modified by an average performance rating, and allowances must be added to obtain a standard time.

**time standard**
Established time for completing a job, used in determining labor costs associated with making a product.

Calculating a **time standard** for a new job using elemental standard-time data tables entails the following steps:

1. Break down the new job into its basic elements.
2. Match these elements to the time for similar elements in the table.

3. Adjust element times for special characteristics of the new job. (In metal cutting, for example, this is often done by a formula that modifies the time required as a function of type of metal, size of the cutting tool, depth of the cut, and so forth.)

4. Add element times together and add delay and fatigue allowances as specified by company policy for the given class of work.

The obvious benefit of elemental standard data is cost savings in that it eliminates the need for a new time study every time there is a new job. This saves staff time and avoids disruption of the workforce. The main practical requirements of the approach is that the elemental data must be kept up to date and easily accessible.

## Work Sampling

**work sampling**
Technique for estimating how workers allocate their time among various activities throughout a workday.

Whereas work measurement is concerned with how long it takes to perform a specific task or activity, **work sampling** is primarily concerned with how workers spend their time among several tasks or activities. For example, we may want to know how much time workers spend on indirect activities such as material handling to determine whether or not more cost-efficient material handling equipment should be purchased. Work sampling provides us with a method for determining the time spent on these activities, and involves observing a portion or sample of the work activity. Then, based on the findings in this sample, some statements can be made about how the employee or employees spend their time.

For example, if we were to observe a fire department rescue squad 100 random times during the day and found that it was involved in a rescue mission for 30 of the 100 times (en route, on site, or returning from a call), we would estimate that the rescue squad spends 30 percent of its time directly on rescue mission calls. (The time it takes to make an observation depends on what is being observed. Often only a glance is needed to determine the activity, and the majority of studies require only several seconds' observation.)

Observing an activity even 100 times may not, however, provide the accuracy desired in the estimate. To refine this estimate, three main issues must be decided (these points are discussed later in this section, along with an example):

1. What level of statistical confidence is desired in the results?
2. How many observations are necessary?
3. Precisely when should the observations be made?

The number of observations required in a work sampling study can be fairly large, ranging from several hundred to several thousand, depending on the activity and the desired degree of accuracy. The formula for computing the required number of observations is:

$$N = \frac{Z^2 p(1 - p)}{E^2} \tag{S9.3}$$

where

$N$ = Number of observations to be made.

$Z$ = Number of standard deviations associated with a given confidence level.

$p$ = Estimated proportion of time that the activity being measured occurs.

$E$ = Absolute error that is desired.

Example

For example, we want to determine what percentage of time clerks at a hotel registration desk are idle. We want our results to be 95 percent confident within an error of 3 percent. Our initial estimate of the clerks' idle time is 20 percent.

In this example:

$Z = 1.96$ (corresponding to 95% confidence).
$p = 0.20$ (estimated percentage idle time).
$E = 0.03$ (absolute error).

**Solution**        Substituting these values into the above formula, we obtain the following:

$$N = \frac{(1.96)^2(0.2)(1-0.2)}{(0.03)^2}$$

$$N = \frac{(3.84)(0.16)}{(0.0009)}$$

$N = 682.95$ or 683 observations. (Note: We always round up here to ensure we meet the minimum requirements of the study.)

Thus, with the above work sampling study, we can state that we are 95 percent confident that the true percentage of time that the clerks are idle falls within 3 percent of the study results.

However, we don't always have an estimate of the proportion of time spent on a given activity (in fact, that is often why we are doing the work sampling study in the first place!). In these situations, we use $p = 0.5$ which will give us a worst case scenario. (If $p$ is equal to anything other than 0.5 we have, in effect, overestimated the sample size.)

Suppose in the above example we don't have any estimate for the proportion of time the clerks are idle. In this case we would use $p = 0.5$, and the calculation of the sample size would be as follows:

$$N = \frac{(1.96)^2(0.5)(1-0.5)}{(0.03)^2}$$

$$N = \frac{(3.84)(0.25)}{(0.0009)}$$

$N = 1,067.11$ or 1,068 observations.

The specific steps involved in conducting a work sampling study are:

1. Identify the specific activity or activities that are the main purpose for the study. For example, determine the percentage of time equipment is working, idle, or under repair.

2. If it is possible, estimate the proportion of time of the activity of interest to the total time (e.g., that the equipment is working 80 percent of the time). These estimates can be made from the analyst's knowledge, past data, reliable guesses from others, or a pilot work-sampling study. If no estimate can be made, assume, as stated above, that the proportion is 0.50.

3. State the desired accuracy in the study results.

4. Determine the specific times when each observation is to be made.

5. If you are using an estimated time, recompute the required sample size at two or three intervals during the study period by using the data collected thus far. Adjust the number of observations if appropriate.

The number of observations to be taken in a work sampling study is usually divided equally over the study period. Thus, if 500 observations are to be made over a 10-day period, the observations are usually scheduled at 500/10, or 50 per day. Each day's observations are then assigned a specific time by using a random number generator. The need to divide the observations equally over the data collection period is even more important in service operations where workers can be extremely busy during certain periods and less busy at other times.

Example

There has been a long-standing argument that a large amount of nurses' hospital time is spent on non-nursing activities. This, the argument goes, creates an apparent shortage of well-trained nursing personnel, a significant waste of talent, a corresponding loss of efficiency, and increased hospital costs because nurses' wages are the highest single cost in the operation of a hospital. Further, pressure is growing for hospitals and hospital administrators to contain costs. With that in mind, let us use work sampling to test the hypothesis that a large portion of nurses' time is spent on non-nursing duties.

Assume at the outset that we have made a list of all the activities that are part of nursing and will make our observations in only two categories: nursing and non-nursing activities. (An expanded study could list all nursing activities to determine the portion of time spent in each.) Therefore, when we observe nurses during the study and find them performing one of the duties on the nursing list, we simply place a tally mark in the nursing column. If we observe a nurse doing anything besides nursing, we place a tally mark in the non-nursing column.

Solution

We can now proceed to design the work sampling study. Assume that we (or the nursing supervisor) estimate that nurses spend 60 percent of their time in nursing activities. Also assume that we would like to be 95 percent confident that the findings of our study are within the absolute error range of plus or minus 3 percent. In other words, if our study shows nurses spend 60 percent of their time on nursing duties, we are 95 percent confident that the true percentage lies between 57 and 63 percent. Using the above formula, we calculate that 1,025 observations are required for 60 percent activity time and ±3 percent error. If our study is to take place over 10 days, we start with 103 observations per day.

To determine when each day's observations are to be made, we assign specific numbers to each minute and a random number table to set up a schedule. If the study extends over an eight-hour shift, we can assign numbers to correspond to each consecutive minute. The list in Exhibit S9.8 shows the assignment of numbers to corresponding minutes. For simplicity, because each number corresponds to one minute, a three-number scheme is used, with the second and third number corresponding to the minute of the hour. A number of other schemes would also be appropriate. (If a number of studies are planned, a computer program may be used to generate a randomized schedule for the observation times.)

If we refer to a random number table and list three-digit numbers, we can assign each number to a time. The random numbers shown in Exhibit S9.9 demonstrate the procedure for seven observations.

This procedure is followed to generate 103 observation times, and the times are rearranged chronologically for ease in planning. Rearranging the times determined in Exhibit S9.9 gives the total observations per day shown in Exhibit S9.10 (for our sample of seven).

To be perfectly random in this study, we should also "randomize" the nurse we observe each time (the use of various nurses minimizes the effect of bias). In this study, our first observation is made at 7:13 AM for Nurse X. We walk into the nurse's area and check either a nursing or a non-nursing activity, depending on what we observe. Each observation need be only long enough to determine the class of activity—in most cases only a glance. At 8:04 AM we observe Nurse Y. We continue in this way to the end of the day and the 103 observations. At the end of the second day (and 206 observations), we decide to check for the adequacy of our sample size.

Let's say that we made 150 observations of nurses working and 64 of them not working, which gives 70.1 percent working. Again, using the formula given above, we calculate that the required number of observations is now 895. Inasmuch as we have already taken 206 observations, we only need to take another 689 over the next eight days or 86 per day. This recalculation of the sample size should be done several times during the data collection period.

If at the end of the study we find that 66 percent of nurses' time is involved with what has been defined as nursing activities, there should be an analysis to identify the remaining 34 percent. Approximately 12 to 15 percent is justifiable for coffee breaks and personal needs, which leaves 20 to 22 percent of the time that must be justified and compared to what the industry considers ideal levels of nursing activity. To identify the non-nursing activities, a more detailed breakdown could have been originally built into the sampling plan. Otherwise, a follow-up study may be in order.

---

**EXHIBIT S9.8**

Assignment of Numbers to Corresponding Minutes

| Time | Assigned Numbers |
|------|------------------|
| 7:00– 7:59 AM | 100–159 |
| 8:00– 8:59 AM | 200–259 |
| 9:00– 9:59 AM | 300–359 |
| 10:00–10:59 AM | 400–459 |
| 11:00–11:59 AM | 500–559 |
| 12:00–12:59 PM | 600–659 |
| 1:00– 1:59 PM | 700–759 |
| 2:00– 2:59 PM | 800–859 |

**EXHIBIT S9.9**

Determination of Observation Times

| Random Number | Corresponding Time from the Preceding List |
|---------------|--------------------------------------------|
| 669 | Nonexistent |
| 831 | 2:31 PM |
| 555 | 11:55 AM |
| 470 | Nonexistent |
| 113 | 7:13 AM |
| 080 | Nonexistent |
| 520 | 11:20 AM |
| 204 | 8:04 AM |
| 732 | 1:32 PM |
| 420 | 10:20 AM |

---

**EXHIBIT S9.10**

Observation Schedule

| Observation | Scheduled Time | Nursing Activity (✓) | Non-Nursing Activity (✓) |
|-------------|----------------|----------------------|--------------------------|
| 1 | 7:13 AM | | |
| 2 | 8:04 AM | | |
| 3 | 10:20 AM | | |
| 4 | 11:20 AM | | |
| 5 | 11:55 AM | | |
| 6 | 1:32 PM | | |
| 7 | 2:31 PM | | |

ployees, the privately held company, which is based in Greenwich, Connecticut, has grown highly profitable despite stiff competition. In fact, UPS is one of the most efficient companies anywhere, productivity experts say.

"You never see anybody sitting on his duff at UPS," says Bernard La Londe, a transportation professor at The Ohio State University. "The only other place you see the same commitment to productivity is at Japanese companies."

## GETTING UP TO SPEED

At UPS, more than 1,000 industrial engineers use time studies to set standards for a myriad of closely supervised tasks. Drivers are instructed to walk to a customer's door at the brisk pace of three feet per second and to knock first lest seconds be lost searching for the doorbell. Supervisors then ride with the "least best drivers" until they learn to finish on time. "It's human nature to get away with as much as possible," says Michael Kamienski, a UPS district manager. "But we bring workers up to our level of acceptance. We don't go down to their level."

If UPS isn't quite a throwback to old-time work measurement, it nevertheless runs counter to the drift of many U.S. companies. To increase productivity, others are turning more often to employee-involvement techniques that stress consultation and reject the rigid monitoring of workers.

"Workers are better educated and want more to say about what happens to them," says Roger Weiss, a vice president of H. B. Maynard & Co., a consulting concern. "Time study is a dark-ages technique, and it's dehumanizing to track someone around with a stopwatch."

UPS dismisses the criticism. "We don't use the standards as hammers, but they do give accountability," says Larry P. Breakiron, the company's senior vice president for engineering. "Our ability to manage labor and hold it accountable is the key to our success."

## NEW COMPETITION

Those techniques are about to be tested. Long engaged in a battle for parcels with the U.S. Postal Service, UPS recently has charged into overnight delivery against Federal Express Corporation, Purolator Courier, Airborne Freight, Emery Air Freight and others. What's more, it now is being challenged on its own turf by Roadway Services Inc., which in the early 1990s started a parcel delivery company called Roadway Package System that is implementing management ideas of its own.

The upstart competitor boasts that its owner-operator drivers, unlike UPS's closely scrutinized, but highly paid and unionized, drivers, are motivated by the challenge of running their own business. "Our people don't drive brown

trucks; they own their trucks," says Ivan Hoffman, a vice president of Roadway.

Roadway also is trying to gain the edge in productivity by eliminating people as much as possible through automation. Its package hubs use bar codes, laser scanners, computers, and special mechanical devices to sort packages, a task still handled at UPS by armies of workers. UPS calls its rival's methods unreliable, inflexible, and expensive. Those are the same epithets that Roadway hurls at UPS's human sorters.

The outcome of this budding competition interests package shippers. "UPS has taken the engineering of people as far as it can be taken," says Michael Birkholm, the director of transportation of American Greetings Corporation. "But the question is whether technologically sophisticated Roadway can dent the big brown UPS machine."

## BURGEONING COMPETITION

If the competition intensifies, productivity improvements will be at the heart of UPS's counterattack. Indeed, UPS long has used efficiency to overcome rivals. Founded in Seattle in 1907 as a messenger service, UPS over the years won parcel deliveries from department stores and captured package business once handled by the U.S. Postal Service because of its lower rates and superior service.

UPS's founder, James E. Casey, put a premium on efficiency. In the 1920s, he turned to Frank B. Gilbreth and other pioneers of time study to develop techniques to measure the time consumed each day by each UPS driver. Later, UPS engineers cut away the sides of a UPS delivery truck, or "package car" as the company calls the vehicle, to study a driver at work. Resultant changes in package loading techniques increased efficiency 30 percent.

Mr. Casey also shaped the company culture, which stresses achievement and teamwork in addition to efficiency. Copies of his tract, "Determined Men," and of "Pursuit of Excellence," a pamphlet written by one-time UPS Chairman George Smith, are handed out to the company's managers. "We still use Jim's and George's quotes in everything we do," says George Lamb, Jr., a UPS director and past chairman.

Another guiding principle: a fair day's work for a fair day's pay. The company's drivers, all of them Teamsters, earn wages of $15 an hour, about $1 more than the best-paid drivers at other trucking companies earn. With overtime, many UPS drivers gross $35,000 to $40,000 a year.

In return, UPS seeks maximum output from its drivers, as is shown by the time study Mrs. Cusack is conducting. On this day in suburban Whippany, she determines time allowances for each of Polise's 120 stops while watching for inefficiency in his methods. "What are you doing, Joe?"

she asks as Mr. Polise wastes precious seconds handling packages more than once. She says that a mere 30 seconds wasted at each stop can snowball into big delays by day's end.

Some UPS drivers with nicknames like Ace, Hammer, Slick, and Rocket Shoes take pride in meeting the standards day after day. "We used to joke that a good driver could get to his stop and back to the car before the seat belt stopped swaying," Mrs. Cusack says. (UPS has since redesigned its seat belts to eliminate sway.)

But not all UPS drivers enjoy the pace. For example, Michael Kipila, a driver in East Brunswick, New Jersey, says, "They squeeze every ounce out of you. You're always in a hurry, and you can't work relaxed." Some drivers say they cut their breaks in order to finish on time.

UPS officials maintain that the company's work standards are not just a matter of increasing output, but of making the job easier. "If you do it our way, you'll be less tired at the end of the day," says a UPS spokesman.

## Had Enough

The pressure causes some UPS employees—supervisors and drivers alike—to quit. Jose Vega, a former UPS supervisor, says he would ride with one New York driver, noting each time "pace too slow, customer contact too long." Vega says he tried to embarrass the driver so as to speed him up: "Are you falling asleep? Do you want a sleeping bag?" After a while, "it's like you're abusing this person," says Vega, who now drives for Roadway.

"There's a fine line between motivation and harassment, and many times UPS crosses that line," says Mario Perrucci, the secretary-treasurer of Teamsters Local 177 in Hillside, New Jersey, Mr. Perrucci has battled UPS for years over a requirement that drivers tap their horns when they approach a stop in the hopes that the customer will hurry to the door seconds sooner.

UPS's efforts to increase productivity get mixed reactions from the Teamsters union. While some local Teamsters officials such as Perrucci say that UPS is driving its workers "beyond endurance," the union's national executives are grateful that the company is successful. "I'd rather see UPS pushing the men too hard," says a Team-

sters official in Washington, "than see UPS in bankruptcy court."

Many trucking companies employing Teamsters are shutting down or, like Roadway Package System, turning to nonunion workers. But, UPS continues to be the largest single employer of Teamsters members, with more than 100,000 unionized workers, a 33 percent rise since 1980.

## A Game of Inches

To sustain growth, UPS executives are looking for new efficiencies. For example, they are seeking to make work standards for truck mechanics more exact. And at UPS's Parsippany, New Jersey, package sorting hub, 1 of more than 100 that the company operates, officials are making the most of space by parking delivery trucks just five inches apart. But productivity has its price. New York City says that UPS drivers have received more than $1 million in unpaid parking tickets since March 1985 while making local deliveries. A company attorney says the amount is "much too high." UPS has contested the fines.

The new competition from Roadway Package System also looms large. Roadway is cutting labor expenses 20 percent to 30 percent by using independent drivers. Because Roadway drivers buy their own trucks, uniforms, and insurance, Roadway is saving money that it is using to automate package sorting. "We'll use technology to be the low-cost producer," says Bram Johnson, a Roadway vice president.

Roadway says it reduced personnel 25 percent at its five sorting hubs through automation. At its York, Pennsylvania, hub, for example, a moving belt of tilt trays following instructions from a computer drops packages down a series of chutes.

## Question

What are the advantages and disadvantages of the UPS approach to job design and work measurement?

Source: Daniel Machalaba, "Up to Speed: United Parcel Service Gets Deliveries Done by Driving Its Workers." Reprinted by permission of *The Wall Street Journal* (April 22, 1986), p. 1. © 1986 Dow Jones & Company, Inc. All rights reserved worldwide.

## Selected Bibliography

Adler, Paul S. "Time and Motion Regained." *Harvard Business Review* 71, no. 1 (January–February 1993), pp. 97–110.

Adler, Paul S. "The Return of the Stopwatch." *The Economist,* January 23, 1993, p. 69.

Barnes, Ralph M. *Motion and Time Study: Design and Measurement of Work.* 8th ed. New York: John Wiley & Sons, 1980.

Barnes, Frank C. "Principles of Motion Economy: Revisited, Reviewed and Restored." *Proceedings of the Southern Management Association Annual Meeting,* Atlanta, GA, 1983, p. 298.

Chakravarty, Subrata N. "Hit 'em Hardest with the Mostest." *Forbes,* September 16, 1991, p. 51.

Globerson, Shlomo, and Robert Parsons. "Multi-factor Incentive Systems: Current Practices." *Operations Management Review* 3, no. 2 (Winter 1985).

Lawler, E. E., III. "Paying for Organizational Performance." Report G 87–1 (92), Center for Effective Organizations, University of Southern California, 1987.

Machalaba, Daniel. "Up to Speed: United Parcel Service Gets Deliveries Done by Driving Its Workers." *The Wall Street Journal,* April 22, 1986, p. 1.

Niebel, Benjamin W. *Motion and Time Study.* 7th ed. Homewood, IL: Richard D. Irwin, 1982.

Niles, John L. "To Increase Productivity, Audit the Old Incentive Plan." *Industrial Engineering* (January 1980), pp. 20–23.

"The Promise of Reengineering." *Fortune* (May 3, 1993), p. 96.

Smalley, Harold E., and John Freeman. *Hospital Industrial Engineering.* New York: Reinhold, 1966, p. 409.

# PROJECT MANAGEMENT

## Chapter Objectives

- Recognize that project management involves both people skills to coordinate and motivate individuals from a range of disciplines and technical skills to properly plan and schedule a project.

- Explain the role of the project manager in organizing and coordinating all activities performed in a project.

- Introduce critical path scheduling as a tool for identifying activities that require attention.

- Identify the time–cost trade-offs involved in expediting the completion of a project

- Discuss some of the criticisms often associated with project management techniques.

## EXHIBIT 10.2

A Sample of Graphic Project Reports

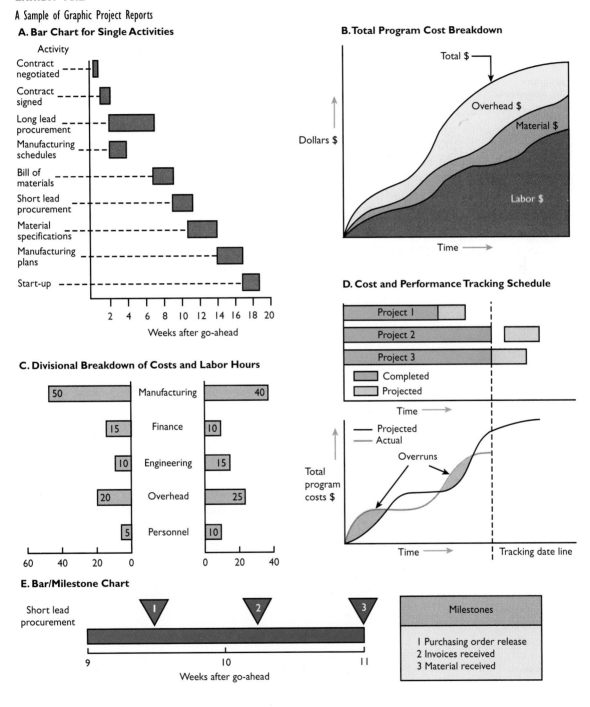

**A. Bar Chart for Single Activities**

**B. Total Program Cost Breakdown**

**C. Divisional Breakdown of Costs and Labor Hours**

**D. Cost and Performance Tracking Schedule**

**E. Bar/Milestone Chart**

Milestones
1 Purchasing order release
2 Invoices received
3 Material received

# CRITICAL PATH SCHEDULING

*Critical path scheduling* refers to a set of graphic techniques used in planning and controlling projects. In any given project, the three factors of concern are time, cost, and resource availability. Critical path techniques have been developed to deal with each of these, individually and in combination.

**PERT (program evaluation and review technique)**
Technique developed by the U.S. Navy for planning the Polaris missile project.

**CPM (critical path method)**
Technique to schedule preventive maintenance shutdowns of chemical processing plants.

**PERT (Program Evaluation and Review Technique)** and **CPM (Critical Path Method),** the two best-known techniques, were both developed in the late 1950s. PERT was developed under the sponsorship of the U.S. Navy Special Projects Office in 1958 as a management tool for scheduling and controlling the Polaris missile project. CPM was developed in 1957 by J. E. Kelly of Remington-Rand and M. R. Walker of Du Pont to aid in scheduling maintenance shutdowns of chemical processing plants.

Critical path scheduling techniques display a project in graphic form and relate its individual tasks in a way that focuses attention on those tasks that are critical to the project's completion. For critical path scheduling techniques to be most applicable, a project must have the following characteristics:

1. It must have well-defined jobs or tasks whose completion marks the end of the project.
2. The jobs or tasks are independent; they may be started, stopped, and conducted separately within a given sequence.
3. The jobs or tasks are ordered; certain ones must follow others in a given sequence.

The construction, aerospace, and shipbuilding industries commonly meet these criteria, and critical path techniques find wide application within them. We previously noted also that the applications of project management and critical path techniques are becoming much more common within firms in rapidly changing industries.

Project management techniques are also becoming more common in health care, with the objective of reducing a patient's overall stay in a hospital. Here, each patient is viewed as a project and the various procedures he or she undergoes are considered to be the tasks in that project. (It should be noted that there is a growing trend toward defining "care paths"

At Boeing, effective project management techniques were essential both in setting up the 777 assembly system and in scheduling and manufacturing the plane. Twenty percent of the 777 is built in Japan, along with manufacturing help from Australia (rudder), Northern Ireland and Singapore (nose gear), Korea (wingtip), Brazil (fin and wingtip assembly), and Italy (outboard wing flaps).

which provide standard steps that all patients follow. For example, Massachusetts General Hospital has established a paper checklist of what should happen with a patient on each day of a five-day stay for coronary artery bypass graft surgery.)

# TIME-ORIENTED TECHNIQUES

The basic forms of PERT and CPM focus on identifying the longest time-consuming path through a network of tasks as a basis for planning and controlling a project. Both PERT and CPM use nodes and arrows for display. Originally, the basic differences between PERT and CPM were that PERT used the arrow to represent an activity and CPM used the node. The other original difference between these two techniques was that PERT used three estimates—optimistic, pessimistic, and best—of an activity's required time, whereas CPM used just a single, best time estimate. This distinction reflects PERT's origin in scheduling advanced scientific projects (like the lunar missions) that are characterized by uncertainty and CPM's origin in the scheduling of the fairly routine activity of plant maintenance. Thus PERT was often used when the primary variable of interest was time, whereas CPM was used when the primary variable of interest was cost. As years passed, these two features no longer distinguished PERT from CPM. This is because CPM users started to use three time estimates and PERT users often placed activities on the nodes.

We believe the activity on the node is much easier to follow logically than the activity on the arrow. However, the three time estimates are often very valuable in obtaining a measure of the probability of completion times. Therefore, in this chapter we use the activity on the node and either a single estimate for activity time or three time estimates, depending on our objective. We use the terms *CPM* and *PERT* interchangeably and mean the same thing, although we tend to use the term *CPM* more frequently.

In a sense, both techniques owe their development to their widely used predecessor, the Gantt chart. While the Gantt chart is able to relate activities to time in a visually usable fashion for very small projects, the interrelationship of activities, when displayed in this format, becomes extremely difficult to visualize and to work with for projects with more than 25 or 30 activities. Moreover, the Gantt chart provides no direct procedure for determining the critical path, which, despite its theoretical shortcomings, is of great practical value.

## CPM with a Single Time Estimate

With the following as an example, we will develop the typical approach taken in project scheduling. The times for each activity have been given as a most likely estimate (rather than three estimates, which will be discussed in a later example).

Example

Many firms that have tried to enter the portable computer market have failed. Suppose your firm believes that there is a big demand in this market because existing products have not been designed correctly. They are either too heavy, too large, or too small to accommodate a standard-size keyboard. Your intended computer will be small enough to carry inside a jacket pocket if need be. The ideal size will be no larger than 4 inches × 9½ inches × 1 inch with a standard typewriter keyboard. It should weigh no more than 15 ounces, have a 4 to 8 line × 80 character back-lit display, have a micro disk drive, and a micro printer. It should be aimed primarily toward word processing use but have plug-in ROMs to accommodate an assortment of computer languages and programs.

These characteristics should appeal to traveling business people, but then could also have a much wider market. If it can be priced to sell retail in the $175–$200 range, the computer should appeal to a wide market.

The project, then, is to design, develop, and produce a prototype of this portable computer. In the rapidly changing computer industry, it is crucial to hit the market with a product of this type in less than a year. Therefore, the project team has been allowed approximately nine months, or 39 weeks, to produce the prototype.

The first assignment of the project team is to develop a project network chart to determine whether or not the prototype computer can be completed within the 39 weeks. Let's follow the steps in the development of this network.

**Solution**

### Step 1: Activity identification

The project team decides that the following activities constitute the major components of the project: (A) designing the computer, (B) constructing the prototype, (C) evaluating automatic assembly equipment, (D) testing the prototype, (E) preparing an assembly equipment study report, (F) writing methods specifications (to be summarized in a report), and (G) preparing a final report summarizing all aspects of the design, equipment, and methods.

### Step 2: Activity sequencing and network construction

On the basis of discussion with her staff, the project manager develops the precedence table and sequence network shown in Exhibit 10.3. Activities are indicated as nodes while arrows show the sequence in which the individual activities must be completed.

Using the precedence table, we can construct a network diagram, taking care to ensure that the activities are in the proper order and that the logic of their relationships is maintained. For example, it would be illogical to have a situation where Event A precedes Event B, B precedes C, and then C precedes A.

---

**EXHIBIT 10.3**

CPM Network for Computer Design Project

| | CPM Activity/Designations and Time Estimates | | |
|---|---|---|---|
| **Activity** | **Designation** | **Immediate Predecessors** | **Time in Weeks** |
| Design | A | — | 21 |
| Build prototype | B | A | 4 |
| Evaluate equipment | C | A | 7 |
| Test prototype | D | B | 2 |
| Write equipment report | E | C, D | 5 |
| Write methods report | F | C, D | 8 |
| Write final report | G | E, F | 2 |

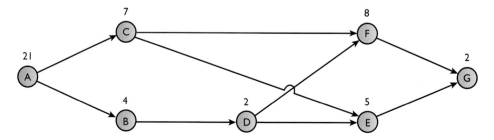

**EXHIBIT 10.5**

Typical Beta Curves

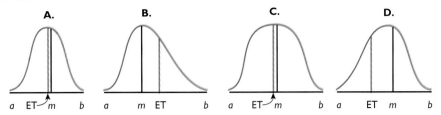

Curve A indicates very little uncertainty about the activity time, and since it is symmetrical, the expected time (ET) and the most likely or modal time (m) fall along the same point.

Curve B indicates a high probability of finishing the activity early, but if something goes wrong, the activity time could be greatly extended.

Curve C is almost a rectangular distribution, which suggests that the estimator sees the probability of finishing the activity early or late as equally likely, and $m \cong$ ET.

Curve D indicates that there is a small chance of finishing the activity early, but it is more probable that it will take an extended period of time.

**EXHIBIT 10.6**

Activity Expected Times and Variances

| Activity | Activity Designation | Time Estimates | | | Expected Times (ET) $\dfrac{a + 4m + b}{6}$ | Activity Variances ($\sigma^2$) $\left(\dfrac{b - a}{6}\right)^2$ |
|---|---|---|---|---|---|---|
| | | a | m | b | | |
| Design | A | 10 | 22 | 28 | 21 | 9.00 |
| Build prototype | B | 1 | 4 | 7 | 4 | 1.00 |
| Evaluate equipment | C | 4 | 6 | 14 | 7 | 2.78 |
| Test prototype | D | 1 | 2 | 3 | 2 | 0.11 |
| Write report | E | 1 | 5 | 9 | 5 | 1.78 |
| Write methods report | F | 7 | 8 | 9 | 8 | 0.11 |
| Write final report | G | 2 | 2 | 2 | 2 | 0.00 |

As you can see, the variance is the square of one sixth the difference between the two extreme time estimates, and, of course, the greater this difference, the larger the variance. A summary of the expected time and variance for each activity involved in making the portable computer discussed previously is presented in Exhibit 10.6.

### Step 6: Identify all of the paths in the network and their estimated completion times and variances

Using the data in Exhibit 10.6, the expected completion time for each path is simply the sum of the expected completion times for the activities that are on that path. Likewise, to calculate the variance for each path we simply add together the variances of the activities on the path. Again using the data in Exhibit 10.6, the path variances are calculated, and summarized in Exhibit 10.7, along with the path expected completion times.

### Step 7: Determine the probability of completing the project by a given date

The probability of completing the project by a given date is dependent on the probability of each path in the network being completed by that date. In our example, the desired completion time for the project is 39 weeks. In other words, we want to calculate the probability of completing the project in 39 weeks or less. To do this we need to calculate the probability of each of the paths in the network being completed in 39 weeks or less. All of the paths need to be completed in 39 weeks or less for the project to be completed within that same time period. Thus, the probability of the project being completed within a given time is equal to the minimum of the probabilities of the different paths.

**EXHIBIT 10.7**

Path Estimated Completion
Times and Variances

| Path | Expected Completion Time (in weeks) | Variance ($\sigma_p^2$) |
|------|:---:|:---:|
| A–C–E–G | 35 | 13.56 |
| A–B–D–F–G | 37 | 10.22 |
| A–B–D–E–G | 34 | 11.89 |
| A–C–F–G | 38 | 11.89 |

**EXHIBIT 10.8**

Probability of Each Path
Being Completed in
39 Weeks or Less

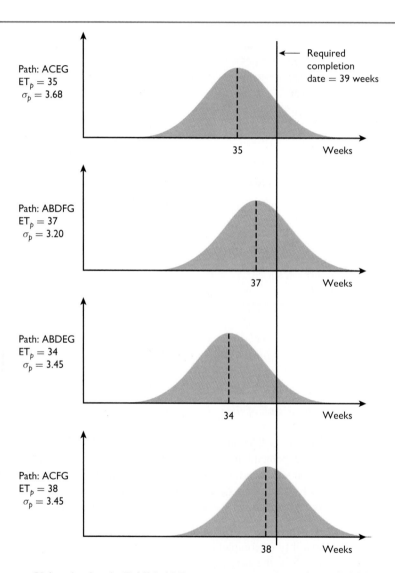

Path: ACEG
$ET_p = 35$
$\sigma_p = 3.68$

Path: ABDFG
$ET_p = 37$
$\sigma_p = 3.20$

Path: ABDEG
$ET_p = 34$
$\sigma_p = 3.45$

Path: ACFG
$ET_p = 38$
$\sigma_p = 3.45$

Required completion date = 39 weeks

Using the data in Exhibit 10.7 we can now construct the probability distribution for each path and calculate the probability of each path being completed in 39 weeks or less. This is shown graphically in Exhibit 10.8. Note that in order to calculate the probability of completing each path in 39 days or less we use $\sigma_p$, which is the square root of the variance, $\sigma_p^2$.

In Exhibit 10.8, the shaded area to the left of the line representing 39 weeks is the probability of that path being completed within the 39 week period. To obtain the value of that

| Activity | Normal Time* | Normal Costs† | Crash Time‡ | Crash Costs¶ |
|---|---|---|---|---|
| 1. Board of Trustees approval | 4 | $ 10 | 2 | $ 16 |
| 2. Obtain building permits | 2 | 5 | 2 | 5 |
| 3. Construct building | 21 | 1,500 | 17 | 1,700 |
| 4. Request bids for furniture | 4 | 3 | 4 | 3 |
| 5. Recruit faculty | 30 | 150 | 27 | 165 |
| 6. Order furniture | 16 | 200 | 12 | 240 |
| 7. Complete interiors | 6 | 110 | 3 | 131 |
| 8. Landscape site | 4 | 68 | 2 | 80 |
| 9. Obtain certificate of occupancy | 1 | 2 | 1 | 2 |
| 10. Final cleanup | 2 | 20 | 1 | 26 |
| 11. Install furniture | 1 | 12 | 1 | 12 |
| 12. Building occupied | — | — | — | — |
| Totals: | | 2,080 | | 2,380 |

*Times listed are in weeks.
†Costs listed are in thousands of dollars.
‡Crash time is the minimum time in which an activity can be completed.
¶Crash costs are the total costs associated with the acceleration of an activity. The weekly increase in costs for a given activity is assumed to be constant.

## QUESTIONS

1. What is the minimum time and overall cost in which the addition to Harvey Hall can be occupied by faculty under normal times and costs?

2. If you were operating under a very limited budget, how could you reduce the overall length of the project by one week at the least cost? By two weeks?

3. If John decides to complete this project in the shortest time possible, what is the minimum time and associated costs that the project can be completed (without incurring any unnecessary costs)?

4. After receiving approval from the school's board in the normal time of four weeks, John ran into a problem obtaining the necessary building permits. The original 125 acres on which the current campus is located was initially subdivided into one acre housing lots. As a result, permits are required for each of the building lots on which the addition was to be built, along with any immediately adjacent lots. These additional permits required an additional two weeks to obtain and increased the cost of obtaining the permits by $4,000. If John wants to complete the project in the original time that was determined in question 1, what specific actions must he now take to minimize costs while still completing the building as scheduled?

Source: © Mark M. Davis.

## SELECTED BIBLIOGRAPHY

Cleland, David I., and William R. King. *Project Management Handbook.* New York: Van Nostrand Reinhold, 1983.

Hughes, Michael William. "Why Projects Fail: The Effects of Ignoring the Obvious." *Industrial Engineering* 18, no. 4 (April 1986), pp. 14–18.

Kerzner, Harold. *Project Management for Executives.* New York: Van Nostrand Reinhold, 1984.

Shtub, A.; J. F. Bard; and S. Globerson. *Project Management: Engineering, Technology and Implementation.* Englewood Cliffs, NJ: Prentice Hall, 1994.

Thamhain, Hans J. "Effective Leadership Style for Managing Project Teams." In *Handbook of Program and Project Management,* ed. P. C. Dinsmore. New York: AMACOM, 1992.

Thamhain, Hans J. "Managing Technologically Innovative Team Efforts Towards New Product Success." *Journal of Production Innovation Management* 7, no. 1 (March 1990).

Wheelwright, S., and J. Weber. "Massachusetts General Hospital: CABG Surgery (A)." Boston, MA: Harvard Business School Publishing, 1997.

# Chapter 11

# SUPPLY CHAIN MANAGEMENT

## Chapter Objectives

- Introduce the concept of supply chain management and describe how it has changed the supplier relationship.

- Present the different factors that have had an impact on the supply chain in recent years.

- Identify the requirements for the establishment of a successful supply chain.

- Define in-transit inventory costs and show their impact on the purchasing decision.

- Introduce the concept of disintermediation as a current trend that affects the structure of the supply chain.

# PROBLEMS

1. An automobile company in Ohio currently purchases 100,000 tires a year from a manufacturer located 50 miles from its assembly plant. The price per tire is $40. Because of the close proximity of the two plants, the vendor delivers these tires free of charge. The purchasing agent has recently been approached by a tire manufacturer in Asia who has agreed to provide these tires for $35 each. Through inquiries, the purchasing agent has determined that it will cost an additional $4.50 per tire to ship the tires from Asia to the plant in Ohio. In addition, it will take approximately six weeks for a shipment to arrive. Currently the cost of capital for the automobile company is 20 percent per year. Which vendor should the purchasing agent buy tires from?

2. A computer company in the greater Boston area currently buys electronic modules at a price of $26 per unit from a vendor located in Tijuana, Mexico. The firm's buyer is currently evaluating two alternative modes for transporting these modules. The first way is overland on a trailer truck. The cost with this method is $2.50 per module and takes approximately two weeks. The second way is to ship the modules air freight, which takes only two days to deliver at a cost of $3 per unit. Currently the computer maker is buying 25,000 modules per year. The cost of capital for the firm is estimated at 18 percent per year. Which mode of transportation do you recommend?

3. As the purchasing agent for a small company located in central France, Laurence Garreau has recently sent out a request for proposal for a small motor used in a subassembly that her firm manufactures for the automobile industry. The annual requirement for this motor is 25,000 units, and she has estimated the cost of in-transit inventory to be 25 percent per year.

   The first quotation she receives is from a company in Southeast Asia. The unit price per motor from this firm is 45 FF (French francs). In addition, the transportation cost per unit is 4 FF. The transit time from Southeast Asia, using an ocean freighter, is estimated to be 50 days in total. The second quotation she receives is from a company in Mexico that is very anxious to do business in Europe. The unit price per motor from this company is 43 FF, and the transportation cost per unit is 6,5 FF, but it will only take 10 days in total to deliver the motors because the company will be using air freight. (Note: In Europe, a comma is used instead of a decimal point to indicate less than a whole unit.)

   *a.* Evaluate each of these two proposals to determine which is the most economical alternative. What is your recommendation? (Be specific and show all of your calculations.)

   *b.* What factors, in addition to cost, need to be taken into consideration in arriving at a final decision as to which supplier to use?

# SELECTED BIBLIOGRAPHY

Bowersox, Donald J., and David J. Closs. *Logistical Management: The Integrated Supply Chain Process.* New York: McGraw-Hill, 1996.

Cooke, James A. "The $30 Billion." *Traffic Management,* December 1993, pp. 57–61.

Coyle, J. J.; E. J. Bardi; and C. John Langley Jr. *The Management of Business Logistics.* 6th ed. Minneapolis/St. Paul, MN: West, 1996.

Davis, Stanley M. *Future Perfect.* Reading, MA: Addison-Wesley, 1987.

Dixon, Lance E. *JIT II*®. Bose Corporation.

Fabey, Michael. "Time Is Money: Seamless Logistics Are in Demand." *World Trade,* July 1997, pp. 53–54.

"Going Beyond EDI: Wal-Mart Cited for Vendor Links." *Chain Store Age Executive,* March 1993, pp. 150–51.

Jenkins, David B. "Jenkins Leads EDI Effort." *Chain Store Age Executive,* March 1993, p. 147.

Leenders, Michiel R., and Harold E. Fearon. *Purchasing and Supply Management.* 11th ed. Burr Ridge, IL: Irwin/McGraw-Hill, 1997.

Lima, Edvaldo Pereira. "VW's Revolutionary Idea." *Industry Week,* March 17, 1997.

Reitman, Valerie. *The Wall Street Journal,* May 8, 1997, p. A1.

Schemo, Diana J. "Is VW's New Plant Lean, or Just Mean?" *The New York Times,* November 19, 1996.

# Just-in-Time Systems

## Chapter Outline

## Chapter Objectives

- Introduce the underlying concepts of just-in-time (JIT) and the Japanese approach to improving productivity.
- Identify the differences between Japanese companies and U.S. firms with respect to implementing JIT, and explore why these differences exist.
- Identify the various elements that need to be included to successfully implement JIT within an organization.
- Illustrate how many JIT concepts have been implemented in services.

The 100 Yen Sushi House is no ordinary sushi restaurant. It is the ultimate showcase of Japanese productivity. As we entered the shop, there was a chorus of *"iratsai,"* a welcome from everyone working in the shop—cooks, waitresses, the owner, and the owner's children. The house features an ellipsoid-shaped serving area in the middle of the room, where three or four cooks were busily preparing sushi. Perhaps 30 stools surrounded the serving area. We took seats at the counters and were promptly served with a cup of "misoshiru," which is a bean paste soup, a pair of chopsticks, a cup of green tea, a tiny plate to make our own sauce, and a small china piece to hold the chopsticks. So far, the service was average for any sushi house. Then, I noticed something special. There was a conveyor belt going around the ellipsoid service area, like a toy train track. On it I saw a train of plates of

sushi. You can find any kind of sushi that you can think of—from the cheapest seaweed or octopus kind to the expensive raw salmon or shrimp dishes. The price is uniform, however, 100 yen per plate. On closer examination, while my eyes were racing to keep up with the speed of the traveling plates, I found that a cheap seaweed plate had four pieces, while the more expensive raw salmon dish had only two pieces.

I saw a man with eight plates all stacked up neatly. As he got up to leave, the cashier looked over and said, "800 yen, please." The cashier had no cash register, since she could simply count the number of plates and then multiply by 100 yen. As the customer was leaving, once again we heard a chorus of *"Arigato Gosaimas"* (thank you), from all the workers.

The owner's daily operation is based on a careful analysis of information. The owner has a complete summary of demand information about different types of sushi plates, and thus he knows exactly how many of each type of sushi plates he should prepare and when. Furthermore, the whole operation is based on the repetitive manufacturing principle with appropriate just-in-time and quality control systems. For example, the store has a very limited refrigerator capacity (we could see several whole fish or octopus in the glassed chambers right in front of our counter). Thus, the store uses the just-in-time inventory control system. Instead of increasing the refrigeration capacity by purchasing new refrigeration systems, the company has an agreement with the fish vendor to deliver fresh fish several times a day so that materials arrive just in time to be used for sushi making. Therefore, the inventory cost is minimum.

In the just-in-time operation system, the safety stock principle is turned upside down. In other words, the safety stock is deliberately removed gradually, to uncover problems and their possible solutions. The available floor space is for workers and their necessary equipment but not for holding inventory. In the 100 Yen Sushi House, workers and their equipment are positioned so close that sushi making is passed on hand to hand rather than as independent operations. The absence of walls of inventory allows the owner and workers to be involved in the total operation, from greeting the customer to serving what is ordered. Their tasks are tightly interrelated and everyone rushes to a problem spot to prevent the cascading effect of the problem throughout the work process.

The 100 Yen Sushi House is a labor-intensive operation, which is based mostly on simplicity and common sense rather than high technology, contrary to American perceptions. I was very impressed. As I finished my fifth plate, I saw the same octopus sushi plate going around for about the thirtieth time. Perhaps I had discovered the pitfall of the system. So I asked the owner how he takes care of the sanitary problems when a sushi plate goes around all day long, until an unfortunate customer eats it and perhaps gets food poisoning. He bowed with an apologetic smile and said, "Well, sir, we never let our sushi plates go unsold longer than about 30 minutes." Then he scratched his head and said, "Whenever one of our employees takes a break, he or she can take off unsold plates of sushi and either eat them or throw them away. We are very serious about our sushi quality." As we laughed, he laughed, along with a 90-degree bow.  ∎

Source:  Sang M. Lee, "Japanese Management and the 100 Yen Sushi House," *Operations Management Review* 1, no. 2 (Winter 1983), pp. 45–48.

# JIT LOGIC

**JIT (just-in-time)**
A coordinated approach that continuously reduces inventories while also improving quality.

**JIT ( just-in-time)** is an integrated set of activities designed to achieve high-volume production using minimal inventories of raw materials, work in process, and finished goods. Parts arrive at the next workstation "just in time" and are completed and move through the operation quickly. Just-in-time is also based on the logic that nothing will be produced until it is needed. Exhibit 12.1 illustrates the process. Need is created by the product being pulled toward the user. When an item is sold, in theory, the market pulls a replacement from the last position in the system—final assembly in this case. This triggers an order to the factory production line where a worker then pulls another unit from an upstream station in the flow to replace the unit taken. This upstream station then pulls from the next station further upstream and so on back to the release of raw materials. To enable this pull process to work smoothly, JIT demands high levels of quality at each stage of the process, strong vendor relations, and a fairly predictable demand for the end product.

JIT can be viewed colloquially as "big JIT" and "little JIT." Big JIT (often termed lean production[1]) is the philosophy of operations management that seeks to eliminate waste in all aspects of a firm's production activities: human relations, supplier relations, technology, and the management of materials and inventories. Little JIT focuses more narrowly on scheduling goods inventories and providing service resources where and when needed. For example, companies such as Manpower Temporary Services and Pizza Hut essentially use

[1]Paul H. Zipkin, "Does Manufacturing Need a JIT Revolution?" *Harvard Business Review* (January–February 1991), p. 41.

**EXHIBIT 12.1**

Pull System

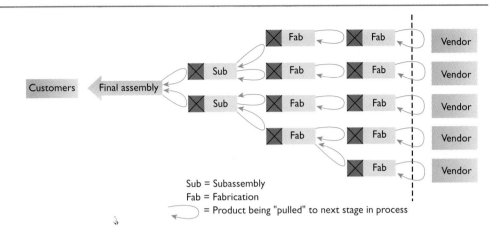

Sub = Subassembly
Fab = Fabrication
⌒ = Product being "pulled" to next stage in process

pull signals to fill orders for replacement workers or Sicilian pizzas, respectively. However, they do not necessarily integrate operations around other aspects of the JIT philosophy.

# THE JAPANESE APPROACH TO PRODUCTIVITY[2]

To fully appreciate the elements of Big JIT, it is useful to review the history and philosophy of its application in Japan. The ability of Japanese manufacturers to compete in high-quality, low-cost production which was widely publicized in the 1970s and early 1980s (see Exhibits 12.2 and 12.3) still holds despite their current economic problems. Indeed, the Japanese retain the market dominance in televisions, VCRs, cameras, watches, motorcycles, and shipbuilding that they established over 20 years ago—in large part due to JIT.

Many people believe these accomplishments are attributable to cultural differences. They envision the Japanese dedicating their lives to their companies and working long hours for substandard wages, which would be unthinkable in America. The evidence, however, is contrary to these distorted notions. Consider the following: In 1977, a Japanese company named Matsushita purchased a television plant in Chicago from a U.S. company. In the purchase contract, Matsushita agreed that all the hourly personnel would be retrained. Two years later, they still had essentially the same 1,000 hourly employees and had managed to reduce the indirect staff by 50 percent (see Exhibit 12.4). Yet, during that period, daily production had doubled. The quality, as measured by the number of defects per 100 TV sets built, improved 40-fold. Outside quality indicators also improved. Where the U.S. company (Motorola) had spent an average amount of $16 million a year on warranty costs, Matsushita's expenditures were $2 million. (That's for twice as many TV sets, so it's really a 16-to-1 ratio.) These are big differences—differences achieved here in the United States with American workers. The issue is, how do the Japanese do this and what can we learn from them?

As a starting point, it's important to understand that the Japanese, as a nation, have had one fundamental economic goal since 1945: full employment through industrialization. The strategy employed to achieve this goal called for obtaining market dominance in very select product areas. They very carefully chose those industries in which they believed they could become dominant and concentrated on them, rather than diluting their efforts over a broader spectrum.

---

[2]Adapted from Kenneth A. Wantuck, "The Japanese Approach to Productivity," Southfield, MI: Bendix Corporation, 1983.

**EXHIBIT 12.2**

1977 Hertz Repair Study

| Model | Repairs per 100 Vehicles |
|-------|--------------------------|
| Ford | 326 |
| Chevrolet | 425 |
| Pinto | 306 |
| Toyota | 55 |

This study, undertaken by Hertz, was the first widely publicized evidence of the Japanese quality superiority in automobiles.

**EXHIBIT 12.3**

Comparative U.S. and Japanese Inventory Turnover Rates for 15 Industries

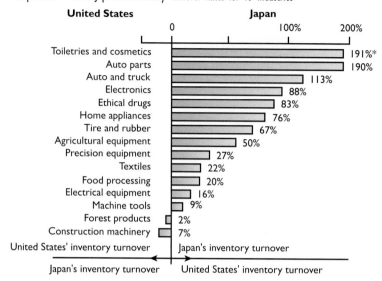

\* Inventory turnover of Japanese firms in this industry is 191% of that of U.S. firms.
Source: Booz, Allen & Hamilton Survey of 1,500 Companies, 1981.

**EXHIBIT 12.4**

Quasar Plant Productivity

|  | Under Motorola | Under Matsushita* |
|--|----------------|-------------------|
| Direct labor employees | 1,000 | 1,000[†] |
| Indirect employees | 600 | 300 |
| Total employees | 1,600 | 1,300 |
| Daily production | 1,000 | 2,000 |
| Defect rate per 100 TV sets | 160 | 4 |
| Annual warranty cost ($ millions) | $16 | $2 |

*2 years later.
[†] Same people.

The tactics of the Japanese were threefold: (*a*) They imported their technology. (The entire Japanese semiconductor industry was built around a $25,000 purchase from Texas Instruments for the rights to the basic semiconductor process.) Instead of reinventing the wheel, they avoided major R&D expenditures and the associated risks, then negotiated license agreements to make successful, workable new products. (*b*) They concentrated their ingenuity on the factory to achieve high productivity and low unit cost. The best engineering talent available was directed to the shop floor, instead of the product design department. (*c*) Finally, they embarked on a drive to improve product quality and reliability to the highest possible levels, to give their customers product reliability that competitors were not able to supply.

The implementation of these tactics by the Japanese was governed by two fundamental concepts (most of us agree with these concepts in principle, but the difference is the degree to which the Japanese practice them):

**eliminate waste**
Eliminate everything not essential to production, including safety stocks, waiting times, and extra labor.

1. They are firm believers that in every way, shape, and form you must **eliminate waste.**

2. They have a great respect for people.

## Elimination of Waste

When the Japanese talk about waste, the definition given by Fujio Cho, from the Toyota Motor Company, probably states it as well as anyone. He calls it "anything other than the *minimum* amount of equipment, materials, parts, and workers (working time) which are *absolutely essential* to production." That means no surplus, no safety stock. That means nothing is banked for future use. If you can't use it now you don't make it now because that is considered waste. There are seven basic elements under this concept:

1. Focused factory networks.
2. Group technology.
3. *Jidoka*—quality at the source.
4. Just-in-time production.
5. Uniform plant loading.
6. Kanban production control system.
7. Minimized setup times.

**focused factory networks**
Groups of small plants, each highly specialized in products they manufacture.

**Focused Factory Networks**   The first element is **focused factory networks.** Instead of building a large manufacturing plant that does everything (i.e., a highly vertically integrated facility), the Japanese build small plants that are highly specialized. There are several reasons for doing this. First, it's very difficult to manage a large installation; the bigger it gets the more bureaucratic it gets. The Japanese style of management does not lend itself to this kind of environment.

Second, when a plant is specifically designed for one purpose it can be constructed and operated more economically than its universal counterpart. It's comparable to buying a special machine tool to do a very specific job instead of trying to adapt a general purpose tool. Fewer than 750 plants in Japan have as many as 1,000 or more employees. The bulk of them, some 60,000 plants, have between 30 and 1,000 workers and over 180,000 have fewer than 30 employees. When we talk about the Japanese approach to productivity and the impressive things they're doing, we're talking primarily about the middle group, in which most of their model manufacturing plants are located.

Two illustrative examples have been cited by the Ford Motor Company: The Escort automobile needed a transaxle, which was going to require a $300 million expansion at the Ford plant in Batavia, Ohio. Ford asked the Japanese for an equivalent quotation and Tokyo–Kogyo offered to construct a brand-new plant with the same rate of output at a competitive unit price for $100 million, a one-third ratio. A second example relates to Ford's Valencia engine plant, which produces two engines per employee per day, and requires 900,000 square feet of floor space. An almost identical engine is produced by the Toyota Motor Company in Japan, where they make nine engines per employee per day in a plant that has only 300,000 square feet of space. The issue is not only productivity per person but also a much lower capital investment to achieve this manufacturing capability.

**group technology**
Clustering dissimilar machines and operations in one area of the plant to manufacture one family of products.

**Group Technology**   Inside the plant the Japanese employ a technique called **group technology.** Group technology is nothing new to America; it was invented here, like so many of the techniques the Japanese successfully employ, but only relatively recently has been practiced widely in the United States. A simplified diagram of the technique is shown in Exhibit 12.5. The lower portion shows the way we operate our plants today. Most companies process a job and send it from department to department because that's the way our plants are organized (sheetmetal department, grinding department, etc.). Each machine in those departments is usually staffed by a worker who specializes in that function. Getting a job through a shop can be a long and complicated process because there's a lot of waiting time and moving time involved (usually between 90 percent and 95 percent of the total processing time).

**EXHIBIT 12.5**

Group Technology versus
Departmental Specialty

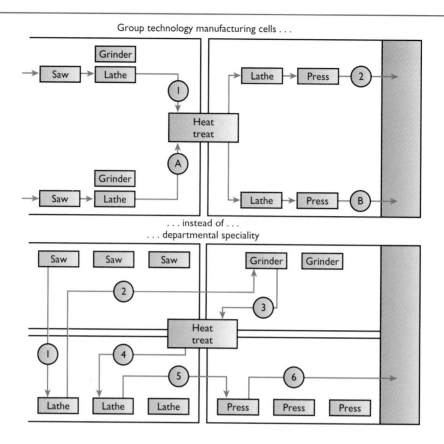

Group technology manufacturing cells . . .

. . . instead of . . .
. . . departmental speciality

The Japanese, on the other hand, consider all the operations required to make a part and try to group those machines together. The upper part of Exhibit 12.5 shows clusters of dissimilar machines designed to be work centers for given parts or families of parts. One operator runs all three machines shown in the upper-left corner, increasing the utility of the individual operator and eliminating the move and queue time between operations in a given cluster. Thus, not only does productivity go up but the work-in-process (WIP) inventory also comes down dramatically.

To achieve this, people have to be flexible; to be flexible, people must identify with their companies, have a high degree of job security, and undergo continuous training.

### Jidoka—Quality at the Source

**Jidoka**
Japanese concept focusing on controlling the quality of a product at its source.

When management demonstrates a high degree of confidence in people, it is possible to implement a quality concept that the Japanese call **Jidoka.** The word means "Stop everything when something goes wrong." It can be thought of as controlling quality at the source. (In the photo, air bag crash sensors are being inspected by workers at the TRW plant in

which makes the set of cards in the rack a dispatch list. Many firms use withdrawal cards only. Under the simplest form of one-card system, the worker at the assembly line (or more likely a material handler) walks to the machine center with an empty container and a withdrawal Kanban. He or she would then place the empty container at a designated spot, attach the withdrawal card to a filled container, and carry it back to the assembly line. The worker at the machining center would know that a refill is required. This type of system is appropriate where the same part is made by the same people every day.

If it turns out that the demand for Part A is greater than planned and less than planned for Part B, the system self-regulates to these changes because there can be no more parts built than called for by the Kanban cards in circulation. Mix changes of 10 to 20 percent can easily be accommodated because the shifts are gradual and the increments are small. The ripple effect upstream is similarly dampened.

The same approach is used to authorize vendor shipments. When both the customer and the vendor are using the Kanban system, the withdrawal Kanban serves as the vendor release/shipping document while the production Kanban at the vendor's plant regulates production there.

The whole system hinges on everyone doing exactly what is authorized and following procedures explicitly. In fact, the Japanese use no production coordinators on the shop floor, relying solely on supervisors to ensure compliance. Cooperative worker attitudes are essential to its success.

Results can be impressive. Jidosha Kiki, a Bendix braking components affiliate in Japan, installed the Kanban/just-in-time system in 1977 with the help of its customer, Toyota. Within two years they had doubled productivity, tripled inventory turnover, and substantially reduced overtime and space requirements. Jidosha Kiki stated that this was a slow and difficult learning process for its employees, even considering the Japanese culture, because all the old rules of thumb had to be tossed out the window and deep-rooted ideas had to be changed.

**Minimized Setup Times**    The Japanese approach to productivity demands that production be run in small lots. This is impossible to do if machine setups take hours to accomplish. In fact, many companies in the United States use the economic order quantity (EOQ) formula to determine what quantity to make in order to absorb a long and costly setup time.

The Japanese have the same formula, but they've turned it around. Instead of accepting setup times as fixed amounts, they fixed the lot sizes (very small) and then went to work to reduce setup time.

That is a crucial factor in the Japanese approach. Their success in this area has received widespread acclaim. Many Americans have been to Japan and witnessed a team of press operators change the dies on an 800-ton press in 10 minutes. Compare their data with those of U.S. firms, as shown in Exhibit 12.10. The Japanese aim for single-digit setup times (i.e., less than 10 minutes) for every machine in their factories. They've addressed not only big things, like presses, but small molding machines and standard machines tools as well.

---

**EXHIBIT 12.10**

Minimizing Setup Time—
Hood and Fender Press
Comparison (800-ton press)

|  | Toyota | USA | Sweden | Germany |
|---|---|---|---|---|
| Setup time | 10 minutes | 6 hours | 4 hours | 4 hours |
| Setups/day | 3 | 1 | — | ½ |
| Lot size | 1 day* | 10 days | 1 month | — |

*For low-demand items (less than 1,000 month), as large as seven days.

Successful setup time reduction is easily achieved when approached from a methods engineering perspective. The Japanese separate setup time into two segments: *internal*—that part that must be done while a machine is stopped, and *external*—that part that can be done while the machine is operating. Simple things, such as the staging of replacement dies in anticipation of a change, fall into the external category, which, on the average, represents half of the usual setup time.

Another 50 percent reduction can usually be achieved by the application of time and motion studies and practice. (It is not unusual for a Japanese setup team to spend a full Saturday practicing changeovers.) Time-saving devices like hinged bolts, roller platforms, and folding brackets for temporary die staging are commonly seen, all of which are low-cost items.

Only then is it necessary to spend larger sums, to reduce the last 15 percent or so, on things such as automatic positioning of dies, rolling bolsters, and duplicate tool holders. The result is that 90 percent or *more* of the setup times can be eliminated if we have a desire to do so.

Referring again to the Jidosha Kiki Corporation (JKC), Exhibit 12.11 shows the remarkable progress the company made in just four years. These data relate to all the machines in the factory. It's interesting to note that while we are quite impressed that two thirds of their equipment can be changed over in less than 2 minutes, the company is embarrassed that 10 percent still takes more than 10 minutes!

The savings in setup time are used to increase the number of lots produced, with a corollary reduction in lot sizes. This makes the use of just-in-time production principles feasible, which in turn makes the Kanban control system practical. All the pieces fit together.

## Respect for People

**respect for people**
Principal of Japanese management where mutual respect is shown between management and workers.

The second guiding principle for the Japanese, along with elimination of waste, is **respect for people.** This principle, also, has seven basic elements:

1. Lifetime employment.
2. Company unions.
3. Attitude toward workers.
4. Automation/robotics.
5. Bottom-round management.
6. Subcontractor networks.
7. Quality circles.

**EXHIBIT 12.11**

Setup Reduction Results at JKC

| Setup Time | Percent Reduction | | |
|---|---|---|---|
| | 1976 | 1977 | 1980 |
| >60 minutes | 30% | 0% | 0% |
| 30–60 minutes | 19 | 0 | 0 |
| 20–30 minutes | 26 | 10 | 3 |
| 10–20 minutes | 20 | 12 | 7 |
| 5–10 minutes | 5 | 20 | 12 |
| 100 second–5 minutes | 0 | 17 | 16 |
| <100 seconds | 0 | 41 | 62 |

**Lifetime Employment**   Much has been written about the Japanese concept of lifetime employment. When Japanese workers are hired for permanent positions with a major industrial firm, they have jobs with that company for life (or until retirement age) provided they work diligently. If economic conditions deteriorate, the company maintains the payroll almost to the point of going out of business. We should understand, though, that these kinds of benefits apply only to permanent workers, who constitute about one third of the workforce in Japan. What's important is that the concept is pervasive. When people can identify with the company as the place they're going to spend their working life, not just an interim place to get a paycheck, then they have a tendency to be more flexible and to want to do all they can do to help achieve the company's goals.

**Company Unions**   When General Douglas MacArthur introduced the union concept to Japan during the post-World War II reconstruction period, he undoubtedly had in mind trade unions, but the Japanese didn't think that way. Japanese workers at Toyota were concerned about Toyota. They really didn't identify with the other automobile manufacturing employees in the rest of the country. They identified not with the kind of work they were doing but rather with the company for which they were working. So Toyota formed a union that included everybody who worked for Toyota, no matter what their skills were. The objective of both the union and management was to make the company as healthy as possible so there would be benefits accruing to the people in a secure and shared method. The resulting relationship was cooperative, not adversarial.

The Japanese system of compensation reinforces these goals because it is based on company performance bonuses. Everybody in a Japanese company, from the lowest employee to the highest, gets a bonus twice a year. In good times the bonus is high (up to 50 percent of their salaries), while in bad times there may be no bonus. As a result, the employees have an attitude that says, "If the company does well, I do well," which is important from the standpoint of soliciting the workers' help to improve productivity.

**Attitude toward Workers**   The attitude of management toward the workers is also critical. The Japanese do not look at people as human machines. As a matter of fact, they believe that if a machine can do a job, then a person *shouldn't* do it because it's below his or her dignity. A corollary concept says that if workers are really important as people, you must also believe that they can do much more than you are now giving them the opportunity to do.

The Japanese say, "What workers are doing today is only tapping their capability. We must give them an opportunity to do more." Thus, a third and most significant attitude requires that the management system provides every worker with an opportunity to display his or her maximum capabilities. These concepts are practiced, not just discussed, and the Japanese spend more for employee training and education—at all levels—than any other industrial nation.

**Automation/Robotics**   When people feel secure, identify with the company, and believe that they are being given an opportunity to fully display their talents, the introduction of automation and robotics is not considered as a staff-cutting move. The Japanese feel that this is a way to eliminate dull jobs so people can do more important things, and they have been making major capital investments in these areas. Interestingly enough, Japan has invested one-third or 33 percent of its gross national product in capital improvements over the last 20 years, compared to about 19 percent for the United States during the same period.

In automation, the Japanese have invested first in low-cost enhancements to existing or standard equipment, using some clever approaches. In the capital area they have been concentrating on programmable robots. A recent survey showed that Japan had approximately five times the number of programmable robots (some of them quite simple) as the United States. It is interesting to note that most of those robots were built in the United States. Again, we shipped our technology to Japan where it was used to build products to compete with us. Today, Japan is building its own robots at a rapid pace and has become both the leading robot producer and robot user in the world.

Because the Japanese honestly believe that robots free people for more important tasks, there is little worker resistance to the robotics implementation. In fact, workers go out of their way to figure out how to eliminate their jobs, if they find them dull, because they know the company will find something better and more interesting for them to do.

**Bottom-Round Management**   This mutual reliance between workers and management is a manifestation of the management style the Japanese call **bottom-round management.** It's also been identified as *consensus management* or *committee management.* It is an innate part of the Japanese culture because they have grown up with the concept that the importance of the group supercedes that of the individual. Consider that in Japan more than 124 million people are crowded on a tiny island group about the size of California, 80 percent of which is mountainous. In those circumstances, its citizens must have considerable respect for their neighbors, or social survival would be impossible. This cultural concept is ideal in a manufacturing environment because the process requires that people work together in a group to make a product. The individual cannot function independently, without concern for others, because he or she would only get out of synchronization with the rest of the group and disrupt the process.

Bottom-round management is a slow decision-making process. In attempting to arrive at a true consensus, not a compromise, the Japanese involve all potentially interested parties, talk over a problem at great length, often interrupt the process, seek out more information, and retalk the problem until everyone finally agrees. While we have often criticized the slowness of this method, the Japanese have an interesting response.

They say, "You Americans will make an instant decision and then you'll take a very long time to implement it. The decision is made so quickly, without consulting many of the people it's going to affect, that as you try to implement it you begin to encounter all sorts of unforeseen obstacles. Now, in our system, we take a long time to make a decision, but it only takes a short time to implement it because by the time we've finally reached a conclusion, everybody involved has had their say."

A key to bottom-round management is that decisions are made at the lowest possible level. In essence, the employees recognize a problem, work out a potential solution with their peers, and make recommendations to the next level of management. They, in turn, do the same thing and make the next recommendation up the line. And so it goes, with everyone participating in the process. As a result, top management teams in Japanese companies make very few day-to-day operating decisions, their time being almost totally devoted to strategic planning. Note, though, that the use of bottom-round management makes it extremely difficult to manage a large, complex manufacturing organization. That's another reason why the Japanese build focused factories.

**Subcontractor Networks**   The specialized nature of Japanese factories has fostered the development of an enormous subcontractor network; most subcontractors have fewer than 30 employees. More than 90 percent of all Japanese companies are part of the supplier network, which is many layers deep, because there is so little vertical integration in Japanese factories.

There are two kinds of suppliers: specialists in a narrow field who serve multiple customers (very much like U.S. suppliers), and captives, who usually make a small variety of

**bottom-round management**
Mutual reliance between management and workers focusing on reaching consensus or agreement.

MANAGEMENT

parts for a single customer. The second kind is more prevalent in Japan. Of course, this idea of sole-sourcing suppliers is diametrically opposite to the U.S. multisource concept. Sole-sourcing arrangements work in Japan because the relationships are based on a tremendous amount of mutual trust. They seek long-term partnerships between customer and supplier. Americans who do business with Japanese companies know that the very first stages of negotiation involve an elaborate ceremony of getting to know one another to determine whether there is a potential long-term relationship in the picture. Japanese businesspeople are rarely interested in a one-time buy, so it's a different way of doing business for Americans.

Suppliers in Japan consider themselves part of their customers' families. Very often key suppliers are invited to company functions such as picnics or parties. In return, suppliers deliver high-quality parts many times per day, often directly to the customer's assembly line, bypassing receiving and inspection. A typical scenario would have the supplier's truck arriving at a precise time of day, the driver unloading the truck, transporting the parts into the factory and delivering them to the assembly line at a given station, depositing the parts, picking up the empty containers, loading them into the truck, and leaving, without any interference. No receiving, no incoming inspection, no paperwork, no delays. It's an almost paper-free system, all built on mutual trust.

Trust is a two-way street. Because so many of the suppliers are small and undercapitalized, Japanese customers advance money to finance them, if necessary. Customer process engineers and quality personnel help vendors improve their manufacturing systems to meet the rigid quality and delivery standards imposed. Efforts are also made to help vendors reduce their production process costs to help ensure their profitability. When there is an economic downturn, however, the customers will perform more of the work in-house instead of buying from vendors. They do this to protect their own work forces. Vendors are small and do not have the permanent, lifetime employment guarantees that the major companies do. However, this is known in advance and suppliers consider this an acceptable risk.

**Quality Circles**   Another interesting technique, with which many Americans are already familiar, is **quality circles.** The Japanese call them *small group improvement activities (SGIA).* A quality circle is a group of volunteer employees who meet once a week on a scheduled basis to discuss their function and the problems they're encountering, to try to devise solutions to those problems, and to propose those solutions to their management. The group may be led by a supervisor or a production worker. It usually includes people from a given discipline or a given production area, like Assembly Line A or the machining department. It can also be multidisciplinary, consisting, for instance, of all the material handlers who deliver materials to a department and the industrial engineers who work in that department. It does have to be led, though, by someone who is trained as a group leader. The trainers are facilitators, and each one may coordinate the activities of a number of quality circles. Westinghouse Electric Corporation, for example, has 275 quality circles and about 25 facilitators.

The quality circle really works because it's an open forum. It takes some skill to prevent it from becoming a gripe session, but that's where the trained group leaders keep the members on target. Interestingly enough, only about one third of the proposals generated turn out to be quality related. More than half are productivity oriented. It's really amazing how many good ideas these motivated employees can contribute toward the profitability and the improved productivity of their companies. Quality circles are actually a manifestation of the consensus, bottom-round management approach but are limited to these small groups.

**quality circles**
Groups of workers who meet to discuss their common area of interest and problems they are encountering.

# JIT IN THE UNITED STATES

 JIT evolved in Japan in great part due to the unique characteristics of that country. Japan is a very small country in area. Distances between most of the major cities are, therefore, relatively short. In addition, a large proportion of its geographic area is mountainous. Consequently, most of Japan's population lives in a relatively small area, with space at a premium. In addition, the Japanese tend to have a strong paternalistic, family-oriented culture that extends to the relationship between large and small companies.

Consequently, the vast majority of Japanese suppliers to the major companies are usually located within a 25-mile radius of the major firms' manufacturing facilities. In addition, most of the sales of these small firms tend to be to a single large customer, thereby making these small companies highly dependent.

In contrast, the United States has a very large geographic area. Suppliers are, therefore, often located thousands of miles away from production facilities. (As companies continue to extend their supply chains globally, their suppliers will become even more remotely located.) In addition, the paternalistic relationship between large companies and small does not exist to the same extent that it does in Japan. Finally, most U.S. firms have a much wider customer base, with any one customer representing only a small percentage of its sales. For these and various other reasons, JIT is practiced differently in the United States than it is in Japan.

"JIT in the United States often stands for *Jumbo-Inventory-Transfer*," said Peter Frasso, vice president and general manager of Varian Vacuum Products in Lexington, Massachusetts, at the April 1996, Annual Meeting of the Operations Management Association in Boston, Massachusetts. In other words, there are many large companies in the United States that, instead of working with suppliers to synchronize operations, will often try to force suppliers to maintain large stocks of inventory rather than keep these inventories at their own facilities. Thus, while the large firms practice JIT within their own facilities, their suppliers deliver raw material and components from buffer inventories that are frequently located nearby. With this approach, transferring the inventory from the manufacturer to the supplier improves the performance of the large firm at the expense of the smaller supplier, which absorbs all of the risks and costs associated with these inventories. The large distances that often exist between suppliers and customers in the United States also precludes the ability to provide products in small lot sizes at short time intervals (that is, several times a day, as is often the case in Japan).

Nevertheless, other aspects or elements of JIT, such as: (*a*) working with suppliers in a partnership relationship rather than an adversarial one, (*b*) reducing setup times and thus lot sizes, (*c*) encouraging worker participation, and (*d*) reducing inventories and waste, are being adopted by the better companies, with recognizable benefits. A survey of U.S. manufacturers indicated that 86 percent of the respondents acknowledged some benefits from implementing JIT.[3]

Because of these differences, many U.S. companies have adopted an MRP system (as discussed later in Chapter 15) in working with their suppliers. The MRP system provides the suppliers with a forecast of the raw material and component requirements. Typically these requirements are *frozen* for the immediate future, but can change the further out the requirements are. For example, the orders placed with a supplier might be fixed for the next six weeks, but the requirements may change beyond this six-week window. This approach allows suppliers to schedule work efficiently within their own facilities. As illustrated in

---

[3]Richard E. White, "An Empirical Assessment of JIT in U.S. Manufacturers," *Production and Inventory Management Journal* 34, no. 2 (1993), pp. 38–42.

_____. *Attaining Manufacturing Excellence.* Homewood, IL: Dow Jones-Irwin, 1987.

Halverson, R. "Logistical Supremacy Secures the Base—But Will It Translate Abroad?" *Discount Store News* 33, no. 23 (1994), pp. 107–8.

Inman, R. Anthony, and Satish Mehra. "The Transferability of Just-in-Time Concepts to American Small Business," *Interfaces* 20, no. 2 (March–April 1990), pp. 30–37.

Klein, Janice. "A Re-examination of Autonomy in Light of New Manufacturing Practices." *Human Relations* 43 (1990).

Lee, J. Y. "JIT Works for Services Too." *CMA Magazine* 6 (1990), pp. 20–23.

Lee, Sang M. "Japanese Management and the 100 Yen Sushi House." *Operations Management Review* 1, no. 2 (Winter 1983), pp. 45–48.

Ohno, Taiichi. *Toyota Production System: Beyond Large-Scale Production.* Cambridge, MA: Productivity Press, 1988.

Ohno, Taiichi, and Setsuo Mito. *Just-in-Time for Today and Tomorrow.* Cambridge, MA: Productivity Press, 1988.

Rata, Ernest. "Saturn: Rising Star," *Purchasing* (September 9, 1993), pp. 44–47.

Schneider, B., and D. E. Bowen. *Winning the Service Game.* Cambridge, MA: Harvard Business School Press, 1995.

Schonberger, Richard J. *Japanese Productivity Techniques.* New York: Free Press, 1982.

_____. *World Class Manufacturing: The Lessons of Simplicity Applied.* New York: Free Press, 1986.

_____. *Building a Chain of Customers: Linking Business Functions to Create a World-Class Company.* New York: Free Press, 1989.

Sewell, G. "Management Information Systems for JIT Production." *Omega* 18, no. 5 (1990), pp. 481–503.

Shingo, Shigeo. *A Study of the Toyota Production System from an Industrial Engineering Viewpoint.* Cambridge, MA: Productivity Press, 1989.

Sohal, Amrik, and Keith Howard. "Trends in Materials Management." *International Journal of Production Distribution and Materials Management* 17, no. 5 (1987), pp. 3–41.

Stalk, G., Jr. "Competing on Capabilities: The New Rules of Corporate, Strategy." *Harvard Business Review* 70, no. 2, pp. 57–69.

Suzaki, Kiyoshi. *The New Manufacturing Challenge: Techniques for Continuous Improvement.* New York: Free Press, 1987.

Tatikonda, Mohan V. "Just-in-Time and Modern Manufacturing Environments: Implications for Cost Accounting." *Production and Inventory Management Journal* 28, no. 1 (1988), pp. 1–5.

Wantuck, Kenneth A. "The Japanese Approach to Productivity." Southfield, MI: Bendix Corporation, 1983.

White, Richard E. "An Empirical Assessment of JIT in U.S. Manufacturers." *Production and Inventory Management Journal* 34, no. 2 (1993), pp. 38–42.

Zipkin, Paul H. "Does Manufacturing Need a JIT Revolution?" *Harvard Business Review,* January–February 1991, pp. 40–50.

# AGGREGATE PLANNING

*Chapter Objectives*

- Demonstrate how aggregate planning links long-range strategic planning and short-range scheduling.

- Present alternate strategies for matching supply and demand: adjusting supply (an operations function) or adjusting demand (a marketing function).

- Introduce strategies for developing aggregate plans and ways to identify their strengths and weaknesses.

- Define marginal costs and total costs as they pertain to aggregate planning.

- Introduce the concept of yield management as a tool for matching supply and demand in service operations.

Each year, Janet Cramer, the plant manager at Polaroid's Integral Film Assembly Operation in Waltham, Massachusetts, struggles to identify the most efficient way to meet the forecasted sales for film. Janet's plant is the only film assembly operation in the United States. (There is only one other Polaroid film assembly operation in the world, located in The Netherlands.)

Historically, annual sales of Polaroid film has followed a cyclic pattern, with the maximum sales per month taking place just before Christmas time when retail operations stock their shelves in anticipation of holiday sales. There is also another peak, although somewhat smaller, in late spring and early summer, when customers purchase film for graduations, weddings, and summer vacations.

Four different types of film are assembled at the Waltham plant. The assembly of film into the cartridges for the Polaroid cameras is a highly capital intensive process with very high fixed costs and relatively low variable costs. As a result, Polaroid's operation in Waltham, which includes approximately 470 hourly employees, runs on three shifts, 24 hours a day, five days a week. In addition, the workforce primarily consists of highly skilled individuals who would be difficult to replace.

Even within this highly constrained environment, Janet has several alternatives available to her for scheduling production. The first alternative is to work overtime on Saturdays at a premium pay of 50 percent for all shifts. With this approach, inventory will be carried at an estimated cost of 20 to 25 percent per annum until the peak demand month is reached. The second alternative is to work both Saturdays and Sundays in the months just prior to the peak in order to minimize inventory carrying costs. Working on Sunday pays a premium of double time. However, with this approach there is the concern that worker fatigue (from working seven days a week) will have a negative impact on quality and productivity and, even, on employee morale.

The issues confronting Janet Cramer in selecting an aggregate planning alternative for her operation are typical of those that operations managers face when demand for their products is cyclic. There is often no one right answer, but rather a compromise that takes into consideration all of the various factors that can affect quality, productivity, cost, and employee morale. ∎

Source: Special thanks to Janet Cramer and Laurie Mullane, Polaroid Corp.

The first step in translating long-range strategic plans down to the operational level is the development of an aggregate plan. In essence, aggregate planning is an intermediate- or medium-range planning tool that is used to develop gross requirements, primarily for labor and materials, for the next 12 months. Aggregate planning thus takes a fairly broad view, addressing gross product requirements in total rather than specific products, and determining the number of workers needed in total rather than the number needed in specific skills areas.

In manufacturing, the goal of aggregate planning is to match the demand for the firm's products with its capacity or ability to supply those products, and to do so at minimum cost. The aggregate planning process identifies alternative methods to match supply and demand from the operations management perspective. In services, because the customer interacts directly with the service delivery process, alternative approaches to matching supply and demand are more limited. Thus, for certain types of services, a concept known as *yield management* has been developed which simultaneously manages both supply and demand for a service.

MARKETING

In both manufacturing and services, the marketing function also plays a key role in this matching process through the use of marketing tools such as pricing, advertising, and promotion. Both the marketing and operations management functions need to work together to develop an aggregate plan that is both effective and efficient.

In this chapter we present several quantitative techniques for developing aggregate plans that are applicable to both manufacturing and service organizations.

## OVERVIEW OF OPERATIONAL PLANNING ACTIVITIES

**planning activities:**
**long-range planning**
Focuses on strategic issues relating to capacity, process selection, and plant location.

**medium-range planning**
Focuses on tactical issues pertaining to aggregate workforce and material requirements for the coming year.

**short-range planning**
Addresses day-to-day issues of scheduling workers on specific jobs at assigned work stations.

Every organization must plan its activities at a variety of levels and operate these as a system. Exhibit 13.1 presents an overall view of planning and shows how aggregate production planning relates to other activities of a manufacturing firm. The time dimension is shown as long, medium, and short range.

**Long-range planning** is generally done once a year, focusing on a time horizon that is usually greater than a year. The length of the time horizon will vary from industry to industry. For those industries that require many years to plan and construct plants and facilities, and to install specific processes (e.g., refineries), the time horizon may be 5 to 10 or more years. For other industries where the ability to expand capacity is shorter (e.g., clothing manufacturing and many service industries), the time horizon may be two to five years or less.

**Medium-range planning** usually covers the period from 6 to 18 months in the future, with time increments or "buckets" that are monthly and/or quarterly. (The near-term time increments are often monthly, whereas those at the end of the time horizon tend to be quarterly, as these are usually less accurate.) Medium-range planning is typically reviewed and updated quarterly.

**Short-range planning** covers the period from one day to six months, with the time increment usually being weekly. As with long-range planning, the length of the time horizon for medium- and short-range planning will vary from industry to industry.

### Long-Range Planning

Long-range planning begins with a statement of organizational objectives and goals for the next 2 to 10 years. *Corporate strategic planning* articulates how these objectives and goals are to be achieved in light of the company's capabilities and its economic and political environment as projected by its *business forecasting*. Elements of the strategic plan include

**EXHIBIT 13.1**

Overview of Manufacturing
Planning Activities

```
Long range

    Business          Corporate            Financial
    forecasting  →    strategic     →      planning
                      planning

                      Product and          Resource
                      market       ←        (capacity)
                      planning              planning

Medium range

                      Aggregate
                      production   ←
                      planning

    Item              Master               Rough-cut
    forecasting  ↔    production    ↔       capacity
                      scheduling           planning
                      (MPS)                (RCP)

Short range

    Final             Materials            Capacity
    assembly          requirements  ↔      requirements
    scheduling        planning             planning
    (FAS)             (MRP)                (CRP)

    ┌─────────────────────────────────────────────────┐
    │ Production                      Purchase         │
    │ activity                        planning and     │
    │ control                         control          │
    │ (PAC)                                            │
    │            Input/output planning and control     │
    └─────────────────────────────────────────────────┘
```

product-line delineation, quality and pricing levels, and market penetration goals. *Product and market planning* translates these into individual market and product-line objectives, and includes a long-range production plan (basically a forecast of items to be manufactured for two years or more into the future). *Financial planning* analyzes the financial feasibility of these objectives relative to capital requirements and return on investment goals. *Resource planning* identifies the facilities, equipment, and personnel needed to accomplish the long-range production plan, and thus is frequently referred to as *long-run capacity planning*.

## Medium-Range Planning

**Aggregate Production Planning** As noted in Exhibit 13.1, this activity provides the primary link between the long-range strategic plans and the intermediate- or medium-range planning activities. Aggregate planning specifies monthly or quarterly output requirements by major product groups either in labor hours required or in units of production for up to

Kawasaki Motors USA produces utility vehicles, motorcycles, all-terrain vehicles, and Jet Ski watercraft at its plant in Lincoln, Nebraska.

While the corporate plan would specify how many units in each product line, the aggregate plan would determine how to meet this requirement with available resources.

**aggregate production planning**
Process for determining most cost effective way to match supply and demand over next 12–18 months.

18 months into the future. Its main inputs are the product and market plans and the resource plan. **Aggregate production planning** seeks to find that combination of monthly or quarterly workforce levels and inventory levels that minimizes total production-related costs over the planning period while meeting the forecasted demand for product.

**Item Forecasting**   This provides an estimate of specific products (and replacement parts), which, when integrated with the aggregate production plan, becomes the output requirement for the master production schedule (MPS). The process of monitoring and integrating this information is termed *demand management.*

**master production schedule**
Weekly schedule of specific end product requirements for the next several quarters.

**Master Production Scheduling (MPS)**   The MPS generates for the manufacturer the amounts and dates of specific end products. The **master production schedule** is usually fixed or "frozen" over the short run (six to eight weeks). Beyond six to eight weeks, various changes can be made, with essentially complete revisions possible after six months. As shown in Exhibit 13.1, the MPS depends on the product and market plans and resource plans outlined in the aggregate production plan.

**rough-cut capacity planning**
Determination that adequate production capacity and warehousing are available to meet demand.

**Rough-Cut Capacity Planning**   This reviews the MPS to make sure that no obvious capacity constraints would require changing the schedule. **Rough-cut capacity planning** includes verifying that sufficient production and warehouse facilities, equipment, and labor are available and that key vendors have allocated adequate capacity to provide materials when needed.

## Short-Range Planning

**Materials Planning**   Also known as *material requirements planning (MRP),* which is discussed in Chapter 15, this system takes the end product requirements from the MPS and breaks them down into their subassemblies and component parts. The materials plan specifies when production and purchase orders must be placed for each part and subassembly to complete the products on schedule.

**Capacity Requirements Planning**   Capacity requirements planning (CRP) should really be referred to as capacity requirements *scheduling,* because it provides a detailed schedule of when each operation is to run on each work center and how long it will take to process. The information it uses comes from planned (i.e., forecasted) and open (i.e., existing) orders that are generated by the materials plan. The CRP itself helps to validate the rough-cut capacity plan.

**Final Assembly Scheduling**   This activity identifies the various operations required to put the product in its final form. It is here that customized or final features of the product are scheduled. For example, a printer manufacturer would typically specify from various options a control panel configuration at this scheduling stage.

**Input/Output Planning and Control**   This refers to a variety of reports and procedures focusing on scheduled demands and capacity constraints derived from the materials plan.

**Production Activity Control**   Production activity control (PAC) is a relatively new term that is used to describe scheduling and shop-floor control activities. PAC involves the scheduling and controlling of day-to-day activities on the shop floor. At this point, the master production schedule is translated into the immediate priorities of daily work schedules.

**Purchase Planning and Control**   This activity deals with the acquisition and control of purchased items, again as specified by the materials plan. Input/output planning and control are necessary to make sure that purchasing not only is obtaining materials in time to meet the schedule, but is also aware of those orders that, for various reasons, call for rescheduling the delivery of purchased materials.

   In summary, all the planning approaches attempt to balance capacity required with capacity available, and then schedule and control production in light of changes in the capacity balance. A good planning system is complete without being overwhelming, and has the confidence of its users up and down the organization structure.

# AGGREGATE PRODUCTION PLANNING

**production rate**
Capacity of output per unit of time (such as units per day or units per week).

**workforce level**
Number of workers required to provide a specified level of production.

**inventory on hand**
Amount of inventory carried over from one time period to the next.

Again, aggregate production planning is concerned with setting production rates by product group or other broad categories for the intermediate term (6 to 18 months). Note again from our first exhibit that the aggregate plan precedes the master schedule. *The main purpose of the aggregate plan is to specify that combination of production rate, workforce level, and inventory on hand that both minimizes costs (efficiency) and satisfies the forecasted demand (effectiveness).* **Production rate** refers to the quantity of product completed per unit of time (such as VCRs per hour or automobiles per day). **Workforce level** is the number of workers needed for production. **Inventory on hand** represents the unsold units of product that are carried over from the previous period.

   The process of aggregate planning varies from company to company. In some firms, it is a formalized report containing both planning objectives and the planning premises on which it is based. In other companies, particularly smaller ones, it may be much more informal in the form of verbal communications.

   The process by which the plan itself is derived also varies. One common approach is to develop it from the corporate annual plan, as was shown in Exhibit 13.1. A typical corporate plan contains a section on manufacturing that specifies how many units in each major product line need to be produced over the next 12 months to meet the sales forecast. The planner takes this information and attempts to determine how best to meet these requirements with available resources. Alternatively, some organizations combine output requirements into

**EXHIBIT 13.2**

Required Inputs to the
Production Planning System

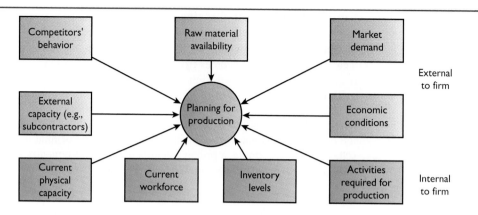

equivalent units and use this as the basis for aggregate planning. For example, a division of
General Motors may be asked to produce a certain number of cars of all types at a particular facility. The production planner would then take the average labor hours required for all
models as a basis for the overall aggregate plan. Refinements to this plan, specifically model
types to be produced, would be reflected in shorter-term production plans. Another approach is to develop the aggregate plan by simulating various master production schedules
and calculating corresponding capacity requirements to see if adequate labor and equipment exist at each work center. If capacity is inadequate, additional requirements for overtime, subcontracting, extra workers, and so forth are specified for each product line and
combined into a rough-cut plan. This plan is then modified by trial-and-error or mathematical methods to derive a final and, one hopes, lower-cost plan.

## Production Planning Environment

Exhibit 13.2 illustrates the internal and external factors that constitute the production planning environment. In general, the external environment is outside the production planner's
direct control. In some firms, demand for the product can be managed, but even so, the production planner must live with the sales projections and orders promised by the marketing
function. This leaves the internal factors as the variables that can be manipulated in deriv-
ing a production plan.

The internal factors themselves differ in their degree of control. Current physical capacity (plant and equipment) is virtually fixed in the short run and, therefore, cannot be increased; union agreements often constrain what can be done in changing the workforce;
and top management may set limits on the amount of money that can be tied up in inventories. Still, there is always some flexibility in managing these factors, and production
planners can implement one or a combination of the **production planning strategies** discussed here.

## Production Planning Strategies

There are essentially three production planning strategies. These strategies involve trade-
offs among workforce size, work hours, inventory, and order backlogs.

1. *Chase strategy.*[1] Match the production rate to exactly meet the order rate by hiring and
   laying off employees as the order rate varies. The success of this strategy depends on

**production planning
strategies:**
  **pure strategy**
  Either a chase strategy
  when production
  exactly matches
  demand or a level
  strategy when
  production remains
  constant over a
  specified number of
  time periods.

  **mixed strategy**
  Combination of chase
  and level strategies to
  match supply and
  demand.

---

[1]No relation to one of the authors of this text.

**EXHIBIT 13.3**

Examples of Pure Chase
and Pure Level Strategies

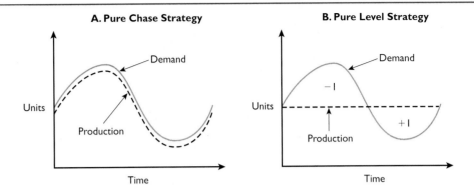

having a pool of easily trained applicants to draw on as order volumes increase. There
are obvious motivational impacts. When order backlogs are low, employees may feel
compelled to slow down out of fear of being laid off as soon as existing orders are
completed.

2. *Stable workforce—variable work hours.* Vary the output by varying the number of
   hours worked through flexible work schedules or overtime. By varying the number of
   work hours, production quantities can be matched, within limits, to existing orders.
   This strategy provides workforce continuity and avoids many of the emotional and
   tangible costs of hiring and firing personnel that are associated with the chase
   strategy.

3. *Level strategy.* Maintain a stable workforce working at a constant output rate.
   Shortages and surpluses are absorbed by fluctuating inventory levels, order backlogs,
   and lost sales. Employees benefit from stable work hours, but inventory costs are
   increased. Another concern is the possibility of inventoried products becoming
   obsolete.

When just one of these variables is used to absorb demand fluctuations, it is termed a
**pure strategy;** one or more used in combination is a **mixed strategy.** As you might sus-
pect, mixed strategies are more widely applied in industry.

Exhibit 13.3A illustrates a pure chase strategy. Here production is in lockstep with demand. In other words, the number of units required in each time interval is the number of
units that production will make. Exhibit 13.3B, on the other hand, demonstrates a pure
level strategy. Here production is held constant, regardless of what the demand is. The difference between demand and production is accounted for in a "buffer" inventory of finished goods. When demand exceeds production, the difference is taken out of finished
goods inventory (−I); when demand is less than production, the difference is placed back
into inventory (+I). (It is assumed that when demand exceeds production in the initial
cycle, as shown in Exhibit 13.3B, that there is sufficient inventory on hand at the beginning
of the aggregate planning period to supply the required number of units.)

Certain industries, due to their inherent operating characteristics, often favor one type of
strategy over the other. For example, services tend to follow a chase strategy because the
customer is involved in the service delivery process. (If your restaurant is too crowded on
a Saturday night, customers will not wait until Monday morning when you have more than
enough capacity available to serve them!) Process-oriented facilities, on the other hand,
such as breweries and refineries, tend to follow a level strategy because the high fixed costs
associated with them require that they operate at a high level of capacity utilization.

Specialty outsourcing companies are being increasingly used to satisfy the needs of companies. Here Norrell Services in Memphis, Tennessee, provides training to temporary workers in high-speed packing techniques. These workers will eventually work for Nike.

**Subcontracting**   In addition to these strategies, managers may also choose to subcontract some portion of production. This strategy is similar to the chase strategy, but hiring and laying off is translated into subcontracting and not subcontracting. Some level of subcontracting can be desirable to accommodate demand fluctuations. However, unless the relationship with the supplier is particularly strong, a manufacturer can lose some control over schedule and quality. For this reason, extensive subcontracting may be viewed as a high-risk strategy.

## Relevant Costs

ACCOUNTING

There are four costs relevant to aggregate production planning. These are:

1. *Basic production costs.* These are the fixed and variable costs incurred in producing a given product type in a given time period. Included are material costs, direct and indirect labor costs, and regular as well as overtime compensation.

2. *Costs associated with changes in the production rate.* Typical costs in this category are those involved in hiring, training, and laying off personnel. Additional one-time costs might also be associated with adding another shift.

3. *Inventory holding costs.* A major component is the cost of capital tied up in inventory. Other components include storage, insurance, taxes, spoilage, and obsolescence.

4. *Backlogging costs.* Usually these costs are very difficult to measure and include costs of expediting, loss of customer goodwill, and loss of sales revenues resulting from cancelled orders because the product is not available.

ACCOUNTING
FINANCE

**Budgets**   To receive funding, operations managers are generally required to submit annual, and sometimes quarterly, budget requests. Aggregate planning activities are key to the success of the budgeting process. Recall that the goal of aggregate planning is to meet forecasted product demand while minimizing the total production-related costs over the planning horizon by determining the optimal combination of workforce levels and inventory levels. Thus, aggregate planning provides justification for the requested budget amount.

Accurate medium-range planning increases both the likelihood of receiving the requested budget and operating within the limits of the budget.

In the next section, we provide examples of medium-range planning in both a manufacturing and a service setting. These examples illustrate the trade-offs associated with different production planning strategies.

# AGGREGATE PLANNING TECHNIQUES

Companies still use simple trial-and-error charting and graphic methods to develop their aggregate plans. Computer spreadsheets and graphics packages are now available to facilitate the process. A trial-and-error approach involves costing out various production planning alternatives and selecting the one with the lowest cost. In addition to the trial-and-error method, there are more sophisticated approaches, including linear programming, the Linear Decision Rule, and various heuristic methods. Of these, only linear programming has seen broad application.

## A Trial-and-Error Example: The C&A Company

A firm with pronounced seasonal variation normally plans production with a 12-month time horizon in order to capture the extremes in demand during the busiest and slowest months. However, it is possible to illustrate the general concepts involved in aggregate planning with a shorter time horizon. Suppose we wish to set up a production plan for the C&A Company for the next six months. We are given the information shown in Exhibit 13.4.

**EXHIBIT 13.4**

Forecasted Demand and Workdays for the C&A Company

| | Jan. | Feb. | Mar. | Apr. | May | June | Total |
|---|---|---|---|---|---|---|---|
| Demand forecast (units) | 2,200 | 1,500 | 1,100 | 900 | 1,100 | 1,600 | 8,400 |
| Working days (per month) | 22 | 19 | 21 | 21 | 22 | 20 | 125 |

| Costs | |
|---|---|
| Material cost | $100/unit |
| Inventory holding cost | $1.50/unit-month |
| Stockout cost | $5/unit/month |
| Subcontracting cost | $125/unit |
| Hiring and training cost | $200/worker |
| Layoff cost | $250/worker |
| Labor required per unit | 5 hours |
| Labor cost (first 8 hours each day) | $4/hour |
| Overtime cost (time and a half) | $6/hour |

| Inventory | |
|---|---|
| Beginning inventory | 400 units |

| Workforce | |
|---|---|
| Number of workers currently employed | 30 |

Before we solve this problem, we need to first recognize the differences between full costs and marginal or incremental costs. Full costs are all of the actual, out-of-pocket costs associated with a particular aggregate plan. Included in full costs are the costs of material, labor, and other direct, variable costs. Full costs are often used for developing a projected labor and material budget that will support an aggregate plan.

Marginal or incremental costs are only those unique costs that are different for a particular aggregate plan. Here we assume that the total number of products forecasted over the time horizon need to be built, regardless of the alternative selected. The incremental costs are, therefore, only those costs that are above and beyond those required to build the product by its most economical means (which is usually on the first shift in-house). Included in marginal costs are hiring and firing costs, inventory carrying costs, and overtime and/or second- and third-shift premium costs. To demonstrate the difference, we will use both the full-cost and marginal-cost methods to solve the aggregate planning problem for the C&A Company. You will note that both methods result in selecting the same alternative plan, based on lowest cost. The different alternatives are also ranked in the same order with both methods of costing. The advantage in using the marginal-cost approach is that we do not have to include a lot of numerical figures that have no impact on the final decision.

To properly develop and evaluate an aggregate plan, we need to first divide it into two stages. The first stage is the development of a feasible plan that provides the required number of products under the conditions stated. After this aggregate plan has been developed, the next step is to determine the costs associated with the plan. This is the approach we have taken with the C&A Company. Each alternative aggregate plan is accompanied by both its full and marginal costs.

Many of the costs included in an aggregate plan are presented in a form that is typically not found in the accounting records of a firm. For example, there is usually no cost of carrying inventory. Instead, the individual component costs associated with carrying inventory are listed in separate categories (e.g., the cost of storage is rent, insurance, taxes, etc.; the cost of obsolescence is reflected in higher material and labor costs, etc.).

The first step in evaluating alternative production plans is to convert the demand forecast into production requirements. This is accomplished by subtracting out the amount of inventory on hand at the beginning of the forecast period. In the C&A example, the beginning inventory on hand is 400 units.

Now we are ready to formulate and evaluate alternative aggregate or production plans for the C&A Company. Although one could develop a large number of alternative aggregate plans, we have identified four plans that we will evaluate with the objective of selecting that one with the lowest costs.

*Plan 1.* Produce to exact monthly production requirements using a regular eight-hour day by varying workforce size (pure chase strategy).

*Plan 2.* Produce to meet expected average demand over the next six months by maintaining a constant workforce. This constant number of workers is calculated by *averaging* the demand forecast over the horizon. Take the total production requirements for all six months and determine how many workers would be needed if each month's requirements were the same [(8,400 − 400) units × 5 hours per unit ÷ (125 days × 8 hours per day) = 40 workers]. Inventory is allowed to accumulate, and shortages, when they occur, are filled from next month's production by back ordering (pure level strategy).

*Plan 3.* Produce to meet the minimum expected demand (April) using a constant workforce on regular time. Subcontract to meet additional output requirements. The number of workers is calculated by identifying the minimum monthly production requirement and determining how many workers would be needed for that month [(900 units × 6 months × 5 hours per unit) ÷ (125 days × 8 hours per day) = 27 workers] and subcontracting any

EXHIBIT 13.5

First Alternative: Pure Chase
Strategy

| | Jan. | Feb. | March | April | May | June | Total |
|---|---|---|---|---|---|---|---|
| Demand forecast | 2,200 | 1,500 | 1,100 | 900 | 1,100 | 1,600 | 8,400 |
| Initial inventory | 400 | | | | | | |
| Production requirements | 1,800 | 1,500 | 1,100 | 900 | 1,100 | 1,600 | 8,000 |
| **Aggregate plan** | | | | | | | |
| Workers required | 51 | 49 | 33 | 27 | 31 | 50 | |
| Workers hired | 21 | 0 | 0 | 0 | 4 | 19 | |
| Workers fired | 0 | 2 | 16 | 6 | 0 | 0 | |
| Units produced | 1,800 | 1,500 | 1,100 | 900 | 1,100 | 1,600 | 8,000 |
| **Costs—full** | | | | | | | |
| Regular production | 36,000 | 30,000 | 22,000 | 18,000 | 22,000 | 32,000 | 160,000 |
| Material costs | 180,000 | 150,000 | 110,000 | 90,000 | 110,000 | 160,000 | 800,000 |
| Hiring costs | 4,200 | 0 | 0 | 0 | 800 | 3,800 | 8,800 |
| Firing costs | 0 | 500 | 4,000 | 1,500 | 0 | 0 | 6,000 |
| Total full costs | 220,200 | 180,500 | 136,000 | 109,500 | 132,800 | 195,800 | 974,800 |
| **Costs—incremental** | | | | | | | |
| Hiring costs | 4,200 | 0 | 0 | 0 | 800 | 3,800 | 8,800 |
| Firing costs | 0 | 500 | 4,000 | 1,500 | 0 | 0 | 6,000 |
| Total incremental costs | 4,200 | 500 | 4,000 | 1,500 | 800 | 3,800 | 14,800 |

EXHIBIT 13.6

Second Alternative:
Pure Level Strategy

| | Jan. | Feb. | March | April | May | June | Total |
|---|---|---|---|---|---|---|---|
| Demand forecast | 2,200 | 1,500 | 1,100 | 900 | 1,100 | 1,600 | 8,400 |
| Initial inventory | 400 | | | | | | |
| Production requirements | 1,800 | 1,500 | 1,100 | 900 | 1,100 | 1,600 | 8,000 |
| **Aggregate plan** | | | | | | | |
| Workers required | 40 | 40 | 40 | 40 | 40 | 40 | |
| Workers hired | 10 | 0 | 0 | 0 | 0 | 0 | |
| Workers fired | 0 | 0 | 0 | 0 | 0 | 0 | |
| Units produced | 1,408 | 1,216 | 1,344 | 1,344 | 1,408 | 1,280 | 8,000 |
| Monthly inventory | (392) | (284) | 244 | 444 | 308 | (320) | |
| Cumulative inventory | (392) | (676) | (432) | 12 | 320 | 0 | |
| **Costs—full** | | | | | | | |
| Regular production | 28,160 | 24,320 | 26,880 | 26,880 | 28,160 | 25,600 | 160,000 |
| Material costs | 140,800 | 121,600 | 134,400 | 134,400 | 140,800 | 128,000 | 800,000 |
| Hiring costs | 2,000 | 0 | 0 | 0 | 0 | 0 | 2,000 |
| Firing costs | 0 | 0 | 0 | 0 | 0 | 0 | 0 |
| Inventory carrying costs | 0 | 0 | 0 | 18 | 480 | 0 | 498 |
| Stockout costs | 1,960 | 3,380 | 2,160 | 0 | 0 | 0 | 7,500 |
| Total full costs | 172,920 | 149,300 | 163,440 | 161,298 | 169,440 | 153,600 | 969,998 |
| **Costs—incremental** | | | | | | | |
| Hiring costs | 2,000 | 0 | 0 | 0 | 0 | 0 | 2,000 |
| Firing costs | 0 | 0 | 0 | 0 | 0 | 0 | 0 |
| Inventory carrying costs | 0 | 0 | 0 | 18 | 480 | 0 | 498 |
| Stockout costs | 1,960 | 3,380 | 2,160 | 0 | 0 | 0 | 7,500 |
| Total incremental costs | 3,960 | 3,380 | 2,160 | 18 | 480 | 0 | 9,998 |

**EXHIBIT 13.7**

Third Alternative: Minimum Workforce with Subcontracting Strategy

| | Jan. | Feb. | March | April | May | June | Total |
|---|---|---|---|---|---|---|---|
| Demand forecast | 2,200 | 1,500 | 1,100 | 900 | 1,100 | 1,600 | 8,400 |
| Initial inventory | 400 | | | | | | |
| Production requirements | 1,800 | 1,500 | 1,100 | 900 | 1,100 | 1,600 | 8,000 |
| **Aggregate plan** | | | | | | | |
| Workers required | 27 | 27 | 27 | 27 | 27 | 27 | |
| Workers hired | 0 | 0 | 0 | 0 | 0 | 0 | |
| Workers fired | 3 | 0 | 0 | 0 | 0 | 0 | |
| Units produced | 950 | 821 | 907 | 907 | 950 | 864 | 5,399 |
| Monthly inventory | 0 | 0 | 0 | 7 | 0 | 0 | |
| Units subcontracted | 850 | 679 | 193 | 0 | 143 | 736 | 2,601 |
| **Costs—full** | | | | | | | |
| Regular production | 19,000 | 16,420 | 18,140 | 18,140 | 19,000 | 17,280 | 107,980 |
| Material costs | 95,000 | 82,100 | 90,700 | 90,700 | 95,000 | 86,400 | 539,900 |
| Hiring costs | 0 | 0 | 0 | 0 | 0 | 0 | 0 |
| Firing costs | 750 | 0 | 0 | 0 | 0 | 0 | 750 |
| Inventory carrying costs | 0 | 0 | 0 | 11 | 0 | 0 | 11 |
| Subcontracting costs | 106,250 | 84,875 | 24,125 | 0 | 17,875 | 92,000 | 325,125 |
| Total full costs | 221,000 | 183,395 | 132,965 | 108,851 | 131,875 | 195,680 | 973,766 |
| **Costs—incremental** | | | | | | | |
| Hiring costs | 0 | 0 | 0 | 0 | 0 | 0 | 0 |
| Firing costs | 750 | 0 | 0 | 0 | 0 | 0 | 750 |
| Inventory carrying costs | 0 | 0 | 0 | 11 | 0 | 0 | 11 |
| Subcontracting costs | 4,250 | 3,395 | 965 | 0 | 715 | 3,680 | 13,005 |
| Total incremental costs | 5,000 | 3,395 | 965 | 11 | 715 | 3,680 | 13,766 |

monthly difference between requirements and production (minimum workforce with subcontracting strategy).

*Plan 4.* Produce to meet expected demand for all but the first two months using a constant workforce on regular time. Use overtime to meet additional output requirements (constant workforce with overtime strategy).

The number of workers needed in this alternative is determined as follows:

$$1,100 + 900 + 1,100 + 1,600 = 4,700 \text{ units (March–June)}$$

$$4,700 \text{ units} \times 5 \text{ labor hours per unit} = 23,500 \text{ worker-hours}$$

$$23,500 \text{ worker-hours/8 hours per day} = 2,938 \text{ worker-days}$$

$$2,938 \text{ worker-days/84 days (March–June)} \cong 35 \text{ workers}$$

Having identified each of the four alternatives, the next step is to develop an aggregate plan for each alternative, showing all of the detailed calculations. These are presented in Exhibits 13.5, 13.6, 13.7, and 13.8. Once the details of each production plan have been developed, we can then determine the costs associated with each plan. These costs (both full

**EXHIBIT 13.8**

Constant Workforce with Overtime Strategy

| | Jan. | Feb. | March | April | May | June | Total |
|---|---|---|---|---|---|---|---|
| Demand forecast | 2,200 | 1,500 | 1,100 | 900 | 1,100 | 1,600 | 8,400 |
| Initial inventory | 400 | | | | | | |
| Production requirements | 1,800 | 1,500 | 1,100 | 900 | 1,100 | 1,600 | 8,000 |
| **Aggregate plan** | | | | | | | |
| Workers required | 35 | 35 | 35 | 35 | 35 | 35 | |
| Workers hired | 5 | 0 | 0 | 0 | 0 | 0 | |
| Workers fired | 0 | 0 | 0 | 0 | 0 | 0 | |
| Units produced—regular | 1,232 | 1,064 | 1,176 | 1,176 | 1,232 | 1,120 | 7,000 |
| Units produced—overtime | 568 | 436 | | | | | 1,004 |
| Monthly inventory | 0 | 0 | 76 | 276 | 132 | (480) | |
| Cumulative inventory | 0 | 0 | 76 | 352 | 484 | 4 | |
| **Costs—full** | | | | | | | |
| Regular production | 24,640 | 21,280 | 23,520 | 23,520 | 24,640 | 22,400 | 140,000 |
| Overtime production | 17,040 | 13,080 | 0 | 0 | 0 | 0 | 30,120 |
| Material costs | 180,000 | 150,000 | 117,600 | 117,600 | 123,200 | 112,000 | 800,400 |
| Hiring costs | 1,000 | 0 | 0 | 0 | 0 | 0 | 1,000 |
| Firing costs | 0 | 0 | 0 | 0 | 0 | 0 | 0 |
| Inventory carrying costs | 0 | 0 | 114 | 528 | 726 | 6 | 1,374 |
| Total full costs | 222,680 | 184,360 | 141,234 | 141,648 | 148,566 | 134,406 | 972,894 |
| **Costs—incremental** | | | | | | | |
| Overtime production | 5,680 | 4,360 | 0 | 0 | 0 | 0 | 10,040 |
| Hiring costs | 1,000 | 0 | 0 | 0 | 0 | 0 | 1,000 |
| Firing costs | 0 | 0 | 0 | 0 | 0 | 0 | 0 |
| Inventory carrying costs | | | 114 | 528 | 726 | 6 | 1,374 |
| Total incremental costs | 6,680 | 4,360 | 114 | 528 | 726 | 6 | 12,414 |

**EXHIBIT 13.9**

Summary of Costs for Alternative Aggregate Plans

| Alternative | Full Costs | Marginal Costs |
|---|---|---|
| Pure chase | $974,800 | $14,800 |
| Pure level | $969,998 | $ 9,998 |
| Minimum workforce with subcontracting | $973,766 | $13,766 |
| Constant workforce with overtime | $972,894 | $12,414 |

costs and marginal costs) are also included in their respective exhibits. A summary of these costs is presented in Exhibit 13.9, showing that the pure level strategy is the lowest cost alternative.

Example Matt Koslow is the operations manager for the New England Shirt Company. In this capacity he is required to develop an aggregate plan for the next six months with the goal of meeting demand during this period and minimizing costs at the same time. As a first step in developing this plan he obtained from the marketing department the following forecast for shirts:

| January | February | March | April | May | June |
|---------|----------|-------|-------|-----|------|
| 2,400 | 1,200 | 2,800 | 3,600 | 3,200 | 3,600 |

Matt has estimated the following production data:

| | |
|---|---|
| Inventory carrying cost | $1.50 per shirt per month |
| Stockout cost | $3.00 per shirt per month |
| Hiring cost | $200 per employee |
| Firing cost | $300 per employee |
| Labor per shirt | 2 hours |
| Hourly wage | $8.00 per hour |
| Beginning employment level | 30 employees |
| Beginning inventory level | 0 shirts |
| Hours per employee per day | 8 hours |
| Work days per month | 20 days |

Using marginal costs, develop both a chase strategy and a level strategy to determine which is the more economical.

**Solution**    a.  See the spreadsheet for marginal cost of chase strategy.

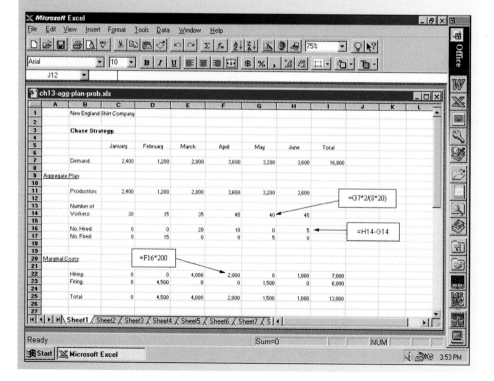

b. See the spreadsheet for marginal cost of level strategy.

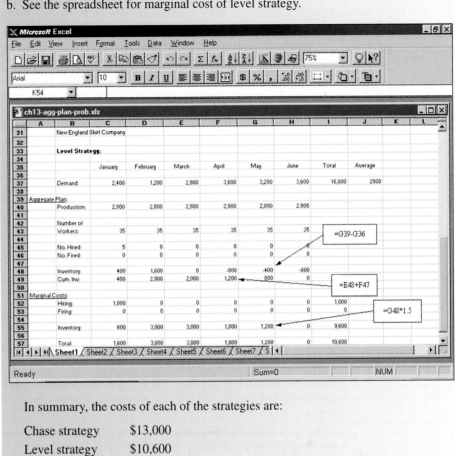

In summary, the costs of each of the strategies are:

Chase strategy     $13,000
Level strategy     $10,600

Therefore, Matt should elect to go with the level strategy.

## Aggregate Planning Applied to Services: Tucson Parks and Recreation Department

Charting and graphic techniques are also very useful for aggregate planning in service applications. The following example shows how a city's parks and recreation department could use the alternatives of full-time employees, part-time employees, and subcontracting to meet its commitment to provide service to the city.

The Tucson Parks and Recreation Department is responsible for developing and maintaining open space, all public recreational programs, adult sports leagues, golf courses, tennis courts, pools, and so forth. There are 336 full-time-equivalent employees (FTEs). Of these, 216 are full-time permanent personnel who provide the administration and year-round maintenance to all areas. The remaining 120 year-long FTE positions are part time, with about 75 percent of them being used during the summer and the remaining 25 percent being used in the fall, winter, and spring seasons. The 75 percent (or 90 FTE positions) show up as approximately 800 part-time summer jobs: lifeguards, baseball umpires, and instructors in summer programs for children. The 800 part-time jobs are derived from 90 FTEs because many of these positions last only for a month or two while the FTEs are a year long.

Currently, the parks and recreation work that is subcontracted amounts to less than $100,000. This is for the golf and tennis pros and for grounds maintenance at the libraries and veterans cemetery.

Because of the nature of city employment, the probable bad public image, and civil service rules, the option to hire and fire full-time help daily and/or weekly to meet seasonal demand is pretty much out of the question. However, temporary part-time help is authorized and traditional. Also, it is virtually impossible to have regular (full-time) staff for all of the summer jobs. During the summer months, the approximately 800 part-time employees are staffing many programs that occur simultaneously, prohibiting level scheduling over a normal 40-hour week. Also, a wider variety of skills is required than can be expected from full-time employees (e.g., umpires; coaches; lifeguards; teachers of ceramics, guitar, karate, belly dancing, and yoga).

Under these conditions, the following three options are open to the department in its aggregate planning.

1. The present method, which is to maintain a medium-level full-time staff and schedule work during off seasons (such as rebuilding baseball fields during the winter months) and to use part-time help during peak demands.

2. Maintain a lower level of staff over the year and subcontract all additional work presently done by full-time staff (still using part-time help).

3. Maintain an administrative staff only and subcontract all work, including part-time help. (This would entail contracts to landscaping firms, pool-maintenance companies, and to newly created private firms to employ and supply part-time help.)

The common unit of measure of work across all areas is full-time equivalent jobs or employees (referred to as FTEs). For example, assume in the same week that 30 lifeguards worked 20 hours each, 40 instructors worked 15 hours each, and 35 baseball umpires worked 10 hours each. This is equivalent to $(30 \times 20) + (40 \times 15) + (35 + 10) = 1{,}550 \div 40 = 38.75$ FTE positions for that week. Although a considerable amount of workload can be shifted to the off season, most of the work must be done when required.

Full-time employees consist of three groups: (a) the skeleton group of key department personnel coordinating with the city, setting policy, determining budgets, measuring performance, and so forth; (b) the administrative group of supervisory and office personnel who are responsible for or whose jobs are directly linked to the direct-labor workers; and (c) the direct-labor workforce of 116 full-time positions. These workers physically maintain the department's areas of responsibility, such as cleaning up, mowing golf greens and ballfields, trimming trees, and watering grass.

Cost information needed to determine the best alternative strategy is

**Full-Time Direct-Labor Employees**

| | |
|---|---|
| Average wage rate | $8.90 per hour |
| Fringe benefits | 17% of wage rate |
| Administrative costs | 20% of wage rate |

**Part-Time Employees**

| | |
|---|---|
| Average wage rate | $8.06 per hour |
| Fringe benefits | 11% of wage rate |
| Administrative costs | 25% of wage rate |
| Subcontracting all full-time jobs | $3.2 million |
| Subcontracting all part-time jobs | $3.7 million |

June and July are the peak demand seasons in Tucson. Exhibit 13.10 shows the high seasonal requirements for June and July personnel. The part-time help reaches 575

## EXHIBIT 13.10

Actual Demand Requirement for Full-Time Direct Employees and Full-Time Equivalent (FTE) Part-Time Employees

|  | Jan. | Feb. | March | April | May | June | July | Aug. | Sept. | Oct. | Nov. | Dec. | Total |
|---|---|---|---|---|---|---|---|---|---|---|---|---|---|
| Days | 22 | 20 | 21 | 22 | 21 | 20 | 21 | 21 | 21 | 23 | 18 | 22 | 252 |
| Full-time employees | 66 | 28 | 130 | 90 | 195 | 290 | 325 | 92 | 45 | 32 | 29 | 60 | |
| Full-time days* | 1,452 | 560 | 2,730 | 1,980 | 4,095 | 5,800 | 6,825 | 1,932 | 945 | 736 | 522 | 1,320 | 28,897 |
| Full-time-equivalent part-time employees | 41 | 75 | 72 | 68 | 72 | 302 | 576 | 72 | 0 | 68 | 84 | 27 | |
| FTE days | 902 | 1,500 | 1,512 | 1,496 | 1,512 | 6,040 | 12,096 | 1,512 | 0 | 1,564 | 1,512 | 594 | 30,240 |

Note: Some workweeks are staggered to include weekdays, but this does not affect the number of workdays per employee.

*Full-time days are derived by multiplying the number of days in each month by the number of workers.

## EXHIBIT 13.11

Three Possible Plans for the Parks and Recreation Department

**Alternative 1:** Maintain 116 full-time regular direct workers. Schedule work during off seasons to level workload throughout the year. Continue to use 120 full-time-equivalent (FTE) part-time employees to meet high demand periods.

| Costs | Days per Year (Exhibit 13.9) | Hours (employees × days × 8 hours) | Wages (full-time, $8.90; part-time, $8.06) | Fringe Benefits (full-time, 17%; part-time, 11%) | Administrative Cost (full-time, 20%; part-time, 25%) |
|---|---|---|---|---|---|
| 116 full-time regular employees | 252 | 233,856 | $2,081,318 | $353,824 | $416,264 |
| 120 part-time employees | 252 | 241,920 | 1,949,875 | 214,486 | 487,469 |
| Total cost = $2,751,619 | | | $4,031,193 | $568,310 | $903,733 |

**Alternative 2:** Maintain 50 full-time regular direct workers and the present 120 FTE part-time employees. Subcontract jobs releasing 66 full-time regular employees. Subcontract cost, $2,200,000.

| Costs | Days per Year (Exhibit 13.9) | Hours (employees × days × 8 hours) | Wages (full-time, $8.90; part-time, $8.06) | Fringe Benefits (full-time, 17%; part-time, 11%) | Administrative Cost (full-time, 20%; part-time, 25%) | Subcontract Cost |
|---|---|---|---|---|---|---|
| 50 full-time employees | 252 | 100,800 | $ 897,120 | $152,510 | $179,424 | $2,200,000 |
| 120 FTE part-time employees subcontracting cost | 252 | 241,920 | 1,949,875 | 214,486 | 487,469 | |
| Total cost = $3,040,443 | | | $2,846,995 | $366,996 | $666,893 | $2,200,000 |

**Alternative 3:** Subcontract all jobs previously performed by 116 full-time regular employees. Subcontract cost $3,200,000. Subcontract all jobs previously performed by 120 full-time-equivalent part-time employees. Subcontract cost $3,700,000.

| Cost | Subcontract Cost |
|---|---|
| 0 Full-time employees | |
| 0 Part-time employees | |
| Subcontract full-time jobs | $3,200,000 |
| Subcontract part-time jobs | 3,700,000 |
| Total cost | $6,900,000 |

**EXHIBIT 13.12**

Comparison of Costs for All Three Alternatives

|  | Alternative 1:<br>116 Full-Time<br>Direct Labor<br>Employees, 120 FTE<br>Part-Time Employees | Alternative 2:<br>50 Full-Time<br>Direct Labor<br>Employees, 120 FTE<br>Part-Time Employees,<br>Subcontracting | Alternative 3:<br>Subcontracting Jobs<br>Formerly Performed<br>by 116 Direct Labor<br>Full-Time Employees<br>and 120 FTE<br>Part-Time Employees |
|---|---|---|---|
| Wages | $4,031,193 | $2,846,995 | — |
| Fringe benefits | 568,310 | 366,996 | — |
| Administrative costs | 903,733 | 666,893 | — |
| Subcontracting, full-time jobs |  | 2,200,000 | $3,200,000 |
| Subcontracting, part-time jobs |  |  | 3,700,000 |
| Total | $5,503,236 | $6,080,884 | $6,900,000 |

fulltime-equivalent positions (although in actual numbers, this is approximately 800 different employees). After a low fall and winter staffing level, the demand shown as "full-time direct" reaches 130 in March when grounds are reseeded and fertilized and then increases to a high of 325 in July. The present method levels this uneven demand over the year to an average of 116 full-time year-round employees by early scheduling of work. As previously mentioned, no attempt is made to hire and lay off full-time workers to meet this uneven demand.

Exhibit 13.11 shows the cost calculations for all three alternatives. Exhibit 13.12 compares the total costs for each alternative. From this analysis, it appears that the department is already using the lowest-cost alternative (Alternative 1).

# YIELD MANAGEMENT

**yield management**
Concept used in certain service operations that attempts to match supply and demand.

Aggregate planning in services is very different from that in manufacturing. This is due, in large part, to the fact that the capacity of service operations is often viewed as highly perishable because it cannot be saved or inventoried for future use. For example, the empty seats in a restaurant on Monday morning cannot be saved for use on Saturday night when it is very busy. Thus services do not have the luxury to choose between chase and level strategies, as do manufacturing firms, but rather must always use the chase strategy. In other words, capacity must be available when the customer wants it.

However, even within this constraint, the service manager has considerable latitude in planning. For those services that have high fixed costs and low variable costs, it is important to maximize capacity utilization even if it means reducing prices to attract additional customers during slow periods of demand. This method, known as **yield management** or *revenue management,* attempts to simultaneously integrate demand management (by changing prices) and supply management (by controlling availability). The goal of yield management is to sell all available capacity, even at discount prices but, at the same time, not turn away a full paying customer because the capacity had been previously sold to a bargain hunter. Examples of industries that apply yield management concepts include airlines that offer discounts for advanced reservations, and car rental agencies and hotels that offer discounts on weekends. (See OM in Practice on National Car Rental.) The concept of yield management is introduced in this chapter; the detailed mathematical theory behind yield management is explained in the next chapter. It is also mentioned in the forecasting chapter.

# Operations Management in Practice

## YIELD MANAGEMENT AT NATIONAL CAR RENTAL

Faced with possible liquidation in 1993 by General Motors, its parent company, National Car Rental was under significant pressure to produce both a substantial and sustainable profit. To accomplish this, management decided to adopt a comprehensive revenue management system. Instead of a constant car rental price all the time, the revenue management system demonstrated that a variable pricing policy which would fluctuate with demand would result in significantly higher profits.

The revenue management system was implemented in two phases. The first phase was introduced in July, 1993, with the goal of showing immediate profits, which it did. The sec-

ond phase focused on developing a state-of-the-art revenue management system for the car rental industry. This phase was successfully implemented in July 1994.

As a result of this revenue management system, profits were significantly increased, and General Motors was able to sell National Car Rental in 1995 for an amount in excess of $1 billion.

Sources: Ernest Johnson, "1994 Trophy Award: National Car Rental Systems, Inc." *Scorecard: The Revenue Management Quarterly*, First Quarter, 1995. M. K. Geraghty and Ernest Johnson, "Revenue Management Saves National Car Rental," *Interfaces* 27, no. 1 (January–February 1997), pp. 107–27.

After yield management has been applied to a service operation, the service manager would then determine the aggregate workforce requirements in a manner similar to that described previously for a manufacturing company.

In order to take maximum advantage of yield management, a service should have the following characteristics: (*a*) the ability to segment its markets, (*b*) high-fixed and low-variable costs, (*c*) product perishability, and (*d*) the ability to presell capacity.[2]

### Market Segmentation

A major issue in the successful implementation of yield management is the ability of the firm to segment its markets. Proper segmentation will prevent all of the firm's customers from taking advantage of price reductions when they are offered to fill available capacity.

Market segmentation can be done in several ways. The first is to impose significant restrictions on customers who use the lower prices. For example, airlines require customers to stay over a Saturday night or to purchase their tickets from 7 to 30 days in advance to qualify for lower airfares. These very same conditions, however, prevent the business traveler, who usually travels midweek on short notice, from taking advantage of the lower fares.

Another method of segmentation is to limit lower prices to specific days of the week or times of the day. Movie theaters offer reduced ticket prices for matinees, which senior citizens can take advantage of during weekdays. Similarly, downtown hotels typically offer discounts on weekends when business travelers are home, as an incentive for tourists.

### High-Fixed and Low-Variable Costs

High-fixed and low-variable costs allow a firm to offer significant discounts while still being able to cover variable costs. When a service firm has this type of cost profile, profits are directly related to sales. In other words, the more sales generated, the more profits made.

For example, if the variable cost associated with having a hotel room cleaned is estimated at $25 (which would include the labor to clean the room and the replacement of any material that was consumed, such as soap and shampoo, as well as fresh sheets and towels),

---

[2]Sheryl E. Kimes, "Yield-Management: A Tool for Capacity-Constrained Service Firms," *Journal of Operations Management* 8, no. 4 (October 1989).

then any price that the hotel could get for the room above the $25 variable cost would be financially beneficial (as opposed to leaving the room empty for the night).

### Product Perishability

The underlying reason that yield management can be applied to many types of services is the perishability of service capacity. In other words, service capacity cannot be saved for future use. (Wouldn't it be great if the airlines could save all of their empty seats during the year for use during the Thanksgiving and Christmas periods!) Given that capacity in a service operation is perishable, the service manager should try and maximize capacity utilization whenever possible, even if it means offering large discounts to attract customers—provided that the discounted prices exceed the variable cost.

### Presold Capacity

A final requirement for the successful implementation of yield management is that the lower-priced capacity can be sold in advance. This limits the availability of capacity to the higher priced market segments. As an illustration, hotels usually work with conference planners several years in advance of a conference, offering a given number of rooms at the lowest room rates. Travel groups usually plan tours within a year before they need them and therefore also receive a discount. Finally, the last-minute customer, or "walk-in," will pay top dollar or the "rack-rate" for a hotel room.

## CONCLUSION

Aggregate planning provides the link between the corporate strategic and capacity plans and workforce size, inventory quantity, and production levels. It does not involve detailed planning. It is also useful to point out some practical considerations in aggregate planning.

First, demand variations are a fact of life, so the planning system must include sufficient flexibility to cope with such variations. Flexibility can be achieved by developing alternative sources of supply, cross-training workers to handle a wide variety of orders, and engaging in more frequent replanning during high-demand periods.

Second, decision rules for production planning should be adhered to once they have been selected. However, they should be carefully analyzed prior to implementation by such checks as using simulation of historical data to see what really would have happened if these rules had been in operation in the past.

 Services typically require a chase strategy due to the customer's direct involvement with the service delivery system. However, services, under certain conditions, can successfully apply the concept of yield management, which simultaneously adjusts customer demand and the operation's capacity with the goal of maximizing the firm's profit.

## KEY TERMS

# REVIEW AND DISCUSSION QUESTIONS

1. What are the basic controllable variables of a production planning problem? What are the four major costs?

2. Distinguish between pure and mixed strategies in production planning.

3. Compare the best plans in the C&A Company and the Tucson Parks and Recreation Department. What do they have in common?

4. How does forecast accuracy relate, in general, to the practical application of the aggregate planning models discussed in the chapter?

5. In which way does the time horizon chosen for an aggregate plan determine whether or not it is the best plan for the firm?

6. Under what conditions is the concept of yield management must appropriate for service operations?

# SOLVED PROBLEM

### Problem

Jason Enterprises (JE) is producing video telephones for the home market. Quality is not quite as good as it could be at this point, but the selling price is low and Jason has the opportunity to study market response while spending more time in additional R&D work.

At this stage, however, JE needs to develop an aggregate production plan for the six months from January through June. As you can guess, you have been commissioned to create the plan. The following information is available to help you:

|  | Jan. | Feb. | March | April | May | June |
|---|---|---|---|---|---|---|
| **Demand data** | | | | | | |
| Beginning inventory | 200 | | | | | |
| Forecast demand | 500 | 600 | 650 | 800 | 900 | 800 |
| **Cost data** | | | | | | |
| Holding cost | $10/unit/month | | | | | |
| Stockout cost | $20/unit/month | | | | | |
| Subcontracting cost/unit | $100 | | | | | |
| Hiring cost/worker | $50 | | | | | |
| Layoff cost/worker | $100 | | | | | |
| Labor cost/hour—straight time | $12.50 | | | | | |
| Labor cost/hour—overtime | $18.75 | | | | | |
| **Production data** | | | | | | |
| Labor hours/unit | 4 | | | | | |
| Workdays/month | 22 | | | | | |
| Current workforce | 10 | | | | | |

What is the cost of each of the following production strategies?

*a.* Chase strategy; vary workforce (assuming a starting workforce of 10).

*b.* Constant workforce; vary inventory and stockout only (assuming a starting workforce of 10).

*c.* Level workforce of 10; vary overtime only; inventory carryover permitted.

*d.* Level workforce of 10; vary overtime only; inventory carryover not permitted.

*Solution*

a. Plan 1: Chase strategy; vary workforce (assume 10 in workforce to start).

| Month | (1) Production Requirement | (2) Production Hours Required (1) × 4 | (3) Hours/Month per Worker 22 × 8 | (4) Workers Required (2) ÷ (3) | (5) Workers Hired | (6) Workers Fired |
|---|---|---|---|---|---|---|
| January | 300 | 1,200 | 176 | 7 | 0 | 3 |
| February | 600 | 2,400 | 176 | 14 | 7 | 0 |
| March | 650 | 2,600 | 176 | 15 | 1 | 0 |
| April | 800 | 3,200 | 176 | 18 | 3 | 0 |
| May | 900 | 3,600 | 176 | 20 | 2 | 0 |
| June | 800 | 3,200 | 176 | 18 | 0 | 2 |

| Month | (7) Hiring Cost (5) × $50 | (8) Layoff Cost (6) × $100 | (9) Straight-Time Cost (2) × $12.50 |
|---|---|---|---|
| January | 0 | $300 | $ 15,000 |
| February | 350 | 0 | 30,000 |
| March | 50 | 0 | 32,500 |
| April | 150 | 0 | 40,000 |
| May | 100 | 0 | 45,000 |
| June | 0 | 200 | 40,000 |
| | $650 | $500 | $202,500 |

Total cost for plan:

| | |
|---|---|
| Hiring cost | $    650 |
| Layoff cost | 500 |
| Straight-time cost | 202,500 |
| Total | $203,650 |

b. Plan 2: Constant workforce; vary inventory and stockout only.

| Month | (1) Cumulative Production Requirement | (2) Production Hours Available 22 × 8 × 10 | (3) Units Produced (2) ÷ 4 | (4) Cumulative Production |
|---|---|---|---|---|
| January | 300 | 1,760 | 440 | 440 |
| February | 900 | 1,760 | 440 | 880 |
| March | 1,550 | 1,760 | 440 | 1,320 |
| April | 2,350 | 1,760 | 440 | 1,760 |
| May | 3,250 | 1,760 | 440 | 2,200 |
| June | 4,050 | 1,760 | 440 | 2,640 |

| Month | (5) Units Short (1) − (4) | (6) Shortage Cost (5) × $20 | (7) Units in Excess (4) − (1) | (8) Inventory Cost (7) × $10 | (9) Straight-Time Cost (2) × $12.50 |
|---|---|---|---|---|---|
| January | $   0 | 0 | 140 | 1,400 | $ 22,000 |
| February | 20 | 400 | 0 | 0 | 22,000 |
| March | 230 | 4,600 | 0 | 0 | 22,000 |
| April | 590 | 11,800 | 0 | 0 | 22,000 |
| May | 1,050 | 21,000 | 0 | 0 | 22,000 |
| June | 1,410 | 28,200 | 0 | 0 | 22,000 |
| | | $66,000 | | $1,400 | $132,000 |

Total cost for plan:

| | |
|---|---|
| Shortage cost | $ 66,000 |
| Inventory cost | 1,400 |
| Straight-time cost | 132,000 |
| Total | $199,400 |

c. Plan 3: Level workforce of 10; vary overtime only; inventory carryover permitted.

| Month | (1)<br>Production<br>Requirement | (2)<br>Standard Time<br>Hours Available<br>22 × 8 × 10 | (3)<br>Standard Time<br>Units Produced<br>(2) ÷ 4 | (4)<br>Overtime<br>Required<br>in Units<br>(1) − (3) |
|---|---|---|---|---|
| January | 300 | 1,760 | 440 | 0 |
| February | 460* | 1,760 | 440 | 20 |
| March | 650 | 1,760 | 440 | 210 |
| April | 800 | 1,760 | 440 | 360 |
| May | 900 | 1,760 | 440 | 460 |
| June | 800 | 1,760 | 440 | 360 |
| | | | | 1,410 |

*600 − 140 units of beginning inventory in February.

| Month | (5)<br>Overtime<br>Required<br>in Hours<br>(4) × 4 | (6)<br>Overtime<br>Cost<br>(5) × $18.75 | (7)<br>Straight-<br>Time Cost<br>(2) × $12.50 | (8)<br>Excess<br>Inventory Costs<br>(3) − (1) × $10 |
|---|---|---|---|---|
| January | 0 | $ 0 | $ 22,000 | $1,400 |
| February | 80 | 1,500 | 22,000 | |
| March | 840 | 15,750 | 22,000 | |
| April | 1,440 | 27,000 | 22,000 | |
| May | 1,840 | 34,500 | 22,000 | |
| June | 1,440 | 27,000 | 22,000 | |
| | | $105,750 | $132,000 | $1,400 |

Total cost for plan:

| | |
|---|---|
| Straight-time cost | $132,000 |
| Overtime cost | 105,750 |
| Inventory cost | 1,400 |
| Total | $239,150 |

d. Plan 4: Constant workforce of 10; vary overtime only; inventory carryover not permitted.

| Month | (1)<br>Production<br>Requirement | (2)<br>Standard-Time<br>Hours Available<br>22 × 8 × 10 | (3)<br>Standard-Time<br>Units Produced<br>Min. [(2) ÷ 4; (1)] | (4)<br>Overtime<br>Required<br>in Units<br>(1) − (3) |
|---|---|---|---|---|
| January | 300 | 1,760 | 300 | 0 |
| February | 600 | 1,760 | 440 | 160 |
| March | 650 | 1,760 | 440 | 210 |
| April | 800 | 1,760 | 440 | 360 |
| May | 900 | 1,760 | 440 | 460 |
| June | 800 | 1,760 | 440 | 360 |

| Month | (5) Overtime Required in Hours (4) × 4 | (6) Overtime Cost (5) × $18.75 | (7) Standard-Time Cost (2) × $12.50 | (8) Excess Inventory Costs (3) − (1) × $10 |
|---|---|---|---|---|
| January | 0 | $0 | $22,000 | $1,400 |
| February | 640 | 12,000 | 22,000 | |
| March | 840 | 15,750 | 22,000 | |
| April | 1,440 | 27,000 | 22,000 | |
| May | 1,840 | 34,500 | 22,000 | |
| June | 1,440 | 27,000 | 22,000 | |
| | | $116,250 | $132,000 | $1,400 |

Total cost for plan:

| | |
|---|---|
| Straight-time cost | $132,000 |
| Overtime cost | 116,250 |
| Excess inventory cost | 1,400 |
| | $249,650 |

## PROBLEMS

1. Develop a production plan and calculate the annual cost for a firm whose unit demand forecast is fall, 10,000; winter, 8,000; spring, 7,000; summer, 12,000. Inventory at the beginning of fall is 500 units. At the beginning of fall you currently have 30 workers, but you plan to hire temporary workers at the beginning of summer and lay them off at the end of summer. In addition, you have negotiated with the union an option to use the regular workforce on overtime during winter or spring if overtime is necessary to prevent stockouts at the end of those quarters. Overtime is *not* available during the fall. Relevant costs are: hiring, $100 for each temp; layoff, $200 for each regular worker laid off; inventory holding, $5 per unit per quarter; back order, $10 per unit; straight time, $5 per hour; overtime, $8 per hour. Assume that worker productivity is two hours per unit, with eight hours per day and 60 days per season.

2. Develop an aggregate production plan for a four-month period: February through May. For February and March, you should produce to exactly meet the demand forecast. For April and May, you should use overtime and inventory with a stable workforce. However, government constraints put a maximum of 5,000 hours of overtime labor per month in April and May (zero overtime in February and March). If demand exceeds supply, then back orders occur. There are 100 workers on January 31. You are given the following unit demand forecast: February, 80,000; March, 64,000; April, 100,000; May, 40,000. Worker productivity is four units per hour. Assume eight hours per day, 20 days per month and zero inventory on February 1. Costs are: hiring, $50 per new worker; layoff, $70 per worker laid off; inventory holding, $10 per unit per month; straight-time labor, $10 per hour; overtime, $15 per hour; backorder, $20 per unit. Find the total cost of this plan.

3. Develop an aggregate production plan for the next year. The unit demand forecast is spring, 20,000; summer, 10,000; fall, 15,000; winter, 18,000. At the beginning of spring you have 70 workers and 1,000 units in inventory. The union contract specifies that you may lay off workers only once a year, at the beginning of summer. Also, you may hire new workers only at the end of summer to begin regular work in the fall. The number of workers laid off at the beginning of summer and the number hired at the end of summer should result in planned production levels for summer and fall that equal the demand forecasts for summer and fall respectively. If demand exceeds supply, use overtime in spring only, which means that back orders could occur in winter. You are given these costs: hiring, $100 per new worker; layoff,

$200 per worker laid off; holding, $20 per unit per quarter; back-order costs, $8 per unit; straight-time labor, $10 per hour; overtime, $15 per hour. Worker productivity is two hours per unit. Assume eight hours per day and 50 days per quarter. Find the total cost.

4. DAT, Inc. needs to develop an aggregate plan for its product line. Relevant data are:

| | |
|---|---|
| Production time | 1 hour per unit |
| Average labor cost | $10 per hour |
| Work-week | 5 days, 8 hours each day |
| Days per month | Assume 20 work days per month |
| Beginning inventory | 500 units |
| Safety stock | One-half of monthly forecast |
| Shortage cost | $20 per unit per month |
| Inventory carrying cost | $5 per unit per month |

The forecast for January to December 1998 is:

| Jan. | Feb. | March | April | May | June | July | Aug. | Sept. | Oct. | Nov. | Dec. |
|---|---|---|---|---|---|---|---|---|---|---|---|
| 2,500 | 3,000 | 4,000 | 3,500 | 3,500 | 3,000 | 3,000 | 4,000 | 4,000 | 4,000 | 3,000 | 3,000 |

Management prefers to keep a constant workforce and production level, absorbing variations in demand through inventory excesses and shortages. Demand that is not met is carried over to the following month.

Develop an aggregate plan that will meet the demand and other conditions of the problem. Do not try to find the optimum; just find a good solution and state the procedure you might use to test for a better solution. Make any necessary assumptions.

5. Shoney Video Concepts produces a line of CD players to be linked to personal computers for video games. CDs have much faster access time than do tape. With such a computer/CD link, the game becomes a very realistic experience. In a simple driving game where the joystick steers the vehicle, for example, rather than seeing computer graphics on the screen, the player is actually viewing a segment of a CD shot from a real moving vehicle. Depending on the action of the player (hitting a guard rail, for example) the disc moves virtually instantaneously to that segment and the player becomes part of an actual accident of real vehicles (staged, of course).

Shoney is trying to determine a production plan for the next 12 months. The main criterion for this plan is that the employment level is to be held constant over the period. Shoney is continuing in its R&D efforts to develop new applications and prefers not to cause any adverse feeling with the local workforce. For the same reasons, all employees should put in full work weeks, even if this is not the lowest-cost alternative. The number of CD players forecast for the next 12 months is:

| Month | Forecast Demand | Month | Forecast Demand |
|---|---|---|---|
| January | 600 | July | 200 |
| February | 800 | August | 200 |
| March | 900 | September | 300 |
| April | 600 | October | 700 |
| May | 400 | November | 800 |
| June | 300 | December | 900 |

Manufacturing cost is $200 per player, equally divided between materials and labor. Inventory storage costs are $5 per CD player per month. A shortage results in lost sales and is estimated to cost an overall $20 per unit short. (Shortages are not carried forward since the sales are lost.)

The inventory on hand at the beginning of the planning period is 200 units. Ten labor hours are required per CD player. The workday is eight hours.

Develop an aggregate production schedule for the year using a constant workforce. For simplicity, assume 22 working days each month except July, when the plant closes down for three weeks' vacation (leaving seven working days). Make any assumptions you need.

6. The Bentley Chemical Company (BCC) is vitally concerned about generating a production schedule for their products for the coming fiscal year (July–June). The operations manager at BCC, Mr. Perspa Cassidy, has been charged with generating an aggregate plan for this time period so that BCC can meet their demand with the minimum utilization of resources.

Mr. Cassidy first aggregates the various products which BCC sells into a single "aggregate" production unit and forecasts the demand for the following four quarters:

| Quarter | Quarter #1 Jul/Aug/Sept | Quarter #2 Oct/Nov/Dec | Quarter #3 Jan/Feb/Mar | Quarter #4 Apr/May/June |
|---|---|---|---|---|
| Demand forecast | 10,000 | 9,800 | 9,400 | 10,200 |

On March 1 (prior to quarter #1) there were 1,200 units in BCC's inventory and the forecast demand for the fourth quarter of the previous year is 9,900 units. Mr. Cassidy knows that to keep one unit in inventory for one month costs $5; further, BCC uses average inventory when computing inventory costs. The workforce on March 1 consisted of 40 employees, each of whom produces exactly four (4) units in an 8-hour day. For the coming four quarters, Mr. Cassidy has determined the number of productive days for each quarter to be as follows:

| Quarter | Quarter #1 Jul/Aug/Sept | Quarter #2 Oct/Nov/Dec | Quarter #3 Jan/Feb/Mar | Quarter #4 Apr/May/June |
|---|---|---|---|---|
| Number of productive days | 56 | 60 | 61 | 63 |

Each of the regular employees is paid at the rate of $53 per day; however, overtime is available at the rate of $80 per day. BCC has a very strict quality control policy and does not allow any subcontracting. In addition, BCC wishes to maintain their reputation with their customers and has adopted a policy that *all* demand must be met on time.

Mr. Cassidy recognizes that meeting all demand can be difficult. He is faced with two limitations: (1) he is using aggregate units, and (2) he has only his forecasts as a basis for his aggregate plan. However, he believes that his forecasts are quite good and decides to use his figures objectively (i.e., he decides not to keep any safety stock).

The workforce can be increased or decreased at the discretion of Mr. Cassidy, but no more than a 25 percent increase or decrease (using integer values) is allowed in any given quarter due to union regulations. Mr. Cassidy knows that should he wish to hire and/or fire, that the total increase/decrease in the workforce (when using whole people) cannot exceed the 25 percent mark. Fortunately, BCC is located in an area where there is no shortage of skilled labor.

To hire a new individual and train him/her requires exactly one quarter and costs $1,200. All new employees always start on the first day of a given quarter. Hence, they cannot be considered part of the productive labor force until after their first quarter. To fire an individual costs $1,000, and when an individual is fired, he remains part of the productive workforce until the end of the quarter in which he was fired.

Mr. Cassidy believes that he has all the data he needs; hence, he starts to determine the aggregate capacity plan. He selects a strategy of trying to maintain a relatively stable workforce, while letting the inventory levels fluctuate.

*a.* Perform the initial calculations Mr. Cassidy would need prior to completing the grid that follows.

*b.* Develop an aggregate plan for Mr. Cassidy by filling in the grid.

*c.* What is the total cost of Mr. Cassidy's plan?

| (1) Qtr. | (2) Demand | (3) Prod. Hours Req. (2) × 2 | (4) Prod. Days per Qtr. | (5) Prod. Hrs. per Qtr. per Worker (4) × 8 | (6) No. of Empls. | (7) Total Prod. Hrs. Avail. per Qtr. (5) × (6) | (8) Straight-Time Cost (4) × (6) × $53 | (9) No. of Units Short | (10) Short Cost | (11) No. of OT Units Req. | (12) No. of OT Days Req. (11)/4 |
|---|---|---|---|---|---|---|---|---|---|---|---|
| NOW | 9,900 | 19,800 | 63 | 504 | 40 | 20,160 | $133,560 | 0 | $0 | 0 | 0 |
| 1 | 10,000 | | 56 | | | | | | 0 | | |
| 2 | 9,800 | | 60 | | | | | | 0 | | |
| 3 | 9,400 | | 61 | | | | | | 0 | | |
| 4 | 10,200 | | 63 | | | | | | 0 | | |

| (13) Overtime Cost (12) × $80 | (14) No. of Unit Sub. | (15) Sub. Cost. | (16) No. of Empls. Hired | (17) Hiring Cost (16) × $1200 | (18) No. of Empls. Fired | (19) Firing Cost (18) × $1000 | (20) Begin. Inv. | (21) End. Inv. | (22) Ave. Inv. (20) + (21) / 2 | (23) Inv. Cost (22) × $15 |
|---|---|---|---|---|---|---|---|---|---|---|
| $0 | 0 | $0 | 0 | $0 | 0 | $ 0 | 1,200 | 1,380 | 1,290 | $19,350 |
| | | | | | | | 1,380 | | | |
| | | | | | | | | | | |
| | | | | | | | | | | |
| | | | | | | | | | | |

# CASE: XYZ BROKERAGE FIRM

Consider the national operations group of the XYZ brokerage firm. The group, housed in an office building located in the Wall Street area, handles the transactions generated by registered representatives in more than 100 branch offices throughout the United States. As with all firms in the brokerage industry, XYZ's transactions must be settled within five trading days. This five-day period allows operations managers to smooth out the daily volume fluctuations.

Fundamental shifts in the stock market's volume and mix can occur overnight, so the operations manager must be prepared to handle extremely wide swings in volume. For example, on the strength of an international peace rumor, the number of transactions or XYZ rose from 5,600 one day to 12,200 the next.

Managers of XYZ, not unlike their counterparts in other firms, have trouble predicting volume. In fact, a ran-

dom number generator can predict volume a month or even a week into the future almost as well as the managers can.

How do the operations managers in XYZ manage capacity when there are such wide swings? The answer differs according to the tasks and constraints facing each manager. Here's what two managers in the same firm might say:

**Manager A:** The capacity in our operation is currently 12,000 transactions per day. Of course, what we should gear up for is always a problem. For example, our volume this year ranged from 4,000 to 15,000 transactions per day. It's a good thing we have a turnover rate, because in periods of low volume it helps us reduce our personnel without the morale problems caused by layoffs. [The labor turnover rate in this department is over 100 percent per year.]

**Manager B:** For any valid budgeting procedure, one needs to estimate volume within 15 percent. Correlations between actual and expected volume in the brokerage industry have been so poor that I question the value of budgeting at all. I maintain our capacity at a level of 17,000 transactions per day.

Why the big difference in capacity management in the same firm? Manager A is in charge of the cashiering operation—the handling of certificates, checks, and cash. The personnel in cashiering are messengers, clerks, and supervisors. The equipment—file cabinets, vaults, calculators—is uncomplicated.

Manager B, however, is in charge of handling orders, an information-processing function. The personnel are data-entry clerks, EDP specialists, and systems analysts. The equipment is complex—computers, LANs, file servers, and communication devices that link national operations with the branches. The employees under B's control had performed their tasks manually until decreased volume and a standardization of the information needs made it worthwhile to install computers.

Because the lead times required to increase the capacity of the information-processing operations are long, however, and the incremental cost of the capacity to handle the last 5,000 transactions is low (only some extra peripheral equipment is needed), Manager B maintains the capacity to handle 17,000 transactions per day. He holds to this level even though the average number of daily transactions for any month has never been higher than 11,000 and the number of transactions for any one day has never been higher than 16,000.

Because a great deal of uncertainty about the future status of the stock certificate exists, the situation is completely different in cashiering. Attempts to automate the cashiering function to the degree reached by the order-processing group have been thwarted because the high risk of selecting a system not compatible with the future format of the stock certificate.

In other words, Manager A is tied to the chase demand strategy, and his counterpart, Manager B in the adjacent office, is locked into the level capacity strategy. However, each desires to incorporate more of the other's strategy into his own. A is developing a computerized system to handle the information-processing requirements of cashiering; B is searching for some variable costs in the order-processing operation that can be deleted in periods of low volume.

### Questions

1. What appear to be the primary differences between these two departments?

2. Do these differences eliminate certain strategy choices for either manager?

3. Which factors cause the current strategy to be desirable for each manager?

4. What are the mixed or subcontracting possibilities?

5. What are the problems associated with low standardization?

Source: *Management of Service Operations*, 1/E, by Sasser/Olsen/Wykoff, © 1978. Reprinted by permission of Prentice Hall, Inc., Upper Saddle River, NJ.

# CASE: LA BUENA COMPAÑÍA DE ESPAÑA, S.A.

La Buena Compañía de España, S.A., (LBC) located just outside of Barcelona, Spain, produces kitchen tables that it sells throughout Western Europe. Sales have been increasing steadily over the past several years, due in large part to the free trade among Western European countries that has resulted from the formation of the European Union (EU).

Jordi Garolera, the operations manager at LBC, is currently developing an aggregate plan for the next six months. In order for him to be able to evaluate alternative plans, Jordi has collected the following information:

### Production Data

20 work days per month.

7.5 hours per work day.

2.5 labor-hours per table (average).

On-hand inventory: 300 tables.

Current workforce: 25 workers.

### Cost Data

Hourly wages: 800 pesetas (ptas.) per hour.

Hiring costs: 20.000 ptas. per employee.*

---

*In Europe, decimals are separated from whole numbers by a comma, whereas, thousands and millions are separated by periods which is just the reverse of the practice in the United States. Thus US$5,000.00 in the United States would be written as US$5.000,00 in Europe.

Firing costs: 70.000 ptas. per employee.

Material cost per table: 10.000 ptas.

Overtime costs: 50 percent premium.

Inventory carrying costs: 200 ptas. per unit per month.

Stockout costs: 1.000 ptas. per unit per month.

Jordi has just returned from a meeting with the marketing manager who provided him with a sales forecast for the next six months of 12.960 tables, which is broken down as follows by month:

| Month | Jan. | Feb. | Mar. | Apr. | May | June |
|-------|------|------|------|------|-----|------|
| Forecast (Tables) | 1.740 | 1.740 | 2.460 | 3.240 | 2.220 | 1.860 |

## QUESTIONS

1. Using Excel or a similar spreadsheet, compare the costs of a pure chase strategy and a pure level strategy. Which type of strategy would you recommend?

2. As another alternative, Jordi was considering using a level workforce of 30 employees and working overtime to eliminate any stockouts. Evaluate this alternative and compare it to the pure strategies.

3. What alternative aggregate plans could you suggest to Jordi? What are the relative strengths and weaknesses of these plan(s)?

Source: © 1997 by Mark M. Davis.

## SELECTED BIBLIOGRAPHY

Fisk, J. C., and J. P. Seagle. "Integration of Aggregate Planning with Resource Requirements Planning." *Production and Inventory Management,* Third Quarter 1978, p. 87.

Geraghty, M. K., and Ernest Johnson. "Revenue Management Saves National Car Rental." *Interfaces* 27, no. 1 (January–February 1997), pp. 107–27.

Johnson, Ernest. "1994 Trophy Award: National Car Rental Systems, Inc." *Scorecard: The Revenue Management Quarterly,* First Quarter, 1995.

Kimes, Sheryl E. "Yield-Management: A Tool for Capacity-Constrained Service Firms." *Journal of Operations Management* 8, no. 4 (October 1989).

McLeavy, D., and S. Narasimhan. *Production Planning and Inventory Control.* Boston: Allyn & Bacon, 1985.

Plossl, G. W. *Production and Inventory Control: Principles and Techniques.* 2nd ed. Englewood Cliffs, NJ: Prentice Hall, 1985.

Sasser, W. E.; R. P. Olsen; and D. D. Wyckoff. *Management of Service Operations.* Boston: Allyn & Bacon, 1978.

Silver, E. A., and R. Peterson. *Decision Systems for Inventory Management and Production Planning.* 2nd ed. New York: John Wiley & Sons, 1985.

Vollmann, T. E.; W. L. Berry; and D.C. Whybark. *Manufacturing Planning and Control Systems.* 3rd ed. Homewood, IL: Richard D. Irwin, 1992.

*Chapter*

# INVENTORY SYSTEMS FOR INDEPENDENT DEMAND

## Chapter Outline

## Chapter Objectives

- Introduce the different types of inventories that can exist in an organization and provide a rationale for why companies maintain inventories.

- Identify the various costs associated with carrying and maintaining inventories.

- Define the classical inventory models and the conditions necessary for them to be applicable.

- Show how the economic order quantity is calculated for each of the different inventory models.

- Introduce the single-period inventory model and the concept of yield management with respect to service operations.

- Present some of the current inventory management trends and issues that exist in companies today.

The senior executives of Alpha Numerics were having their annual retreat to review accomplishments of the past year and to discuss major policy issues for the coming year.* As was the norm, the retreat was held at a small hotel in the mountains of eastern Pennsylvania, well removed from the company's actual manufacturing facility.

The first day's meeting had gone well, but in the early evening, after dinner, the subject of inventory control and the number of shortages that had occurred over the past year came up for discussion. The vice president of engineering

*"Something's got to go, Fenton. You, me or this inventory—and it's not going to be me."*

suggested that, as a solution to the shortage problem, purchasing should order all of the projected material requirements at the beginning of the year.

The vice president of manufacturing was so taken back by this suggestion that, to the amazement of the others in the room, he leaped onto the conference table and shouted out, "Inventory is evil!" He turned to the president and said, "If we were to follow this suggestion, Mr. President, do you have an extra 25,000 square feet of warehouse space where we can store the material?" The president shook his head no. "And do you, Mr. Vice President of Finance, have an extra $5 million dollars to buy all this material?" The VP of finance similarly shook his head.

"And are you, Mr. Vice President of Marketing, going to provide me with a perfect forecast of the products we expect to sell for the next year?" The VP of marketing said, "No, of course not. That would be impossible." And turning to the VP of engineering who had made the initial proposal, he said, "And you'll keep the same designs in the coming year without making any changes, won't you?" The VP of engineering said, "That would be very unrealistic." All of the individuals in the room then looked up to the VP of manufacturing still standing on the conference table and said, "We see what you mean. Inventory is indeed evil!" ∎

---

*This meeting of senior corporate executives actually took place, although the name of the firm has been disguised.

461

In the past, inventory was perceived as an asset to an organization inasmuch as it appeared as an asset in its financial reports. This view, as shown in the opening vignette, is no longer the accepted norm. With product life cycles becoming increasingly shorter, product obsolescence also becomes more likely. In addition, we now recognize that inventories, particularly work-in-process inventories, tend to conceal problems. Maintaining inventories can also be very expensive. The average annual cost of maintaining inventories across all manufacturing firms is estimated to be 30 to 35 percent of its value, and could even be higher for some products. For these and other reasons, inventory is now seen to be a liability, something to be reduced or eliminated to the greatest extent possible as also shown by this GE advertisement that explains their ability to set up electronic links with suppliers, manufacturers, and distributors to avoid costly inventory.

As a result, probably no topic in operations today is more often discussed or perceived to be more important than inventory. The name of the game is to reduce inventory quantities on hand at all levels: in raw materials and purchased parts through direct delivery by the vendor (often directly to the production line); in work in process by techniques such as just-in-time production or scheduling with small batch sizes; and finally, in finished goods through a better matching of output to market requirements, and shipments to those markets as soon as possible. The growing effort to reduce all inventory is inspired by new measurements and performance evaluation based not on the percentage of resource utilization, but rather on inventory turns and product quality.

There are also changing views concerning the teaching of classical inventory models. On one side, some claim that economic order quantity (EOQ) models are invalid in actual application; others defend their use. While one must be careful when using them, there do exist situations where EOQ models can be successfully applied. More important, from a learning perspective, these models provide a basic framework for understanding the difficult issues involved in inventory management. Just-in-time manufacturing (JIT), for example, is based on the classical production-consumption model.

In this chapter, we present fixed-order and fixed-time period models. Also included are special purpose models, such as the quantity discount model, as well as the ABC technique for classifying items in inventory. We also present the single-period model which addresses highly perishable products as well as inventory issues in services through a discussion of yield management. In addition, we discuss the questions of inventory accuracy and show simple applications of the models in the real-world environment.

## DEFINITION OF INVENTORY

*Inventory* is defined as the stock of any item or resource used in an organization. An *inventory system* is the set of policies and controls that monitors levels of inventory and determines (*a*) what levels should be maintained, (*b*) when stock should be replenished, and (*c*) how large orders should be.

# Operations Management in Practice

## THE APPLICATION OF YIELD MANAGEMENT AT AMERICAN AIRLINES

Yield management is widely used today in the airline industry to maximize revenues and profits. American Airlines was one of the first companies to use yield management to (a) establish prices, (b) determine for a given flight what percentage of capacity it should allocate to each price, and (c) determine the restrictions necessary to segment the markets. Listed below is a sampling of the different prices for a round-trip flight between Boston, Massachusetts and London, England.

| Fare | Season | Day of Week | Advanced Purchase (days) | Other Restrictions |
|------|--------|-------------|--------------------------|--------------------|
| $324 | Low | MW | 90 | 5 day min.; 45 max. |
| $374 | Low | WE | 90 | 5 day min.; 45 max. |
| $472 | Low | MW | 21 | 7 day min.; 21 max. |
| $523 | Low | WE | 21 | 7 day min.; 21 max. |
| $454 | Shoulder | MW | 90 | 5 day min.; 45 max. |
| $504 | Shoulder | WE | 90 | 5 day min.; 45 max. |
| $575 | Shoulder | MW | 21 | 7 day min.; 21 max. |
| $620 | Shoulder | WE | 21 | 7 day min.; 21 max. |
| $599 | High | MW | 90 | 5 day min.; 45 max. |
| $649 | High | WE | 90 | 5 day min.; 45 max. |
| $740 | High | MW | 21 | 7 day min.; 21 max. |
| $801 | High | MW | 21 | 7 day min.; 21 max. |
| $2,364 | | | | Unrestricted coach |
| $5,260 | | MW | | Business class |
| $8,552 | | WE | | First class |

**Definitions:**

| | |
|---|---|
| Low season: | November 1–December 17 |
| | January 6–March 15 |
| Shoulder season: | September 30–October 31 |
| | March 16–June 15 |
| High season: | December 18–January 5 |
| | June 16–September 29 |
| Midweek (MW): | Monday–Thursday |
| Weekend (WE): | Friday–Sunday |

Source: Based on telephone conversations on August 8, 1997, with "Joyce" and "Linda," reservation agents with American Airlines.

At the same time, however, the service manager does not want to turn away a last-minute customer who usually pays the full rate because the capacity had been previously sold at a discounted rate. When this happens, opportunity costs are incurred. The methodology for determining the percentage of capacity to allocate to each market segment or price is referred to as yield management or revenue management. By using yield management, the service manager is simultaneously managing both the supply and demand for the firm's capacity. Demand is controlled by the different price structures: lower prices increase demand; higher prices decrease demand. Supply is controlled by limiting the capacity available at each of the different price structures.

As an illustration of how a service firm will use pricing to manage demand, the accompanying OM in Practice provides a sampling of the different airfares that American Airlines offers between Boston, Massachusetts, and London, England, and the restrictions associated with each airfare. It is important to note that while the level of service is significantly different for first class and business class passengers, the passengers receive the exact same level of service for all other fares. (There are also 7-day advanced purchase prices beginning at $619 round trip and 14-day advanced purchase prices beginning at $544 round trip. The 7-day requires a Saturday night stay over with a 6-month maximum stay and the 14-day has a minimum stay of 7 days with a maximum of 60 days. In addition, there are frequently special fares from time to time when demand is lower than forecast.)

As discussed in detail in the previous chapter, a service should have certain characteristics in order to take full advantage of yield management.

**Example**

Jacob and Evan Raser own a small hotel with 65 rooms in western Massachusetts. During the summer, there are many cultural activities going on in this region, including the Boston Symphony Orchestra at Tanglewood. The maximum room rate they charge during this time is $150 per night. However, while the hotel is usually sold out on weekends, it is never sold out during the week. From historical data, the two brothers have developed the following probability table with respect to the number of rooms occupied during a weeknight (i.e., Sunday through Thursday nights):

| Number of Rooms Occupied | Probability |
|---|---|
| 45 | 0.15 |
| 50 | 0.30 |
| 55 | 0.20 |
| 60 | 0.35 |

The variable cost to clean an occupied room is estimated to be $25. The two brothers have recently been approached by a group representing retired people, who are on limited incomes. The group is doing a special promotion for their spring newsletter and want to include a hotel that would offer reduced room rates during the week if the retirees made reservations at least one month in advance. The group assures Jacob and Evan that if the rate was $95 per night, they could sell all the rooms available on a weekday night. How many rooms should Jacob and Evan allocate to this lower rate for weeknights?

**Solution**

As with the Christmas tree problem, we construct the following payoff table:

| Probability | 0.15 | 0.30 | 0.20 | 0.35 | |
|---|---|---|---|---|---|
| Customer Demand | 45 | 50 | 55 | 60 | |
| Number of Rooms Available at $150 | | | | | Expected Profit |
| 45 | 7,025 | 6,750 | 6,475 | 6,200 | $6,543.75 |
| 50 | 6,325 | 7,300 | 7,025 | 6,750 | 6,906.25 |
| 55 | 5,625 | 6,600 | 7,575 | 7,300 | 6,893.75 |
| 60 | 4,925 | 5,900 | 6,875 | 7,850 | 6,640.00 |

11.  Mike Coggins, owner of Bagel Maker bakery, is trying to decide how many bagels he should make each morning. He currently sells fresh bagels for $5.25 per dozen. Any bagels that are left over at the end of the day are sold the next day as "yesterday's bagels" for $3.00 per dozen. Mike estimates that the material and labor to make a dozen bagels is $3.75. To help him decide how many bagels to make each morning he has collected the following information based on historical data:

| | Dozens of Bagels Sold | | | | | | |
|---|---|---|---|---|---|---|---|
| | 12 | 14 | 16 | 18 | 20 | 22 | 24 |
| | Probability | | | | | | |
| Weekdays (Monday–Friday) | .15 | .25 | .25 | .20 | .15 | .00 | .00 |
| Weekends (Saturday–Sunday) | .05 | .15 | .15 | .25 | .20 | .15 | .05 |

*a.* How many dozens of bagels should Mike make weekday mornings?

*b.* How many dozens of bagels should Mike make on weekend mornings?

12.  Sonia Groves owns a parking lot in downtown Boston with 100 spaces. She can offer an "early bird" special for $12.00 a day and she knows she can attract as many customers who work in downtown Boston as she is willing to allocate parking spaces at this low daily rate. The hourly rate that she charges is $6.00 and the average customer stays for about 3½ hours. Sonia has collected the following data on how many parking spaces a day she has had occupied at the hourly rate:

| Parking spaces | 65 | 70 | 75 | 80 | 85 |
|---|---|---|---|---|---|
| Probability | .15 | .20 | .25 | .30 | .10 |

If we assume that only one hourly customer per day occupies a given parking space, how many spaces should Sonia allocate for the early bird special in order to maximize her profits?

# SELECTED BIBLIOGRAPHY

Anderson, Edward J. "Testing Feasibility in a Lot Scheduling Problem." *Operations Research,* November–December 1990, pp. 1079–89.

Bernhard, Paul. "The Carrying Cost Paradox: How Do You Manage It?" *Industrial Engineering,* November 1989, pp. 40–46.

Davis, Samuel G. "Scheduling Economic Lot Size Production Runs." *Management Science,* August 1990, pp. 985–99.

Fitzsimmons, James, and Mona Fitzsimmons. *Service Management: Operations, Strategy, and Information Technology.* New York: McGraw-Hill, 1998.

Fogarty, Donald W.; John H. Blackstone; and Thomas R. Hoffmann. *Production and Inventory Management.* 2nd ed. Cincinnati, OH: South-Western Publishing, 1991.

Freeland, James R.; John P. Leschke; and Elliott N. Weiss. "Guidelines for Setup Reduction Programs to Achieve Zero Inventory." *Journal of Operations Management,* January 1990, pp. 75–80.

Harris, Ford Whitman. "How Many Parts to Make at Once." *Operations Research,* November–December 1990, pp. 947–51.

Kimes, Sheryl E., "Yield-Management: A Tool for Capacity-Constrained Service Firms." *Journal of Operations Management* 8, no. 4 (1989).

Tersine, Richard J. *Principles of Inventory and Materials Management.* 3rd ed. New York: North-Holland, 1988.

Vollmann, T. E.; W. L. Berry; and D. C. Whybark. *Manufacturing Planning and Control Systems.* 3rd ed. Homewood, IL: Richard D. Irwin, 1992.

Weiss, Elliott N. "Lot Sizing Is Dead: Long Live Lot Sizing." *Production and Inventory Management Journal,* First Quarter 1990, pp. 76–78.

Young, Jan B. *Modern Inventory Operations: Methods for Accuracy and Productivity.* New York: Van Nostrand Reinhold, 1991.

# INVENTORY SYSTEMS FOR DEPENDENT DEMAND

## Chapter Outline

## Chapter Objectives

- Define the various elements that comprise a materials requirements planning (MRP) system.

- Introduce the fundamental concepts and calculations that drive an MRP system.

- Identify some of the more common problems that confront managers when installing an MRP system.

- Describe how MRP-related systems are used in service operations.

- Introduce some of the more recent manufacturing-oriented systems that have been developed.

**F**MC Corp. is a $3.75 billion global producer of food machinery, chemicals, and defense equipment. Already skilled at producing high-quality, low-cost products, the company now wants to take advantage of emerging, worldwide markets while being its customers' best supplier.

To do that, FMC plans to supply the sales force with up-to-date information about the markets, the company's product lines, and product availability across their plants. This will allow the sales force to access current information from 112 plants in 20 countries.

In addition, sales representatives will be given tools to analyze available inventory, capacity, cost, and currency considerations in order to achieve the most favorable economics in delivering products to customers. But first, FMC needs to get the right information from the company's multiple ManMan MRP II systems from The Ask Cos. Currently, FMC is working with Ask to develop the capabilities to support its goals.

Customer service is the primary focus at Dow Corning Corp. The company has launched 30 cross-functional teams across five of its eight divisions. These teams are working to change Dow's operational processes, work flows, and the way people perform to increase customer satisfaction and reduce resource consumption.

Of utmost importance is shortening the time-to-market of new products and placing operational activities, such as order entry, into the hands of customers. Key to these plans is an EDI system for the entire supply chain. Dow also plans to replace its 20-year-old, in-house–developed MRP II system with an advanced system that can balance its production resources across all of its divisions.  ■

Source: Alice Greene, "Two Ready for the Next Generation," *Computerworld,* June 8, 1992, p. 77.

All of the inventory models presented in the previous chapter operate under an inherent assumption: Demand is independent and constant. However, there are often times when this assumption is not valid. This is particularly true when we are dealing with subassemblies and component parts, the demand for which is often variable and highly dependent on the demand for the final or end product in which they are used. For example, the demand for automobile tires is dependent on the demand for the autos themselves. Once the demand for the autos has been established, the demand for the tires is easily calculated.

**materials requirements planning (MRP)** Determines the number of subassemblies, components, and raw materials required and their build dates to complete a given number of end products by a specific date.

Consequently, the classical inventory models previously presented are not appropriate under these circumstances. To address these types of inventory issues, we use a concept known as **materials requirements planning,** or **MRP.**

Today, MRP systems, in part or in whole, are used in manufacturing firms both large and small. Exhibit 15.1 shows the percentage of companies within various industries in the United States that have installed MRP II-type systems. The reason is that MRP is a logical and readily understandable approach to the problem of determining the number of parts, components, and materials needed to produce each end item. MRP also provides the time schedule specifying when each of these materials, parts, and components should be ordered or produced.

The original MRP planned only materials. However, as computer power and speed increased over the past 20 or so years and applications expanded, so did the breadth of MRP. Soon it considered resources as well as materials; now MRP also stands for *manufacturing resource planning (MRP II),* which will be discussed later in this chapter.

The main purpose of this chapter is to present an overview of MRP and its underlying logic, and to demonstrate its use through several illustrations. We also discuss samples of existing MRP programs currently in use in industry. Finally, we show that just-in-time (JIT) systems and MRP are not necessarily competing ways for production but can work effectively together.

**EXHIBIT 15.1**

Percentage of Companies in 11 Industries with Installed MRP II Systems

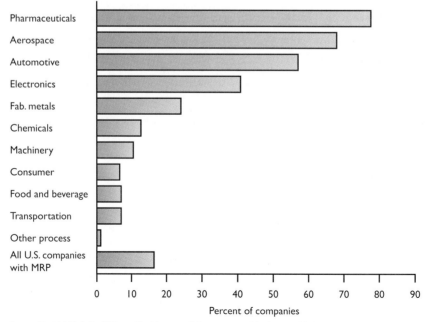

Source: David A. Turbide, *MRP + : The Adaptation, Enhancement, and Application of MRP II* (New York: Industrial Press, 1993), p. 11.

# MASTER PRODUCTION SCHEDULE

**master production schedule (MPS)**
Production plan that specifies how many of, and when to build, each end item.

The aggregate production plan, as presented in Chapter 13, specifies product groups. It does not specify exact items. The next level down in the planning process after the development of the aggregate plan is the master production schedule. The **master production schedule (MPS)** is the time-phased plan specifying how many and when the firm plans to build each specific end item. For example, the aggregate plan for a furniture company may specify the total volume of mattresses it plans to produce over the next month or next quarter. The MPS goes to the next step down and identifies the exact size of the mattresses and their models. All the mattresses sold by the company would be specified by the MPS. The MPS also states period by period (which is usually weekly) how many and when each of these mattress types is needed.

Still further down the disaggregation process is the MRP program, which calculates and schedules all of the raw materials, parts, and supplies needed to make each of the different mattresses specified in the MPS.

## Time Fences

The question of flexibility within an MPS depends on several factors including: production lead time, the commitment of parts and components to a specific end item, the relationship between the customer and vendor, the amount of excess capacity, and the reluctance or willingness of management to make changes.

Exhibit 15.2 shows an example of a master production schedule time fence. Management defines *time fences* as periods of time, with each period having some specified level of opportunity for the customer to make changes. (The customer may be the firm's own marketing department, which may be considering product promotions, broadening variety, etc.) Note in the exhibit that for the next eight weeks the MPS for this particular firm is frozen. Each firm has its own time fences and operating rules. Under these rules, *frozen* could be defined as anything from absolutely no changes in one firm to only the most minor of changes in another. *Moderately firm* may allow changes in specific products within a product group, so long as parts are available. *Flexible* may allow almost any variations in products, with the provision that capacity remains about the same and that there are no long lead time items involved.

The purpose of time fences is to maintain a reasonably controlled flow through the production system. Unless some operating rules are established and adhered to, the system could be chaotic and filled with overdue orders and constant expediting.

**EXHIBIT 15.2**

Master Production Schedule Time Fences

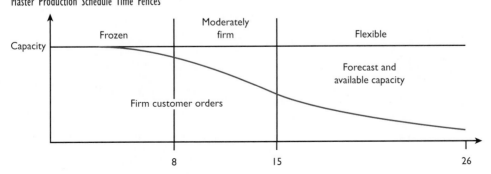

# MATERIAL REQUIREMENTS PLANNING (MRP) SYSTEMS

Using an MPS that is derived from an aggregate plan, *a material requirements planning (MRP)* system can then create schedules identifying the specific parts and materials necessary to produce the end items required, the exact numbers of each that are needed, and the dates when orders for these materials should be released and be received or completed within the production cycle. Today's MRP systems use a computer program to carry out these operations. Most firms have used computerized inventory systems for years, but they were independent of the scheduling system; MRP links these two elements together.

Material requirements planning is not new in concept. Logic dictates that the Romans probably used it in their construction projects, the Venetians in their shipbuilding, and the Chinese in building the Great Wall. Building contractors have always been forced into planning for material to be delivered when needed and not before, because of space limitations. What is new is the larger scale and the more rapid changes that can be made through the use of computers. Now firms that produce many products involving thousands of parts and materials can take advantage of MRP.

## Purposes, Objectives, and Philosophy of MRP

The main purposes of an MRP system are to control inventory levels, assign operating priorities to items, and plan capacity to load the production system. These may be briefly expanded as follows:

**Inventory**

Order the right part.

Order the right quantity.

Order at the right time.

**Priorities**

Order with the right due date.

Keep the due date valid.

The MRP system at Allen-Bradley, a manufacturer of circuit boards, receives an order and schedules appropriate production. Board panels are automatically routed to the required process, such as this robotic cell that inserts nonstandard components.

# Operations Management in Practice

## FURNITURE MANUFACTURER USES MRP II TO CUT DELIVERY TIME

In 1988, Harpers, Inc., an office furniture manufacturer located in California, was experiencing sustained growth in sales, but profits continued to fall. To reverse the downward trend in profits, management determined that it would have to reduce manufacturing costs by 15 percent, reduce product delivery times from six weeks (which was the industry standard) to three weeks, and reduce the new product time-to-market from three years to six months.

At the same time, Harpers recognized the need to focus its efforts on one segment of the office furniture market which was "custom furniture solutions." To accomplish all of this, Harper needed a flexible manufacturing system that would allow customers to change the features of any furniture configuration.

The heart of its manufacturing system was centered around an MRP II system that would "integrate our engineering, marketing, manufacturing, and accounting efforts, and simultaneously engineer and deliver those custom products," said Joe Wisniewski, executive vice president and general manager at Harpers.

The system was installed and running by 1990, and by the end of 1991, 20 percent of the company's furniture was shipping within two weeks, with the remaining orders shipping in four weeks.

Source: Adapted from Robert M. Knight, "Furniture Maker Uses MRP II to Cut Lead Time," *Computerworld*, June 8, 1992, p. 80.

---

MRP II systems are run on minicomputers or mainframes because of the very large data storage requirements and the number of program modules involved. Lease costs may range from $30,000 to $500,000 per year; however, technology is changing rapidly, with a consequent drop in cost. In terms of additional personnel needed, the experiences of many companies indicate that the overall net change in personnel is close to zero. Companies simply switch people from existing areas into MRP system roles.

The typical MRP II system takes about 18 months to install. However, this can vary widely depending on the size of the application, the condition of the existing databases and how much they may have to be revised, the quality of the bills of materials, routing sheets and inventory records, and the amount of personnel training required. Another factor is whether the firm has already been using an MRP system and is switching to an MRP II system. The entire range of time can vary from as little as several months to as much as three years.

Payback for an MRP installation can be quite short. When larger companies first installed MRP systems some years ago, they realized an average annual return on investment of about 300 percent.[2]

When we think of MRP II, we tend to think of large computer programs with applications confined to business giants. In fact, however, MRP II is also economically feasible for manufacturing companies with annual sales of less than $1 million. In addition, much of the current software is user-friendly and easy to operate.

Prices and quality of software vary widely and not necessarily in a direct relationship. Customer support is another very important factor. This is a buyer beware market, and care should be taken in selecting a program because it is a long-term commitment.

## MRP IN SERVICES

In general, MRP systems have not made significant inroads in service operations. This is due, in part, to the belief that MRP is strictly a manufacturing tool. However, modified versions of MRP are used in service operations where an actual product is manufactured as part of the service delivery process. Examples of these quasi-manufacturing services, as

[2]Ibid., pp. 34–35.

stated in an earlier chapter, include restaurants and bakeries where food is prepared on-site. In these types of service operations, the inventory management system usually consists of one or more point-of-sale (POS) terminals (or cash registers) that are connected to a central computer. This computer can be located either on-site at the retail operation or at a remote regional or headquarters location.

The POS terminals are designed for *single item pricing,* where the cashier simply pushes a single key on the terminal that represents a specific item on the menu. The computer system then automatically posts the price of that item. At the same time, within the central computer system, is the bill-of-materials (or recipe) for the item that has just been sold. All of the ingredients that go into that item are subtracted out from the inventory records file. The computer inventory files are then compared against the actual physical inventories on a periodic basis. Typically these systems have reorder points built into them which will automatically signal when a specific item is running low.

Some of these service operations also use this modified MRP system to order raw ingredients to meet future sales, in a manner similar to that of an MRP system in a manufacturing environment. First, a forecast of end items to be sold is generated (for example, hamburgers). The forecasted demand for these items is then "exploded" against the bills of materials (or recipes) for the end items to determine the gross requirements. Finally these requirements are compared to on-hand inventories to determine the actual amounts of raw ingredients to be ordered and the delivery dates for when they are needed.

## MISCELLANEOUS MRP ISSUES

### Problems in Installing and Using MRP Systems

MRP is very well developed technically, and implementation of an MRP system should be pretty straightforward. Yet there are many problems with existing MRP systems and many "failures" in trying to install them. Why do such problems and outright failures occur with a "proven" system?

The answer partially lies with organizational and behavioral factors. Three major causes of failure have been identified: (*a*) the lack of top management commitment, (*b*) the failure to recognize that MRP is only a software tool and that it needs to be used correctly, and (*c*) the ability to properly integrate MRP and JIT.

Part of the blame for the lack of top management's commitment may be MRP's image. It sounds like a manufacturing system rather than a business plan. However, an MRP system is used to plan resources and develop schedules. And a well-functioning schedule effectively uses the firm's assets with the result of increased profits. MRP should be presented to top management as a planning tool with specific reference to profit results. Intensive executive education is needed, emphasizing the importance of MRP as a closed-loop, integrated, strategic planning tool.

The second cause of the problem concerns the MRP advocates that overdid themselves in selling the concept. MRP was presented and perceived as a complete, stand-alone system to run a firm, rather than part of the total system. The third issue is how MRP can be made to function with JIT. JIT and MRP can live together, but there are few rules as to how they should be integrated. The total system consists of the functional areas of engineering, marketing, personnel, and manufacturing, as well as techniques and concepts such as quality circles, CAD/CAM, and robotics. MRP needs to be *part* of the total system, not the total system by itself.

In many meetings that we have attended, both professional and industrial, we have heard similar installation and operational problems. These problems distill down to the fact that the MRP system essentially runs the firm; its main objective is simply to meet the schedule. As a result, people become subservient to the MRP system. Even such simple decisions as determining a lot size cannot be made outside the system.

As it stands now, MRP is a very formal system that requires strict adherence to its rules in order to function properly. Often supervisors and workers develop an informal system for getting the job done. Their argument is that this informal system arises because the existing formal system is too rigid or inadequate to deal with real inventory scheduling problems. However, when these rules are not adhered to within the formal system, incorrect data is often reported and, as a consequence, worker confidence in the formal system begins to deteriorate. In any event, it appears that employees at all levels must change—from the company president to the lower-level employees. Even though MRP currently does work in many installations, its good features and its shortcomings should be thoroughly understood.

Other problems encountered in using MRP include:

1. *The fallacy of static lead time.* MRP software programs treat lead time as a fixed number, while in reality lead time changes for a variety of reasons, such as normal variation in processing time, waiting for parts, delays in processing due to expedited jobs, breakdown or normal maintenance of machines, and so on.

2. *The misdefinition of lead time.* Manufacturing lead time consists of:
    *a.* Make-ready time—to write order, enter, prepare job packet, release order, and issue material.
    *b.* Queue time—time at the operation center waiting for operations to begin.
    *c.* Setup time—to prepare equipment for operations.
    *d.* Run time—to perform operations (produce product).
    *e.* Wait time—time waiting after operation ends.
    *f.* Move time—to physically move between operations.

3. *Lead time versus fabrication/production quantity.* MRP software, because it considers lead time fixed, does not account for the fact that run time (part of the lead time) varies depending on the quantity of units to be produced.

4. *Bills of materials.* MRP software programs use the bills of materials as a bottoms-up product structure representing the ways firms manufacture products. For many firms, however, especially those producing on an assembly line, products may be produced in a very different sequence than the engineering bills of materials.

5. *Material revision control.* Many MRP programs do not easily allow changes to be made to part numbers or in the way the product is produced.

6. *Lead time versus routing.* Since many MRP programs use the bills of materials structure to schedule the shop floor, poor schedules may result. For example, there may be several routing steps at the same bill of materials level, which require more time than allowed.

7. *Fallacy of infinite capacity planning.* Few MRP programs can recognize a shop overload and reschedule.

8. *The real story of rough-cut planning.* While rough-cut capacity planning was taught as the solution to overloaded work centers, in reality rough-cut capacity planning lies somewhere between the difficult and the impossible. In effect, master schedulers are expected to perform MRP and CRP explosions in their heads. Technically, the only way to really do rough-cut capacity planning is to run the MRP and CRP (capacity requirement plan) each time a change is made in the master schedule. The required computer time makes this impossible.

9. *Capacity planning versus MRP logic.* Because MRP and CRP are not run together when changes are made in the MPS, such changes often create "floating bottlenecks." Bottlenecks appear and disappear, depending on the master production schedule.

10. *MRP logic—a user confuser.* MRP logic differs from system to system. The user should test how the system reacts to, say, accelerating, decelerating, or canceling an order.[3]

## Criticisms of the MRP Concept

In addition to the problems previously mentioned with respect to installing and using an MRP system, there are other criticisms as well. Many critics state that MRP schedules are either impossible or are only true on the day that they were created. Too many changes take place in the system for MRP to be able to adjust to all of them.

**Accuracy Requirements**  Because MRP uses detailed files to schedule, MRP cannot tolerate inaccuracies. In fact, for many years since MRP was introduced, companies have been rated and grouped by class based on the accuracy of their records. Class A companies, for example, have more than 99-percent accuracy. MRP's failures in its scheduling performance had been blamed on inaccurate records. Now we recognize that inaccuracy was not completely to blame; the MRP scheduling technique was also at fault.

MIS  **Top Management Commitment**  This is not so much a criticism of MRP, but of top management. As in the case of many programs, MRP needs to be endorsed and continually supported by top management. An MRP system is doomed to failure if management believes its responsibilities end with authorizing purchase of the program and turning over responsibility for running the computer system to the MIS group. Continuous reinforcement and encouragement are needed; everyone must be convinced that the system is worth its time and expense. It also means spending money on training, and perhaps changing the internal measurement and reward system. If this is not done, shop-floor personnel ignore MRP schedules and use their own priorities in doing job selection and in determining process batch sizes.

 **MRP as a Database**  Although MRP has been criticized for its questioned accuracy in providing workable schedules, MRP has been highly complimented for its detailed database. MRP's database extends throughout the entire facility and is linked through numerous modules. Even if a firm decides to discontinue using MRP to schedule its facilities, it would more than likely continue to maintain MRP files for their informational value.

## Safety Stock

Ordinarily, adding a safety stock to required quantities is not advised in an MRP system that is based on derived demand. There is some feeling, however, that when the availability of parts could suffer from a long and inflexible lead time or is subject to strikes or cancellation, a safety stock offers some protection against production delays. A safety stock is sometimes intentionally created by planning for excess. One of the main arguments against using safety stock is that the MRP system considers it a fixed quantity, and the safety stock is never actually used.

## Lot Sizing in MRP Systems

The determination of lot sizes in an MRP system is a complicated and difficult problem. Lot sizes are the part quantities issued in the planned order receipt and planned order

---

[3]Adapted from Gus Berger, "Ten Ways MRP Can Defeat You," *Conference Proceedings, American Production and Inventory Control Society* (1987), pp. 240–43.

release sections of an MRP schedule. For parts produced in house, lot sizes are the production quantities or batch sizes. For purchased parts, these are the quantities ordered from the supplier. Lot sizes generally meet part requirements for one or more periods.

Most lot-sizing techniques deal with how to balance the setup or order costs and holding costs associated with meeting the net requirements generated by the MRP planning process. Many MRP systems have options for computing lot sizes based on some of the more commonly used techniques. It should be obvious, though, that the use of lot-sizing techniques increases the complexity in generating MRP schedules. When fully exploded, the numbers of parts scheduled can be enormous.

We present four lot-sizing techniques using a common example. The lot-sizing techniques presented are lot-for-lot (L4L), economic order quantity (EOQ), least total cost (LTC), and least unit cost (LUC).

Consider the following MRP lot-sizing problem; the net requirements are shown for eight scheduling periods:

| | |
|---|---|
| Cost per item | $10.00 |
| Order or setup cost | $47.00 |
| Inventory carry cost/period | 0.5% |

Period net requirements:

| 1 | 2 | 3 | 4 | 5 | 6 | 7 | 8 |
|---|---|---|---|---|---|---|---|
| 50 | 60 | 70 | 60 | 95 | 75 | 60 | 55 |

**Lot-for-Lot**  Lot-for-lot (L4L) is the most common technique; it:

- Sets planned orders to exactly match the net requirements.
- Produces exactly what is needed each period with none carried over into future periods.
- Minimizes carrying cost.
- Does not take into account setup costs or capacity limitations.

Many times producing enough product to last several periods and incurring holding costs may be cheaper than producing in every period and incurring repeated setup costs. In the case of parts produced in house, the setup cost represents time that resources are not operating but getting ready to produce. This is lost capacity. Not only are setup costs higher, but requiring setups in every period a part is needed also reduces the time available to produce other products.

Exhibit 15.15 shows the lot-for-lot calculations. In each period the lot size exactly matches the net requirements. A setup cost is charged for each period. The lot-for-lot

---

**EXHIBIT 15.15**

Lot-for-Lot Run Size for an MRP Schedule

| Period | Net Requirements | Production Quantity | Ending Inventory | Holding Cost | Setup Cost | Total Cost |
|---|---|---|---|---|---|---|
| 1 | 50 | 50 | 0 | $0.00 | $47.00 | $ 47.00 |
| 2 | 60 | 60 | 0 | 0.00 | 47.00 | 94.00 |
| 3 | 70 | 70 | 0 | 0.00 | 47.00 | 141.00 |
| 4 | 60 | 60 | 0 | 0.00 | 47.00 | 188.00 |
| 5 | 95 | 95 | 0 | 0.00 | 47.00 | 235.00 |
| 6 | 75 | 75 | 0 | 0.00 | 47.00 | 282.00 |
| 7 | 60 | 60 | 0 | 0.00 | 47.00 | 329.00 |
| 8 | 55 | 55 | 0 | 0.00 | 47.00 | 376.00 |

**EXHIBIT 15.16**

Economic Order Quantity
Run Size for an MRP
Schedule

| Period | Net Requirements | Production Quantity | Ending Inventory | Holding Cost | Setup Cost | Total Cost |
|--------|------------------|---------------------|------------------|--------------|------------|------------|
| 1 | 50 | 351 | 301 | $15.05 | $47.00 | $ 62.05 |
| 2 | 60 | 0 | 241 | 12.05 | 0.00 | 74.10 |
| 3 | 70 | 0 | 171 | 8.55 | 0.00 | 82.65 |
| 4 | 60 | 0 | 111 | 5.55 | 0.00 | 88.20 |
| 5 | 95 | 0 | 16 | 0.80 | 0.00 | 89.00 |
| 6 | 75 | 351 | 292 | 14.60 | 47.00 | 150.60 |
| 7 | 60 | 0 | 232 | 11.60 | 0.00 | 162.20 |
| 8 | 55 | 0 | 177 | 8.85 | 0.00 | 171.05 |

| EOQ assumptions: | |
|---|---|
| Total requirements | 525 |
| Average requirements | 65.6 |
| Annual holding cost per unit | $2.60 |
| Annual demand | 3,412.5 |
| EOQ | 351.25 |

technique, while minimizing holding costs, orders far too often because it places an order every time a net requirement occurs.

**Economic Order Quantity**   In Chapter 14 we discussed the EOQ model that explicitly balances setup and holding costs. An inherent assumption in the EOQ model is that there is either fairly constant demand or that safety stock must be kept to accommodate any variability in demand. The EOQ model uses an estimate of total annual demand, the setup or order cost, and the annual holding cost. EOQ was not designed for a system with discrete time periods such as MRP. The lot-sizing techniques used for MRP assume that part requirements are satisfied at the start of the period. Holding costs are then charged only to the ending inventory for the period, not to the average inventory used in the EOQ model. EOQ assumes that parts are used on a continuous basis during the period. The lot sizes generated by EOQ do not always cover the entire number of periods. For example, the EOQ might provide the requirements for 4.6 periods.

Exhibit 15.16 shows the EOQ lot size calculated for this part. Several assumptions are made to determine the EOQ. EOQ requires an estimate of both annual demand and annual holding cost. Since the holding cost per period is $0.05 and the MRP schedule is weekly, the annual holding cost per unit is $2.60 ($0.05 × 52 weeks). Annual demand is computed by multiplying the average weekly demand for the eight periods by 52 weeks (525/8 × 52 = 3,412.5). The resulting EOQ is 351 units. The EOQ lot size in Period 1 is enough to meet requirements for Periods 1 through 5 and a portion of Period 6. Then, in Period 6 another EOQ lot is planned to meet the requirements for Periods 6 through 8. Notice that the EOQ plan leaves some inventory at the end of Period 8 to carry forward into Period 9.

**Least Total Cost**   The least total cost method (LTC) is a dynamic lot-sizing technique that calculates the order quantity by comparing the order cost and the holding costs for various lot sizes and then selects the lot in which these are most nearly equal.

Exhibit 15.17 shows the least total cost lot size results. The procedure to compute least total cost lot sizes is to compare order costs and holding costs for various numbers of periods. For example, costs are compared for producing in Period 1 to cover the requirements for Period 1; producing in Period 1 for Periods 1 and 2; producing in Period 1 to cover

**EXHIBIT 15.17**

Least Total Cost Run Size for an MRP Schedule

| Period | Net Requirements | Production Quantity | Ending Inventory | Holding Cost | Setup Cost | Total Cost |
|---|---|---|---|---|---|---|
| 1 | 50 | 335 | 285 | $14.25 | $47.00 | $ 61.25 |
| 2 | 60 | 0 | 225 | 11.25 | 0.00 | 72.50 |
| 3 | 70 | 0 | 155 | 7.75 | 0.00 | 80.25 |
| 4 | 60 | 0 | 95 | 4.75 | 0.00 | 85.00 |
| 5 | 95 | 0 | 0 | 0.00 | 0.00 | 85.00 |
| 6 | 75 | 190 | 115 | 5.75 | 47.00 | 137.75 |
| 7 | 60 | 0 | 55 | 2.75 | 0.00 | 140.50 |
| 8 | 55 | 0 | 0 | 0.00 | 0.00 | 140.50 |

| Periods | Quantity Ordered | Carrying Cost | Order Cost | Total Cost | |
|---|---|---|---|---|---|
| 1 | 50 | $ 0.00 | $47.00 | $ 47.00 | |
| 1–2 | 110 | 3.00 | 47.00 | 50.00 | |
| 1–3 | 180 | 10.00 | 47.00 | 57.00 | |
| 1–4 | 240 | 19.00 | 47.00 | 66.00 | |
| 1–5 | 335 | 38.00 | 47.00 | 85.00 | ←Least total cost |
| 1–6 | 410 | 56.75 | 47.00 | 103.75 | |
| 1–7 | 470 | 74.75 | 47.00 | 121.75 | |
| 1–8 | 525 | 94.00 | 47.00 | 141.00 | |
| 6 | 75 | 0.00 | 47.00 | 47.00 | |
| 6–7 | 135 | 3.00 | 47.00 | 50.00 | |
| 6–8 | 190 | 8.50 | 47.00 | 55.50 | ←Least total cost |

Periods 1, 2, and 3, and so on. The correct selection is that lot size where the ordering costs and holding costs are approximately equal. In Exhibit 15.17 that lot size is 335, because the difference between a $38 carrying cost and a $47 ordering cost is closer than $56.25 and $47. This lot size covers requirements for Periods 1 through 5. Unlike EOQ, the lot size covers only whole numbers of periods.

Based on the Period 1 decision to place an order to cover 5 periods, we are now located in Period 6, and our problem is to determine how many periods into the future we can provide for from here. Exhibit 15.17 shows that holding and order costs are closest in the quantity that covers requirements for Periods 6 through 8. Notice that the holding and order costs here are far apart. This is because our example extends only to Period 8. If the planning horizon were longer, that lot size planned for Period 6 would likely cover more periods into the future beyond Period 8. This brings up one of the limitations of both LTC and LUC (discussed below). Both techniques are influenced by the length of the planning horizon.

**Least Unit Cost** The least unit cost method (LUC) is a dynamic lot-sizing technique that adds ordering and inventory carrying cost for each trial lot size and divides by the number of units in each lot size, picking the lot size with the lowest unit cost. In the example in Exhibit 15.18, the lot size of 410 covers Periods 1 through 6. The lot size planned for Period 7 covers through the end of the planning horizon.

**Which Lot Size To Choose** Using the lot-for-lot method, the total cost for the eight periods is $376; the EOQ total cost is $171.05; the least total cost method is $140.50; and the least unit cost is $209. The lowest cost was obtained using the least total cost method of $140.50. If there were more than eight periods, the method with the lowest cost could be different.

**EXHIBIT 15.18**

Least Unit Cost Run Size for an MRP Schedule

| Period | Net Requirements | Production Quantity | Ending Inventory | Holding Cost | Setup Cost | Total Cost |
|--------|------------------|---------------------|------------------|--------------|------------|------------|
| 1 | 50 | 410 | 360 | $18.00 | $47.00 | $ 65.00 |
| 2 | 60 | 0 | 300 | 15.00 | 0.00 | 80.00 |
| 3 | 70 | 0 | 230 | 11.50 | 0.00 | 91.50 |
| 4 | 60 | 0 | 170 | 8.50 | 0.00 | 100.00 |
| 5 | 95 | 0 | 75 | 3.75 | 0.00 | 103.75 |
| 6 | 75 | 115 | 115 | 5.75 | 47.00 | 156.50 |
| 7 | 60 | 0 | 55 | 2.75 | 0.00 | 159.25 |
| 8 | 55 | 55 | 55 | 2.75 | 47.00 | 209.00 |

| Periods | Quantity Ordered | Carrying Cost | Order Cost | Total Cost | Unit Cost | |
|---------|------------------|---------------|------------|------------|-----------|---|
| 1 | 50 | $ 0.00 | $47.00 | $ 47.00 | $0.9400 | |
| 1–2 | 110 | 3.00 | 47.00 | 50.00 | 0.4545 | |
| 1–3 | 180 | 10.00 | 47.00 | 57.00 | 0.3167 | |
| 1–4 | 240 | 19.00 | 47.00 | 66.00 | 0.2750 | |
| 1–5 | 335 | 38.00 | 47.00 | 85.00 | 0.2537 | |
| 1–6 | 410 | 56.75 | 47.00 | 103.75 | 0.2530 | ←Least unit cost |
| 1–7 | 470 | 74.75 | 47.00 | 121.75 | 0.2590 | |
| 1–8 | 525 | 94.00 | 47.00 | 141.00 | 0.2686 | |
| 7 | 60 | 0.00 | 47.00 | 47.00 | 0.7833 | |
| 7–8 | 115 | 2.75 | 47.00 | 49.75 | 0.4326 | ←Least unit cost |

The advantage of the least unit cost method is that it provides a more complete analysis, taking into account ordering or setup costs that might change as the order size increases. If the ordering or setup costs remain constant, the lowest total cost method is more attractive because it is simpler and easier to compute; yet it would be just as accurate under that restriction.

# INSTALLING AN MRP SYSTEM

The average time for a company to effectively install an MRP system seems to range from 18 to 24 months—not for the software, but because so much other preparation and training must take place. At the risk of being redundant, we repeat some cautions about installing an MRP system.

## Preparation Steps

**Bills of Materials**   The BOM lists all of the materials required to create a product in a hierarchical form, which is usually the way in which a product is produced. The BOM is an extremely important element in an MRP system and, as a consequence, inaccuracies here cannot be tolerated. Without an MRP or some such computer system, BOM accuracy is not critical and firms can live with some errors. A first step prior to installing an MRP system is to review the BOM for all products to ensure that they are correct.

**Routing Sheets and Processing Times**   Similar to the BOM, many firms previously did not need to be specific about which machine or process should be used, since adjustments could always be made manually on the shop floor. The same goes for processing; with the usual longer times in the shop (as opposed to MRP installations) there are opportunities to make up discrepancies (in spite of the fact that the data for accounting purposes would be in error).

**Inventory Stock**   Most firms have errors in their inventory records. Oftentimes it is because no one wants to take the time necessary to count and verify records and physical stock. Another reason is that often inventory stock is old or obsolete; bringing records up to date may mean that much inventory carried on company books as assets may have to be declared scrap. Few managers are willing to bite the bullet and do this. Reducing inventory directly impacts the bottom line and quickly catches the attention of top management. However, installing an MRP system means that errors must be removed and the inventory carried must be of usable quality.

**Procedures**   In addition to the actual records previously mentioned, procedures and/or new software must be installed to keep these records up to date. Examples are adding stock to inventory when received from vendors and making appropriate changes when issuing stock to production. Also, ways of handling changes to the bills of materials, routing, or processing times need to be decided.

 **Training**   Everyone—from top management through to the purchasing staff, supervisors, and the workers on the shop floor—must be trained in the effective use of an MRP system—how to read its reports, which leeways are allowable in quantity or schedule variations, and what results can be expected. People, by nature, are reluctant to change. Throughout MRP's history of more than two decades, we have blamed people whenever poor performance occurred in their MRP system (lack of understanding, lack of top management support, lack of adequate discipline, etc.). While this is now recognized as a problem caused in large part by the MRP itself (noted elsewhere in this chapter), nevertheless without support of all the individuals involved, MRP would be doomed to failure.

## Advanced MRP-Type Systems

 For more than two decades, MRP systems were the first choice for firms that focused at the plant production level. MRP took as its input the product demands, inventory levels and resource availability, and produced production schedules as well as inventory ordering quantities. During this time the world was changing, with new global competition, multiplant international sites, wide global product demand, international subcontracting, and varying political environments and currency markets. Existing MRP software programs in their standard form could not handle these widened applications.

In today's environment, MRP users want instant access to information on customers' needs, which plants can meet these needs, and companywide inventory levels and available capacity throughout the supply chain.

What has been the response to these needs? There are more than 300 vendors for MRP systems. While most of these were involved with MRP systems from years ago and are still selling and maintaining their existing systems, many others are changing their systems to accommodate the new requirements; other firms are at the state-of-the-art in developing new advanced systems based on MRP logic. In an expected response, many existing firms are modifying their current software programs while others are making major changes in the basic logic and databases.

Various names have been given to this new generation of MRP. The Gartner Group called the new MRP *Enterprise Resource Planning (ERP).* To fully operate in an enterprise sense,

FINANCE
MARKETING
ACCOUNTING
MIS

there needs to be distributed applications for planning, scheduling, costing, and so on to the multiple layers of the organization: work centers, sites, divisions, corporate. Multiple languages and currencies are also being included for global applications.

Advanced MRP systems (also called next-generation MRP II) will (or now) include[4]

Client/server architecture.

Relational database with SQL.

Graphic user interface.

Multiple database support.

Front-end systems for decision support.

Automated EDI.

Interoperability with multiple platforms.

Standard application programming interfaces.

Electronic data interchange (EDI) needs to be included for better communication with both customers and suppliers.

### Distributed MRP Processing versus Centralized Processing

Many companies want to retain their mainframes and centralized processing systems. To do this and be able to give users throughout the firm reliable real-time information, relational databases are being implemented. Oracle Corp., for example, has a widely used relational database system and fourth-generation language that is being incorporated to enhance existing MRP systems. Sequent Computer Systems is using Oracle's manufacturing software on its computer and is expanding into other areas as the need arises, such as JIT (just-in-time manufacturing) and TQI (total quality through incremental improvements).

Existing MRP systems are limited in access and quite self-contained.

A *centralized process operation* controls such features as engineering, production scheduling, forecasting, order processing, purchasing, and materials planning for multiple plants at one central location. A *decentralized processing operation* distributes these responsibilities among the plants for autonomous operation. A *distributed processing operation* uses a combination of centralized and decentralized controls to allocate resources where they are logically needed and where they can be executed most efficiently.[5]

In distributed MRP processing, remote stations can access data, manipulate it, do local processing, and feed it back into the system. High-performance workstations such as Hewlett-Packard and Sun Microsystems are based on Unix, allowing fairly open communications and exchange. Mainframes, minicomputers, and microcomputers are a mixture that will become common in a truly distributed environment. Other open communication systems include IBM's OS/2 and Hewlett-Packard's MPE/iX.

Focus is on the total organization, but local computation and control are allowed. Local managers get quicker feedback on their performance and can therefore improve themselves by doing their own analysis.

There are two opposing views about centralization versus decentralization. One argument is that shifting to global manufacturing will encourage more decentralized MRP to allow more local control. The counterargument is that global manufacturing will cause centralization since more decision making will take place concerning multiple markets, customers, sources, and so on. Both can be satisfied perhaps by using an OSI (open systems

---

[4]Alice Greene, "MRP II: Out with the Old," *Computerworld,* June 8, 1992, p. 74.

[5]Richard Costello, "Available: Real-Time EDI, Multiplant Functions, More," *Computerworld,* June 8, 1992, p. 79.

interconnect) providing for a fully distributed system. OSI uses a common data architecture that permits both decentralization and data sharing.[6]

## SAP America, Inc.'s R/3

SAP America, Inc., has come out with its R/3 MRP software package for open systems. It is a client/server application. The software includes a full variety of manufacturing and financial applications (such as financial and fixed asset accounting), materials management, sales and distribution, human resources, production planning, quality assurance, and plant maintenance. R/3 runs on UNIX, HP MPE/IX, and IBM OS/2.

Many companies are justifiably reluctant to install drastically new systems. They know that being first in new software applications has more disadvantages than advantages. Previously unknown system bugs and errors in logic creep in and can create havoc during the installation and startup phases. Rather than adopting the R/3 package, many firms are installing SAP's earlier R/2 instead. SAP's R/2 system is used by more than 4,000 customers as of 1997. Many of these will switch over to R/3 as needs arise. OS/2-based R/3 software improves the graphic user interface.

Use of R/3 is more widespread in Europe, since SAP AG is a German firm. Companies are responding in different ways. Eastman Chemical, a $3.9-billion company, is installing R/2 and just a very small part of R/3 to see how it runs. However, $40-billion Chevron is using R/3 on a corporatewide basis.

## ManMan/X

ManMan/X is a Unix-based software from Ask Computer Systems, Inc. It is based on the Enterprise Resource Planning logic and uses the fourth-generation language (4GL). ManMan/X also supports Hewlett-Packard's MPR/iX, Oracle Corp.'s database, and Informix Inc.'s database.

ManMan/X provides stronger planning and forecasting features (including simulation and net change) than most other MRP systems. ManMan/X will exchange information with other systems. It also includes languages and currency features for global operation.

## COMMS
## (Customer-Oriented Manufacturing Management System)

Vendors are taking many different approaches to develop new MRP-type advanced programs. A new model of an advanced integrated MRP-type system is being created by Advanced Manufacturing Research, Inc. (AMR), a Boston-based consulting firm. AMR's model is called COMMS (Customer-Oriented Manufacturing Management System). COMMS has added in real-time interaction with the manufacturing plants throughout the supply chain. Currently in development, this model is shown in Exhibit 15.19. It places the customer in the center with the objective of giving customers what they want, when, how, where, and at the price they want. This is a distributed-type system.

The firms that AMR represents believe that we are entering an era of "customerized" manufacturing where the customer can specify anything and the manufacturer must be able to respond quickly to remain competitive. Note that Exhibit 15.19 shows AMR's COMMS model uniting the departments of the chain around the customer. In practice, when a customer's order is taken, the salesperson can give all the necessary information to the customer: any engineering changes, the schedule, price, and so on. This is possible because the salesperson has direct access to all the databases and schedules.

[6]William F. McSpadden, "OSI, Distributed MRP II and You," *Industrial Engineering*, February 1992, pp. 38–39.

**EXHIBIT 15.19**

A Customer-Oriented
Manufacturing Management
System (COMMS)

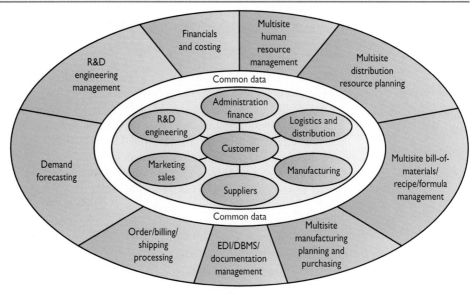

Source: Chris Staiti, "Customers Drive New Manufacturing Software." *Datamation*, November 15, 1993, p. 72. Reprinted with permission. © 1993 by Cahners Publishing Co.

### EDI (Electronic Data Interchange)

Roughly 80 percent of MRP packages have an EDI module that allows manufacturers to import and export documents. The new addition to EDI is that it is beginning to be *real-time* interchange rather than batch processing. It is valuable for multiplant MRP. EDI vendors include American Software, IBM, Andersen Consulting, and Symix Computer Systems.

About 85 percent of MRP II packages include an interface with at least one CAD (computer-aided design) system. The CAD integration solutions such as those by Cincom and Micro-MRP are two of the most popular.

### Transition to Advanced MRP-Type Systems

How do firms change from existing MRP systems to the advanced ones? That depends on the new system they want. Some systems are easier to use than others, such as Cincom's Control Manufacturing, which uses existing data and transaction processing methods. Others (such as Datalogix and Dunn and Bradstreet software) are more difficult in requiring re-implementation. Still other firms are waiting by the sidelines until more clear paths and possible results are visible. Most larger firms eventually will have to update and expand their MRP system to remain competitive.

## CONCLUSION

Since the 1970s, MRP has grown from its purpose of determining simple time schedules, to its present advanced types that tie together all major functions of an organization. During its growth and its application, MRP's disadvantages as a scheduling mechanism have been well recognized. This is largely because MRP tries to do too much in light of the dynamic, often jumpy environment in which it is trying to operate.

MRP is recognized, however, for its excellent databases and linkages within the firm. MRP also does a good job in helping to produce master schedules. Many firms in repetitive manufacturing are installing JIT systems to link with the MRP system. JIT takes the master production schedule as its pulling force but does not use MRP's generated schedule. Results indicate that this is working very well.

Many newer MRP-type software programs have been developed since the early 1990s. Several others are currently in the development stage. These allow more open exchange of data than the earlier systems, embrace a larger part of the firm's operation (such as multiple sites, global customers, languages, and currency rates), and operate in real time.

MRP's service applications have not fared as well, although it is making inroads in various forms in quasi-manufacturing service operations such as restaurants and bakeries. The MRP approach would appear to be valuable in producing services since service scheduling consists of identifying the final service and then tracing back to the resources needed, such as equipment, space, and personnel. Consider, for example, a hospital operating room planning an open-heart surgery. The master schedule can establish a time for the surgery (or surgeries, if several are scheduled). The BOM could specify all required equipment and personnel—MDs, nurses, anesthesiologist, operating room, heart/lung machine, defibrillator, and so forth. The inventory status file would show the availability of the resources and commit them to the project. The MRP program could then produce a schedule showing when various parts of the operation are to be started, expected completion times, required materials, and so forth. Checking this schedule would allow "capacity planning" in answering such questions as "Are all the materials and personnel available?" and "Does the system produce a feasible schedule?"

We still believe that MRP systems will eventually find their way into a greater variety of service applications. One reason for the delay is that even service managers who are aware of it believe that MRP is just a manufacturing tool. Also, service managers tend to be people-oriented and skeptical of tools from outside their industry.

## KEY TERMS

bill of materials (BOM)   p. 501
inventory records file   p. 503
manufacturing resource planning
  (MRP II)   p. 510

master production schedule (MPS)   p. 497
materials requirements planning
  (MRP)   p. 496

## REVIEW AND DISCUSSION QUESTIONS

1. Because MRP appears so reasonable, discuss reasons why it did not become popular until recently.

2. Discuss the meaning of MRP terms such as *planned order releases* and *scheduled order receipts.*

3. Most practitioners currently update MRP weekly or biweekly. Would it be more valuable if it were updated daily? Discuss.

4. What is the role of safety stock in an MRP system?

5. Contrast the significance of the term *lead time* in the traditional EOQ context and in an MRP system.

6. Discuss the importance of the MPS in an MRP system.

7. MRP systems are difficult to install. Identify the various problems that can occur with the system requirements (ignore behavioral problems).

8. "MRP just prepares shopping lists—it doesn't do the shopping or cook the dinner." Comment.

9. What are the sources of demand in an MRP system? Are these dependent or independent, and how are they used as inputs to the system?

10. State the types of data that would be carried in the bill of materials file and the inventory record file.

11. How does MRP II differ from MRP?

12. Why isn't MRP more widespread in services?

# SOLVED PROBLEMS

### Problem 1

Product X is made of two units of Y and three of Z. Y is made of one unit of A and two units of B. Z is made of two units of A and four units of C.

Lead time for X is one week; Y, two weeks; Z, three weeks; A, two weeks; B, one week; and C, three weeks.

a. Draw the product structure tree.

b. If 100 units of X are needed in week 10, develop a planning schedule showing when each item should be ordered and in what quantity.

**Solution**

a.

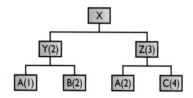

b.

| | | 3 | 4 | 5 | 6 | 7 | 8 | 9 | 10 |
|---|---|---|---|---|---|---|---|---|---|
| X | LT = 1 | | | | | | | 100 | 100 |
| Y | LT = 2 | | | | | 200 | | 200 | |
| Z | LT = 3 | | | | 300 | | | 300 | |
| A | LT = 2 | | 600 | 200 | 600 | 200 | | | |
| B | LT = 1 | | | | 400 | 400 | | | |
| C | LT = 3 | 1200 | | | 1200 | | | | |

### Problem 2

Product M is made of two units of N and three of P. N is made of two units of R and four units of S. R is made of one unit of S and three units of T. P is made of two units of T and four units of U.

a. Show the product structure tree.

b. If 100 Ms are required, how many units of each component are needed?

c. Show both a single-level bill of material and an indented bill of material.

**Solution**

a.

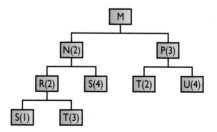

b. $M = 100$       $S = 800 + 400 = 1{,}200$

    $N = 200$       $T = 600 + 1{,}200 = 1{,}800$

    $P = 300$       $U = 1{,}200$

    $R = 400$

*c.* Single-level BOM    Indented BOM

```
M | N              M |
    P                 |
  N                 N |
    |                 |  R
    R                 |     S
    S                 |     T
  R                   |  S
    |                 |
    S               P |
    T                 |  T
  P                   |  U
    |
    T
    U
```

# PROBLEMS

1. In the following MRP planning schedule for Item J, indicate the correct net requirements, planned order receipts, and planned order releases to meet the gross requirements. Lead time is one week.

| Item J | Week Number | | | | | |
|---|---|---|---|---|---|---|
| | 0 | 1 | 2 | 3 | 4 | 5 |
| **Gross requirements** | | | 75 | | 50 | 70 |
| **On hand 40** | | | | | | |
| **Net requirements** | | | | | | |
| **Planned order receipt** | | | | | | |
| **Planned order releases** | | | | | | |

2. Assume that Product Z is made of two units of A and four units of B. A is made of three units of C and four of D. D is made of two units of E.

   The lead time for purchase or fabrication of each unit to final assembly: Z takes two weeks, A, B, C, and D take one week each, and E takes three weeks.

   Fifty units are required in Period 10. (Assume that there is currently no inventory on hand of any of these items.)

   *a.* Draw a product structure tree.

   *b.* Develop an MRP planning schedule showing gross and net requirements, order release and order receipt dates.

   Note: For Problems 3 through 6, to simplify data handling to include the receipt of orders that have actually been placed in previous periods, the six-level scheme shown below can be used. (There are a number of different techniques used in practice, but the important issue is to keep track of what is on hand, what is expected to arrive, what is needed, and what size orders should be placed.) One way to calculate the numbers is as follows:

| | Week | | | | | | | | |
|---|---|---|---|---|---|---|---|---|---|
| Gross requirements | | | | | | | | | |
| Scheduled receipts | | | | | | | | | |
| On hand from prior period | | | | | | | | | |
| Net requirements | | | | | | | | | |
| Planned order receipt | | | | | | | | | |
| Planned order release | | | | | | | | | |

3. One unit of A is made of three units of B, one unit of C, and two units of D. B is composed of two units of E and one unit of D. C is made of one unit of B and two units of E. E is made of one unit of F.

    Items B, C, E, and F have one-week lead times; A and D have lead times of two weeks.

    Assume that lot-for-lot (L4L) lot sizing is used for items A, B, and F; lots of size 50, 50, and 200 are used for items C, D, and E, respectively. Items C, E, and F have on-hand (beginning) inventories of 10, 50, and 150, respectively; all other items have zero beginning inventory. We are scheduled to receive 10 units of A in Week 5, 50 units of E in Week 4, and also 50 units of F in Week 4. There are no other scheduled receipts. If 30 units of A are required in Week 8, use the low-level-coded product structure tree to find the necessary planned order releases for all components.

4. One unit of A is made of two units of B, three units of C, and two units of D. B is composed of one unit of E and two units of F. C is made of two units of F and one unit of D. E is made of two units of D. Items A, C, D, and F have one-week lead times; B and E have lead times of two weeks. Lot-for-lot (L4L) lot sizing is used for Items A, B, C, and D; lots of size 50 and 180 are used for items E and F, respectively. Item C has an on-hand (beginning) inventory of 15; D has an on-hand inventory of 50; all other items have zero beginning inventory. We are scheduled to receive 20 units of Item E in week 4; there are no other scheduled receipts.

    Construct simple and low-level-coded product structure trees and indented and summarized bills of materials.

    If 20 units of A are required in Week 8, use the low-level-coded products structure tree to find the necessary planned order released for all components. (See note prior to Problem 3.)

5. One unit of A is made of one unit of B and one unit of C. B is made of four units of C and one unit of E and F. C is made of two units of D and one unit of E. E is made of three units of F. Item C has a lead time of one week; Items A, B, E, and F have two-week lead times; and Item D has a lead time of three weeks. Lot-for-lot (L4L) lot sizing is used for Items A, D, and E; lots of size 50, 100, and 50 are used for Items B, C, and F, respectively. Items A, C, D, and E have on-hand (beginning) inventories of 20, 50, 100, and 10, respectively; all other items have zero beginning inventory. We are scheduled to receive 10 units of A in week 5, 100 units of C in Week 6, and 100 units of D in Week 4; there are no other scheduled receipts. If 50 units of A are required in Week 10, use the low-level-coded product structure tree to find the necessary planned order releases for all components. (See note prior to Problem 3.)

6. One unit of A is made of two units of B and one unit of C. B is made of three units of D and one unit of F. C is composed of three units of B, one unit of D, and four units of E. D is made of one unit of E. Item C has a lead time of one week; Items A, B, E, and F have two-week lead times; and Item D has a lead time of 3 weeks. Lot-for-lot (L4L) lot sizing is used for Items C, E, and F; lots of size 20, 40, and 160 are used for items A, B, and D, respectively. Items A, B, D, and E have on-hand (beginning) inventories of 5, 10, 100, and 100, respectively; all other items have zero beginning inventories. We are scheduled to receive 10 units of A in Week 3, 20 units of B in Week 7, 60 units of E in week 2, and 40 units of F in Week 5; there are no other scheduled receipts. If 20 units of A are required in Week 10, use the low-level-coded product structure tree to find the necessary planned order releases for all components. (See note prior to Problem 3.)

7. The MRP gross requirements for Item A is shown here for the next 10 weeks. Lead time for A is three weeks and setup cost is $10 per setup. There is a carrying cost of $0.01 per unit per week. Beginning inventory is 90 units.

|  | Week | | | | | | | | | |
|---|---|---|---|---|---|---|---|---|---|---|
|  | 1 | 2 | 3 | 4 | 5 | 6 | 7 | 8 | 9 | 10 |
| Gross requirements | 30 | 50 | 10 | 20 | 70 | 80 | 20 | 60 | 200 | 50 |

Use either the least total cost or the least unit cost lot-sizing method to determine when and for what quantity the first order should be released.

8. (This problem is intended as a very simple exercise to go from the aggregate plan to the master schedule to the MRP.) Gigamemory Storage Devices, Inc. produces CD ROMs (Read Only Memory) and WORMs (Write Once Read Many) for the computer market. Aggregate demand for the WORMs for the next two quarters are 2,100 units and 2,700 units. Assume that the demand is distributed evenly for each month of the quarter.

   There are two models of the WORM: an internal model, and an external model. The drive assemblies in both are the same but the electronics and housing are different. Demand is higher for the external model and currently is 70 percent of the aggregate demand.

   The bill of materials and the lead times follow. One drive assembly and one electronic and housing unit go into each WORM.

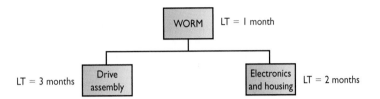

   The MRP system is run monthly. Currently, 200 external WORMs are in stock and 100 internal WORMs. Also in stock are 250 drive assemblies, 50 internal electronic and housing units, and 125 external electronic and housing units.

   Problem: Show the aggregate plan, the master production schedule, and the full MRP with the gross and net requirements and planned order releases.

9. Product A is an end item and is made from two units of B and four of C. B is made of three units of D and two of E. C is made of two units of F and two of E.

   A has a lead time of one week. B, C, and E have lead times of two weeks, and D and F have lead times of three weeks. Currently, there are no units of inventory on hand.

   a. Draw the product structure tree.

   b. If 100 units of A are required in week 10, develop the MRP planning schedule, specifying when items are to be ordered and received.

10. Product A consists of two units of subassembly B, three units of C, and one unit of D. B is composed of four units of E and three units of F. C is made of two units of H and three units of D. H is made of five units of E and two units of G.

   a. Construct a simple product structure tree.

   b. Construct a product structure tree using low-level coding.

   c. Construct an indented bill of materials.

   d. To product 100 units of A, determine the numbers of units of B, C, D, E, F, G, and H required.

11. The MRP gross requirements for Item X are shown here for the next 10 weeks. Lead time for A is two weeks, and setup cost is $9 per setup. There is a carrying cost of $0.02 per unit per week. Beginning inventory is 70 units.

| | Week | | | | | | | | | |
|---|---|---|---|---|---|---|---|---|---|---|
| | 1 | 2 | 3 | 4 | 5 | 6 | 7 | 8 | 9 | 10 |
| Gross requirements | 20 | 10 | 15 | 45 | 10 | 30 | 100 | 20 | 40 | 150 |

   Use either the least total cost or the least unit cost lot-sizing method to determine when and for what quantity the first order should be released.

12. Audio Products, Inc., produces two AM/FM cassette players for automobiles. Both radio/cassette units are identical, but the mounting hardware and finish trim differ. The standard model fits intermediate- and full-size cars, and the sports model fits small sports cars.

Audio Products handles its production in the following way. The chassis (radio/cassette unit) is assembled in Mexico and has a manufacturing lead time of two weeks. The mounting hardware is purchased from a sheet steel company and has a three-week lead time. The finish trim is purchased from a Taiwan electronics company with offices in Los Angeles as prepackaged units consisting of knobs and various trim pieces. Trim packages have a two-week lead time. Final assembly time may be disregarded, since adding the trim package and mounting are performed by the customer.

Audio Products supplies wholesalers and retailers, who place specific orders for both models up to eight weeks in advance. These orders, together with enough additional units to satisfy the small number of individual sales, are summarized in the following demand schedule:

|  | | | | | | Week | | | |
|---|---|---|---|---|---|---|---|---|
| | 1 | 2 | 3 | 4 | 5 | 6 | 7 | 8 |
| Standard model | | | | 300 | | | | 400 |
| Sports model | | | | | 200 | | | 100 |

There are currently 50 radio/cassette units on hand but no trim packages or mounting hardware.

Prepare a material requirements plan to meet the demand schedule exactly. Specify the gross and net requirements, on-hand amounts, and the planned order release and receipt periods for the cassette/radio chassis, the standard trim and sports car model trim, and the standard mounting hardware and the sports car mounting hardware.

13. Brown and Brown Electronics manufactures a line of digital audiotape players. While there are differences among the various products, there are a number of common parts within each player. The product structure, showing the number of each item required, lead times, and the current inventory on hand for the parts and components, follows:

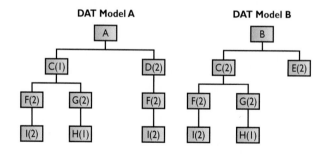

| | Number Currently in Stock | Lead Time (weeks) |
|---|---|---|
| DAT Model A | 30 | 1 |
| DAT Model B | 50 | 2 |
| Subassembly C | 75 | 1 |
| Subassembly D | 80 | 2 |
| Subassembly E | 100 | 1 |
| Part F | 150 | 1 |
| Part G | 40 | 1 |
| Raw material H | 200 | 2 |
| Raw material I | 300 | 2 |

Brown and Brown created a forecast that it plans to use as its master production schedule, producing exactly to schedule. Part of the MPS shows a demand for 700 units of Model A and 1,200 units of Model B in Week 10.

Develop an MRP schedule to meet that demand.

# CASE: NICHOLS COMPANY

This particular December day seemed bleak to Joe Williams, president of Nichols Company (NCO). He sat in his office watching the dying embers of his fireplace, hoping to clear his mind. Suddenly there came a tapping by someone gently rapping, rapping at his office door. "Another headache," he muttered, "tapping at my office door. Only that and nothing more."*

The intruder was Barney Thompson, director of marketing. "A major account has just canceled a large purchase of A units because we are back ordered on tubing. This can't continue. My sales force is out beating the bushes for customers and our production manager can't provide the product."

For the past several months, operations at NCO have been unsteady. Inventory levels have been too high, while at the same time there have been stockouts. This resulted in many late deliveries, complaints, and cancellations. To compound the problem, overtime was excessive.

## HISTORY

Nichols Company was started by Joe Williams and Peter Schaap, both with MBAs from the University of Arizona. Much has happened since Williams and Schaap formed the company. Schaap has left the company and is working in real estate development in Queensland, Australia. Under the direction of Williams, NCO has diversified to include a number of other products.

NCO currently has 355 full-time employees directly involved in manufacturing its three primary products, A, B, and C. Final assembly takes place in a converted warehouse adjacent to NCO's main plant.

## THE MEETING

Williams called a meeting the next day to get input into the problems facing NCO and to lay the groundwork for some solutions. Attending the meeting, besides himself and Barney Thompson, were Phil Bright of production and inventory control, Trevor Hansen of purchasing, and Steve Clark of accounting.

The meeting lasted all morning. Participation was vocal and intense.

Bright said, "The forecasts that marketing sends us are always way off. We are constantly having to expedite one product or another to meet current demand. This runs up our overtime."

Thompson said, "Production tries to run too lean. We need a larger inventory of finished goods. If I had the merchandise, my salespeople could sell 20 percent more product."

Clark said, "No way! Our inventory is already uncomfortably high. We can't afford the holding costs, not to mention how fast technology changes around here causing even more inventory, much of it obsolete."

Bright said, "The only way I can meet our stringent cost requirements is to buy in volume."

At the end of the meeting, Williams had lots of input but no specific plan. What do you think he should do?

Use Case Exhibits 1–4 showing relevant data to answer the specific questions at the end of the case.

## QUESTIONS

Use Excel (or another spreadsheet if you prefer) to solve the Nichols Company case.

*Simplifying assumption:* To get the program started, some time is needed at the beginning because MRP backloads the system. For simplicity, assume that the forecasts (and therefore demands) are zero for Periods 1 through 3. Also assume that the starting inventory specified in Case Exhibit 3 is available from Week 1. For the master production schedule, use only the end Items A, B, and C.

To modify production quantities, adjust only Products A, B, and C. Do not adjust the quantities of D, E, F, G, H, and I. These should be linked so that changes in A, B, and C automatically adjust them.

1. Disregarding machine-center limitations, develop an MRP schedule and also capacity profiles for the four machine centers.

2. Work center capacities and costs follow. Repeat Question 1 creating a *feasible* schedule (within the capacities of the machine centers) and compute the relevant costs. Do this by adjusting the MPS only. Try to minimize the total cost of operation for the 27 weeks.

|  | Capacity | Cost |
|---|---|---|
| Work center 1 | 6,000 hours available | $20 per hour |
| Work center 2 | 4,500 hours available | $25 per hour |
| Work center 3 | 2,400 hours available | $35 per hour |
| Work center 4 | 1,200 hours available | $65 per hour |

**Inventory carrying cost**

| End items A, B, and C | $2.00 per unit |
|---|---|
| Components D, E, F, G, and H | $1.50 per unit |
| Raw material I | $1.00 per unit |

**Back-order cost**

| End items A, B, and C | $20 per unit |
|---|---|
| Components D, E, F, G, and H | $14 per unit |
| Raw material I | $ 8 per unit |

3. Suppose end items had to be ordered in multiples of 100 units, components in multiples of 500 units, and raw materials in multiples of 1,000 units. How would this change your schedule?

---

*With apologies to E.A.P.

**CASE EXHIBIT 1**

Bills of Materials for Products A, B, and C

| Product A | Product B | Product C |
|-----------|-----------|-----------|
| .A | .B | .C |
|   .D(4) |   .F(2) |   .G(2) |
|     .I(3) |   .G(3) |     .I(2) |
|   .E(1) |     .I(2) |   .H(1) |
|   .F(4) | | |

**CASE EXHIBIT 2**

Work Center Routings for Products and Components

| Item | Work Center Number | Standard Time (hours per unit) |
|------|--------------------|--------------------------------|
| Product A | 1 | 0.20 |
| | 4 | 0.10 |
| Product B | 2 | 0.30 |
| | 4 | 0.08 |
| Product C | 3 | 0.10 |
| | 4 | 0.05 |
| Component D | 1 | 0.15 |
| | 4 | 0.10 |
| Component E | 2 | 0.15 |
| | 4 | 0.05 |
| Component F | 2 | 0.15 |
| | 3 | 0.20 |
| Component G | 1 | 0.30 |
| | 2 | 0.10 |
| Component H | 1 | 0.05 |
| | 3 | 0.10 |

**CASE EXHIBIT 3**

Inventory Levels and Lead Times for Each Item on the Bill of Material at the Beginning of Week 1

| Product/Component | On Hand (units) | Lead Time (weeks) |
|-------------------|-----------------|-------------------|
| Product A | 100 | 1 |
| Product B | 200 | 1 |
| Product C | 175 | 1 |
| Component D | 200 | 1 |
| Component E | 195 | 1 |
| Component F | 120 | 1 |
| Component G | 200 | 1 |
| Component H | 200 | 1 |
| I (raw material) | 300 | 1 |

**CASE EXHIBIT 4**

Forecasted Demand for
Weeks 4–27

| Week | Product A | Product B | Product C |
|------|-----------|-----------|-----------|
| 1 | | | |
| 2 | | | |
| 3 | | | |
| 4 | 1,500 | 2,200 | 1,200 |
| 5 | 1,700 | 2,100 | 1,400 |
| 6 | 1,150 | 1,900 | 1,000 |
| 7 | 1,100 | 1,800 | 1,500 |
| 8 | 1,000 | 1,800 | 1,400 |
| 9 | 1,100 | 1,600 | 1,100 |
| 10 | 1,400 | 1,600 | 1,800 |
| 11 | 1,400 | 1,700 | 1,700 |
| 12 | 1,700 | 1,700 | 1,300 |
| 13 | 1,700 | 1,700 | 1,700 |
| 14 | 1,800 | 1,700 | 1,700 |
| 15 | 1,900 | 1,900 | 1,500 |
| 16 | 2,200 | 2,300 | 2,300 |
| 17 | 2,000 | 2,300 | 2,300 |
| 18 | 1,700 | 2,100 | 2,000 |
| 19 | 1,600 | 1,900 | 1,700 |
| 20 | 1,400 | 1,800 | 1,800 |
| 21 | 1,100 | 1,800 | 2,200 |
| 22 | 1,000 | 1,900 | 1,900 |
| 23 | 1,400 | 1,700 | 2,400 |
| 24 | 1,400 | 1,700 | 2,400 |
| 25 | 1,500 | 1,700 | 2,600 |
| 26 | 1,600 | 1,800 | 2,400 |
| 27 | 1,500 | 1,900 | 2,500 |

## SELECTED BIBLIOGRAPHY

Biggs, Joseph R., and Ellen J. Long. "Gaining the Competitive Edge with MRP/MRP II." *Management Accounting,* May 1988, pp. 27–32.

Costello, Richard. "Available: Real-Time EDI, Multiplant Functions, More." *Computerworld,* June 8, 1992, p. 79.

Flapper, S. D. P.; G. J. Miltenburg; and J. Wijngaard. "Embedding JIT into MRP." *International Journal of Production Research* 29, no. 2 (1991), pp. 329–41.

Goodrich, Thomas. "JIT & MRP Can Work Together." *Automation,* April 1989, pp. 46–47.

Greene, Alice. "MRPII: Out with the Old." *Computerworld,* June 8, 1992, p. 74.

Greene, Alice. "Two Ready for the Next Generation." *Computerworld,* June 8, 1992, p. 77.

Knight, Robert M. "Furniture Maker Uses MRP II to Cut Lead Time." *Computerworld,* June 8, 1992, p. 80.

McSpadden, William, F. "OSI, Distributed MRPII and You." *Industrial Engineering,* February 1992, pp. 38–39.

Orlicky, Joseph. *Materials Requirements Planning.* New York: McGraw-Hill, 1975. (This is the classic book on MRP.)

*Production and Inventory Management Journal* and *APICS: The Performance Advantage.* Practitioner journals with numerous articles on MRP and MRP II. Many of these cite the difficulties and experiences of practitioners.

Sipper, Daniel, and Robert Bulfin. *Production Planning, Control and Integration.* New York: McGraw-Hill, 1997.

Staiti, Chris. "Customers Drive New Manufacturing Software." *Datamation,* November 15, 1993, p. 72.

Turbide, David A. *MRP+: The Adaptation, Enhancement and Application of MRP II.* New York: Industrial Press, 1993, p. 11.

Vollmann, Thomas E.; William L. Berry; and D. Clay Whybark. *Manufacturing Planning and Control Systems.* 4th ed. Burr Ridge, IL: Irwin, 1997.

# SCHEDULING

*Chapter Objectives*

- Provide insight into the nature of scheduling and control of intermittent production systems.
- Emphasize the prevalence of job shop environments, notably in the service sector.
- Stress the interaction and dependence of job shop planning and technology.
- Present examples showing the importance of worker scheduling in service sector job shops.
- Identify the major elements of scheduling workers in a service organization.
- Illustrate how technology can facilitate the scheduling of workers.

Many service and production operations need large volumes of standardized manufactured goods; the U.S. Space Program, however, often needs one-of-a-kind items designed for specific aerospace missions. The Teledyne Brown Engineering (TBE) Fabrication and Assembly Plant in Alabama is one firm that helps meet such demand.

The TBE plant layout includes precision equipment that allows their engineers to design and build specific items based on a set of blueprints. Using these blueprints, a planner determines what steps are needed to produce the final product and how these steps should be scheduled. Final products are often flight hardware and launch support equipment for some of TBE's major customers: NASA and the U.S. Air Force.

Because of the unique nature of the products made by TBE and the impact of changing technology, TBE cannot standardize their operations. Thus the required steps and the scheduling of these steps are unique for each product. This make-to-order approach requires a versatile plant layout and equipment that can perform multiple operations in an efficient manner.  ■

Source: Condensed from James B. Dilworth, "Tour of a Job Shop: Teledyne Brown Engineering Fabrication and Assembly Plant I," *Operations Management: Design, Planning and Control for Manufacturing and Services* (New York: McGraw-Hill, Inc., 1992).

Different industries provide different levels of standardization of the goods and services they produce. In the education industry, for example, there are some graduate schools that require students to follow a "lock-step" curriculum with minimal student choice—thus every student receives basically the same education and the same degree. In contrast, the medical care provided in the health care industry is usually customized, based upon an individual patient's symptoms and the severity of the illness. These differences in standardization result in a wide spectrum of processes ranging from intermittent-type processes (such as job shops) to continuous flow operations (such as assembly lines). (Project-type processes are unique in that there is typically only one single product that is produced; this is addressed in Chapter 10 on project management.)

Intermittent flow operations have both the flexibility and capacity to accommodate multiple products that require different operations in different sequences. The manager or dispatcher may try to group work stations or equipment based on either function or process, but scheduling made-to-order products can often be extremely difficult.

Continuous flow operations, on the other hand, are quite inflexible to changes in products and the sequencing of operations. The scheduling of jobs is, therefore, fixed and thus relatively simple.

## THE JOB SHOP DEFINED

**job shop**
Organization whose layout is process-oriented (vs. product-oriented) and that produces items in batches.

A **job shop** is a functional organization whose departments or work centers are organized around particular processes that consist of specific types of equipment and/or operations, such as drilling and assembly in a factory, scanning and printing in a computer laboratory, or specialized examination rooms in a hospital's emergency room. The good produced or

**EXHIBIT 16.1**

Major Attributes of a Job Shop

| Characteristic | In the Job Shop |
|---|---|
| Mission | Sells capacity and skills |
| Item flow | Few or no dominant paths |
| Bottlenecks | Shift frequently |
| Equipment selection | General-purpose, flexible |
| Run length | Short |
| Setup cost | Low |
| Labor content | High |
| Scope of direct jobs | Broad |
| Controller of work pace | Worker, foreman, dispatcher |
| Raw material inventory | Low |
| In-process inventory | High |
| Finished-goods inventory | Low or none |
| Suppliers | Frequent use of multiple suppliers |
| Worker information required for jobs | New instructions needed for each job; specialized training sometimes required. |
| Scheduling | Uncertain, changes are frequent; job components need to be completed at approximately the same time |
| Challenges | Estimating requirements, scheduling, fast response to bottlenecks |
| Response to reduced demand | Lay off workers in affected departments |

Source: Adapted from Robert H. Hayes, and Steven C. Wheelwright, *Restoring our Competitive Edge: Competing Through Manufacturing* (New York: Wiley Publishers, 1984), pp. 180–82.

the service provided is based upon an individual order for a specific customer. Exhibit 16.1 identifies some of the major attributes of a job shop.

## SCHEDULING IN A JOB SHOP

A schedule is a timetable for performing activities, using resources, or allocating facilities. The purpose of operations scheduling in a job shop is to disaggregate the master production schedule (MPS) into time-phased weekly, daily, and/or hourly activities—in other words, to specify in precise terms the planned workload on the production process in the very short run. Operations control entails monitoring job-order progress and, where necessary, expediting orders and/or adjusting system capacity to make sure that the MPS is met.

In designing a scheduling and control system, provision must be made for efficient performance of the following functions:

1. Allocating orders, equipment, and personnel to work centers or other specified locations. Essentially, this is short-run capacity planning.

2. Determining the *sequence* of order performance; that is, establishing job priorities.

3. Initiating performance of the scheduled work. This is commonly termed the **dispatching of orders.**

**dispatching of orders**
Releasing of orders to the factory floor.

4. Shop-floor control (or production activity control), which involves:
   *a.* Reviewing the status and controlling the progress of orders as they are being worked on.
   *b.* **Expediting** late and critical orders.[1]

**expediting**
Checking the progress of specific orders to ensure completion in a timely manner.

5. Revising the schedule to reflect recent changes in order status.

6. Assuring that quality control standards are being met.

A simple job shop-scheduling process is shown in Exhibit 16.2. At the start of the day, the job dispatcher (in this case, a production control person assigned to this department) selects and sequences the available jobs to be run at individual workstations. The dispatcher's decisions would be based on the operations and routing requirements of each job, status of existing jobs on the machines, the queue of work before each machine, job priorities, material availability, anticipated job orders to be released later in the day, and worker and machine capabilities. To help organize the schedule, the dispatcher would draw on shop-floor information from the previous day and external information provided by central production control, process engineering, and so on. The dispatcher would also confer with the foreman or supervisor of the department about the feasibility of the schedule, especially with respect to workforce considerations and identifying potential bottlenecks. Visual schedule boards, as shown in the photo of the Bernard Welding Company, are efficient ways to communicate the priority and status of work.

---

[1]Despite the fact that expediting is frowned on by production control specialists, it is nevertheless a reality of life. In fact, a very typical entry-level job in production control is that of expediter or "stock-chaser." In some companies a good expediter—one who can negotiate a critical job through the system or who can scrounge up materials nobody thought were available—is a prized possession.

**EXHIBIT 16.2**

Typical Scheduling Process

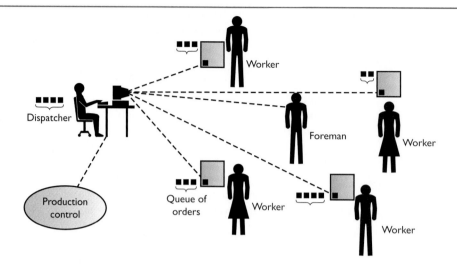

What makes scheduling this job so difficult? Consider the following factors:

- This good/service may never have been done before, so the estimates of the expected length of time for completion of the various components may be quite different from the actual time.

- The sequence of operations is extremely flexible and, with a cross-trained workforce, the number of possible sequences can be huge. Trying to assess the expected results of different sequences with a goal of finding the best sequence is usually very difficult.

- For different operations, the determination of the "best" sequence may vary—for one case it may be the minimization of waste, for another it may be the minimization of idle facilities, for a third it may be the maximization of throughput, and so on. Thus, even with extensive research into the job shop scheduling problem, it is hard to find quantitative or mechanical algorithms that are always appropriate for all situations.

## ELEMENTS OF THE JOB SHOP SCHEDULING PROBLEM

 Job shops exist everywhere and, as a result, examples are plentiful. The emergency room at a hospital may be organized by function: the examination rooms are separate from the x-ray room, which is separate from the waiting room. Depending on the needs of the patient, different jobs are performed at different physical locations within the ER, and in some cases, at locations other than the ER. A riding academy not only boards and exercises the horses, but also provides lessons at different levels to different groups. A ski resort may similarly provide different levels of instruction for different students. The kitchen of a restaurant is also a job shop—different orders come in at different times and the different meals may be prepared by different people.

But all these examples share some common elements:

- The "jobs"—whether they are riding students at an academy or orders for dinner at a restaurant—arrive at the job shop in some pattern.

- The ability of the job shop to complete these "jobs" in a given amount of time is dependent upon the capacity or "machinery" in the shop. For example, the number of students who may take riding lessons is limited by the number of horses present at the riding academy; the number of students who enroll in a given class may be limited by the number of seats available in the classroom.

- The ability of the job shop to complete these "jobs" is also dependent on the ratio of skilled workers to "machines." A riding academy may have lots of horses, but the number of riding students is also limited by the availability of skilled instructors. The number of meals that can be prepared in a timely fashion at a restaurant can be limited by the number of chefs working that evening (in addition to the number of ovens, stoves, and other cooking equipment).

**flow pattern**
Routes that materials follow through a factory to make a product.

- The **flow pattern** of jobs through the shop varies from job to job. At a restaurant, one order might be for a sandwich and salad while another might be for a full seven-course dinner. Consequently, the number and sequence of steps required to fill these two orders is dramatically different.

- Different jobs are often assigned different priorities. Some jobs are marked "rush" or "urgent" and may be from a preferred customer. Medical personnel at the ER in the hospital assign these priorities by performing triage so that the most serious patients are seen first.

- The criteria used to evaluate a given schedule differ from job shop to job shop. A restaurant may try to minimize the wasted food or the idle personnel; Teledyne, in the opening vignette of this chapter, may wish to maximize the reliability of the parts produced.

**Job Arrival Patterns**    Jobs often arrive in a pattern that follows a known statistical distribution (for example, the Poisson distribution is relatively common), or they may arrive in batches (also called "lot" or "bulk" arrivals), or they may arrive such that the time between arrivals is constant. Further, jobs may come with different priorities.

**The "Machinery" in the Shop**    The scheduling problem is also dependent on the number and variety of the equipment or "machines" in the shop. Further, as these "machines" become smarter and are more capable of multitasking, the task of scheduling becomes more complicated.

**machine-limited systems**
Operations where the capacity of the facility is determined by number of machines.

**labor-limited systems**
Operations where the capacity of the facility is determined by number of workers.

**The Ratio of Skilled Workers to Machines**    Job shops can be classified as either **machine-limited** or **labor-limited,** depending on whether the workers outnumber the machines or vice versa. In addition, jobs may be classified as *labor-intensive* or *machine-intensive,* depending on how much of the job may be performed using automated processes.

**The Flow Pattern of Jobs through the Shop**    Exhibit 16.3 shows the various possible flows of jobs through a job shop. In some job shops, all jobs follow the same pattern; in others, the pattern is purely random. Most job shops fall somewhere in between these two extremes. Because of the apparent lack of organization, the flow of material through a job shop is often described as a *jumbled flow.*

## Priority Rules for Allocating Jobs to Machines

**priority rules**
Criteria for determining the sequence or priority of jobs through a facility.

The process of determining which job is started first on some machine or work center is known as sequencing or priority sequencing. **Priority rules** are the rules used to obtain a job sequence. These can be very simple, requiring only that jobs be sequenced according to one piece of data, such as processing time, due date, or order of arrival. Other rules, though equally simple, may require several pieces of information, typically to derive an index number such as in the *least slack rule* and the *critical ratio rule* (both defined later). Still others, such as Johnson's rule (also discussed later), apply to job scheduling on a sequence of machines and require a computational procedure to specify the order of performance. Ten of the more common priority rules are:

1. *FCFS—first come, first-served.* Orders are run in the order they arrive in the department.

**EXHIBIT 16.3**

Material Flows through a
Job Shop

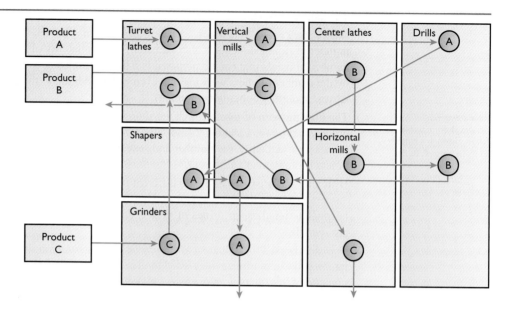

2. *SPT—shortest processing time.* Run the job with the shortest completion time first, next shortest second, etc. This is identical to SOT—shortest operating time.

3. *Due date—earliest due date first.* Run the job with the earliest due date first. DDate—when referring to the entire job; OPNDD—when referring to the next operation.

4. *Start date—due date minus normal lead time.* Run the job with the earliest start date first.

5. *STR—slack time remaining.* This is calculated as the difference between the time remaining before the due date minus the processing time remaining. Orders with the shortest STR are run first.

6. *STR/OP—Slack time remaining per operation.* Orders with shortest STR/OP are run first, calculated as follows:

$$\text{STR/OP} = \frac{\text{Time remaining before due date} - \text{Remaining processing time}}{\text{Number of remaining operations}}$$

7. *CR—critical ratio.* This is calculated as the difference between the due date and the current date divided by the work remaining. Orders with the smallest CR are run first.

8. *QR—queue ratio.* This is calculated as the slack time remaining in the schedule divided by the planned remaining queue time. Orders with the smallest QR are run first.

9. *LCFS—last-come, first-served.* This rule occurs frequently by default. As orders arrive they are placed on the top of the stack and the operator usually picks up the order on top to run first.

10. *Random order—whim.* The supervisors or the operators usually select whichever job they feel like running.[2]

---

[2]This list is modified from Donald W. Fogarty, John H. Blackstone, Jr., and Thomas R. Hoffmann, *Production and Inventory Management* (Cincinnati: South-Western Publishing, 1991), pp. 452–53.

to where we planned to be. Other useful controls devices include the PERT and CPM networks discussed in Chapter 10.

Shop-floor control systems in most modern plants are now computerized, with job status information entered directly into a computer as the job enters and leaves a work center. Some plants have gone heavily into bar coding and optical scanners to speed up the reporting process and to cut down on data-entry errors.[7] As you might guess, the key problems in shop-floor control are data inaccuracy and lack of timeliness. When these occur, the information fed back to the overall planning system is wrong and incorrect production decisions are made. Typical results are excess inventory and/or stockout problems, missed due dates, and inaccuracies in job costing.

Of course, maintaining data integrity requires that a sound data-gathering system be in place; but more important, it requires adherence to the system by everybody interacting with it. Most firms recognize this, but maintaining what is variously referred to as *shop discipline, data integrity,* or *data responsibility* is not always easy. And despite periodic drives to publicize the importance of careful shop-floor reporting by creating data-integrity task forces, inaccuracies can still creep into the system in many ways: A line worker drops a part under the workbench and pulls a replacement from stock without recording either transaction. An inventory clerk makes an error in a cycle count. A manufacturing engineer fails to note a change in the routing of a part. A department supervisor decides to work jobs in a different order than specified in the dispatch list.

## SCHEDULING WORKERS IN SERVICE OPERATIONS

### Why Scheduling Is Important in Services

As discussed previously, one of the main distinctions between manufacturing and service operations is the customer's direct interaction with the service delivery process. Because of this interaction, the determination of the proper number of workers to schedule at any particular time is critical to the success of every service operation. On one hand, scheduling too few workers results in unnecessarily long customer waiting times. On the other hand, scheduling too many workers results in overstaffing and the incurrence of unnecessarily high labor costs, which negatively affect profits. The service manager, consequently, needs to schedule workers in a way that effectively satisfies customer demand while minimizing unnecessary labor costs.

The cost of labor in most services is a major cost component, often running 35 percent of sales and higher. For some services, in fact, virtually all of the direct costs can be considered as labor (examples of these types of services include consulting, legal work, home care nursing and hair salons). Thus a small but unnecessary increase in labor can have a very significant impact on a firm's profits.

### The Sequence for Scheduling Service Workers

Work schedules in service operations are usually developed on a weekly basis for several reasons. First, there are state and federal laws that specify the maximum number of hours and/or days an employee can work in a given week after which overtime premiums must

---

[7]Some companies also use "smartshelves"—inventory bins with weight sensors beneath each shelf. When an item is removed from inventory, a signal is sent to a central computer that notes the time, date, quantity, and location of the transaction.

be paid. Second, the distinction between full-time and part-time workers is often made on the basis of the number of hours worked in a calendar week. Full-time versus part-time status often determines the benefits paid by the employer, and may be related to union contracts that specify the minimum number of hours workers in each category may work. Finally, many workers, especially hourly workers, are paid on a weekly basis that is often mandated by local or state laws.

The sequence for developing a schedule for service workers can be divided into the following four major elements, as illustrated in Exhibit 16.9: (*a*) forecasting customer demand, (*b*) converting customer demand into worker requirements, and (*c*) converting worker requirements into daily work schedules, and converting daily work schedules into weekly work schedules.

**Forecasting Demand**    Since the delivery of most services takes place in the presence of the customer, the customer's arrival directly correlates with the demand level for the service operation. For example, the customer must be present at a restaurant to partake in the meal being served; the patient must be present in the hospital to receive treatment. In addition to the customer's presence at the point of service, the potential for high variability in the pattern of customer demand makes it extremely important for service managers to efficiently schedule workers. The first step, therefore, in developing a schedule that will permit the service operation to meet customer demand is to accurately forecast that demand.

There are several patterns of demand that need to be considered: variation in demand within days (or even hours), variation across days of the week, and seasonal variations. Because demand is often highly variable throughout a day, forecasting within-day variation is usually done in either hour or half-hour increments. Today, with the use of computers and more sophisticated point-of-sale (POS) equipment, the ability to record customer demand in even shorter time increments is possible (for example, 15-minute time intervals).

To develop a forecast we need to collect historical data about customer demand. The actual number of customers expecting service in a given time interval (that is, half-hour or hour) is the preferred data. Fortunately, there is a wide range of POS equipment available

**EXHIBIT 16.9**

The Required Steps in a Worker Schedule

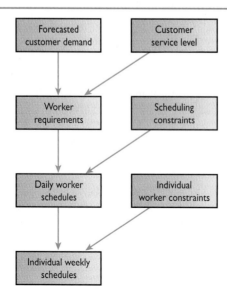

# Negative Exponential Distribution: Values of $e^{-x}$

| x | $e^{-x}$ (value) | x | $e^{-x}$ (value) | x | $e^{-x}$ (value) | x | $e^{-x}$ (value) |
|---|---|---|---|---|---|---|---|
| 0.00 | 1.00000 | 0.50 | 0.60653 | 1.00 | 0.36788 | 1.50 | 0.22313 |
| 0.01 | 0.99005 | 0.51 | .60050 | 1.01 | .36422 | 1.51 | .22091 |
| 0.02 | .98020 | 0.52 | .59452 | 1.02 | .36060 | 1.52 | .21871 |
| 0.03 | .97045 | 0.53 | .58860 | 1.03 | .35701 | 1.53 | .21654 |
| 0.04 | .96079 | 0.54 | .58275 | 1.04 | .35345 | 1.54 | .21438 |
| 0.05 | .95123 | 0.55 | .57695 | 1.05 | .34994 | 1.55 | .21225 |
| 0.06 | .94176 | 0.56 | .57121 | 1.06 | .34646 | 1.56 | .21014 |
| 0.07 | .93239 | 0.57 | .56553 | 1.07 | .34301 | 1.57 | .20805 |
| 0.08 | .92312 | 0.58 | .55990 | 1.08 | .33960 | 1.58 | .20598 |
| 0.09 | .91393 | 0.59 | .55433 | 1.09 | .33622 | 1.59 | .20393 |
| 0.10 | .90484 | 0.60 | .54881 | 1.10 | .33287 | 1.60 | .20190 |
| 0.11 | .89583 | 0.61 | .54335 | 1.11 | .32956 | 1.61 | .19989 |
| 0.12 | .88692 | 0.62 | .53794 | 1.12 | .32628 | 1.62 | .19790 |
| 0.13 | .87809 | 0.63 | .53259 | 1.13 | .32303 | 1.63 | .19593 |
| 0.14 | .86936 | 0.64 | .52729 | 1.14 | .31982 | 1.64 | .19398 |
| 0.15 | .86071 | 0.65 | .52205 | 1.15 | .31664 | 1.65 | .19205 |
| 0.16 | .87514 | 0.66 | .51685 | 1.16 | .31349 | 1.66 | .19014 |
| 0.17 | .84366 | 0.67 | .51171 | 1.17 | .31037 | 1.67 | .18825 |
| 0.18 | .83527 | 0.68 | .50662 | 1.18 | .30728 | 1.68 | .18637 |
| 0.19 | .82696 | 0.69 | .50158 | 1.19 | .30422 | 1.69 | .18452 |
| 0.20 | .81873 | 0.70 | .49659 | 1.20 | .30119 | 1.70 | .18268 |
| 0.21 | .81058 | 0.71 | .49164 | 1.21 | .29820 | 1.71 | .18087 |
| 0.22 | .80252 | 0.72 | .48675 | 1.22 | .29523 | 1.72 | .17907 |
| 0.23 | .79453 | 0.73 | .48191 | 1.23 | .29229 | 1.73 | .17728 |
| 0.24 | .78663 | 0.74 | .47711 | 1.24 | .28938 | 1.74 | .17552 |
| 0.25 | .77880 | 0.75 | .47237 | 1.25 | .28650 | 1.75 | .17377 |
| 0.26 | .77105 | 0.76 | .46767 | 1.26 | .28365 | 1.76 | .17204 |
| 0.27 | .76338 | 0.77 | .46301 | 1.27 | .28083 | 1.77 | .17033 |
| 0.28 | .75578 | 0.78 | .45841 | 1.28 | .27804 | 1.78 | .16864 |
| 0.29 | .74826 | 0.79 | .45384 | 1.29 | .27527 | 1.79 | .16696 |
| 0.30 | .74082 | 0.80 | .44933 | 1.30 | .27253 | 1.80 | .16530 |
| 0.31 | .73345 | 0.81 | .44486 | 1.31 | .26982 | 1.81 | .16365 |
| 0.32 | .72615 | 0.82 | .44043 | 1.32 | .26714 | 1.82 | .16203 |
| 0.33 | .71892 | 0.83 | .43605 | 1.33 | .26448 | 1.83 | .16041 |
| 0.34 | .71177 | 0.84 | .43171 | 1.34 | .26185 | 1.84 | .15882 |
| 0.35 | .70469 | 0.85 | .42741 | 1.35 | .25924 | 1.85 | .15724 |
| 0.36 | .69768 | 0.86 | .42316 | 1.36 | .25666 | 1.86 | .15567 |
| 0.37 | .69073 | 0.87 | .41895 | 1.37 | .25411 | 1.87 | .15412 |
| 0.38 | .68386 | 0.88 | .41478 | 1.38 | .25158 | 1.88 | .15259 |
| 0.39 | .67706 | 0.89 | .41066 | 1.39 | .24908 | 1.89 | .15107 |

| $x$ | $e^{-x}$ (value) | $x$ | $e^{-x}$ (value) | $x$ | $e^{-x}$ (value) | $x$ | $e^{-x}$ (value) |
|---|---|---|---|---|---|---|---|
| 0.40 | .67032 | 0.90 | .40657 | 1.40 | .24660 | 1.90 | .14957 |
| 0.41 | .66365 | 0.91 | .40252 | 1.41 | .24414 | 1.91 | .14808 |
| 0.42 | .65705 | 0.92 | .39852 | 1.42 | .24171 | 1.92 | .14661 |
| 0.43 | .65051 | 0.93 | .39455 | 1.43 | .23931 | 1.93 | .14515 |
| 0.44 | .64404 | 0.94 | .39063 | 1.44 | .23693 | 1.94 | .14370 |
| 0.45 | .63763 | 0.95 | .38674 | 1.45 | .23457 | 1.95 | .14227 |
| 0.46 | .63128 | 0.96 | .38289 | 1.46 | .23224 | 1.96 | .14086 |
| 0.47 | .62500 | 0.97 | .37908 | 1.47 | .22993 | 1.97 | .13946 |
| 0.48 | .61878 | 0.98 | .37531 | 1.48 | .22764 | 1.98 | .13807 |
| 0.49 | .61263 | 0.99 | .37158 | 1.49 | .22537 | 1.99 | .13670 |
| 0.50 | .60653 | 1.00 | .36788 | 1.50 | .22313 | 2.00 | .13534 |

# ANSWERS TO SELECTED PROBLEMS

**Supplement 3**

2. *a.*

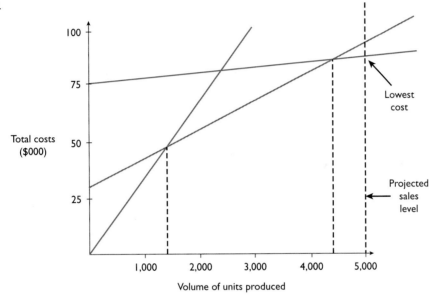

*b.* Break-even between Alternatives 1 and 2:

$$32x = 30,000 + 12x$$
$$20x = 30,000$$
$$x = 1,500 \text{ units}$$

Break-even between Alternatives 2 and 3:

$$30,000 + 12x = 75,000 + 2x$$
$$10x = 45,000$$
$$x = 4,500 \text{ units}$$

*c.* Based on lowest total costs, The company should choose Alternative 3, which is to invest the $75,000 in fixed costs and use unskilled labor.

7. The straight-line depreciation method yields a 15.9 percent return. The sum-of-the-years' digits yields a 17.1 percent return. Thus, neither method of depreciation will provide the minimum 20 percent return.

**Chapter 5**

1. *a.* Not inspecting cost = $20/hour. Cost to inspect = $9/hour. Therefore, inspect.
   *b.* $.18 each.
   *c.* $.22 per unit.

**Supplement 5**

1. *a.* $C_{pk} = .889$.
   *b.* $C_{pk} = 1.11$.
   The process is capable but needs to adjust mean downward to achieve 100 percent perfect quality.

2. *a.* $p = .067$.
   UCL = .194.
   LCL = 0.
   *b.* Stop the process. There is wide variation and two are out of limits.

**Chapter 6**

2. *a.* 15.
   *b.* 14.3.
   *c.* 13.4.
   *d.* $Y = a + bX = 10.8 + .77X$.
   *e.* $Y = 10.8 + .77(7) = 16.2$.

9. MAD = 58.3
   TS = −6
   Model is poor at giving a good forecast.

## Chapter 7

1. Output/day: 24B + 24D.
   Process times: 12 min./B and 8 min./D.
   BB/DDD BB BB/DDD repetitively.

2. *a.* 27 seconds.
   *b.* 7 stations.
   *c.* 78.3 percent.
   *d.* Reduce cycle time to 25 seconds and work 8½ minutes overtime.

4. $44,500.

## Supplement 8

1. $\bar{t}_s = 4.125$ minutes.
   $\bar{n}_j = 4.05$ cars.
   $\bar{n}_s = 4.95$ cars.

2. *4 spaces:* Stand busy 67.2 percent
   *5 spaces:* Stand busy 69.6 percent
   *6 spaces:* Stand busy 71.15 percent
   *7 spaces:* Stand busy 72.22 percent
   *8 spaces:* Net loss = $160;
   7 spaces should be leased.

## Supplement 9

1. *a.* 1.65 minutes.
   *b.* 1.90 (minutes rounded).
   *c.* $56.93.

5. *a.* $NT = .9286$ minute/part.
   *b.* $ST = 1.0679$ minute/part.
   *c.* Daily output = 449.50.
   Day's wages = $44.49.

## Chapter 10

1. *b.* A–C–D–E–G.
   *c.* 26 weeks.
   *d.* 6 weeks (15 − 9).

8. *a.* Critical path is A–C–D–F–G.
   *b.*

   | Day | Cost | Activity |
   |---|---|---|
   | First | $1,000 | A |
   | Second | 1,200 | C |
   | Third | 1,500 | D (or F) |
   | Fourth | 1,500 | F (or D) |
   | | $5,200 | |

## Chapter 11

1.

   | Transportation Costs | Carrying Costs |
   |---|---|
   | TC = $450,000.00 | $80,547.95 |
   | = $530,547.95 | |

   Cost per tire: $5.305479
   Total cost: $40.30548

   Continue buying from current supplier at $40.00 per tire delivered.

## Chapter 13

1. Total cost = $413,600.

4. Ending inventory = safety stock.
   Inventory cost includes forecast and safety stock.
   Shortage cost is only based on the forecast.
   Total cost = $413,750.

## Chapter 14

1. TC = $24,254.50.
   Q at 200 is the optimum order size.

4. TC = $56,370.
   1,000 at a time.

5. *a.* A (4, 13, 18), B (2,5,8,10,11,14,16), C (remainder).
   *b.* Classify as A.

## Chapter 15

2.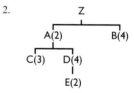

7. Least total cost method: Order 250 units in period one for periods 1–8;
   Least unit cost method: Order 450 units in period one for periods 1–9.

10. *c.* .A
   .B(2)
   .E(4)
   .F(3)
   .C(3)
   .D(3)
   .H(2)
   .E(5)
   .G(2)
   .D(1)

*d.* Level 0    100 units of A

Level 1    200 units of B

               300 units of C

Level 2    600 units of F

               600 units of H

              1000 units of D

Level 3    3800 units of E

              1200 units of G

## Chapter 16

1.

| Car | Priority |
|-----|----------|
| C | First |
| A | Tie for second |
| B | Tie for second |

4. Average totals: 10,600; 8,800.

   Aggregate runout time = 2.295 weeks.

7. Johnson's method: E, A, B, D, C.

# UNIFORMLY DISTRIBUTED RANDOM DIGITS

| | | | | | | | | |
|---|---|---|---|---|---|---|---|---|
| 56970 | 10799 | 52098 | 04184 | 54967 | 72938 | 50834 | 23777 | 08392 |
| 83125 | 85077 | 60490 | 44369 | 66130 | 72936 | 69848 | 59973 | 08144 |
| 55503 | 21383 | 02464 | 26141 | 68779 | 66388 | 75242 | 82690 | 74099 |
| 47019 | 06683 | 33203 | 29603 | 54553 | 25971 | 69573 | 83854 | 24715 |
| 84828 | 61152 | 79526 | 29554 | 84580 | 37859 | 28504 | 61980 | 34997 |
| | | | | | | | | |
| 08021 | 31331 | 79227 | 05748 | 51276 | 57143 | 31926 | 00915 | 45821 |
| 36458 | 28285 | 30424 | 98420 | 72925 | 40729 | 22337 | 48293 | 86847 |
| 05752 | 96045 | 36847 | 87729 | 81679 | 59126 | 59437 | 33225 | 31280 |
| 26768 | 02513 | 58454 | 56958 | 20575 | 76746 | 40878 | 06846 | 32828 |
| 42613 | 72456 | 43030 | 58085 | 06766 | 60227 | 96414 | 32671 | 45587 |
| | | | | | | | | |
| 95457 | 12176 | 65482 | 25596 | 02678 | 54592 | 63607 | 82096 | 21913 |
| 95276 | 67524 | 63564 | 95958 | 39750 | 64379 | 46059 | 51666 | 10433 |
| 66954 | 53574 | 64776 | 92345 | 95110 | 59448 | 77249 | 54044 | 67942 |
| 17457 | 44151 | 14113 | 02462 | 02798 | 54977 | 48340 | 66738 | 60184 |
| 03704 | 23322 | 83214 | 59337 | 01695 | 60666 | 97410 | 55064 | 17427 |
| | | | | | | | | |
| 21538 | 16997 | 33210 | 60337 | 27976 | 70661 | 08250 | 69509 | 60264 |
| 57178 | 16730 | 08310 | 70348 | 11317 | 71623 | 55510 | 64750 | 87759 |
| 31048 | 40058 | 94953 | 55866 | 96283 | 40620 | 52087 | 80817 | 74533 |
| 69799 | 83300 | 16498 | 80733 | 96422 | 58078 | 99643 | 39847 | 96884 |
| 90595 | 65017 | 59231 | 17772 | 67831 | 33317 | 00520 | 90401 | 41700 |
| | | | | | | | | |
| 33570 | 34761 | 08039 | 78784 | 09977 | 29398 | 93896 | 78227 | 90110 |
| 15340 | 82760 | 57477 | 13898 | 48431 | 72936 | 78160 | 87240 | 52710 |
| 64079 | 07733 | 36512 | 56186 | 99098 | 48850 | 72527 | 08486 | 10951 |
| 63491 | 84886 | 67118 | 62063 | 74958 | 20946 | 28147 | 39338 | 32109 |
| 92003 | 76568 | 41034 | 28260 | 79708 | 00770 | 88643 | 21188 | 01850 |
| | | | | | | | | |
| 52360 | 46658 | 66511 | 04172 | 73085 | 11795 | 52594 | 13287 | 82531 |
| 74622 | 12142 | 68355 | 65635 | 21828 | 39539 | 18988 | 53609 | 04001 |
| 04157 | 50070 | 61343 | 64315 | 70836 | 82857 | 35335 | 87900 | 36194 |
| 86003 | 60070 | 66241 | 32836 | 27573 | 11479 | 94114 | 81641 | 00496 |
| 41208 | 80187 | 20351 | 09630 | 84668 | 42486 | 71303 | 19512 | 50277 |
| | | | | | | | | |
| 06433 | 80674 | 24520 | 18222 | 10610 | 05794 | 37515 | 48619 | 62866 |
| 39298 | 47829 | 72648 | 37414 | 75755 | 04717 | 29899 | 78817 | 03509 |
| 89884 | 59651 | 67533 | 68123 | 17730 | 95862 | 08034 | 19473 | 63971 |
| 61512 | 32155 | 51906 | 61662 | 64430 | 16688 | 37275 | 51262 | 11569 |
| 99653 | 47635 | 12506 | 88535 | 36553 | 23757 | 34209 | 55803 | 96275 |
| | | | | | | | | |
| 95913 | 11085 | 13772 | 76638 | 48423 | 25018 | 99041 | 77529 | 81360 |
| 55804 | 44004 | 13122 | 44115 | 01601 | 50541 | 00147 | 77685 | 58788 |
| 35334 | 82410 | 91601 | 40617 | 72876 | 33967 | 73830 | 15405 | 96554 |
| 57729 | 88646 | 76487 | 11622 | 96297 | 24160 | 09903 | 14047 | 22917 |
| 86648 | 89317 | 63677 | 70119 | 94739 | 25875 | 38829 | 68377 | 43918 |
| | | | | | | | | |
| 30574 | 06039 | 07967 | 32422 | 76791 | 30725 | 53711 | 93385 | 13421 |
| 81307 | 13114 | 83580 | 79974 | 45929 | 85113 | 72268 | 09858 | 52104 |
| 02410 | 96385 | 79067 | 54939 | 21410 | 86980 | 91772 | 93307 | 34116 |
| 18969 | 87444 | 52233 | 62319 | 08598 | 09066 | 95288 | 04794 | 01534 |
| 87863 | 80514 | 66860 | 62297 | 80198 | 19347 | 73234 | 86265 | 49096 |
| | | | | | | | | |
| 08397 | 10538 | 15438 | 62311 | 72844 | 60203 | 46412 | 65943 | 79232 |
| 28520 | 45247 | 58729 | 10854 | 99058 | 18260 | 38765 | 90038 | 94209 |
| 44285 | 09452 | 15867 | 70418 | 57012 | 72122 | 36634 | 97283 | 95943 |
| 86299 | 22510 | 33571 | 23309 | 57040 | 29285 | 67870 | 21913 | 72958 |
| 84842 | 05748 | 90894 | 61658 | 15001 | 94005 | 36308 | 41161 | 37341 |